I0606031

THE 5-MINUTE BIBLE STUDY PLAN FOR MEN

THE 5-MINUTE BIBLE STUDY PLAN FOR MEN

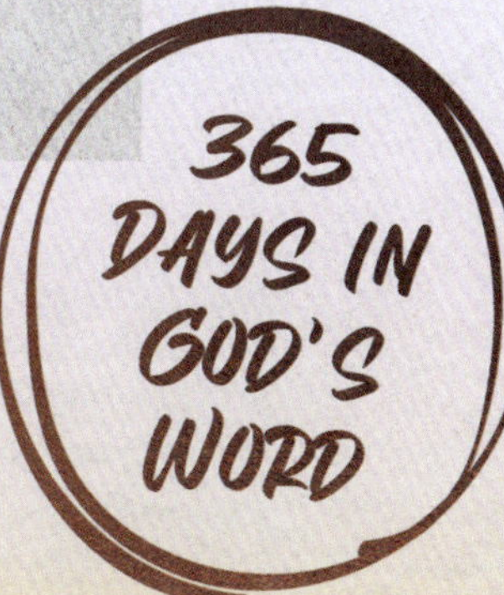

YOU are the reason we do what we do here at Barbour Publishing. We promise that we will always use our God-given talents to produce content with you in mind—and that we will remain biblically faithful, no matter what.

Thank you for being the heart of our business.

ISBN 979-8-89151-244-3

Text compiled from *The 5-Minute Bible Study for Men*, *The 5-Minute Bible Study for Men: Mornings in God's Word*, *The 5-Minute Bible Study for Men: Pursuing God*, and *The 5-Minute Bible Study for Men: Seeking God's Wisdom*, all published by Barbour Publishing, Inc.

Cover Design: Greg Jackson, Thinkpen Design

Published by Barbour Publishing, Inc., 1810 Barbour Drive, Uhrichsville, Ohio 44683, www.barbourbooks.com.

Our mission is to inspire the world with the life-changing message of the Bible.

Printed in China.

Do you find it hard to make time for Bible study? You intend to do it, but the hours turn into days. . .and before you know it, another week has passed and you have not picked up God's Word. This book was designed to help you develop a healthy Bible study habit. It provides an avenue for you to open the Bible regularly and dig into a passage—even if you have only five minutes!

Minutes 1–2: ***Read.*** Carefully review the scripture passage for each day's Bible study.

Minute 3: ***Understand.*** Ponder a couple of prompts designed to help you apply the verses from the Bible to your own life. Consider these throughout your day as well.

Minute 4: ***Apply.*** Read a brief devotional based on the day's scripture. Think about what you are learning and how to apply the scriptural truths to your own life.

Minute 5: ***Pray.*** A prayer starter will help you begin a time of conversation with God. Remember to allow time for Him to speak into your life as well.

May *The 5-Minute Bible Study Plan for Men* help you to establish the discipline of studying God's Word. Make that first five minutes of your day count—or use these studies to end your day strong. You will find that spending even five minutes focused on scripture and prayer has the power to make a huge difference. Soon you will want to make even more time for God's Word.

HOW TO SUCCEED AT BIBLE STUDY

Read 1 Thessalonians 3:1–13

KEY VERSE

May [the Lord]. . .make your hearts strong, blameless, and holy as you stand before God our Father when our Lord Jesus comes again with all his holy people. Amen.
1 THESSALONIANS 3:13 NLT

UNDERSTAND

- *How much have you studied scripture in the past?*
- *How much do you want to study the Bible in the future?*

APPLY

In your heart, you want to be successful at Bible study. Here are five keys:

1. *Make a goal.* Your goal might be to finish every Bible study in this book in a year. If you miss a day, don't worry. You can squeeze in an extra five minutes tomorrow. Worst case? You can catch up a whole week's worth of Bible studies in thirty-five minutes. You can do this!
2. *Divide and conquer.* If your schedule doesn't allow for daily Bible study, figure out what else might work. The National Guard achieves its objectives one weekend per month through most of the year. During this particular season, what would work best for you?
3. *Study with your head and heart.* If you don't understand something, it's okay to ask questions. But as you read and study, focus on what *is* clear.
4. *Pick a favorite verse to make your own.* A good friend of mine picked 1 Thessalonians 3:13 as a prayer focus for the year. Do you have a favorite? If so, great! If not, you might discover it in this book.
5. *Talk to the Lord as you study His Word.* Literally say, "Yes, Lord, I want to live for You as Abraham and Joseph, and as Peter and Paul, did."

The master key? Taking scripture seriously. After all, it is God's Word!

PRAY

Yes, Lord, as You know, I have already said "Yes!" to reading and studying the Bible. That's why I'm spending these minutes with You again today.

SAYING "WOW!"

Read Psalm 8:1–9

KEY VERSE

O Lord, our Lord, your majestic name fills the earth! Psalm 8:1 NLT

UNDERSTAND

- *Where are some of the most picturesque places you've ever been?*
- *Where are two or three of your all-time favorite places to visit?*

APPLY

Imagine today that you have to drive quite a ways into the countryside. You can't help feeling nostalgic about some of the most beautiful places you'll pass along the way. Seeing a strikingly beautiful place for the first time stirs feelings of transcendence, of "Wow!"

Conversely, spoiled creation produces embarrassment or disgust at the wasteful, sinful actions of other men. Yet many awe-inspiring places still remain. Each place speaks to you in a deep and mysterious way. Often, it's the Holy Spirit inside you, lifting your heart with a fresh revelation of the Lord God's infinite, eternal power and glory.

True, creation can't tell us everything about God, but what it says is of first importance. The Lord God could but speak the word and create the entire universe. And yes, He made you, planted the seed of faith in your heart, helped you understand the good news of Jesus Christ, and is at work in your heart and life to this day.

Saying "Wow!" when you see the marvels of creation is important because it draws your heart closer to God. May you experience "Wow!" even more frequently as you see amazing God-inspired truths in scripture during this next year.

Along the way, you'll have opportunities to say "Wow!" to God's inspiration of the Bible, preservation of the scriptures, the miracle of translation, and much more.

PRAY

Yes, Lord, I want to say "Wow!" for Your majestic name! I also want to say "Wow!" for all You have in store for me as I read Your Word. Please keep changing me from the inside out.

DAY 3

BIBLE STUDY ISN'T TOO DIFFICULT

Read Deuteronomy 29:9–30:16

KEY VERSE

The secret things belong to the Lord *our God, but the things revealed belong to us and to our children forever, that we may follow all the words of this law.* Deuteronomy 29:29 NIV

UNDERSTAND

- *Which Bible translations have you used?*
- *Which Bible translation do you find is the easiest to understand?*

APPLY

Some guys allege that reading and studying the Bible is too hard. Wow, nothing could be further from the truth!

If Moses were here, he would shake his head and ask, "Are God's blessings only for the elite?" Instead, in Deuteronomy 29:29, he says that what God has revealed in scripture belongs to everyone, including your children. Granted, the Bible doesn't record everything God knows—not by a long shot! But scripture is everything He's given mankind: It's eternal, and it's designed as a divine imperative to action. (*Do* is the operative word!)

A few paragraphs earlier, in Deuteronomy 29:9–15, Moses said that the person who knows, respects, preserves, and carefully follows God's Word will "prosper in everything [he does]." You don't need a theological degree to read, understand, and apply the Bible to your life.

A few paragraphs later, in Deuteronomy 30:11–16, Moses said God's Word is clear enough for anyone to understand and obey—and reap God's blessings in every area of life.

The reality is that the Bible is available in several wonderful, accurate, highly readable English translations. Translations are nothing new. Jesus and the apostles read and quoted from the Greek translation of the Hebrew scriptures, since Greek was the common language of their day.

More than ever, the scriptures are accessible to anyone and everyone, including you!

PRAY

Yes, Lord, I want to say "Thank You!" for making the riches of Your Word accessible to guys like me. I'm motivated to keep going because I want to reap Your blessings in every area of my life. Help me recognize each of those blessings in the days and weeks ahead.

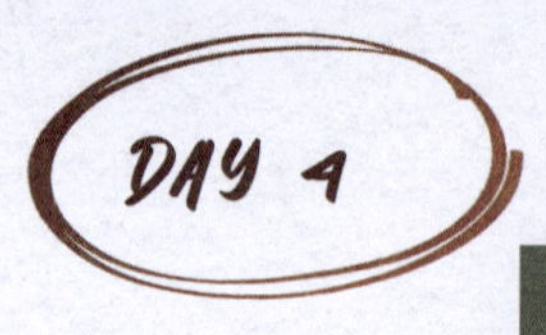

LOVE LEADS TO GENEROSITY

Read 1 John 3

KEY VERSES

We know what real love is because Jesus gave up his life for us. So we also ought to give up our lives for our brothers and sisters. If someone has enough money to live well and sees a brother or sister in need but shows no compassion—how can God's love be in that person?
1 John 3:16–17 NLT

UNDERSTAND

- *How does John want his readers to apply the example of Jesus to their own lives?*
- *If John believes that generosity comes from the presence of God's love in your life, how does someone receive God's love in the first place?*
- *What does today's scripture reading say about how Christians should treat one another?*

APPLY

At the foundation of John's first epistle is God's love for you. If you are aware of that love and received that love, John wrote, then your life should be changed, different from what it was before. John offers the example of Jesus as both the *proof* of just how deep God's love is for you and the *example* of how to love others sacrificially. When you have the foundation of God's love built up within, you can then more fully express love and generosity to others.

John expects you to follow Jesus' example and lay down your own needs and desires for others, and he uses the example of financial generosity to make that point. Christians should be aware of the needs of others, and when they are, the love of God will compel them to meet those needs. This type of concern for others is evidence that you have truly been touched by God's love.

Your actions serve as the ultimate clue that you have received and been transformed by God's love. If you find yourself consumed with yourself, seek God and experience His love for you. Let the Lord transform you from the inside, and then the loving acts for others will follow.

PRAY

Thank You, Father, for Your deep love for me and for the sacrifice of Jesus on my behalf. Thank You for seeking me when I was far from You. May Your love transform my life and enable me to more fully love others. Amen.

LEAVE JUDGMENT TO GOD

Read 1 Corinthians 4:1–13

KEY VERSES

I am not aware of anything against myself, but I am not thereby acquitted. It is the Lord who judges me. Therefore do not pronounce judgment before the time, before the Lord comes, who will bring to light the things now hidden in darkness and will disclose the purposes of the heart. Then each one will receive commendation from God.

1 Corinthians 4:4–5 NRSV

UNDERSTAND

- *Why would Paul write that he does not even judge himself but leaves the judgment to God alone?*
- *What are the benefits of waiting for God to bring judgment on yourself or someone else?*
- *How does God's knowledge of the hidden purposes of your heart change the choices you make today?*

APPLY

Conflict with others can lead to assumptions, judgment, and second-guessing—and Paul was no stranger to that with the churches he founded. Although it's helpful to assess yourself, to evaluate your motives, and to listen to the advice of people you trust, Paul cautions that these measures aren't the very best approach. In fact, escaping the scrutiny of others is hardly proof of innocence.

It is far more useful to examine your conscience before God and to seek to prove yourself before Him. There is nothing you can hide from God, and so you can believe that God's judgment will be true and just.

If thoughts of God's judgment leave you unsettled, just remember that you can trust in His willingness to forgive your sins and to wipe them away when you repent. When you "come clean" with God, you can be assured that you are free from judgment and don't have to live in uncertainty. Even better, when God's Spirit guides you, you will live in the freedom and peace Jesus promised His followers. That doesn't mean you'll be free from conflict and misunderstanding, but in the Spirit, you'll have the guidance God provides.

PRAY

Thank You, Father, for Your Spirit's guidance and for Your Son's sacrifice, which saves me from judgment. May I live today with purity of heart and intention so that I can serve others freely and bring unity to Your people. Amen.

DAY 6

WHY THE BIBLE IS INSPIRED BY GOD

Read Psalm 119:1–24

KEY VERSE

Open my eyes, that I may behold wondrous things out of your law. PSALM 119:18 ESV

UNDERSTAND

- *What does it look like when a creative person is inspired?*
- *What did it look like when God inspired the biblical writers? Any guesses?*

APPLY

When you decide to study the Bible, you want to know for certain that it's inspired by God, not mere mortals. Here are four compelling reasons to say "Wow!"

1. *Scripture is consistently called "the Word of God."* Psalm 119 best demonstrates this by using ten different terms for God's Word. What's more, the prophets indirectly identify their writings as God's Word by using introductory phrases such as "The Lord said to me" and "The Word of the Lord came to . . ." The authors knew they were speaking God's words (Deuteronomy 18:15–22; Jeremiah 36:27).

2. *Scripture states directly that it is inspired by God.* Second Timothy 3:16 uses the word *inspiration* (*God-breathed* in the New International Version), and other passages strongly support this truth. Second Peter 1:20–21 teaches that men "moved" ("carried along" in the NIV) by the Holy Spirit wrote scripture. Jesus and Peter said inspiration is God's choosing to communicate *His* message through *men* (Mark 12:36; Acts 4:25; 2 Peter 1:21).

3. *Scripture is spoken of as if it were God.* See Galatians 3:8 and Genesis 12:1–3. Conversely, God is spoken of as if He is scripture (see Hebrews 3:7 with Psalm 95:7). This shows the close, intimate connection between God and His Word.

4. *Old Testament authors recognized God as their source.* Moses told the people of Israel that what he had commanded them was from the Lord God (Deuteronomy 4:2). In 2 Samuel 23:2, King David on his deathbed stated that the Spirit of the Lord had spoken through him.

There's more!

PRAY

Yes, Lord, I want to say "Wow!" for inspiring every page in my Bible. I'm so glad I can read it with confidence.

DAY 7

MORE REASONS WHY THE BIBLE IS INSPIRED

Read Mark 12:18–37

KEY VERSE

Jesus replied, "Are you not in error because you do not know the Scriptures or the power of God?" MARK 12:24 NIV

UNDERSTAND

- *Humanly speaking, who is the most creative, artistic, and inspired person you know?*
- *To what degree do you think the Bible is inspired by God? Books? Chapters? Verses? Words?*

APPLY

You can know for certain that the Bible is divinely inspired for two more compelling reasons:

5. *Jesus Christ fully supported all of scripture.* See Matthew 5:17–19. He confirmed its historical accuracy, down to the tense of a verb (Mark 12:26). He declared that scripture is permanent (Matthew 5:17–18), is inspired by the Holy Spirit (Mark 12:36), contains enough information to support our faith (Luke 16:29–31), is unbreakable (John 10:35), and agrees with His teachings (John 5:46–47; Luke 24:27, 44).

6. *The New Testament writers viewed both testaments as the Word of God.* Peter affirmed that the Holy Spirit inspired the Old Testament (Acts 4:25). He compared the commandments of Jesus Christ, which the apostles taught, with the words the holy prophets spoke (2 Peter 3:2). He declared that the gospel that was preached to them was the Word of the Lord (1 Peter 1:23, 25). Peter also recognized Paul's writings as part of scripture (2 Peter 3:15–16).

The apostle Paul confirmed that the Old Testament is accurate in its historical details (1 Corinthians 10:1–11). Paul cited the Old Testament and Gospels as scripture (1 Thessalonians 5:18). He went on to state forcefully that he preached God's Word, not his own message (1 Thessalonians 2:13). The New Testament authors knew that God had entrusted them with His Word (1 Timothy 4:1–3; Titus 1:3; Revelation 1:1–3). Wow, indeed!

PRAY

Yes, Lord, I want to say "Thank You!" for these further proofs that You inspired every page in my Bible. I can call it God's Word knowing that's exactly what it is.

DAY 8

EXCUSES FOR NOT STUDYING THE BIBLE

Read Matthew 15:1–20

KEY VERSE

Then Jesus called to the crowd to come and hear. "Listen," he said, "and try to understand." MATTHEW 15:10 NLT

UNDERSTAND

- *How much can personal issues color or cloud a man's understanding of God's Word?*
- *How willing are you to believe what Jesus says?*

APPLY

What are some excuses guys give for not studying the Bible?

1. *"No one studies the Bible."* The truth is, one in five American adults say they read and study the Bible regularly. If you don't know anyone who does, ask around. If someone you ask says they don't study the Bible, ask if they would be interested in studying it with you. Don't be surprised if several say yes! When they do, encourage them to buy this book and go through it along with you.
2. *"No time to study the Bible."* This is like saying you don't have time to eat, drink, or sleep. Are you willing to take five minutes to read and study scripture daily? If so, in a year you'll finish every Bible study in this book. This is doable!
3. *"The Bible is full of errors."* Actually, this line of thinking is what's in error. The Bible is completely accurate and wholly trustworthy.
4. *"It makes me feel guilty."* Now here's an honest excuse! It's true, but it's important to note that God's purpose isn't to make you feel guilty. Instead, in Psalm 119:9–11, you read that scripture keeps you pure. In John 15:3 and 17:17, Jesus reiterated the truth that God's Word makes you holy.

Ultimately, there's no good excuse for not studying the Bible—and plenty of good reasons to study it!

PRAY

Yes, Lord, I want to say no to any and all excuses that might tempt me to stop reading and studying Your Word. Instead, I'm saying yes to You again today.

DAY 9

THE BEST FASTING BENEFITS OTHERS

Read Isaiah 58

KEY VERSES

"Is not this the kind of fasting I have chosen: to loose the chains of injustice and untie the cords of the yoke, to set the oppressed free and break every yoke? Is it not to share your food with the hungry and to provide the poor wanderer with shelter—when you see the naked, to clothe them, and not to turn away from your own flesh and blood?" Isaiah 58:6–7 niv

UNDERSTAND

- *In today's scripture reading, what is the condition God gives for acknowledging His people's prayers?*
- *What does this passage say about the value of religious practice that tolerates oppression and ignores suffering?*
- *How could this passage change the way you worship God this week?*

APPLY

There is certainly a place for "religious" practices such as fasting and humbling yourself before God in prayer, but in today's scripture reading, the prophet Isaiah tells God's people to never substitute these practices for dealing with injustice, oppression, and the needs of others. God is far more concerned with how you treat others than with the details of how you worship.

Putting this another way, caring for others is a kind of worship. If you want to demonstrate your commitment to God, care for others in the same way He cares for you. When you have abundance or extra resources, share them with others so that they can benefit from the blessings you've received.

The result of this kind of worship is that God will hear your prayers and honor them. If you are generous with others, God will be generous with you. In fact, you will find new dimensions of joy in God as you enter into the kind of life that God imagines for His people.

PRAY

Thank You, Lord, for Your generosity to Your people and for Your concern for others who don't yet know You. May I learn to care for others and to share from my abundance with them so that they can benefit from the blessings You have so generously given to me. Amen.

JESUS CARES FOR YOUR WELL-BEING

Read John 10:1–15

KEY VERSES

"The man runs away because he is a hired hand and cares nothing for the sheep. I am the good shepherd; I know my sheep and my sheep know me." JOHN 10:13–14 NIV

UNDERSTAND

- *Today's scripture reading recounts a conversation between Jesus and the Pharisees. What point does Jesus make when He compares the good shepherd to the hired hand who runs away?*
- *What difference does it make in your life that Jesus is your good shepherd?*
- *What does it mean to you that Jesus, the good shepherd, knows you as His "sheep."*

APPLY

As a follower of Jesus, you are His sheep and He is your loving shepherd. Being a part of Jesus' flock means that you follow Him and that He cares for you and protects you. In fact, Jesus is so committed to your well-being and safety that He is willing to lay down His life for you. Jesus doesn't lead you and protect you because of what He can gain for Himself—He leads and protects because He is genuinely committed to your safety and thriving.

There may have been moments in your life when someone who should have cared for you didn't, preferring to place his own interests ahead of yours. But in the safety of Jesus' presence, you won't be neglected or discarded.

Jesus wants you to listen for His voice and to respond to it. There are many different ways to be attentive to Jesus' voice. You may be especially attuned to Him when you read scripture each day, or you may wait on the Lord in silent but hopeful expectation as you pray. However you listen for God's direction in your life, He will show up to lead you forward in very much the same way an earthly shepherd leads his sheep.

PRAY

Help me, Jesus, to listen intently and consistently for Your voice so that I can respond to Your call in my life. May I avoid the deception of self-serving hired hands and remain in the security of Your flock. Amen.

DAY 11

WHERE ARE YOUR ROOTS?

Read Colossians 2:6–15

KEY VERSES

As you therefore have received Christ Jesus the Lord, continue to live your lives in him, rooted and built up in him and established in the faith, just as you were taught, abounding in thanksgiving. See to it that no one takes you captive through philosophy and empty deceit, according to human tradition, according to the elemental spirits of the universe, and not according to Christ. COLOSSIANS 2:6–8 NRSV

UNDERSTAND

- *What are the advantages of staying rooted in Jesus?*
- *What is the role of thanksgiving in remaining rooted in Jesus?*
- *Paul was concerned about the influence of Greek philosophy on his original audience. What could be a comparable dead-end system of religious belief today?*

APPLY

Having a strong start with Jesus is a great thing, but the apostle Paul wrote about the importance of making sure that you grow roots that go deep with Him. He wanted his readers to keep returning to the basics of the faith, such as loving God and living by faith. But he also wanted them to seek to go deeper by applying the teachings of Jesus to their lives and by learning to keep in touch with the Spirit.

It's easy for alternative belief systems to creep in and replace your roots in Christ. Whether that outside influence comes from a political system, philosophy, or cultural movement, your roots in Christ must be tended and cared for, while the threats of other belief systems should be uprooted as soon as possible.

The idea of "living your life" in Christ may appear to be a vague concept. So how can you live "in" a God you can't see? It's most likely that Paul is referring to the orientation of your heart, desires, and mind. He wants you to keep Jesus at the forefront of how you live each day, remaining mindful of Him and desiring quiet intimacy with Him.

PRAY

Jesus, thank You for receiving me and connecting me with the Father so that I can live by faith in Your care, love, and power. May I continue to rely on You and not any alternative foundation. Amen.

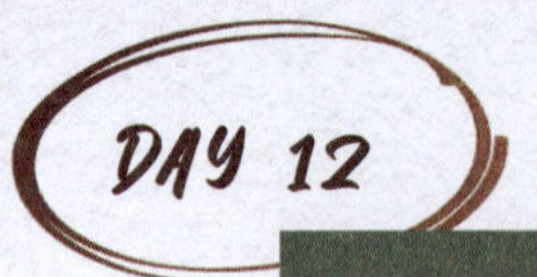

THE BIBLICAL HEROES HILKIAH AND EZRA

Read 2 Kings 22:1–23:3

KEY VERSE

The king stood by the pillar and renewed the covenant in the presence of the Lord—to follow the Lord and keep his commands, statutes and decrees with all his heart and all his soul, thus confirming the words of the covenant written in this book. Then all the people pledged themselves to the covenant. 2 Kings 23:3 NIV

UNDERSTAND

- *Why do you think God preserved the Hebrew scriptures?*
- *Does anyone need to wonder or worry about lost books of the Bible?*

APPLY

Again, it's common to wonder, "Do we have all the right books in God's Word?" Thankfully, the books of the Old Testament were miraculously preserved despite persecution and national apostasy.

Wicked King Manasseh reigned over Judah hundreds of years after Moses, David, and many of the other Old Testament writers. Manasseh considered nothing sacred. You could compare him to the wicked sorcerer in *Indiana Jones and the Temple of Doom*—but instead of sacrificing other people's children, he passed his own son through the fire (2 Kings 21:6)—as well as any copies of the scriptures he could find, it seems.

A generation later, not even the high priest in Jerusalem had a copy of God's Word, until the day Hilkiah the high priest exclaimed, "I have found the Book of the Law" (2 Kings 22:8). This occurred just before the Babylonian captivity of the nation of Israel in 386 BC.

Fortunately, the Israelites took the then-completed books of the Old Testament to Babylon and preserved them throughout their captivity. Hilkiah's family apparently retained the rediscovered scriptures and passed them down from generation to generation.

Hilkiah's great-grandson Ezra had a copy of the scriptures with him when he returned with the released captives to Jerusalem. He was known as a man of the Word (Ezra 7:10; Nehemiah 8:1–3).

PRAY

Yes, Lord, I want to say "Thank You!" for preserving each and every book of the Bible. Even in the worst of times, You used Hilkiah and Ezra in remarkable ways.

DAY 13

THE REWARDS OF PERSISTENT, HUMBLE PRAYER

Read Matthew 15:21–31

KEY VERSES

She replied, "That's true, Lord, but even dogs are allowed to eat the scraps that fall beneath their masters' table." "Dear woman," Jesus said to her, "your faith is great. Your request is granted." And her daughter was instantly healed. MATTHEW 15:27–28 NLT

UNDERSTAND

- *In what areas of your life do you feel the greatest need for Jesus to step in and help you?*
- *What does the story told in today's scripture reading teach about persistent, humble prayer?*
- *This story takes place during a time of tension between Jews and Gentiles. What should the Gentile woman's interaction with Jesus imply about welcoming people from other cultures as brothers and sisters in Christ?*

APPLY

Humility and prayer go hand in hand. When you approach God, it is essential to know your place before your Creator. While God's mercy and grace are abundant, there also is no guarantee that your prayer request and God's desires are going to match up. So if you approach prayer with a humble understanding that God is not obligated to grant your request, it's actually more likely that He will grant it.

The story about Jesus at first ignoring a Gentile woman's desperate plea for help can feel jarring. But her persistence in the face of what seems like rejection teaches us that we sometimes have to stick with it in our prayers, knowing that God won't ignore us but may be waiting to give us what we've asked for. There's no magic number of days to persist in prayer. It's possible that we may have to persist in prayer for years before God moves on our behalf.

As you humbly seek God and bring your requests to Him, you can rest in His goodness and compassion. He welcomes your persistent prayers. One day, maybe not until you are in the glory of God's presence, you will see the rewards of your perseverance.

PRAY

Jesus, thank You for hearing my prayers and honoring my humble perseverance. Help me to continue to pray in faith for myself and for others so that we can draw closer to You and enjoy relief from our struggles in this world. Amen.

EFFECTIVE WISDOM

Read Ecclesiastes 9:7–18

KEY VERSES

Now there lived in that city a man poor but wise, and he saved the city by his wisdom. But nobody remembered that poor man. So I said, "Wisdom is better than strength." But the poor man's wisdom is despised, and his words are no longer heeded. The quiet words of the wise are more to be heeded than the shouts of a ruler of fools. Wisdom is better than weapons of war, but one sinner destroys much good. ECCLESIASTES 9:15–18 NIV

UNDERSTAND

- *Why is wisdom considered better than strength but many still neglect it?*
- *How do the shouts of a ruler of fools, who is presumed to be a fool as well, drown out the quiet words of the wise?*
- *What does it mean to you that one sinner can destroy much good?*

APPLY

Wisdom is a powerful resource that comes from God's Spirit and can bring many benefits. While you likely aren't tasked with saving a city from an attacking army, the wisdom of God can have a tremendous impact in your life—if you value it and seek it out as if it were a precious treasure that could change everything for you.

Wisdom is a quiet power that is easily neglected and even scorned by those who pay heed to those who lead with loud shouts and agitating comments. Wisdom is often valued most when you need it desperately. But when other concerns take over in life, wisdom can fall by the wayside.

One of the most compelling reasons to cling to the wisdom of God is the potential damage sin can do. One sinner can destroy a lot of good, and so can one sin. Wisdom can help you spot the threats to your stability in the Lord. Without God's steady hand of wisdom guiding you forward, it's all the more likely that you'll go astray from His path for your life. But when you heed and live in His wisdom, He'll keep you on course.

PRAY

Lord, I ask for the guidance of Your Holy Spirit to lead me forward in Your wisdom so that I will not fall into the trap of sin or the ignorance of my own judgments. May I remember the benefits of Your wisdom and seek it throughout my day today. Amen.

DAY 15

GOD'S JUSTICE WILL WIN

Read Habakkuk 2:12-20

KEY VERSES

"What sorrow awaits you who say to wooden idols, 'Wake up and save us!' To speechless stone images you say, 'Rise up and teach us!' Can an idol tell you what to do? They may be overlaid with gold and silver, but they are lifeless inside. But the Lord *is in his holy Temple. Let all the earth be silent before him."* Habakkuk 2:19–20 NLT

UNDERSTAND

- *Why would people create idols and then rely on them for their security and prosperity?*
- *What are some examples of modern idols that people may rely on to save them?*
- *What are the differences between the people who rely on idols and the people who worship the Lord?*

APPLY

The prophet Habakkuk warned his audience that the consequences for their reliance on false gods would soon be revisited upon them. That message also applies today.

There is no escaping the moment when God returns to earth in order to set things right. What you invest in today will be revealed for what it is on the day Jesus returns. There is no deceiving God, and so your best option today is to seek God with all your heart.

Consider that while some call out to their idols for help, the followers of the Lord are told to be silent before the temple. The Lord is present in the earth even if you can't see Him or look at an image of Him. You can only trust in faith that the Lord is with you and that you can't do anything to make Him more real or more present. The Lord will act to save His people and to bring justice to the earth, and nothing can stand in His way when the time comes.

As you pray today, consider where you place your trust and what you rely on. Then seek God's presence with quiet confidence. You don't have to shout in order for God to hear you. In fact, you may not need to say anything at all.

PRAY

Lord, You are the Creator of the earth, the keeper of the universe, and the one truly just judge who will one day restore the earth. As I look to You in silent adoration today, I am grateful to be counted as one of Your children. Amen.

YOUR RESPONSE TO SCRIPTURE

Read Daniel 9:1–19

KEY VERSES

I, Daniel, learned from reading the word of the LORD, as revealed to Jeremiah the prophet, that Jerusalem must lie desolate for seventy years. So I turned to the Lord God and pleaded with him in prayer and fasting. DANIEL 9:2–3 NLT

UNDERSTAND

- *How easy or difficult is it for you to take God at His word?*
- *What would make it easier for you?*

APPLY

Do you remember who always rides along with you? Imagine asking the Lord, "Would You please read today's passage to me?" Jesus smiles and says yes. When He finishes, He doesn't close your Bible and give it back to you. Instead, He looks back at you and smiles again.

You wait expectantly, but the Lord doesn't say anything. Then it occurs to you, *Oh, He wants* me *to say something. He wants to know my response to what He just spoke to my heart.*

The easiest response is to pray: "Lord, I thank You for Daniel 9:2–3, which says, 'I, Daniel, learned from reading the word of the LORD. . .'"

Even better? To pray: "Lord, I thank You for Daniel 9:2–3, which tells me that Daniel read a portion of the book of Jeremiah, took that portion's sober and hope-filled truths to heart, and then turned to You in earnest, serious, and wholehearted prayer."

In the end, all Bible study is a conversation. It's the Lord speaking to your heart, and then you responding in prayer. That's why every Bible study in this book ends with a prayer!

PRAY

Yes, Lord, I want to say "Thank You!" for today's Bible reading and key verse. Like Daniel, I want to take You at Your word and pray every day.

DAY 17

MERCY BELONGS TO EVERYONE

Read Matthew 18:21–35

KEY VERSES

"'Shouldn't you have had mercy on your fellow servant just as I had on you?' In anger his master handed him over to the jailers to be tortured, until he should pay back all he owed. This is how my heavenly Father will treat each of you unless you forgive your brother or sister from your heart." MATTHEW 18:33–35 NIV

UNDERSTAND

- *Why does Jesus insist that His followers show mercy to others?*
- *How does your treatment of others impact your relationship with God?*
- *What does it mean to forgive someone "from your heart"?*

APPLY

If you come to God in search of mercy and forgiveness, the good news of the gospel is that the Lord is merciful and ready to restore your relationship with Him.

The debt described in the parable in today's scripture reading was impossible to pay back. Although the indebted servant was likely irresponsible and reckless with the money loaned to him, he still had the audacity to ask for forgiveness, and the master had the kindness to grant it. Even a massive debt is within the reach of God's mercy.

Grace and forgiveness should lead to transformation in how you relate to other imperfect humans. God expects you to dwell on the mercy and grace you have received. So consider how lost you would be without His mercy, and then extend that same consideration to others who are in your debt.

Forgiving a debt can be costly. You may have to swallow your pride, and you may feel like someone has bested or exploited you in some way. Forgiveness doesn't mean that you need to be taken advantage of again, but you do need to let go of your right to demand some kind of payment for a wrong done to you. Holding on to unforgiveness is certainly a temptation, but it isn't an option when you have received God's mercy on such generous terms.

PRAY

Thank You, Lord, for the mercy You show in forgiving my debts and freeing me to serve You and others. May I show the same mercy and kindness to others so they can gain a glimpse of Your grace. Amen.

GODLY SORROW

Read 2 Corinthians 7:2–12

KEY VERSES

Yet now I am happy, not because you were made sorry, but because your sorrow led you to repentance. For you became sorrowful as God intended and so were not harmed in any way by us. Godly sorrow brings repentance that leads to salvation and leaves no regret, but worldly sorrow brings death. 2 Corinthians 7:9–10 NIV

UNDERSTAND

- *What are the benefits that Paul attaches to godly sorrow?*
- *How do people typically view sorrow today?*
- *How did Paul handle his responsibility to both tell the Corinthians hard things while also encouraging them and caring for their souls?*

APPLY

Consider how sorrow has impacted you. Perhaps you still feel a lingering sense of regret or shame, so you know that sorrow is hardly a pleasant experience. No one wants to mess up. And being the person who has to point out the failure or misdeeds of another brings a sense of sorrow.

Paul encourages us to think of sorrow as a catalyst for a fresh start. He held that we can move on beyond our failures and the weight of our sorrows if we're willing to go to the Lord and repent. In fact, Paul encourages us not to dwell on our sorrows—beyond looking ahead to the ways we can make things right.

Moving beyond your sorrows today is a chance to open your life to God's healing and transformation. If you never want to feel the weight of sorrow again, you can imitate the determination of the Corinthians to change their ways. God is always ready to forgive and to aid those who are willing to turn to Him for a fresh start.

PRAY

Jesus, help me to both feel the weight of my sorrow over my sins and to move beyond my sorrow to the new life You offer as I repent. May I remember to show grace to those who are also moving through their sorrow and seeking Your renewal. Amen.

BLESSINGS IN HARDSHIPS

Read Philippians 1:12–20

KEY VERSES

What then? Only that in every way, whether in pretense or in truth, Christ is proclaimed, and in this I rejoice. But not only that, I also will rejoice, for I know that this will turn out for my deliverance through your prayers and the provision of the Spirit of Jesus Christ.
PHILIPPIANS 1:18–19 NASB

UNDERSTAND

- *Why would Paul rejoice over his imprisonment and over those who were preaching the gospel based on wrong motives?*
- *In what did Paul place his faith during his time of suffering and captivity?*
- *What was Paul's main goal in his ministry, and how did that lead to freedom and joy?*

APPLY

In Paul's letter to the Philippian church, he describes a path to joy, freedom, and blessing that may seem counterintuitive. Yet Paul himself is an example of its effectiveness.

Paul endured suffering very few can even imagine. Yet he never complained but continued doing what God had called him to do—even in the face of sometimes frightening opposition. Through everything, Paul made the cause of the gospel and the reputation of Jesus his top priority. Paul was our example of remaining focused on Jesus and His message no matter what it cost him.

This isn't to say that you should *desire* the kinds of struggles Paul endured. You can ask God to protect you from difficulties, but you should also be aware that He can meet you and bless you in the midst of hardship and struggles. God can work in you and for your benefit as well as for the benefit of those around you in any life situation.

If you can link your desires with God's, you'll have a better perspective on life. When you care deeply about seeing other people enjoy liberty in Christ, the stakes of life will look very different. You'll find it easier to endure suffering and to find a silver lining in your struggles when you remember that God is with you through whatever you endure.

PRAY

Jesus, help me to leave behind my desire for an easy life so that I can better advance the cause of Your kingdom and share Your message boldly with others. Amen.

SANCTIFIED TO SERVE

Read John 17:1-19

KEY VERSES

"I am not asking you to take them out of the world, but I ask you to protect them from the evil one. They do not belong to the world, just as I do not belong to the world. Sanctify them in the truth; your word is truth. As you have sent me into the world, so I have sent them into the world." JOHN 17:15–18 NRSV

UNDERSTAND

- *What did Jesus mean when He said that His disciples "do not belong to the world, just as I do not belong to the world"?*
- *How does being sanctified—made holy—affect the choices you make today?*
- *Jesus has sent you into the world and prayed for your protection from the evil one. How does that encourage you and give you confidence today?*

APPLY

If you belong to Jesus, you will always feel a bit out of place in this world, which is filled with people who hold different values than you and who aren't guided by the Holy Spirit. If we're not careful, our not belonging to this world can create adversarial feelings toward those who aren't in a relationship with Jesus. But that is counterproductive to the mission Jesus has given you—namely, the command to go into the world to share His message of salvation through faith in Him.

God has made you holy by His Word and by the Holy Spirit so that you can reveal Jesus to others. For that reason, you don't conform to the standards of the world. Instead, you let Jesus transform your life so you can share that transformation with others.

Even though some will respond to you sharing the gospel message with hostility, Jesus calls you to continue loving, serving, and sharing His message with others. You can find encouragement and empowerment to do those things because Jesus has prayed for your protection as you go about His mission in the world.

PRAY

Jesus, I ask for Your protection, transformation, and guidance as I go out into the world to share the hope of Your message with others. Help me to view others with compassion and mercy so that I can be an effective ambassador for You. Amen.

DAY 21

HOW TO EXPERIENCE THE BIBLE'S VISTAS AND REWARDS

Read Colossians 3:1–17

KEY VERSE

Let the word of Christ dwell in you richly. Colossians 3:16 esv

UNDERSTAND

- *What's the biggest difference when a Christian and an atheist study the Bible?*
- *When does a Christian see the most in scripture?*

APPLY

Remember how you feel when you see a strikingly beautiful place for the first time? When you study the Bible, you want to do so with your spiritual eyes wide open. How do you do that?

First, you come to God in prayer. You can worship God, thank Him for His Word, and then ask Him to remove anything that would cloud your heart and mind as you read and study the Bible.

Second, you ask God for the Holy Spirit's illumination as you read each passage of scripture. You can read the same passage of scripture two, three, four, or more times and still make new discoveries with each new reading.

Third, you come to the Bible with a strong sense of expectancy, determination, and persistence. You want to look closely at scripture. The goal of such careful observation is to discover more and more of what the Word says.

You're not doing a superficial once-over, like you're taking a cursory glance around the room to find your shoes. Instead, you're looking intently at God's Word. What awe-inspiring vistas and rewards He has in store for you in the days ahead!

PRAY

Yes, Lord, I want to say "Thank You!" for the vistas and rewards of reading and studying the Bible. I can't wait to see what You have in store for me in the days ahead.

A COUNTERCULTURAL LIFE

Read Romans 12:9–21

KEY VERSES

Be devoted to one another in brotherly love; give preference to one another in honor, not lagging behind in diligence, fervent in spirit, serving the Lord; rejoicing in hope, persevering in tribulation, devoted to prayer, contributing to the needs of the saints, practicing hospitality. Bless those who persecute you; bless and do not curse. Rejoice with those who rejoice, and weep with those who weep. ROMANS 12:10–15 NASB

UNDERSTAND

- *How can you show preference to fellow Christians in brotherly love?*
- *Which of the actions in this passage do you find most challenging, and how can you experiment with incorporating them into your life a little bit more today?*
- *Why is it so important to bless those who persecute you and to overcome evil with good?*

APPLY

Paul maps out a series of practices for Christians that are extremely countercultural—and even counterintuitive. Giving generously to those in need and showing hospitality to others are two ways that have always been vital to supporting others. Both acts require faith that God will provide for your needs when you remain faithful and take care of others. It's surely more acceptable today to think of ways you can stockpile savings and other assets to protect yourself from uncertainty, but Paul says that Christians should be so devoted to the well-being of others that they give generously of their finances and homes to ensure that fellow Christians receive God's care.

Should hard times and even persecution come your way, the Lord doesn't want you to give up or to shrink back in fear. Cling to the hope He has given you and continue to devote yourself to prayer. It's certainly not easy to endure hardships, but if you place your hope in God and continue to pray, you'll have the strength to continue.

The guiding principle for most of today's scripture reading is to seek the best for others, whether that's sharing in their joys or in their sorrows. Seek the best for others even when they curse you, blessing them in return. As you devote yourself to caring for others, you'll find freedom from the self-centeredness that ensnares so many today, and you'll draw near to God's heart for the world.

PRAY

Jesus, help me to see others the way You see them, to care for their needs as if they were my own, and to give generously to those in need. I trust that You can provide what I need in order to be generous and that You will care for me when I bless my opponents. Amen.

DAY 23

LOOK FOR GOD'S NEW THING

Read Isaiah 43:14–25

KEY VERSES

Thus says the Lord, who makes a way in the sea, a path in the mighty waters, who brings out chariot and horse, army and warrior; they lie down, they cannot rise, they are extinguished, quenched like a wick: Do not remember the former things, or consider the things of old. I am about to do a new thing; now it springs forth, do you not perceive it? I will make a way in the wilderness and rivers in the desert. Isaiah 43:16–19 NRSV

UNDERSTAND

- *Are you expecting God to do a new thing or to do only what you can imagine possible?*
- *How could you begin to expect God to do something new?*
- *How can today's passage help expand your understanding of God's power and strength?*

APPLY

The Lord wants you to remember the things He has done in the past, but we should also be on the lookout for Him to do new things today as well. God isn't content with you learning about the past and stopping there. Each generation has its own calling to be aware of Him and fresh challenges to meet in the moment.

God's promise to do new things means that you have a calling to remain attentive and aware of what He is doing. Thankfully, it's not up to you to create the new things of God. You only need to remain aware of Him, pay attention, and follow where He leads you. Most importantly, don't be surprised if God's new thing feels uncomfortable or unfamiliar. If anything, that may be a sign that you're on the right track and needing to live by faith even more.

You can find hope in the story of God's people who also have had to leave the familiar behind and take up the path He had set before them. The Lord is great and powerful, and He will remain with you through the uncertainty of the days ahead.

PRAY

Lord, help me to rely on Your power and wisdom and not on my own understanding or ability. May I look beyond what I know and what feels comfortable so that I can move into the new thing that You've called me to. Amen.

DAY 24

NATURAL AND SUPERNATURAL REVELATIONS

Read Titus 1:1–2:15

KEY VERSES

Teach them to know the truth that shows them how to live godly lives. This truth gives them confidence that they have eternal life, which God—who does not lie—promised them before the world began. TITUS 1:1–2 NLT

UNDERSTAND

- *Which kind of general revelation do you value the most?*
- *Which kind of special revelation do you value the most?*

APPLY

It's common to ask, "What else did God give us besides the Bible?" Thankfully, God has chosen to reveal Himself in many ways.

General revelation is God's self-disclosure through *natural* means to all men. Four examples follow below:

- *Creation (Psalm 19:1–6; Romans 1:18–21). Why is there an ordered universe?*
- *Preservation (Colossians 1:17). Why doesn't it all fall apart?*
- *Conscience (Romans 2:15). Why do we have a sense of right and wrong?*
- *Reason (Acts 17:16–34). What is "obvious" about the unknown God?*

Special revelation is God's self-disclosure of His message through *supernatural* means to some for all mankind. Here are four examples:

- *Theophanies, or special appearances by the Lord (Genesis 18:1–2; 19:1). The Lord revealed Himself in the form of men and angels.*
- *Visions (1 Samuel 3:1–4; Acts 16:9). The Lord speaks in dreams and angelic appearances.*
- *Jesus Christ (John 1:1–18; Hebrews 1:1–2). After speaking to the Old Testament saints in many ways, God spoke through His Son.*
- *Prophecies (1 Kings 17:1; Titus 1:1–3). The Lord spoke to the prophets, giving oral messages to Israel and the nations.*

You might be tempted to envy those who received theophanies, visions, and prophecies from the Lord. Yet in a real way, you are more privileged than those of any other age, because you have free access to the entire inspired Word of God.

PRAY

Lord, thank You for revealing Yourself in so may ways!

CHOSEN TO BE FRUITFUL

Read John 15:12–17

KEY VERSES

"You did not choose Me but I chose you, and appointed you that you would go and bear fruit, and that your fruit would remain, so that whatever you ask of the Father in My name He may give to you. This I command you, that you love one another." JOHN 15:16–17 NASB

UNDERSTAND

- *What did Jesus say is the purpose for your life as His follower?*
- *What condition did Jesus place on prayer requests to the Father?*
- *What did Jesus mean when He commanded the disciples to "love one another, just as I have loved you"?*

APPLY

Jesus chose you to have a long-lasting impact in this world. That means that you have the tremendous privilege of praying to God as a beloved child, as well as the great responsibility to align your desires and will to Jesus' desires and will. God has chosen you to bear "fruit" for Him. That is part of your identity as a follower of Jesus.

Jesus is so committed to helping you bear fruit for Him and for the benefit of others that He has given you the privilege of making bold prayer requests in His name. He promises that your heavenly Father will give you what you need to accomplish His purposes—if you simply ask in His name. Such a striking promise brings up the key issue at stake: Are your desires in line with Jesus and His will?

You have incredible access to God the Father because you have been united with Him through Jesus. What are you asking Him to do for you today so that you can bear fruit for Him?

PRAY

Thank You, Father, for the incredible access You have granted to me through Your Son, Jesus. May my prayers remain in line with the will of Jesus, and may I bear fruit that endures for years to the benefit of many. Amen.

DAY 26

GOD'S PURPOSE WILL ALWAYS BE ACCOMPLISHED

Read Acts 27:14–26

KEY VERSES

"And yet now I urge you to keep up your courage, for there will be no loss of life among you, but only of the ship. For this very night an angel of the God to whom I belong, whom I also serve, came to me, saying, 'Do not be afraid, Paul; you must stand before Caesar; and behold, God has graciously granted you all those who are sailing with you.' Therefore, keep up your courage, men, for I believe God that it will turn out exactly as I have been told." ACTS 27:22–25 NASB

UNDERSTAND

- *What do you think it was like for Paul to trust that God's purpose for him was stronger than the power of the storm?*
- *Why did Paul speak so boldly to the crew of the ship?*
- *Where did Paul tell the crew on the ship to find their courage?*

APPLY

When God has a mission lined up for you, there is nothing on earth that can stand in the way. Paul witnessed that in a most dramatic way while stuck in a life-threatening storm that eventually left him shipwrecked on a remote island. It's easy to get distracted by the circumstances all around you and the reactions of those in the midst of the storms of life as well. Others may be giving up all hope, and it will be tempting to follow their lead.

You can find confidence in what God has guided you to do and remaining faithful to it. If your life feels chaotic or lacking in direction, this is the day to quietly seek God's wisdom and guidance. Even if you feel like you're in a storm, God's mission for you cannot be overcome. You'll find peace and security in the assurance of God's calling.

When you enjoy the confidence of God's calling in your life, you can share that peace with others. They can learn to grow in their trust in God as you demonstrate faith and hope in uncertain times.

PRAY

Jesus, guide me in the choices I make today so that I won't fall into the trap of relying on my own wisdom. May I find Your path forward, and if I stray far from You, may I have the humility to correct my course. Amen.

HUMBLE FAITH IN GOD

Read Matthew 8:1-13

KEY VERSES

But the officer said, "Lord, I am not worthy to have you come into my home. Just say the word from where you are, and my servant will be healed. I know this because I am under the authority of my superior officers, and I have authority over my soldiers. I only need to say, 'Go,' and they go, or 'Come,' and they come. And if I say to my slaves, 'Do this,' they do it." MATTHEW 8:8–9 NLT

UNDERSTAND

- *Why was it so important to Jesus that a Roman officer had so much faith in His power to heal?*
- *What made this Roman officer's request for a miracle stand out from others recorded in the four Gospels?*
- *How did this Roman officer correctly understand Jesus as a King with authority?*

APPLY

Today's reading offers a helpful balance of faith and humility. Although the Roman officer knew that Jesus had the power to heal his servant, he also didn't think of himself as worthy to ask so great a thing of God's Son, even inviting Him into his home. In fact, his humility was only surpassed by his faith in the power of Jesus to heal.

It is a great and awesome thing to be able to ask things of God. Scripture offers the reminder that people are made from dust and will return to dust and also compares people to grass that quickly withers in the sun. You can make the mistake of assuming too much about your own importance and even end up making demands of God to meet your needs. When your prayers veer in this direction, the story of the Roman officer gives a helpful corrective.

By the same token, Jesus wants us to be bold and courageous when we make requests of God for ourselves or for someone else. No one standing alongside Jesus expected such great faith from a Roman officer, and so there's no reason why you too can't intercede in big ways for others. Prayers that put others first and remember that Jesus is King are the exact type that He longs to hear.

PRAY

Jesus, You are all-powerful and fully able to answer my prayers, bringing healing and restoration to those in need. May I never take Your kindness and generosity for granted as I pray for myself and for others. Amen.

ARE YOUR PRIORITIES CORRECT?

Read 1 Corinthians 13

KEY VERSES

Now we see things imperfectly, like puzzling reflections in a mirror, but then we will see everything with perfect clarity. All that I know now is partial and incomplete, but then I will know everything completely, just as God now knows me completely. Three things will last forever—faith, hope, and love—and the greatest of these is love.

1 CORINTHIANS 13:12–13 NLT

UNDERSTAND

- *What is the correct balance between the pursuit of spiritual gifts and the pursuit of love?*
- *What things did Paul tell the Corinthians to value above prophetic gifts and superior knowledge?*
- *How did Paul find comfort despite all the things he didn't know or understand?*

APPLY

Paul knew that the Corinthians loved higher learning and spectacular spiritual gifts such as prophecy. While he certainly valued these things, he rightly worried that they had put their emphasis in the wrong place.

Consider today what you truly value. What is really important to you in your everyday life, especially your spiritual life? It's easy to get sidetracked by lesser priorities, to make side issues really serious sticking points that sow division in the church, which can cause different groups to take sides, choose leaders, and attack one another endlessly.

Paul's higher road involves faith, hope, and love—things he said would last forever. Faith means living each day in total dependence on God. Hope is a sense of unseen clarity about the future that places it in God's hands. Love, the greatest of the three, means both acceptance by a merciful God and a compassionate and accepting heart attitude toward fellow believers. We should never be so focused on gaining knowledge or spiritual gifts that we miss out on faith, hope, and love.

PRAY

Jesus, help me to put the lesser pursuits of spiritual gifts, prophecies, and knowledge in their proper places so that I can see the purity and power of Your love. May I receive Your love and then share it widely with others. Amen.

DAY 29

ENDURANCE COMES FROM GOD'S POWER

Read Colossians 1:1–14

KEY VERSES

May you be made strong with all the strength that comes from his glorious power, and may you be prepared to endure everything with patience, while joyfully giving thanks to the Father, who has enabled you to share in the inheritance of the saints in the light.
COLOSSIANS 1:11–12 NRSV

UNDERSTAND

- *How can you grow in your strength and endurance?*
- *How does giving thanks to God the Father in the midst of difficulties help you persevere?*
- *Why is it important to keep the rewards of obedience in mind?*

APPLY

Endurance and patience for the trials of life aren't the kinds of things that come naturally. These are fruits of the Spirit that God can develop in you, provided you actively seek them out and ask for them. The strength that God passes on to you has a divine source that you can't earn or develop through willpower. These are all gifts that are given to you based on God's grace.

Although these gifts come through grace, meaning God's unmerited favor, don't overlook the fact that Paul still prayed for these things to be manifested among the Colossian Christians. Being among God's people isn't a guarantee that you'll have instant access to all that God has made available to you. This is where intercession and requests are so important.

Jesus assured you that if you seek, you will find, and He promised that all who are thirsty will be satisfied. Paul's prayer is an invitation for you to actively seek more from God and to fully explore all you have been given through Jesus.

PRAY

Jesus, help me to endure the highs and lows of life with the strength and power You provide. May I keep in mind the hope of Your people who will one day share in Your inheritance because they relied on You above all else. Amen.

SIMPLE AND COMPLEX TRUTHS

Read Isaiah 55:1–13

KEY VERSE

"For as the heavens are higher than the earth, so are my ways higher than your ways and my thoughts than your thoughts." ISAIAH 55:9 ESV

UNDERSTAND

- *Remember phone books? A million facts, but none that could change your life.*
- *The Bible has more than 31,100 verses. How many can change your life?*

APPLY

The Bible is truer than any other book ever published. The Bible was written by God. It will *never* be out of date. Your belief in the Bible is based on the fact that God *always* tells the truth. It is a book of *trustworthy facts about eternal realities.*

As you examine how Jesus and the apostles viewed the Old Testament, you come to understand that they believed the scriptures to be not only a revelation *from* God but also a revelation *of* God. They accepted the factual statements in the Bible at face value and then saw the spiritual implications of its important truths.

In the Bible, you find two kinds of facts: *simple* truths (easily grasped facts) and *complex* truths (facts that exceed your grasp). You will never plumb the depths of the Bible's complex truths. God's thoughts far exceed the collective brainpower of *all* humanity (Isaiah 55:8–9).

It's no wonder that God doesn't pretend to tell you everything (Deuteronomy 29:29). It's also ludicrous to think you can contribute one microscopic atom of truth to what God has known before the beginning of time (Romans 11:33). He is God. You are not!

In coming days, we'll look at how to enjoy and benefit even more from reading and studying scripture:

By asking questions.
By noting specific facts.
By taking God at His word.

PRAY

Yes, Lord, I want to say "Thank You!" for who You are. You are the Lord God, Creator of heaven and earth. Your ways are infinitely higher than my ways. I trust You!

DAY 31

GOD RESPONDS TO CHANGES OF HEART

Read Jonah 3

KEY VERSES

Then the king and his nobles sent this decree throughout the city: "No one, not even the animals from your herds and flocks, may eat or drink anything at all. People and animals alike must wear garments of mourning, and everyone must pray earnestly to God. They must turn from their evil ways and stop all their violence. Who can tell? Perhaps even yet God will change his mind and hold back his fierce anger from destroying us."

JONAH 3:7–9 NLT

UNDERSTAND

- *In what ways did the people of Nineveh have more faith in God than Jonah?*
- *What kinds of changes did the king of Nineveh demand for his people?*
- *What could serve as a sign of repentance today?*

APPLY

Jonah didn't hold out much hope for the people of Nineveh, and their change of heart after hearing the prophet preach shocked him. No matter how far you may have drifted from God, no matter how grievously you've sinned against God, and no matter how much shame you carry, you couldn't top the people of Nineveh. They were so wicked that God threatened to destroy their city.

But the Ninevites had a change of heart and repented. . .and God spared them.

God doesn't overlook a change of heart. If you come to God in repentance today, He will most certainly have mercy on you. There is no point too far from God. The psalms speak of mourning being turned into dancing, and such a turnaround is always possible when God's people confess their sins and seek Him again.

When God saw the Ninevites' change of heart, He had mercy on them. But Jonah, who had reason to dislike the people of Nineveh, was angry because he hoped God would destroy them for their wickedness. Don't be like Jonah! Instead, when you learn that someone—even the worst sinner, the type of [illegible] over that saved soul!

PRAY

Lord, help me to remember that I am never far from mercy and restoration. May I always turn quickly to You after I have sinned so that I can receive Your mercy. May I show that same mercy to others who turn their hearts to You. Amen.

DAY 32

USE WHAT GOD HAS GIVEN TO YOU

Read Matthew 25:14–30

KEY VERSES

"Then he ordered, 'Take the money from this servant, and give it to the one with the ten bags of silver. To those who use well what they are given, even more will be given, and they will have an abundance. But from those who do nothing, even what little they have will be taken away.'" Matthew 25:28–29 NLT

UNDERSTAND

- *The parable recorded in today's scripture reading talks about a master giving his servants money. What do you think God has given to you?*
- *How do you think you can "invest" the gifts God has given you?*
- *What is at stake in this parable concerning the gifts that God has given you?*

APPLY

You may not believe that you have a lot to offer God or other people, but if you view your talents, abilities, and possessions as gifts from the Lord, then you have no reason to neglect them. Even the slightest ability or small portion of free time can be used well to serve or bless others. God has chosen to bless others through your abilities. In addition, He will increase what you have so that you can reach more people for His purposes.

The servant in this parable who is called wicked and lazy didn't use the gifts God had given him and didn't have any plans to use them. The main issue here is neglect. If you neglect what God has given you, why should He give you anything else?

If you desire to be useful to God and a blessing to others, just ask Him to open your eyes to what He's given you, including the abilities you can use for Him. There are opportunities around you right now, and God wants you to use what He's given you to bless others and glorify Him.

PRAY

Jesus, help me to recognize the talents You have given to me. Give me the strength and determination to use them well for Your purposes and to glorify You. Amen.

GENTLE INSTRUCTION

Read 2 Timothy 2:14–25

KEY VERSES

And the Lord's servant must not be quarrelsome but must be kind to everyone, able to teach, not resentful. Opponents must be gently instructed, in the hope that God will grant them repentance leading them to a knowledge of the truth. 2 TIMOTHY 2:24–25 NIV

UNDERSTAND

- *Think of someone who has departed from the truth of Jesus. How do you view that person?*
- *Why would Paul tell Timothy to gently instruct opponents? How could taking the risk of "going easy" on someone in error pay off with a big reward of repentance?*
- *How does Paul's belief that some opponents are deceived by the devil change your view of disagreements over beliefs and theology?*

APPLY

Most people have a lot riding on their religious beliefs. Many people's beliefs are shaped by their personal experiences, stories, teachers, or relationships that nudged them in a particular direction. But that doesn't make their views right. In fact, many hold beliefs that are in absolute opposition to what the Word of God says. These kinds of beliefs are, in a word, *wrong*.

It's human nature to want to blast the views of an opponent to smithereens, to prove him wrong and yourself right. It may appear to be a win/lose situation where only the strong survive. Of course, you could "agree to disagree," but sometimes you'll meet people whose beliefs could do them genuine harm by leading them astray from God. Whether or not you believe they are under the influence of the evil one, you can do them a lot of good by putting your own ego aside and *gently* instructing them in God's truth.

When you talk with someone whose beliefs you know are not in keeping with God's Word, start by putting yourself in their shoes, be willing to engage that person by listening respectfully, and then humbly and gently answer his questions. Above all, remember that speaking the gospel message isn't about you; it's [illegible] have to prove yourself right; you just need to speak God[illegible].

PRAY

Jesus, help me to pursue the best for everyone I meet, especially those who oppose me or who may be in error. Help me to speak with gentleness and humility with others so that I can bring them closer to You and Your truth. Amen.

MERCY LEADS TO REPENTANCE

Read Acts 3:17–26

KEY VERSES

"Now, fellow Israelites, I know that you acted in ignorance, as did your leaders. But this is how God fulfilled what he had foretold through all the prophets, saying that his Messiah would suffer. Repent, then, and turn to God, so that your sins may be wiped out, that times of refreshing may come from the Lord." ACTS 3:17–19 NIV

UNDERSTAND

- *In what way did Peter give his listeners the benefit of the doubt in today's scripture reading?*
- *What does repentance and "turning to God" look like in your life?*
- *What is the promised result of Peter's listeners repenting from their sins?*

APPLY

Humanly speaking, the apostle Peter had every reason to feel angry, even judgmental, toward the people who had either ignored Jesus' message or actively opposed Him. Yet he stuck with Jesus' mission to bring repentance and renewal rather than condemnation.

It's not easy to talk to an indifferent or hostile listener about Jesus, but that is exactly what Peter did in Acts 3. After healing a lame beggar at the temple, he spoke to a group of amazed onlookers, many of whom had probably approved of the crucifixion of Jesus weeks before. Peter's example shows that mercy can win out over judgment, as many of his listeners responded positively to his message.

God's mercy and kindness are well documented throughout scripture, and that kindness leads people to repent of their sins. Just as you have been forgiven by God, you can show the same mercy and forgiveness to others. In fact, Jesus expects just that.

It may feel good in the moment to condemn or judge others, but that won't lead to the refreshment that God desires for the world. The Lord has given each of us a holy calling to show others the path to God. The hope is that their sins can be wiped away for times of refreshing, but sharing that message can be challenging. The grace of God can feel risky and costly, but when others respond to it, it is well worth it.

PRAY

Jesus, help me to remember the ways You have shown grace and mercy to me, freeing me from judgment of others. May I show the same patience and mercy to others so that they can enjoy times of refreshing. Amen.

THE VALUE OF QUESTIONS

Read John 1:19–42

KEY VERSE

Jesus turned and saw them following and said to them, "What are you seeking?" And they said to him, "Rabbi" (which means Teacher), "where are you staying?" John 1:38 ESV

UNDERSTAND

- *In the key verse above, who is "them"?*
- *In that same verse, what does Jesus do right before asking them a question?*

APPLY

As you read and study the Bible, you want to remember that even the smallest details (say, a person's name) often have spiritual undertones.

Here's where you get to turn into a not-so-mild-mannered reporter. Pull out your press card and get ready to ask a stream of questions worthy of the best journalist. You can ask *Who? What? When? Where? Why?* and *How?* questions repeatedly as you read and study God's Word.

You won't ask all of these questions every time you read a scripture verse. But you can ask the most pertinent questions that come to mind after reading it.

By asking lots of *Who? What? When? Where? Why?* and *How?* questions, you get a much better idea of what any given scripture passage says. You also get a good idea of what it *doesn't* say and what you're not yet sure it's saying.

The exciting news throughout scripture is that God promises to bless the man who reads His Word, looks intently at it, interprets it correctly, personalizes it, and applies it to his life. Be that man!

PRAY

Yes, Lord, I want to say "Thank You!" for asking me to engage my brain and ask lots of questions as I read the Bible. No more autopilot for me.

THE LORD DESIRES PEACE FOR HIS PEOPLE

Read Hosea 2:14–23

KEY VERSES

"I will betroth you to Me forever; yes, I will betroth you to Me in righteousness and in justice, in favor and in compassion, and I will betroth you to Me in faithfulness. Then you will know the LORD." HOSEA 2:19–20 NASB

UNDERSTAND

- *How does the Lord speak to the people of Israel in this passage even though they had been rebellious and unfaithful to Him?*
- *What does the image of being "married" to God imply about the kind of relationship God desires to have with you?*
- *How does God's compassion toward His people impact your view of Him?*

APPLY

The sting of betrayal and unfaithfulness is difficult to endure, and the damage done is exceedingly difficult to repair. The key toward reconciliation for a broken relationship is for the betrayed party to extend forgiveness and compassion to the offending person.

In today's scripture reading, we can see God's compassion and mercy on display as He offers complete restoration and a new future of peace to the people of Israel even after generations of unfaithfulness and rebellion. God was eager to get a new start with His people, and the failures and sins of the past weren't going to get in the way of His plans for peace and unity.

You may feel the weight of your past failures and mistakes. Many people do simply because shame and guilt have a way of hanging around. While God wants you to take ownership of those failures, you can trust Him to restore you if you come to Him in confession and accept His forgiveness and mercy.

PRAY

Father, thank You for forgiving and restoring me so that I can move forward in faith and hope for the future. May I enjoy the peace You give Your faithful people. Amen.

HOPE IN GOD ALONE

Read Psalm 71:1–12

KEY VERSES

In you, O Lord, I take refuge; let me never be put to shame. In your righteousness deliver me and rescue me; incline your ear to me and save me. Be to me a rock of refuge, a strong fortress, to save me, for you are my rock and my fortress. Rescue me, O my God, from the hand of the wicked, from the grasp of the unjust and cruel. For you, O Lord, are my hope, my trust, O Lord, from my youth. Psalm 71:1–5 NRSV

UNDERSTAND

- *What are some of the images used in Psalm 71 to describe God? What do those images mean to you?*
- *What kind of adversity are you facing in your life that could apply to the challenges described in this psalm?*
- *What does it mean to be "rescued" by God in your own circumstances today?*

APPLY

The psalms often use images of conflict and battle to describe the threats and challenges of life that oppose the security found in God. But you don't necessarily have to be facing a personal enemy or a difficult relationship in order to feel like you're in the midst of conflict and in need of God's security. The enemy could be a medical diagnosis or a traumatic experience that haunts your thoughts. In each case, you may face adversity that makes it more necessary than ever to rely on God.

There are plenty of places where you can seek refuge. In fact, your greatest temptation may be relying on something other than God for protection in the midst of conflict, suffering, or uncertainty. That is where idolatry comes in, as you find yourself relying more on money, powerful relationships, or your possessions for security. An idol is anything that replaces the role of God in your life and keeps you from intimacy with Him.

Seeing God as your security and hope for the future is a process. Today's psalm tells us about learning to trust in God from the days of one's youth. It's never too soon or too late to start trusting God with the challenges of your life. It is something you learn and cultivate over time. But soon it will become natural to turn to God first when your life is out of sorts and uncertain.

PRAY

Father, You are the true refuge in times of trouble and fear. I can trust that I am safe in Your care because of Your mercy and Your enduring love for me. May I turn away from every false sense of security and rely on You alone. Amen.

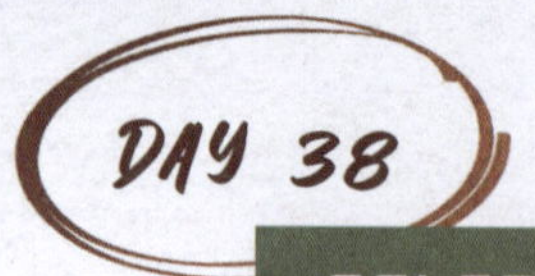

CELEBRATE GENEROUS GRACE FOR OTHERS

Read Matthew 20:1–16

KEY VERSES

"He answered one of them, 'Friend, I haven't been unfair! Didn't you agree to work all day for the usual wage? Take your money and go. I wanted to pay this last worker the same as you. Is it against the law for me to do what I want with my money? Should you be jealous because I am kind to others?'" MATTHEW 20:13–15 NLT

UNDERSTAND

- *What is your reaction to the generosity of the vineyard owner in this parable?*
- *Why does Jesus say the first will be last and the last will be first in God's kingdom?*
- *How does God's generosity run counter to the expectations of society today?*

APPLY

The workers in the vineyard who showed up late needed to receive a full wage in order to feed their families. While it would have technically been just for the vineyard owner to only pay them for the time they worked, such a small payment would not have been very compassionate or in touch with their actual needs. Yet the generosity they received became a point of division with their fellow workers. Seeing mercy and grace shown to others may sometimes become a source of contention.

God sees how humanity has failed and is more than willing to treat people far better than they deserve. That may sound like really great news for you personally, but once you see someone else get the same kind of mercy, you may have a very different view of God. Is God merely giving others a free pass for their sins? Don't the commands of God matter?

Obedience does matter a great deal to God, but so do mercy and restoration. There isn't a limited supply of God's grace. In fact, everyone is treated with more grace than they deserve before God. Jesus doesn't want you to resent anyone else's need of mercy, because without God's grace, they'd have nowhere to go.

PRAY

Jesus, help me to remember the ways You have generously forgiven me and shown me mercy so that I am grateful to You and compassionate toward others. Amen.

DAY 39

ABUNDANT LIFE IS SIMPLE

Read John 15:1-11

KEY VERSES

"Remain in Me, and I in you. Just as the branch cannot bear fruit of itself but must remain in the vine, so neither can you unless you remain in Me. I am the vine, you are the branches; the one who remains in Me, and I in him bears much fruit, for apart from Me you can do nothing." JOHN 15:4–5 NASB

UNDERSTAND

- *What kinds of spiritual practices can you do to "remain" in Jesus?*
- *How does Jesus being the vine and you the branch affect the way you view your own role in producing spiritual growth?*
- *What does it mean for you to be "apart" from Jesus, and how can you prevent that from happening?*

APPLY

Every follower of Jesus bears a measure of responsibility for his choices and actions, but Jesus makes it abundantly clear that you are not solely responsible for producing spiritual growth. Any changes in your life or growth in your spiritual awareness of God comes directly from Jesus. Any benefits that others enjoy because of your abundant life in God can be traced to Jesus' intervention in your life—not your own efforts or willpower.

Jesus invites you to walk a fine line where you must choose to remain in Him. There is a decision and an action in this. If you don't remain in Him, you will surely wither. But if you choose to remain in Him and put in the effort to keep Him at the forefront of your life, He will produce the life of God in you.

Jesus keeps it simple, telling His followers to cultivate a life of faith and dependence on Him. Once you are united with Him, your desires will begin to line up with His, and prayer will become much simpler because you won't have to worry about what to seek from God. The starting point is determining how you can ensure that you are abiding in Jesus today and every day.

PRAY

Jesus, You are my source of life and my hope for the abundant spiritual life You've promised. Help me to abide in You, remaining aware of Your presence and love so that I can bear the fruit of Your Spirit. Amen.

LOOK INTENTLY, BUT THAT'S NOT ALL

Read Psalm 49:1–20

KEY VERSE

But God will ransom my soul from the power of Sheol, for he will receive me. Selah
Psalm 49:15 ESV

UNDERSTAND

- *In Numbers 16:31–32, what terrible judgment did Korah receive?*
- *What lessons did Korah's sons learn from their father's demise?*

APPLY

It can be tempting to think that it's fairly easy to discern the facts in a scripture passage. That's often the case, but not always!

Granted, Psalm 49 isn't one of the most accessible psalms. That's all the more reason to blitz every verse with as many questions as possible, right? You can ask 145 questions over the course of the first six verses alone. Of those 145 questions, only 24 can be answered by observations made within the immediate content. The other 121 questions require interpretative answers. (Thankfully, those interpretative answers exist!)

The key thing to remember is that the goal of Bible study isn't simply to look intently at each passage of scripture. James 1:25 (NKJV) reminds us, "But he who looks into the perfect law of liberty and continues in it, and is not a forgetful hearer but a doer of the work, this one will be blessed in what he does."

Nothing replaces the importance of the Holy Spirit's illuminating your heart and mind. Jesus sent the Spirit to take up residence in every Christian for that very reason. The Holy Spirit's greatest desire is to bring God's Word alive within you so that you can wholeheartedly love the Lord, worship Him, and do what He says!

PRAY

Yes, Lord, I want to say "Thank You!" that the Bible is an incredibly cohesive whole, not a lot of miscellaneous parts. I can learn so much from it.

DAY 41

SEEKING THE RIGHT THING

Read Matthew 6:24-34

KEY VERSES

"No one can serve two masters. For you will hate one and love the other; you will be devoted to one and despise the other. You cannot serve God and be enslaved to money. That is why I tell you not to worry about everyday life—whether you have enough food and drink, or enough clothes to wear. Isn't life more than food, and your body more than clothing?" MATTHEW 6:24–25 NLT

UNDERSTAND

- *How does worrying about your needs impact how you approach the pursuit of wealth versus the pursuit of God?*
- *What line does Jesus draw between the pursuit of wealth as a master and the practical, everyday need to earn money?*
- *How could this passage impact the way you pray about your daily needs?*

APPLY

Jesus goes straight to the root of money's powerful entanglement, and His approach can offer you freedom. . .if you're willing to ask some difficult questions. His probing question "Why do you have so little faith?" addresses the need everyone feels for security and the struggle to trust God with it. Money simply becomes a path toward security, making it possible to eat, to wear nice-looking clothes, and to live secure in a safe home.

The good news is that God knows what you need, and He has much compassion for you as you weigh the burdens of providing for yourself and others. He never leaves you alone, and Jesus assures you that relying on God's provision will pay off.

Relying on money for security can truly backfire, as it can become a cruel master. You will always wonder if you have enough, and your faith in money will replace your faith in God. You can have money while placing your faith in God, but you should always rely on Him, not money, as your source of security.

PRAY

Jesus, help me to bring my worries to You, trusting You to provide for me and leaving behind anything that isn't necessary. May I use money well for my own care and the care of others without letting it dominate my thoughts and desires. Amen.

FAITH OVERCOMES FEAR

Read Nehemiah 4:11–20

KEY VERSES

When I saw their fear, I stood and said to the nobles, the officials, and the rest of the people: "Do not be afraid of them; remember the Lord who is great and awesome, and fight for your brothers, your sons, your daughters, your wives, and your houses." Now when our enemies heard that it was known to us, and that God had frustrated their plan, then all of us returned to the wall, each one to his work. NEHEMIAH 4:14–15 NASB

UNDERSTAND

- *How did Nehemiah respond to the fear of the people when they worried about their enemies attacking them?*
- *Why did Nehemiah give God the credit for frustrating the plans of their enemies?*
- *What is the place of fear when trying to live by faith in God?*

APPLY

In times of uncertainty, even threats to your well-being, the words of Nehemiah cut through the challenges of today: "Remember the Lord who is great and awesome." It's possible to lose perspective and forget who or what is great, awesome, or powerful. You may even feel like your afflictions are greater than God's power and presence.

Feelings of fear aren't unusual even for the man of God, but how we respond to fear and uncertainty will make all the difference.

Consider how Nehemiah sought to remind the people of God's power, to emphasize their reliance on one another, and to help them get back to the work at hand—even if they had to carry weapons while on the job. The people kept working on what God had called them to do, but first they addressed the spiritual and physical elements of their situation.

Afflictions and opposition will come, but that doesn't mean that the Lord has abandoned you. Such difficulties open opportunities for you to rely more completely on God's power and to examine the role of faith in your life. Through living by faith and trusting in God, you'll overcome fear by knowing that the Lord is with you.

PRAY

Help me, Lord, to see Your power and love with greater clarity than anything else in my life. May I commit myself to the work You've given to me and never fall away when adversity comes or affliction threatens my perseverance. Amen.

DAY 43

JESUS CAN SATISFY YOUR DESIRES

Read John 6:25–40

KEY VERSES

"For the bread of God is that which comes down from heaven and gives life to the world." They said to him, "Sir, give us this bread always." Jesus said to them, "I am the bread of life. Whoever comes to me will never be hungry, and whoever believes in me will never be thirsty." John 6:33–35 NRSV

UNDERSTAND

- *How does Jesus' use of physical needs (food) help people understand their need for Him?*
- *What do you think the people talking with Jesus desired to receive from Him?*
- *What does it mean to never be hungry or thirsty when you come to Jesus in faith?*

APPLY

Why are you following Jesus? It's a question many of His earliest followers had to confront. In today's scripture reading, many people wanted a steady supply of food so that they would never go hungry again. Although that's an understandable motivation at a time of Roman oppression, with droughts and famines sometimes making things worse, Jesus wanted them to know they were missing the bigger point of His ministry.

Jesus offers you a chance to consider what you crave today. You can examine your desires and consider whether or not they are drawing you closer to Him. It's possible that you crave something other than what Jesus offers. So do you truly believe that Jesus can give you something better?

The manna God provided in the desert sustained the people of Israel physically, but Jesus, the Bread of Life, offers to sustain you spiritually, leading you to a place of peace and restoration. Jesus is present with you and, much like a loaf of bread dropping from the sky into your lap, His Spirit has come to you so that He can be fully present with you.

PRAY

Jesus, help me to move past the distractions that draw me away from the fulfillment and restoration You offer. May I find satisfaction in You and in the spiritual sustenance You offer. Amen.

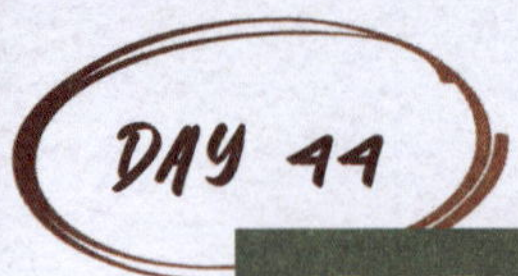

IS YOUR HEART FULLY COMMITTED TO GOD?

Read 2 Chronicles 16:7–14

KEY VERSES

"For the eyes of the Lord range throughout the earth to strengthen those whose hearts are fully committed to him. You have done a foolish thing, and from now on you will be at war." Asa was angry with the seer because of this; he was so enraged that he put him in prison. At the same time Asa brutally oppressed some of the people. 2 Chronicles 16:9–10 NIV

UNDERSTAND

- *What were the consequences of King Asa relying on his own plans in order to solve his problems?*
- *How could Asa have responded more constructively to the prophet's message?*
- *What does this passage teach about what God is looking for?*

APPLY

If you'd like to become better able to confront the challenges you face today, the best course you can take is to address the state of your heart. What is your heart fully committed to right now? Answering that question can help you make an honest assessment of your spiritual state and whether God will be present to strengthen you.

If you persist in going your own way and relying on your own strength and plans, you can expect to be disappointed, even devastated. At some point you will either need to double down on your own ways and the consequences they bring or you will confess your failures. It may be painful to confess the ways you've gone astray, but the sooner you turn back to the Lord, the sooner you'll be back on track with Him.

Even better, the Lord is looking for you to turn back to Him. You don't have to work to get God's attention or act in a certain way. Once you've shifted the orientation of your heart, you'll be ready for His loving gaze, which is already turned your way.

PRAY

Lord, save me from the folly of my own wisdom and the pitfalls of self-reliance. May my heart remain fully loyal to You, committed to Your guidance in my life. Amen.

DAY 45

GOD MEANS WHAT HE SAYS

Read Deuteronomy 18:1–22

KEY VERSE

Moses continued, "The LORD your God will raise up for you a prophet like me from among your fellow Israelites. You must listen to him." DEUTERONOMY 18:15 NLT

UNDERSTAND

- *Based on Acts 3:22–23, who is the "prophet like me"?*
- *Based on Acts 7:37, who is the "prophet like me"?*

APPLY

Thankfully, there's no secret code or formula for understanding the Bible. The world's bestseller is written so people listening to or reading it can grasp what God is saying to them. True, it's possible to misunderstand scripture—men have done that from day one. Still, the Lord wants you to *know* what He's saying!

The "golden rule" of biblical interpretation says God is not trying to mess with our minds. The same goes for Moses, David, Ezra, Malachi, Matthew, Mark, and all the other biblical writers. They expected listeners and readers to understand the meaning of what they wrote.

True, you may not catch everything the first time through. That's why you enjoy listening again to a favorite new song, why you're eager to watch a sports replay, and why you stop to reread something that's profound.

Because God isn't trying to trick anyone, when you're reading scripture you shouldn't try to "decode" it. Unless there's a compelling reason, you should accept the facts the Bible states at face value and embrace the normal meaning of its truths.

PRAY

Yes, Lord, I want to say "Thank You!" for designing the Bible the way You did. You're not trying to mess with me. That means a lot.

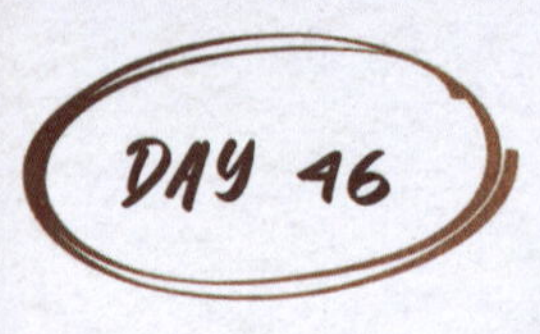

WHAT GOD MEANS TO SAY

Read John 8:12–36

KEY VERSE

"So if the Son sets you free, you will be free indeed." JOHN 8:36 NIV

UNDERSTAND

- *According to John 14:6, who is the truth?*
- *How does He make us free?*

APPLY

Like any great writer, God had specific facts and truths in mind for every verse in scripture. The important question isn't *What does this say to* me? Instead, the question you want to ask is *What did* God *mean*?

Take the famous statement by Jesus, "The truth shall make you free" (John 8:32 NKJV). You could come up with any of a dozen misinterpretations of that verse. But in the end, it doesn't matter what you want that verse to mean.

If you consider yourself an intellectual, you may want "The truth shall make you free" to mean that the more you know and learn, the better your life will be. If you consider yourself an enlightened hedonist, you may want it to mean that you're free to do whatever you want whenever you want as long as it doesn't hurt anyone else. But these popular misinterpretations are *not* what Jesus was saying!

As you read and study the Bible, you want to keep asking, *What did God mean by this statement?* If you're not sure, that's okay! Just write down your questions and then look up the answers later in a study Bible or good Bible commentary.

Studying the Bible isn't a matter of *your* interpretation. Instead, you want to embrace the church's clear understanding of scripture.

PRAY

Yes, Lord, I want to say "Thank You!" that You want me to know what You meant by every chapter, paragraph, and verse of scripture. That's what I want to know.

SEEK TO SERVE GOD ABOVE ALL ELSE

Read 2 Timothy 2:1–13

KEY VERSES

Share in suffering like a good soldier of Christ Jesus. No one serving in the army gets entangled in everyday affairs; the soldier's aim is to please the enlisting officer. And in the case of an athlete, no one is crowned without competing according to the rules.

2 Timothy 2:3–5 NRSV

UNDERSTAND

- *What are the requirements of a soldier, and how did Paul apply them to the Christian life?*
- *Who are you most tempted to please in your life?*
- *Why is it so important for Christians to endure suffering?*

APPLY

The goals of a soldier or athlete are clear and simple. Soldiers obey their commanders, and athletes channel all their energy toward competing for first place. A half measure or divided priorities simply won't work in these situations. You're either "all in" as a soldier or an athlete or ineffectively divided in your commitments.

Paul gave Timothy reminders about his simple gospel message: "Jesus Christ, raised from the dead, a descendant of David." Jesus is alive, the fulfillment of God's promise to raise up a descendant of David to rule with justice and peace. No other person on earth is worthy of our allegiance, and no one else is as intimately aware of us.

Moments of suffering can truly test your commitments and even send you off track with your goals. Suffering may prompt you to look for the easy way out or tempt you to give up. There may not appear to be any point in enduring any longer. Yet if your goal is to win the prize of intimacy with God, then there's no question about enduring hardships. You may have to push yourself beyond what you think your limits may be, but if you can persevere to the end, no one can take away God's reward for you.

PRAY

Jesus, help me to compete for the crown of life You offer and to leave all other distractions and misplaced priorities behind. May I become entangled in only Your loving presence and the work that You have set before me today. Amen.

DAY 48

GOD'S TRUTH ISN'T ALWAYS EASY TO SHARE

Read Jeremiah 28:5–15

KEY VERSES

And Hananiah said again to the crowd that had gathered, "This is what the LORD says: 'Just as this yoke has been broken, within two years I will break the yoke of oppression from all the nations now subject to King Nebuchadnezzar of Babylon.'" . . . Soon after this confrontation with Hananiah, the LORD gave this message to Jeremiah: "Go and tell Hananiah, 'This is what the LORD says: You have broken a wooden yoke, but you have replaced it with a yoke of iron.'" JEREMIAH 28:11–13 NLT

UNDERSTAND

- *Why was Hananiah trying to deceive God's people, sharing a message that he had completely made up?*
- *Why do you think the people listening to the two prophets made up the conflicting messages about deliverance from the Babylonians?*
- *What do you think compelled Jeremiah to share the bad news about Hananiah's false message?*

APPLY

Sometimes the message from God isn't what people want to hear. You may be surrounded by people who are promising that everything is fine and there's no need to make any changes—in fact, things are about to get better! But God sees through attempts to hide sin and disobedience. There's no substitute for an honest assessment of yourself before God and an examination of where you are on the same page with God and where you've gone astray.

Jeremiah offers a challenge to face the brutal, difficult truth. The people of Judah should have repented and accepted the consequences of their unfaithfulness. They couldn't afford to keep limping along in disobedience before God. Yet smooth talkers like Hananiah had an audience because, like today, people don't like being told that they need to make major changes.

If you are willing to follow the example of those few people who listened to Jeremiah's message, you will be on the fast track to restoration and a new future. There's no point in trying to hide what God already knows. And once you come clean before God, you will be prepared to receive His blessings without anything getting in the way.

PRAY

Lord, help me to see my life with clarity and honesty as I come to You in prayer today. I ask for wisdom to discern when I am in keeping with Your direction in my life.

DAY 49

WHOM DO YOU TRUST?

Read Jeremiah 17:5–12

KEY VERSES

"But blessed is the one who trusts in the Lord, *whose confidence is in him. They will be like a tree planted by the water that sends out its roots by the stream. It does not fear when heat comes; its leaves are always green. It has no worries in a year of drought and never fails to bear fruit."* Jeremiah 17:7–8 niv

UNDERSTAND

- *What would it look like to have spiritual security in the Lord regardless of your circumstances in life?*
- *What do you need to entrust to the Lord today?*
- *How does trusting fully in the Lord help you bear spiritual fruit?*

APPLY

What you trust in will go a long way toward determining the amount of turbulence and turmoil in your life. You could trust in money or in powerful relationships, but both could disappear in an instant as they are very much at the mercy of life's circumstances. Ecclesiastes speaks of this approach to the world as a chasing after the wind. There is no foundation and no place to go for security when you trust in the unreliable resources of this world.

By contrast, trusting in the Lord leads to stability, new life, and flourishing. Whether life is difficult or humming along according to plan, you can find a measure of peace and rest by relying on the Lord to direct your paths and to provide what you need. By growing in this trust, you can see your worries and fears fade away.

Besides the benefits you enjoy today by trusting in the Lord, you'll also be rewarded by God according to what you do. God is tuned in to what you're thinking and doing, and if you can live from a foundation of trust in the Lord, you can also look forward to the next life with hope and peace.

PRAY

Lord, I look to You as my source of stability, direction, and joy. Help me to remain rooted in You so that I am not tossed about by the shifting winds of life. May I rest in the confidence of Your reward, which is coming one day. Amen.

WHO'S PURSUING WHOM?

Read John 6:41–45

KEY VERSE

"No one can come to Me unless the Father who sent Me draws him [giving him the desire to come to Me]; and I will raise him up [from the dead] on the last day." JOHN 6:44 AMP

UNDERSTAND

- *What led you to commit your life to follow Christ?*
- *How was God working in your life leading up to that moment?*

APPLY

We tend to pursue God the way we decide to start a hobby. We do the choosing—the activity, time, and place—and think we'll get better at being Christians if we just work at it. But before we can do anything for God, we need to understand that we wouldn't even care about God if He didn't care about us first.

God is all-powerful, all-knowing, and everywhere present. He gave up what is most precious to Him so we might someday understand and respond to His initiative. He enables our goodness and fixes our brokenness. With great acts of power, mercy, and love, He draws us to Himself.

Pursuing God starts by acknowledging He is the original pursuer. It's His overwhelming, all-in love we respond to when we say we're pursuing Him. As 1 John 4:19 (NKJV) notes, "We love Him because He first loved us."

The pursuit of God is comforting and challenging, calming and confounding. But that's God. He is both loving Father and holy Lord of all—closer than a brother and harder to grasp than quantum physics. God sacrificed His precious Son to save you, which imparts both terrible news (you're that much of a sinner) and good news (He thinks you're worth dying for).

PRAY

Thank You, God, for thinking I'm worth pursuing. Help me to see all the times and ways You chased me down. I find comfort in knowing it's not up to me to find You, because You found me first.

SCRIPTURE ITSELF ANSWERS MANY QUESTIONS

Read Jonah 1:1–2:10

KEY VERSE

"But I will offer sacrifices to you with songs of praise, and I will fulfill all my vows. For my salvation comes from the Lord alone." Jonah 2:9 NLT

UNDERSTAND

- *Do you find it easy or difficult to believe today's scripture reading?*
- *What makes it easy or difficult for you?*

APPLY

If you don't have a study Bible, it's time to buy one! If you run into several tough questions, you also can ask your pastor for permission to drop by his office to look up the answers in his commentaries.

Not all Bible commentaries, however, are created equal. In fact, some of them attack the Christian faith. If you're reading a commentary that doesn't (1) worship God, (2) praise the Lord Jesus Christ, and (3) show tremendous respect for God's Word, drop it fast and look for a better one!

Even the best Bible commentators don't have all the answers—not by a long shot. Not every statement in scripture is clear-cut. Some are so poetic that it's hard to tell what the verse or paragraph means. That said, often it's as you keep reading and studying scripture that you realize, *There's the answer to one of my questions!*

Do your best to discover what *God* wants you to know. Most of the answers are right there in His Word. In the end, however, it's okay to list your unanswered questions. In some cases, you'll have to wait until heaven to ask Moses, David, Daniel, or Paul, "What did you mean by this?" or "What did you mean by that?" Imagine how great that will be!

PRAY

Yes, Lord, I want to say "Thank You!" that I can own several Bibles, including one with detailed study notes to help me more readily understand and apply Your Word. And "Thank You!" for motivating me to use this book toward that end.

BEWARE OF OVERCONFIDENCE

Read Luke 22:24–38

KEY VERSES

"But I have pleaded in prayer for you, Simon, that your faith should not fail. So when you have repented and turned to me again, strengthen your brothers." Peter said, "Lord, I am ready to go to prison with you, and even to die with you." LUKE 22:32–33 NLT

UNDERSTAND

- *How do you think Jesus felt when the disciples claimed they would never abandon or betray Him?*
- *How should Peter have responded when Jesus predicted his denial?*
- *What do you think Peter expected would happen when he faced the possibility of death? What could have made him better prepared for that moment?*

APPLY

Following Jesus can be a high-stakes calling that includes both human opposition and spiritual opposition. Like Peter, you may end up in a situation that is far more challenging and stressful than you could ever have predicted. And it's even possible that you will fail at the moment of truth.

One way to guard yourself from opposition is to avoid overconfidence, to humbly assess your weaknesses and confess your struggles to God. Don't assume you'll always make the right choice or always remain on the right path. There is a very real possibility of straying from the truth—or at least making a big, costly mistake.

While you should keep your own weaknesses in mind, the other side of the story is Jesus' intercession for Peter. He will stand by you as well, interceding on your behalf and coming alongside you to help you when you feel like you can't go on (see Hebrews 7:25). And if you should fail, He will restore you—just as He restored Peter at his lowest point of shame and grief.

PRAY

Jesus, help me to view my weaknesses with honesty and clarity so that I can remain careful and attentive while also trusting You to support me when I'm struggling. Amen.

THE BEST TIME

Read Psalm 63:1

KEY VERSE

O God, You are my God; early will I seek You; my soul thirsts for You; my flesh longs for You in a dry and thirsty land where there is no water. PSALM 63:1 NKJV

UNDERSTAND

- *How has God refreshed you—by His Word, through a friend, a moment in nature? What did you learn about Him then?*
- *What time of day do you do your most creative and productive thinking and work?*

APPLY

Hitting that Bible study first thing in the morning is certainly a great way to get your day rolling—if you can still remember what you studied by midmorning. But if you can't—if some aspect of your time with God is not sticking with you throughout the day—there's probably a better time for you to do it.

First, the hard question: Is your time with God just checking a box that makes you feel better about yourself? If it's no different a priority than a workout or taking the dog for a walk, then maybe it's time to rethink it.

Even if you're not at your sharpest in the morning, it's a great idea to start with a few words of thanks and praise. When it comes to focusing on learning about God and His Word, however, it's possible that there are better times than others.

In Psalm 63:1, David writes about seeking God early. However, *early* means more than first thing in the morning; it also means first, as a top priority. Whenever you seek God, be diligent and focused. Dedicate time to pursue Him when you're at your sharpest. Find your best time and give God the first part of it.

PRAY

Lord, I am truly grateful You are there whenever I make time for You. Help me find the best part of my day so I can give the first part of my best, most productive time to You.

BEING FULLY KNOWN

Read Psalm 139:1-6

KEY VERSES

O Lord, You have searched me and known me. You know my sitting down and my rising up; You understand my thought afar off. Psalm 139:1–2 NKJV

UNDERSTAND

- *God knows everything. How does that affect the way you approach relationships, decision-making, work?*
- *When was the last time you thought you knew better than God?*

APPLY

God has perfect knowledge of every subject and topic the human mind can consider, plus far more that we can't. No one teaches God anything; He has nothing to learn and is never surprised. All the folks who think they will have questions for God when they see Him are in for a rude awakening. The superiority of His knowledge beggars the answers they think He owes them.

God knows everything about you. He knows the ways you're different on Sunday morning than Friday night. And He knows when your thoughts wander and where. You can protest what feels like an invasion of privacy, but He knows exactly what you're going to say.

We're contradictory creatures. We hate when people use information about us against us, yet we long to be known and understood by someone who is truly for us. When David wrote in Psalm 139:5 (NKJV), "You have hedged me behind and before, and laid Your hand upon me," he was squirming beneath the weight of God's omniscience, probably because he realized that all his comings and goings—every thought, word, and deed—weren't always pleasing to God.

God knows everything about you and still thinks you were worth dying for. He knows both who you are and who you are becoming in Christ—someone like Jesus, someone beyond your wildest dreams.

PRAY

All-knowing God, I celebrate Your knowledge. You know my sin and my struggles, but You also know my salvation, sanctification, and success in Christ. I lay everything I know (and don't know) at Your feet. Help me know You better.

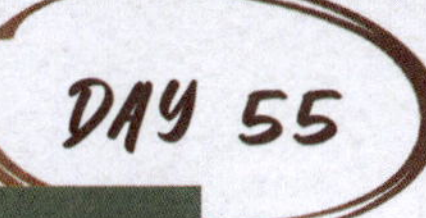

OCCASIONAL SECOND LAYER OF MEANING

Read Psalm 22:1–18

KEY VERSE

They divide my garments among themselves and throw dice for my clothing. PSALM 22:18 NLT

UNDERSTAND

- *Which verses in today's Bible reading remind you of the day Jesus was crucified?*
- *Which verses probably apply only to David's desperate circumstances?*

APPLY

Like any great writer, God occasionally added an important second layer of meaning to a particular word, phrase, sentence, or longer section of scripture. But that second layer of meaning always builds on—and never contradicts—the primary meaning.

In the Old Testament, you see a secondary layer of meaning most often in passages that look forward to the coming of the Messiah, Jesus Christ. Thankfully, Jesus Himself pointed out many of these passages to His disciples after His resurrection (Luke 24:26–27). The apostles studied the Hebrew scriptures diligently after Jesus' ascension (Acts 1:15–22). The apostle Paul did the same thing after his conversion (Acts 9:20–22).

If you think there might be a secondary meaning to a specific Old Testament verse, that's great! Write down your question and then look up the answer in your study Bible or a good commentary.

Just be careful not to spend too much time focused on or worried about possible secondary layers of meaning as you read the Bible. Unless something jumps out at you, keep your focus on the main thing God meant to say.

PRAY

Yes, Lord, I want to say "Thank You!" for the many ways the Old Testament scriptures point to Your Son and my Lord and Savior, Jesus Christ. He's the real hero!

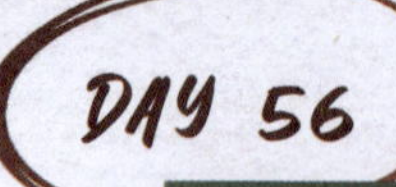

THE EDGY COMFORT OF GOD'S OMNIPRESENCE

Read Psalm 139:7-12

KEY VERSE

Even in darkness I cannot hide from you. To you the night shines as bright as day. Darkness and light are the same to you. PSALM 139:12 NLT

UNDERSTAND

- *When was the last time you behaved as if God couldn't see you?*
- *When was the last time God comforted you in a hard moment?*

APPLY

God knows everything and is present in every place and moment. Does that comfort you or make you nervous? A little tension is good for any relationship—keeping us from taking the other person for granted—but especially with God. We cannot limit Him nor fully understand Him.

In Psalm 139:6 (NLT), David described God's omniscience as "too great for me to understand." He realized there was nowhere he could go where God was not. God is equally and fully present in both light and darkness. We cannot escape accountability to God. The end of this life is the beginning of eternity.

Even for believers, that creates friction. Where is God in our suffering? We take comfort in a Romans 8:28 sense, knowing it's God's specialty to work good things out of bad, straight paths from crooked sticks. But we also know that God demands total control over our entire life. And man, is giving everything over to Him a process!

The Christian life is built on the belief that suffering has value and purpose in God's good hands. We are saved from hell but still challenged by our flesh, the world, and the devil. But even in our darkest hours, we are not hidden from Him. He is making all things right.

PRAY

Ever-present Lord, my humble thanks feel small and insufficient to express what You have done for me. Forgive me for the times I have resisted Your hand honing me into Jesus' image. Today I accept Your attention and trust Your purposes in all that happens.

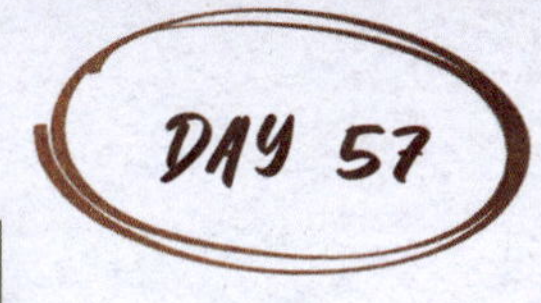

THE REAL WAKE-UP CALL

Read Psalm 139:13-18

KEY VERSE

When I awake, I am still with You. PSALM 139:18 NKJV

UNDERSTAND

- *How does God use His power on your behalf?*
- *When God says He won't ever leave or forsake you, how does that affect your daily life?*

APPLY

God's unmatched power saturates your life, from the moment of your conception through the moment of your death and into eternity. In Psalm 139:13–18, David praises the Lord's hand in creating his life in such an awe-inspiring fashion. God's great power works on the most personal level—the wonders of the cell, of pregnancy, of knowing exactly how long each of us will live. Then David tops it off: "When I awake, I am still with You." He was talking about more than a good night's rest.

Sleep is often a biblical metaphor for both physical and spiritual death. For the Christian, then, to wake up is to step into new life—salvation in this life and eternity with Christ after death. In some sense, David understood that death didn't have to be the final separation from God but a crossing of the threshold into eternal life with Him.

In Psalm 17:15 (NLT), David anticipated that moment: "Because I am righteous, I will see you. When I awake, I will see you face to face and be satisfied." We do the best we can and trust God to make sense of all the hard, broken things in this life. When we die, we will wake up to all that God has for us in eternity, knowing everything we need to know to be satisfied and fulfilled.

PRAY

Father, I am amazed that You use Your unbelievable, unlimited power to make a way in Christ so I can stand in Your presence. Wake me up to Your reality—who You are and what You are doing in, around, and through me. I can't wait to see You.

SHARE WHAT YOU HAVE RECEIVED FROM GOD

Read 1 Peter 4:1–11

KEY VERSES

Above all, maintain constant love for one another, for love covers a multitude of sins. Be hospitable to one another without complaining. Like good stewards of the manifold grace of God, serve one another with whatever gift each of you has received. 1 PETER 4:8–10 NRSV

UNDERSTAND

- *Why does Peter place love above all else?*
- *Why did Peter spell out the need to show hospitality to others without complaining?*
- *How does Peter say you should use the gifts God has given you?*

APPLY

The grace of God is a gift you have been given, but Peter knows that there's a good deal of work and intention that goes into fully enjoying and sharing that gift from the Lord. Prayer requires discipline in order to keep it a top priority, and love calls for perseverance when those around you are engaged in sin. Hospitality will be inconvenient, but it has long been a way to honor others and to care for their needs.

By calling God's people "stewards" of God's grace, Peter is making a point that grace isn't just for us to keep for ourselves but is a gift we should share readily. You have been blessed because God sees the potential in you to carry His influence to others. He sees the potential in you for love, generosity, and peace. When you care for others, you release to them the kindness that God has already given to you.

Your invitation from God today is to find new ways to bless others with the love and mercy He has given you. Along the way, you'll find that people are likely to share that same love and mercy back to you.

PRAY

Jesus, help me to see the love, grace, and favor You have bestowed on me. May I recognize Your gifts and freely share them with others, disciplining myself to pray and to love others with generosity. Amen.

COSTLY TRUST

Read Psalm 139:19-24

KEY VERSES

Search me, O God, and know my heart; try me, and know my anxieties; and see if there is any wicked way in me, and lead me in the way everlasting. PSALM 139:23–24 NKJV

UNDERSTAND

- *What comes to mind when you think of God's holiness?*
- *What are the challenges of asking God to show how you can improve in living His way?*

APPLY

God's most disquieting actions happen because He is holy: His judgment, wrath, justice, jealousy, and even vengeance. His other characteristics are much more comforting; His love, grace, mercy, and faithfulness.

And yet, holiness is the attribute of God mentioned most often in the Bible. And as 1 Peter 1:16 (NKJV) points out, He calls us to be holy: "Be holy, for I am holy." Holiness matters, but how do we practice it?

Like David in Psalm 139, we need to focus on a right relationship with God. Christ makes that possible. In practice, holiness means we love what God loves and hate what He hates—not in a judgmental way, thinking ourselves superior, but understanding that sin has corrupted God's good creation and that we are desperate for Him to make things right.

He makes things right through Jesus. Christ in us makes us holy, set apart by God for God's purposes and pleasure. Our obedience demonstrates our desire to be holy like He is holy. As we do, we join with David, who began Psalm 139:23 (NKJV) by opening himself up for divine scrutiny: "Search me, O God, and know my heart." Where David obeyed in anticipation, we obey in response to Jesus' finished work. When we do, we are His holiness in action.

PRAY

Lord, I take comfort in knowing You are perfect in all of Your ways. I join my voice with the angels praising You, saying, "Holy, holy, holy, is the Lord God Almighty, who was and is and is to come" (Revelation 4:8 ESV).

DAY 60

FIGURES OF SPEECH HAVE KNOWN MEANING

Read John 15:1–17

KEY VERSE

"I am the true grapevine, and my Father is the gardener." JOHN 15:1 NLT

UNDERSTAND

- *In the Old Testament's first five books, God promised to reward His people for doing something. The blessings include fruitful vineyards. What do you think He wanted them to do?*
- *In the Old Testament's second half, God compared His people to vineyards ready to be utterly destroyed. What do you think they did to deserve such severe judgment?*

APPLY

Like any great writer, God used hyperbole, simile, metaphor, and other figures of speech throughout the Old and New Testaments. Not surprisingly, during His time on earth, the Lord Jesus often used figures of speech whenever He spoke to the crowds.

True, figures of speech sometimes confuse listeners and readers. But they're memorable and often cause readers to stop and wonder, *What did Jesus mean by that?* Thankfully, His figures of speech almost always have a known meaning.

If you run across a figure of speech in the Bible that you haven't heard before, try looking it up in your favorite online English-language dictionary. Many English figures of speech have biblical roots. If that doesn't work, look it up in your study Bible.

Five famous figures of speech in the Gospel of Matthew (NKJV) follow below:

- *"Follow Me, and I will make you fishers of men" (4:19).*
- *"You are the salt of the earth" (5:13).*
- *"For John came neither eating nor drinking" (11:18).*
- *"It is easier for a camel to go through the eye of a needle than for a rich man to enter the kingdom of God" (19:24).*
- *"Woe to you, scribes and Pharisees, hypocrites! For you are like whitewashed tombs" (23:27).*

PRAY

Yes, Lord, I want to say "Thank You!" for the creativity built into the design of language. It makes Your Word all the more interesting, provocative, and life-changing.

BELIEVING IS SEEING

Read Hebrews 11:1–6

KEY VERSE

Without faith it is impossible to please him, for whoever would draw near to God must believe that he exists and that he rewards those who seek him. HEBREWS 11:6 ESV

UNDERSTAND

- *To the best of your recollection, list God's characteristics and attributes.*
- *What are the challenges of pursuing an invisible God?*

APPLY

The pursuit of God is sometimes made more challenging by the fact that we can't see Him. It's so much easier to believe in what we can perceive with our senses, even though we know they are limited. But if faith was based only on what we could perceive, it would be science, not faith. And even science has its limits.

God's interactions with us give faith an anchor in history. He made Himself known to people from the beginning and then made Himself visible in Jesus Christ. Even though we don't see the Holy Spirit enter us when we're saved, the proof of His presence is in the way He changes us. Hebrews 11:1 (NIV) says, "Faith is confidence in what we hope for and assurance about what we do not see." When we take that to heart, we don't stay the same. God teaches us to live in light of a greater world. Hebrews 11:16 (NIV) says we long for the reward of "a better country—a heavenly one."

Don't underestimate the anchoring power of that promised reward for the faithful. Believe that everything you go through now is worth it, that God sees you and will reward you for sticking with Him no matter what. Believing is seeing. Believe it now, when your flesh still clouds your eyes, and one day, you will see Him face-to-face.

PRAY

Father, I get stuck in what my senses can perceive. Expand my view of You and all Your ways, seen and unseen. Your invisibility reminds me that You are unlimited, greater than all my senses can perceive.

WORD OF LIFE

Read Psalm 119:1–11

KEY VERSES

Oh, that my actions would consistently reflect your decrees! Then I will not be ashamed when I compare my life with your commands. PSALM 119:5–6 NLT

UNDERSTAND

- *Do you read the Bible with a sense of anticipation that God will tell you something about Himself or your life that you need to hear?*
- *If not, will you commit to asking Him to show up when you spend time in His Word?*

APPLY

Psalm 119 can be pretty intimidating to read and absorb, partly because of its incredible length (it's the longest chapter in the Bible), but also because of its challenging theme: reliance on the Word of God. Almost every verse (176 of them!) mentions some reference to the scriptures—the law of the Lord, His instructions, precepts, statutes, decrees, and commandments.

The unnamed psalmist lays out the theme in Psalm 119:1–2 NLT: "Joyful are people of integrity, who follow the instructions of the LORD. Joyful are those who obey his laws and search for him with all their hearts." Joy is different than happiness. Where happiness comes from fleeting circumstances, joy is a fruit of the Spirit (Galatians 5:22), an attitude that recognizes that God deserves our deepest trust in everything we feel, think, and do.

Taking God's words into your heart is the only endeavor that guarantees a good outcome. Any other may fail—a business, a work of art, a relationship—but walking in God's ways brings (among other good things) freedom, joy, confidence, and comfort.

Even better, no earthly failure can define you. God redeems everything we give to Him, so that we can agree with Psalm 119:71 (NLT): "My suffering was good for me, for it taught me to pay attention to your decrees."

PRAY

Lord God, Your Word is life. Give me a hunger to read it, know You more, and live fruitfully as a result.

DAY 63

UNDERSTANDING LEADS TO FRUITFULNESS

Read Matthew 13:16–23

KEY VERSES

"The seed falling on rocky ground refers to someone who hears the word and at once receives it with joy. But since they have no root, they last only a short time. When trouble or persecution comes because of the word, they quickly fall away. The seed falling among the thorns refers to someone who hears the word, but the worries of this life and the deceitfulness of wealth choke the word, making it unfruitful." MATTHEW 13:20–22 NIV

UNDERSTAND

- *What does it mean for someone who hears God's Word to be fruitful?*
- *Why is it not enough to only receive God's Word with joy in the first place? What gets in the way of joy?*
- *How do worries and the deceit of wealth prevent disciples of Jesus from being fruitful with God's Word?*

APPLY

The words of Jesus have tremendous potential to change your life and the lives of others, but that change isn't going to happen without intentionality on your part. Life is filled with conflict and distractions. You can go off course easily, losing sight of God's wisdom and chasing after something that feels good today but fails you over the long term. Part of the problem for those distracted by the cares of this life is the amount of time given to reflection on Jesus' teachings.

Today you can consider what it looks like to truly understand what Jesus has to say to you. You can pause and dig deeper into your own life today, asking questions or taking an inventory of your soul. What worries you? What do you desire? What are you seeking? There are plenty of ways to uncover what has taken root in your life rather than the words of Jesus.

Once you have an idea of the distractions and challenges you face, you may then consider the ways you can help the words of Jesus take root in your life. How can you keep His message in front of you so that you won't wilt under adversity or toss His promises aside when wealth promises security or prestige?

The fruit of God's Word shows up gradually, but if you invest time today in understanding the message of Jesus, you'll find new growth springing forth in your life.

PRAY

Jesus, help me to hear and meditate deeply on Your words of life. May Your new life rise up in me and lead to fruitfulness that draws me closer to You and prepares me to share Your promises with others. Amen.

FREEDOM REQUIRES SACRIFICE

Read 1 Kings 22:1–8, 26–28, 31–36

KEY VERSE

Jehoshaphat said to the king of Israel, "Inquire first for the word of the Lord."
1 Kings 22:5 esv

UNDERSTAND

- *What does freedom look like to you?*
- *What's your tendency with God: to ask for permission or forgiveness?*

APPLY

Seeking what God has to say *before* you act is great advice, but in context there is a lot more to chew on.

First, look at the history: Jehoshaphat was one of the rare God-honoring kings in Israel and Judah's history, so before he allied himself with King Ahab of Israel, he wanted to see what God had to say to them. In those days, to hear from God, you asked a prophet.

Ahab knew that a true prophet would only have bad things to say to him. So he kept false prophets around: ear-ticklers and sycophants. But real freedom means accepting difficult-to-hear truths. "Inquiring first" of God means being open to His redirection, trusting He knows best.

Next, listen to the right message: Jehoshaphat knew of one prophet, Micaiah, who would speak God's truth no matter the cost to himself. And when Micaiah did, Ahab ordered him to be jailed until he himself returned from battle. Micaiah's response showed his trust in God: If God had spoken through him, Ahab would die in battle; if God hadn't, he wouldn't. It was a simple test he staked his freedom on.

Finally, live in touch with reality: Ahab attempted to disguise himself in battle, but he still died of a seemingly random arrow wound. Since God's will is going to happen whether you're on board or not, why not get on board? Prepare for whatever the day may bring by seeking God first. Offering your time to God with open hands and heart is a sacrifice, but one that pleases Him.

PRAY

Lord God, today I commit myself to Your will. Open my eyes, ears, and heart to You. Show me what pleases You.

THE BIBLE'S RICH VOCABULARY

Read 1 Samuel 15:10–35

KEY VERSE

The LORD regretted that He had made Saul king over Israel. 1 SAMUEL 15:35 NKJV

UNDERSTAND

- *You "hope" the weather is better tomorrow. How is that different from "hope" in the New Testament?*
- *Looking back on your life, you likely have "regrets." How is that different from the Bible saying God "regretted" something?*

APPLY

Like any great writer, God used a rich vocabulary. So, not surprisingly, God's Word will stretch even the most avid reader's vocabulary.

It's important to remember that the biblical author determines the meaning of a given word. What does the Bible mean when it says God "regretted"? Of course, there's more than one meaning for that word. A good dictionary may list five possible definitions. Then again, the Bible may add a sixth meaning.

The good news is you can use a standard collegiate dictionary to look up the meaning of most words you'll find in the Bible. Still, you may run into a few words that you'll find only in a twenty-five-pound unabridged dictionary.

If that's the case, see if your study Bible tells you what it means. Also, read the same verse in one or two other contemporary Bible translations. You may even want to look up the word on BibleGateway.com. It can give you a list of other verses—in one or more Bible translations—that use that same word.

PRAY

Yes, Lord, I want to say "Thank You!" for Your infinite wisdom and way with words. Thank You for the many resources we have to better understand Your Word.

ONE IN A HUNDRED

Read Matthew 18:11–14

KEY VERSE

"If a man has a hundred sheep, and one of them goes astray, does he not leave the ninety-nine and go to the mountains to seek the one that is straying?" MATTHEW 18:12 NKJV

UNDERSTAND

- *How do you react when you're driving and you realize you're lost? Do you keep going or seek directions?*
- *How quick are you to pray when things aren't going well?*
- *Do you realize you are special to God?*

APPLY

Getting spiritually lost looks similar to getting lost while driving. The Bible is your map, and the Holy Spirit is your divine GPS, but you still get off track. You thought you knew the way—how to pray, how to act humbly, how to lead yourself and your family—but then unfamiliar sights started showing up, followed by that nagging feeling that you're off course.

When the kids have gone haywire, communication lines between you and your wife are down, and you're just not feeling like God is there, it's scary, and that fear can easily replace your confidence in God's sovereign care. So you try to course-correct based on your own thoughts and get even more lost.

Whether you get physically lost driving or go spiritually astray, pride is often the biggest obstacle to getting back on track. God knows when you're lost. He also knows how to find you. Whatever may be keeping you from asking for help, your good shepherd is still coming to find you. Stop trying to fix it/hide/act like you're okay. Stand still and call out. You may just be the one in a hundred He is looking for.

PRAY

Father, I should've known better than to let things get this bad. Will You find me where I am and carry me back into Your light so I can see the right way to go again? Forgive my foolish pride and self-reliance—and thanks for always coming after me.

GETTING UNSTUCK

Read Proverbs 8:17

KEY VERSE

I love those who love me; and those who diligently seek me will find me. PROVERBS 8:17 NASB

UNDERSTAND

- *What keeps you from spending as much time praying and reading the Bible as you think you should?*
- *What is your image of God as you spend time with Him? Impatient and frustrated or looking forward to it?*

APPLY

God knows you're busy. While you're busy beating yourself up because you can barely carve out five minutes a day to focus on Him, He loves that you're making time at all. After all, God can do more with five minutes than you can with a whole week.

Don't get stuck thinking that God is tapping His foot, arms folded, thinking you're a doofus because you don't spend enough time building your faith and too much time trying to fix things you can't control.

Instead, picture Him as your Father, waiting with open arms. He is there no matter what, willing and able to comfort, give wisdom, and show grace. He brings challenges sometimes, but everything He does is to help you learn, grow, and know Him better. If anything, He just wishes you would call Him more often, let Him know how you're doing, and thank Him for being a good Father.

If you're stuck in a rut and just need someone who understands that, Jesus does. He got worn out and beaten up too—but He allowed it so He could identify with you in your hard times and give you that deep understanding your soul is dying for. Focus on Him and let Him help you get unstuck.

PRAY

Jesus, You went through the worst moments so I could turn to You when I'm in a bad spot. Thanks for being there for me. Will You keep being patient with me, waiting for me to call, and remind me how much You want to hear from me?

GOD ANSWERS PERSISTENT PRAYER FOR JUSTICE

Read Luke 18:1–8

KEY VERSES

And the Lord said, "Listen to what the unjust judge says. And will not God bring about justice for his chosen ones, who cry out to him day and night? Will he keep putting them off? I tell you, he will see that they get justice, and quickly. However, when the Son of Man comes, will he find faith on the earth?" LUKE 18:6–8 NIV

UNDERSTAND

- *Why would Jesus compare God's answer to prayers to an unjust judge who ignores a woman's pleas for justice?*
- *According to Jesus in today's reading, what is the main problem for God's people?*
- *What kind of approach should you take to prayer requests?*

APPLY

Jesus wants His followers to long for justice, but He also challenges us to live by faith even when life is uncertain. Just as the woman in this parable didn't know if she was going to get justice, you don't know exactly how God will respond to your prayer. Yet Jesus wants you to rest assured that God hears your prayers and is far more compassionate than the unjust judge. The two things you don't know about God's response will be the *timing* and the *details*.

When Jesus tells His followers to be persistent in prayer, He wants them to realize that the problem in prayer isn't God's attentiveness but His people giving up too easily and failing to stay focused and intent on their prayer requests.

Although it's tempting to apply this passage to all kinds of prayers, Jesus specifically mentions the cause of justice and making things right. Whether that's a matter of injustice directed at you or the injustice someone else is enduring, this promise of God's attention to persistent prayer is specifically linked with setting things right.

PRAY

Thank You, Father, for Your attention to the cause of justice in the world and for Your compassion on those who are suffering. May I persist in prayer and share in Your commitment to make things right today. Amen.

QUICK TO FORGIVE

Read Psalm 32

KEY VERSE

Finally, I confessed all my sins to you and stopped trying to hide my guilt. I said to myself, "I will confess my rebellion to the Lord.*" And you forgave me! All my guilt is gone.*

Psalm 32:5 NLT

UNDERSTAND

- *List specific things for which God has forgiven you.*
- *How hard is it for you to forgive others? Why?*

APPLY

In Ephesians 4:32, Paul called us to forgive others to the extent that Jesus has forgiven us. Why, then, do we hang on to how we've been wronged or the wrongs we've done? Accident or not, the damage is real: sleeplessness results, nerves on edge, appetite diminished—we carry the wrongdoing as a physical weight, an emotional millstone. Surely God has more for His children.

And so He does. But it all begins with forgiveness—Him forgiving us. Our problems start when we think we don't have much that needs to be forgiven or we're undeserving of what's happened. We're better than most, aren't we? But as Isaiah 64:6 (AMP) reminds us, "All our deeds of righteousness are like filthy rags."

Psalm 7:11 (NKJV) says, "God is a just judge, and God is angry with the wicked every day." Our offense is always against Him first and foremost—and yet He longs to forgive us. Jesus obeyed the Father's will so we could be forgiven. Forgiveness isn't a matter of feeling but obedience. Especially under grace, we must forgive.

Loving what God loves is learning to forgive, especially when someone doesn't deserve it. When you do that, you will find yourself, as David did, surrounded by mercy. Let God's forgiveness wash over you anew.

PRAY

Lord God, holy and just, forgive me for loving my filthy rags more than Your peace and security. When I value forgiveness like You do, I will be quicker to seek forgiveness and forgive others.

NEW USES FOR OLD WORDS

Read Ephesians 3:1–11

KEY VERSE

This mystery is that through the gospel the Gentiles are heirs together with Israel, members together of one body, and sharers together in the promise in Christ Jesus. EPHESIANS 3:6 NIV

UNDERSTAND

- *What do you think Charles Dickens meant when he quipped, "The life of Shakespeare is a fine mystery"?*
- *What do you think the apostle Paul meant when he used the word* mystery?

APPLY

Like William Shakespeare, Mark Twain, and Ernest Hemingway, God sometimes chose to use an old word in a new way. You see this in Paul's New Testament letters.

Paul used the word *mystery* often. That word already had several definitions. If you look up all of Paul's uses of the word, you'll discover that it referred to the new revelations God had given the apostles through Jesus Christ and the Holy Spirit.

One of those new revelations is the "mystery" that God designed the church to be composed of *all* people—Jewish and Gentile (anyone who's not Jewish), male and female, slave and free.

In other words, God wants everyone to turn from his sins, turn to God, trust Jesus Christ, and instantly become a member of the church, which includes everyone who is a real Christian. You may take that for granted today, but it was a brand-new idea two thousand years ago!

PRAY

Yes, Lord, I want to say "Thank You!" for the many ways the New Testament reveals the transforming power of the gospel of Jesus Christ. That good news has changed my life here and now, and for eternity.

DAY 71

WAITING FOR GOD'S NEW MERCY

Read Lamentations 3:19–38

KEY VERSES

I recall this to my mind, therefore I wait. The Lord*'s acts of mercy indeed do not end, for His compassions do not fail. They are new every morning; great is Your faithfulness. "The* Lord *is my portion," says my soul, "therefore I wait for Him."* Lamentations 3:21–24 NASB

UNDERSTAND

- *What makes it possible to wait for God's mercy in the midst of suffering?*
- *How does making God your portion change the way you view the challenges of life?*
- *What makes waiting especially difficult?*

APPLY

What comes to your mind as you endure suffering or difficulty? You may be so immersed in the lows of today that you struggle to imagine how things could ever get better. But they can!

The world and everything in it are passing away, but you can count on the renewal of God's love and mercy every morning. Waiting will pay off when you rely on a faithful God who will not and cannot forget His own people. When God is your "portion," you will always have something to look forward to even if you have to wait for what He has prepared for you.

When you walk through times of sorrow and loss, turn your eyes to God and His love and consider how you can make Him your portion—the most important priority in your life. When you turn your gaze toward God, you'll find that His gaze has never left you. In that revelation, there is peace and patience abounding that can carry you through the darkest moments—moments that would otherwise feel lonely and hopeless. In God, there is a reason to look forward to each day with hope.

PRAY

Help me, Lord, to see if I'm relying on anything other than You. May I find peace and rest in the promise of Your mercy and compassion so that I can live with joy and peace as I endure even the most trying moments of my life. Amen.

TRUST DESPITE CONFUSION

Read Luke 2:41–52

KEY VERSE

He said to them, "Why did you seek Me? Did you not know that I must be about My Father's business?" LUKE 2:49 NKJV

UNDERSTAND

- *What about God is hardest for you to understand?*
- *How difficult is it for you to trust God fully when you don't understand what He's doing?*

APPLY

Imagine the surge of horror that went through Joseph and Mary's hearts as they realized they had left Jesus behind in the enormous crowds leaving Jerusalem.

When they finally found Jesus, His response was just plain confusing. We've all heard bizarre and infuriatingly patronizing things come from the mouths of twelve-year-olds (if only because we remember being twelve!), but this is an all-timer: "You should've known I'd be hanging out in My (real) Father's house."

On one hand, Mary and Joseph might have been expecting an apology: "Sorry I scared you, Mom and Dad." But then there is the whole reference to Jesus' Father, by which they knew He didn't mean Joseph, which brought up everything that was so alien to them about this boy they had raised and loved.

Sometimes what God's Word says isn't clear, and sometimes it is, but it cuts right to the core of an embarrassing habit. And yet He knows best and cares the most, doesn't He?

Part of pursuing God is learning to deal with that tension. When Jesus confuses you, remember that He always wants His best for you, even when you can't see what He's doing. If you can trust Him at those key moments of uncertainty, fear, and desperate hope, He will not let you down.

PRAY

Father, You're working things together in ways I can't begin to imagine. Help me reconcile what I don't know about what You're doing with what I do know about You. You are holy and just and running over with mercy, love, and grace. I trust You.

THE HORIZON OF RECOVERY

Read Deuteronomy 4:26–31

KEY VERSE

If from there you seek the LORD *your God, you will find him if you seek him with all your heart and with all your soul.* DEUTERONOMY 4:29 NIV

UNDERSTAND

- *What are some ways you seek God?*
- *How hard is it for you to turn back to God when you've strayed away?*

APPLY

Deuteronomy 4:29 (NIV) says, "If from there you seek the LORD"—but where is *there*? At this point in Israel's history, God had delivered the first generation from Egypt after they'd blown it, constantly doubting Him and turning back to their familiar idols. After this latest fresh start, Moses predicted they would blow it again. That's where the *there* comes in: From that next point of sin and distress, they would call out to God.

Fortunately, there was (and is) good news: Deuteronomy 4:31 (NKJV) affirms that even when you blow it (again), God is right there, so that when you turn from your sin and back to Him and His ways, "He will not forsake you nor destroy you, nor forget the covenant of your fathers which He swore to them." God is always faithful to keep His promises, to do what is right. You just have to want it more than anything else.

The trajectory of seeking God has some huge ups and downs. But He is the steady line, the unchanging horizon that helps you reorient yourself and look for Him again. When you make a habit of that—seeking Him and being willing to change based on what you learn—He will reward your faith by anchoring you to Himself.

PRAY

Lord, You are unfailingly merciful and patient. Thank You that You are making me more and more sensitive to my sin, making me hate it while loving You more and that You are always right there when I turn back to You.

SPIRIT AND TRUTH

Read John 4:23–26

KEY VERSE

A time is coming, and even now has arrived, when the true worshipers will worship the Father in spirit and truth; for such people the Father seeks to be His worshipers.
JOHN 4:23 NASB

UNDERSTAND

- *What is your favorite way to worship God?*
- *What distracts you from worshipping God with a full, right heart?*

APPLY

Jesus makes an intriguing statement in John 4:24 in the middle of His discussion with the Samaritan woman at the well: God is looking for those who will worship Him "in spirit and truth." Their talk had turned to worship. The Samaritans had Mount Gerizim, their own local place where they worshipped God, and the Jews had the temple in Jerusalem. This woman wanted to know which was the right place, but she was asking the wrong question.

The question isn't *where* but *whom*. That's what Jesus was getting at—to worship God in the way God approves is to consider twin factors: spirit and truth. There is only one who worships God in this committed, right-hearted way: Jesus Christ Himself. So it is only because we are His that we can be true worshippers.

In worship we should focus on what matters most to the Spirit—the glorification of Jesus Christ. Since Jesus Himself is the only true worshipper, our worship should focus on what means so much to Him: the good news of God's grace.

Anyone gathered in spirit and truth—disregarding barriers of class, gender, age, nationality, and ethnicity—is on track and ready to worship God the way He told us to: focused on God's will and words and celebrated among His people.

PRAY

God, You're great and deserving of all praise, now and forever. I'm so grateful to be covered by the great gift of Jesus' love and sacrifice, so I can be a true worshipper. Help me to worship You the way You said Your people should, in spirit and truth.

DAY 75

OCCASIONAL POWER-PACKED WORDS

Read Galatians 3:1–14

KEY VERSE

And the Scripture, foreseeing that God would justify the Gentiles by faith, preached the gospel beforehand to Abraham, saying, "In you shall all the nations be blessed."
GALATIANS 3:8 ESV

UNDERSTAND

- *Sometimes a single English word, such as fellowship, takes a sentence or two to define. Why is that?*
- *Sometimes a biblical word, such as gospel, takes two or three sentences to define. Why is that?*

APPLY

Sometimes biblical writers chose to cut and paste parts of old words to create a new word. Not surprisingly, you see this in the Old Testament and in Paul's letters.

In Galatians 3:8, Paul used a word that in Greek combines the words "before" and "gospel." You don't find this compound word anywhere else in the Bible. That doesn't mean the early church didn't talk about it!

If you look it up in your Bible, you'll discover this compound term means "preached the gospel beforehand." To communicate that concept succinctly, Paul used what may have been a new word to many of his readers. It was his shorthand way of saying a lot in one power-packed term.

If you look really hard, you'll find only a small handful of biblical words where translators have had to add a footnote saying, in effect, "We don't know for sure what this word means." Many of these words are Hebrew musical terms.

Only one undefined word appears frequently in the Bible, and then almost exclusively in one book. It's the word *selah*, which appears in the text of thirty-nine psalms. Translators have offered several possible meanings for *selah*. Whenever you run into the word, assume it means, "Think about what God is saying in this psalm. Pay attention. Now, keep reading!"

PRAY

Yes, Lord, I want to say "Thank You!" that we can understand 99.99 percent of the Bible's words and sentences in any contemporary English translation. That's amazing.

NOBODY'S LOOKING

Read Psalm 14

KEY VERSES

The Lord *looks down from heaven on the children of man, to see if there are any who understand, who seek after God. They have all turned aside; together they have become corrupt; there is none who does good, not even one.* Psalm 14:2–3 ESV

UNDERSTAND

- *How do you tend to view nonbelievers—as knuckleheads or as lost sheep?*
- *Which describes your general view of God better—wrathful judge or open-armed father?*

APPLY

Some of us are really good at sharing about Jesus, but a lot of us hold back; we're introverts or don't want to be rejected or are worried about blowing our reputation ("Yeah, he's a Christian, but don't worry—he's cool").

Psalm 14 is a wake-up call to stop caring about cool. The world is full of cool people who want nothing to do with God. Some of them hate God and anyone who wants anything to do with Him. Instead, tell them about Jesus.

We each have our stories about how God changed us through the gospel. Your story doesn't have to be spectacular; God's Spirit will make the impact because He knows each person's heart and how to reach everyone. Our part is sharing the gospel. Romans 10:17 (NIV) says, "Faith comes from hearing the message."

Trust the power of the message. Psalm 14:5–6 (ESV) says you are part of the "generation of the righteous," and the "Lord is [your] refuge." When you represent Him to this broken world, He has your back, no matter its reaction. Nobody is looking for Him, but we weren't either until we heard about Jesus.

PRAY

I am so grateful, Father, for Your salvation in Jesus. I want to look for You and what You want to accomplish in this crazy world. Please inflate me with a sense of Your importance, the wonder and joy of what You have done and are doing, so I can't help but tell others about You.

THE MISSION

Read Hebrews 10:23–25

KEY VERSE

Let us not neglect our meeting together, as some people do, but encourage one another, especially now that the day of his return is drawing near. HEBREWS 10:25 NLT

UNDERSTAND

- *What do you see as the value of church?*
- *How has God used other believers to help, build, and heal you?*

APPLY

God is all about relationship. The most harmonious, joyful relationship ever is shared among Father, Son, and Holy Spirit. So it makes sense that something special happens when God's people gather to worship Him and seek His face—that is, with no agenda other than to honor Him and deepen the relationship. Vital things happen in fellowship that can't happen when you're alone.

The church is Christ's body, all the parts working together to accomplish what He, as the head, wants. At church, He wakes us up spiritually, reminding us both that we are separate from the world and of our shared mission to the world. The Spirit encourages us, builds us up, and heals us through worship and the teaching of the Word. God gets us out of our own heads and amplifies our joy because we're sharing it with others who are also relying on Him. These things can't happen anywhere else.

People have all kinds of reasons for attending church less often these days. Without invalidating some of those concerns, let's remember the benefits of church and not give up on gathering. We only have one life to be on mission with God. Let's take advantage of this precious season, lock shields with our brothers and sisters, and see what He does.

PRAY

Lord God, You are worth more than anything this world can offer or threaten to take. You have provided with Your own blood a gathering place for Your people. Forgive me for when I haven't treated church as something essential and precious to You. Give me the hunger to join with Your people to seek Your face.

PRAISE GOD FOR RESTORATION

Read Psalm 68:1–10

KEY VERSES

Father of orphans and protector of widows is God in his holy habitation. God gives the desolate a home to live in; he leads out the prisoners to prosperity, but the rebellious live in a parched land. Psalm 68:5–6 NRSV

UNDERSTAND

- *How does God treat those who are suffering and desolate?*
- *What in particular does this psalm of praise say about God's mercy and power?*
- *How could praising God change the way His people view others?*

APPLY

Today's scripture reading asks readers to shift the way they look at others and what they expect from God. While God will punish those who rebel, there also is blessing for those who are suffering. Perhaps it's easy to overlook those who are suffering—or even to view them as afflicted—but God's desire is for the restoration of those who are most vulnerable.

The place where you can begin today is to praise God for His mercy and restoration. Just as God provided for the people of Israel in the wilderness and restored their lives, He desires to help those who are weighed down and burdened. You don't have to be worthy in any way in order to approach God with confidence and hope. God always looks to those in the greatest need in order to show His mercy.

Look around today at those who are most in need or suffering. These are the people God wants to help and to restore. As you praise God for His mercy and justice, you can also shift your own view of suffering and seek ways to draw near to those who are at the heart of God's desires.

PRAY

Lord, You are compassionate and kind. Help me to see others the way You see them and to approach You in prayer with confidence and hope. Amen.

DAY 79

THE LITMUS TEST FOR TRUSTING GOD

Read Luke 12:29–34

KEY VERSE

Where your treasure is, there your heart will be also. LUKE 12:34 NKJV

UNDERSTAND

- *What is your process for making big decisions—marriage, parenting, jobs, houses, cars, and so on?*
- *What shows you more effectively how God loves you—His provision for what you need or for who you need to be?*

APPLY

Getting vs. giving is the heart issue Jesus deals with in Luke 12, and His words dare us to address a very bottom-line subject: Who is God to us—a loving Father or a means to an end? You can't know what your answer really is until you've given yourself completely over to His priorities—giving because He gives, loving because He loves, serving because He serves.

What kind of God asks for that kind of trust? Only one who has given Himself, His very best, in Jesus Christ. Only one who has given up the worship of heaven for the hatred of men. Only one who chose to become poverty-stricken so you could become a king's heir. God's economy is upside down in the world's eyes—putting yourself last to lift others up, giving to those who can't give back. But we do it because that's what He did.

Embrace Jesus and His counterintuitive ways and, rather than being driven by fear or greed or keeping up, you'll have clarity when financial difficulties arise or a tempting purchase looms. You'll see that your investment in the kingdom is worth more than anything the world can offer—and best of all, unlike wealth or material things, your rewards await you in eternity.

PRAY

Heavenly Father, You are the ultimate provider. You met my greatest need—forgiveness—in Christ, but with You, that's just the beginning of all You have for me. Free me from worry's unending grind by helping me to keep You in Your rightful place on the throne of my heart.

WHAT DOES THE BIBLE MEAN?

Read Genesis 4:1–16

KEY VERSE

Now Cain talked with Abel his brother; and it came to pass, when they were in the field, that Cain rose up against Abel his brother and killed him. Genesis 4:8 NKJV

UNDERSTAND

- *The New King James Version includes the title "Cain Murders Abel" above today's scripture reading. Why do you suppose today's key verse uses the word* killed?
- *Why do you suppose dozens of English Bible translations haven't used the word* murdered *in today's key verse?*

APPLY

Like any great writer, God wrote every word and verse in context. He didn't write in a random, arbitrary manner. God has clearly communicated the meaning of most words and virtually all sentences and paragraphs within the same chapter, book, or section of the Bible. In many cases, you can figure out what God meant if you keep reading.

When you can't figure out the meaning of a statement in its immediate context, you may want to look at the broader context. In the Ten Commandments, God declared, "You shall not murder" (Exodus 20:13; Deuteronomy 5:17 NKJV). Does this verse mean "Don't kill any life form"? No. The broader context is clear. Does it mean "God is against all killing, including war and capital punishment"? No. This commandment says it's against God's law for an individual to maliciously kill another human being. The broader context even goes on to say what to do if someone accidentally kills another human being.

In the Gospels, Jesus declared, "I am the bread of life" (John 6:35 NKJV). Without even studying the context, you know Jesus was using a figure of speech. Every figure of speech has a known meaning. You can determine that meaning by reading what Jesus said in context. The immediate context tells you that Jesus was saying, in effect, "I have come from God to offer you new, eternal life. You can receive that life by believing Me!"

PRAY

Yes, Lord, I want to say "Thank You!" that the Bible itself answers most of the questions I might ask. That's why I want to keep reading and studying it. The more questions I raise, the better.

WRESTLING WITH GOD

Read Genesis 32:24-26

KEY VERSE

He said, "Let Me go, for the day breaks." But [Jacob] said, "I will not let You go unless You bless me!" Genesis 32:26 NKJV

UNDERSTAND

- *When has God used something hard to draw you closer to Him?*
- *How relentless are you in seeking God's blessing?*

APPLY

Jacob was a religious dude from a religious family. All his life, he had heard about his dad's and grandfather's encounters with God—the miraculous deliverances, the life-changing tests of faith, the blessings of provision and purpose. And yet from the moment of his birth, Jacob's behavior was characterized by sneakiness, lies, and thievery.

God wasn't real to him. While Jacob had no reason to doubt the stories his dad and grandpa told, for him that's all they were—stories. Jacob did what was required to honor God, at least superficially, and that was enough for him. But that wasn't enough for God.

God literally got in his face and grappled with him because He knew that's what it would take to break through Jacob's self-reliance—and boy did He break through! Once Jacob realized who he was battling, he wouldn't let go until God blessed him, but he didn't walk away unscathed. God touched Jacob's hip and *pop!* Game over. Jacob walked with a limp for the rest of his life.

Hardship and hard questions remind you that God exists and that He wants you to seek Him. Let Him cut away everything that's keeping you from really knowing Him, even if what He prunes seems like a good thing. If you trust Him no matter what, you've moved from religion to relationship. Don't let go until He blesses you.

PRAY

Almighty God, You made me with a purpose, and You reserve the right to break me for the same purpose—to know You more. Let me see Your face in the hard times, and strengthen me to endure in expectation of Your blessing.

GOD LOVES AN UNDERDOG

Read 2 Corinthians 5:14–19

KEY VERSES

If anyone is in Christ, he is a new creation. The old has passed away; behold, the new has come. All this is from God, who through Christ reconciled us to himself and gave us the ministry of reconciliation. 2 Corinthians 5:17–18 ESV

UNDERSTAND

- *Do you prefer underdogs or favorites?*
- *What do you think it means to let the love of Christ control you?*

APPLY

We know God loves an underdog—just look at David, chosen because, as 1 Samuel 16:7 (MSG) declares, "God judges persons differently than humans do. Men and women look at the face; God looks into the heart."

David's whole story, though, reveals the trap we often fall into as Christians: We come to faith because we see ourselves properly in relation to God, as massive underdogs. Then we get comfortable being on the winning side and start to view ourselves as favorites, like the job's done. That's where David got into trouble; he got comfortable and took his favored status with God for granted.

To live life well, we need a growing relationship with Jesus. We must make a priority of what matters most to Him—seeking the highest good of as many others as we can so we can help populate His kingdom. As Paul noted in 2 Corinthians 5:14 (ESV), "The love of Christ controls us."

Jesus died for everyone so that as many as possible can live for Him. Since God doesn't see us the way the world does, we can't look at anyone else the way the world does—no quick judgments, no assuming the worst, only the effort to see others through God's eyes of love and grace.

PRAY

I praise You, Lord, for saving me—for becoming human, setting Yourself up as the greatest underdog ever. Increase my compassion for the lost by reminding me of how You rescued me when I was lost.

COURAGE IMAGINES A NEW FUTURE

Read Haggai 2:1–9

KEY VERSES

"'But now take courage, Zerubbabel,' declares the Lord, 'take courage also, Joshua son of Jehozadak, the high priest, and all you people of the land take courage,' declares the Lord, 'and work; for I am with you,' declares the Lord of armies. 'As for the promise which I made you when you came out of Egypt, My Spirit remains in your midst; do not fear!'"
Haggai 2:4–5 NASB

UNDERSTAND

- *How does God speak to the leaders of Israel at a moment when the people are complaining about the failures of the present and the lack of hope for the future?*
- *Why is remembering God's past actions so important when seeking His guidance in a situation that seems hopeless?*
- *What hasn't changed for the people of Israel despite all of their failures?*

APPLY

You may find yourself focused on the ways you don't measure up today or the ways you've failed in the past. But God is calling you to take a courageous view of the future. Then you can find courage as you look to the ways God has helped others and on the promises He has made to you. Courage may not come easy or even feel natural.

Consider all of the ways that the people of Israel failed to listen to God and suffered exile as a result. Yet God's Spirit remained with His people. There was hope simply because God's faithfulness was far greater than the faith of His people. Just as the people couldn't go beyond the hope of God's restoration, you also can't move beyond a certain place without hope in the Lord.

It's easy to get weighed down by what others think. But God is calling you to make the courageous choice that asks, "What is God asking me to believe?" Despite what others say, there is a long history of God's people looking forward in hope, despite what seems like impossible odds.

PRAY

Lord, help me to ignore my doubts and the negative thoughts of others so that I can seek You and Your will alone. May I have faith in You to make the courageous choice that rests fully in You and Your faithful Spirit. Amen.

NO HOLDING BACK

Read Psalm 37:1–6

KEY VERSE

Delight yourself in the Lord*; and He will give you the desires of your heart.* Psalm 37:4 NASB

UNDERSTAND

- *What do you think it means to delight in the Lord?*
- *Do you ever catch yourself holding something back from God—a habit, thought, or decision? If so, what's your response?*

APPLY

The movie *Gattaca* is the story of two brothers, one genetically perfected in the womb (Anton), the other (Vincent) left to his own inferior natural devices. As boys, they test each other by swimming out into the ocean as far as they dare in a game of chicken. Anton always wins. As adults, they engage in one final swim, and Anton almost drowns. Vincent, his substandard brother, saves him. When Anton asks how he pulled it off, Vincent replies, "I never saved anything for the swim back."

A model of manhood has always been marked by self-sufficiency, by the will to do what is necessary to succeed, sometimes at any cost. A so-called real man puts his stamp on the world, even if other, weaker people end up getting stamped along the way. Those are the men David referred to in Psalm 37 as evildoers and fools because they rejected God in favor of self-sufficiency.

If your goals center on honoring God in all you do, you can run your race with boldness and confidence. Keep pushing to love well, to honor God, because you know He is with you. When Jesus came, that was God saving nothing for the swim back. He matches you stroke for stroke and keeps your head above water when you need Him most. Delight in Him because He delights in you—and keep swimming.

PRAY

I need You today, Jesus. The race is long and hard, and I'm worn out. Remind me that You are with me and for me. Renew my delight in You and Your ways. Strengthen my trust in Your presence and provision. Help me to swim without fear.

JOSEPH AND GOD-INSPIRED DREAMS

Read Genesis 37:1–26

KEY VERSE

Soon Joseph had another dream, and again he told his brothers about it. "Listen, I have had another dream," he said. "The sun, moon, and eleven stars bowed low before me!"
GENESIS 37:9 NLT

UNDERSTAND

- *When it comes to new novels and movies, are you for or against spoiler alerts?*
- *Do you remember reading Genesis 37–50 for the first time? If so, what surprised you the most?*

APPLY

Like Shakespeare, Twain, and Hemingway, God sometimes says something you don't understand until later in the book. In Genesis 37, you meet Joseph as a seventeen-year-old and are immediately told about two God-inspired dreams. Both have a single interpretation that inflames the hatred of his brothers, who sell Joseph into slavery in Egypt. Joseph's dreams are utterly destroyed. Worse, after being falsely accused of a terrible crime, Joseph spends years in prison.

More than a decade later, two of Joseph's fellow prisoners tell him about their dreams. The dreams sound similar, but Joseph interprets them in two very different ways. Two years later, Joseph is called before Pharaoh to interpret two very disturbing dreams.

This dream motif continues until you get to the climax of Joseph's story in Genesis 45. Finally, trembling and bowing before Pharaoh's right-hand man in Egypt, absolutely afraid for their lives, Joseph's brothers receive the shock of their lives. Joseph's teenage dreams had come true before their very eyes!

Like any great book, the Bible is meant to be read over and over. Better yet, think of it like watching one of your all-time favorite movies. Remember all the "aha!" moments you had the second time you watched the movie? If you keep looking at the context, you can also have "aha!" moments every time you read and study a particular scripture passage.

PRAY

Yes, Lord, I want to say "Thank You!" for the dynamic storytelling power of many big blocks of scripture in both the Old Testament and the New Testament.

HIGHER WAYS, HIGHER THOUGHTS

Read Isaiah 55:6–11

KEY VERSES

"For my thoughts are not your thoughts, neither are your ways my ways," declares the LORD. *"As the heavens are higher than the earth, so are my ways higher than your ways and my thoughts than your thoughts."* ISAIAH 55:8–9 NIV

UNDERSTAND

- *Think of a time when God seemed to let you down. How did you get back on track with Him?*
- *What is the difference between certainty in what God does versus trust in who God is?*

APPLY

Only a dishonest Christian says he has never been disappointed with God's response to a prayer. There is an ebb and flow to walking with God, times when He feels wonderfully near and other times when He seems nowhere to be found. When you're in the groove with God, nothing's better. Why can't it be like that all the time?

The Bible makes it clear that God is always near. We're the ones who move away from Him. Maybe He allows it for a season and a purpose, the way He did in Genesis 40 when Joseph was seemingly forgotten in jail. Or maybe we've slipped and He's course-correcting us.

When we believe we have God figured out and then He does something we don't understand, it's easy to become bitter. Some even leave the faith because they think God's view of people is less loving, less righteous, and less merciful than theirs. But we cannot forget who God is, that even in our confusion and frustration, He never wastes our pain, and He never forsakes us.

No matter how far you have drifted from Him, turn to Him without hesitation or reservation. Isaiah 55:7 (NLT) says God "will forgive generously." He just wants you back on board.

PRAY

Lord, today I trust in who You are and who I am to You. Forgive me for thinking I've got You completely figured out. Your ways and thoughts are higher than mine. Bring me back into Your presence. I need You.

ON THE STRAIGHT AND NARROW

Read Luke 13:24–27

KEY VERSE

"Strive to enter through the narrow gate, for many, I say to you, will seek to enter and will not be able." LUKE 13:24 NKJV

UNDERSTAND

- *What parts of worldly thinking and living do you find most attractive?*
- *In what area of your life is it hardest to submit to God?*

APPLY

What difference does it make whether we believe in God or not? Do the details of our spirituality really matter? Wouldn't it be easier to just let folks live the best lives they could?

At first, yes, much easier. However, that way of thinking and living is what Jesus called the wide gate "that leads to destruction" (Matthew 7:13 NIV). If all those good people were being honest, they would probably agree that, for all their virtuous behavior, life's meaning is still confusing, and going with the flow is ultimately empty. But they still dismiss God as a solution. Ultimately, God will honor their free will by giving them an eternity without Him.

But what do we do with Luke 13:27 (NKJV), where we see people who call themselves Christians being rejected by Jesus as "workers of iniquity"? Luke 13 points to the heart of the problem—the appearance of righteousness versus actual righteousness.

God alone knows the difference because He alone is actually righteous. That's why the gate that leads to life is narrow—the width of a man hanging on a cross. Only Jesus walked a straight and true path—the one He paved for any who would follow Him. We can't love God without loving His rescue plan, without loving others and wanting to see them get through that narrow gate.

PRAY

You alone are deserving of praise and glory, Almighty God. You alone are good, and You alone are worthy of my trust. You alone can save me. Lead me on the narrow path, for Your glory and my best life.

TRUST IN GOD'S FUTURE, NOT IN YOUR PAST

Read Zechariah 8:1–13

KEY VERSES

"This is what the LORD of Heaven's Armies says: All this may seem impossible to you now, a small remnant of God's people. But is it impossible for me? says the LORD of Heaven's Armies. This is what the LORD of Heaven's Armies says: You can be sure that I will rescue my people from the east and from the west. I will bring them home again to live safely in Jerusalem. They will be my people, and I will be faithful and just toward them as their God."
ZECHARIAH 8:6–8 NLT

UNDERSTAND

- *Why would God's people doubt that He could restore Jerusalem to safety as they struggled to rebuild the temple?*
- *How did past experiences shape the way the people of Jerusalem understood Zechariah's message from the Lord?*
- *How could the obedience and courage of God's people bring benefits to others as well?*

APPLY

When you're rebuilding or starting over after a season of loss or suffering, it's hard to look forward in hope, even when God has promised good things. The sting of the past and the consequences of poor decisions can be overwhelming.

But how can you begin to trust God's hope for the future when everything in the present seems to be wrong? There aren't easy answers in today's passage. Zechariah asks the people of Israel to trust in God's message and to keep building things one day at a time. Hope doesn't come with the snap of a finger. You'll have to take a leap into the unknown and commit to the long-term work of faithfulness.

Yet as one day leads to another, God can bring change and renewal into your life. A new story can be written, and you'll find that the failures of the past are farther in the distance as new memories take their place. As you find your way forward with God, your trust will be rewarded and His faithfulness will become clear. What had seemed impossible can gradually lead to hopeful change and restoration.

PRAY

Help me, Lord, to look at Your character and Your promises with faith and hope so that I can put my complete trust in You today. May I find Your strength to live in obedience and to write a new story of restoration that rights the wrongs of the past. Amen.

THE ROOT OF FEAR

Read Psalm 34:1–9, 1 Samuel 21:10–15

KEY VERSE

I sought the LORD and He answered me, and rescued me from all my fears. PSALM 34:4 NASB

UNDERSTAND

- *What frightens you the most?*
- *When was the last time you worried about people's opinions more than God's?*

APPLY

David wrote Psalm 34 when Saul tried to kill him. Saul was jealous that God had chosen someone else to be king. Both men were reacting to frightening situations, but the contrast between their responses is telling.

David faced trouble by relying on God, but Saul chose his own devices, which separated him more and more from God. David feared God more than men; it was the opposite for Saul. David cared more about what God thought of him than his reputation or standing before people, even though it meant going on the run; Saul chose expedience at every turn. In the end, only David had the strength to stand.

For so many men, fear is one of their strongest motivators. We're afraid of failure, often of intimacy, of being revealed to be a fraud (especially when we've been successful). We avoid situations where we might not succeed because we're afraid our failures would define us. We don't let people get to know us because they might reject us. We don't dare admit we don't know how to do something at work because our boss might think it was a bad move to promote us. But God has more for us than that.

David admitted he was afraid and gave the situation to God, who helped him get through it and ultimately vindicated him. When you hold nothing back from God, fear loses its grip and faith takes hold.

PRAY

Father, I confess I'm slow to admit what frightens me. I want to live boldly, trusting in Your love, strength, and provision. Help me to work hard at what I can control and leave the rest to You.

HARD WORDS TO STOMACH

Read John 6:33–40

KEY VERSES

Jesus said to them, "I am the bread of life. He who comes to Me shall never hunger, and he who believes in Me shall never thirst. But I said to you that you have seen Me and yet do not believe." John 6:35–36 NKJV

UNDERSTAND

- *How do you view tension—as a necessary source of growth or something to be avoided as a show of faith?*
- *Why is Jesus a leader worth following?*

APPLY

Kingdom values look upside down compared to the ways and means of the world. From a human perspective, it doesn't make much sense to put yourself last so you can be first. Letting God vindicate you when you've been wronged requires ridiculous patience. Forgiving people—taking the burden of their wrongdoing on your shoulders—when they don't even acknowledge they've wronged you just isn't natural.

But everything Jesus asks you to do, He has done first. He gave up the eternal, loving community of the Trinity and the praise of heaven to draw us into relationship. He endured the most unjust punishment in history, choosing at Gethsemane to give God the final word on the third day. Even on the cross, He asked His Father to forgive His killers.

You may feel crushed, abandoned, and weak, but because of God's power in you, you are not. You are strong enough because He is. The supernatural is in you today and every day. Don't diminish its small movements or less flashy manifestations—faithful prayer, hopeful expectation, spiritual fruit. All of that is where you'll connect with God's heart, and that's the greatest miracle of all.

PRAY

Lord God, You can do anything and everything that aligns with who You are and what You want. Because Your power is in me, I can follow Your example in trusting God and loving others. Open my eyes to see You at work all around me in big and small ways.

DAY 91

GOD WANTED THE BIBLE TO HAVE REPETITION

Read Hebrews 1:1–2:4

KEY VERSE

Long ago, at many times and in many ways, God spoke to our fathers by the prophets.
HEBREWS 1:1 ESV

UNDERSTAND

- *An old Latin proverb says, "Repetition is the mother of learning." Why do you think that is?*
- *When you read the Gospels, what do you think about parallel accounts of Jesus' teachings and miracles?*

APPLY

Like any great writer, God wrote more than one work. Since the Bible is a collection of sixty-six God-inspired books with a unified theme and purpose, it's well worth your time comparing one scripture passage with other related passages.

Many study Bibles provide a list of cross-references for any given scripture verse. The cross-references show how other verses address the same theme. In addition, most study Bibles let you know whenever there's a parallel passage to the one you're reading. For example:

- *You'll find that Moses covers many of the events and laws in Exodus, Leviticus, and Numbers all over again in Deuteronomy.*
- *You'll find many of the events in 1 and 2 Samuel and 1 and 2 Kings covered again from a different perspective in 1 and 2 Chronicles.*
- *You'll find many direct and indirect Old Testament quotations throughout the New Testament. Many show that Jesus is the promised Messiah.*
- *You'll find a number of Jesus' miracles and teachings covered from different perspectives in two or three Gospels.*
- *You'll find a number of the apostles' teachings and instructions covered from different perspectives in multiple New Testament letters.*

The good news is that the more time you spend seeking to understand scripture correctly, the easier it gets. God designed it that way!

PRAY

Yes, Lord, I want to say "Thank You!" for letting me know the important themes in scripture by repeating them and expressing them in so many different ways.

LET IT RIP, THEN LIFT HIM UP

Read Lamentations 5:15–22

KEY VERSE

Restore us, O Lord, and bring us back to you again! Give us back the joys we once had!
Lamentations 5:21 NLT

UNDERSTAND

- *What do you tend to do when God seems far away?*
- *How often do you get angry, and what happens when you do? Do you clam up or blow up (or clam up until you blow up)?*

APPLY

As we look at our wounded world, Jeremiah's lament is a good model for us. He was honest about the hurt and anger he felt, but mostly he identified with his people, using *us* as he asked God why He had abandoned and rejected His people.

When we cry out to God, He can handle it. He isn't obligated to do what we ask, but He can understand why we're angry, sad, and fed up. Sin angers Him all the time—but love is His very nature. Even when God punishes His people, He does so with higher purposes in mind—restoration, reconciliation, redemption.

Go ahead and get angry that the world's gone mad. Then remember David's words in Psalm 4:4 (NKJV): "Be angry, and do not sin." Let God channel your anger into a focus on obedience and justice, on pursuing right standing with Him and those around you. You're a new creation, after all. You're no longer bound by the idea that good Christians don't get mad. Don't go nuts, but don't clam up till you blow up. Instead, stand on Christ's righteous foundation, take on His mission, and do something about the problems you see.

PRAY

God, You are the only one who is good, righteous, just, and loving. Please help me to see people through Your eyes and with Your heart; we are broken and riddled with sin and its consequences but still beloved and precious to You. Forgive me, forgive my country, forgive us all, merciful God, and bring our hearts into unity with Yours. Start with me.

JUST KEEP PLOWING

Read Hosea 10:12–13

KEY VERSE

"Plant the good seeds of righteousness, and you will harvest a crop of love. Plow up the hard ground of your hearts, for now is the time to seek the LORD, that he may come and shower righteousness upon you." HOSEA 10:12 NLT

UNDERSTAND

- *How regularly do you rely on God's righteousness to give you faith in hard times?*
- *How often do you think of your role as God's ambassador in the world?*

APPLY

Hosea is one of those no-holds-barred OT prophets who made it clear that if even God's people reject Him long enough, He will let them have what they want. Case in point, the Babylonian exile—one of the lowest points in Israel's history. Hosea 10:13 (NKJV) describes the root of all Israel's sins: "You have eaten the fruit of lies, because you trusted in your own way."

Only God can insert a ray of hope into a message of dire judgment and mean it. But the fact that He does should inspire us to keep hope's flame burning in a darkening world. Even as Israel's doom was laid out, Hosea passed along a message of hope—Hosea 10:12's promise of God's faithfulness at all times. When we seek God's righteousness, He is faithful to bless us with all we need to do His work.

That's the only hopeful verse in a chapter of violent darkness, but it reminds us that no matter how overwhelmingly bad things get, God's light is never completely extinguished. Your part is to keep plowing the fields, to keep sowing His good news, especially when the light seems dimmest. Remind yourself and others that as bad as things get, God has provided a harvest—hope now and life forever.

PRAY

Lord God, You remain faithful in every age. You are just in Your judgments, and Your mercies are truly astounding. These are troubled times, and I admit I'm often overwhelmed. Remind me today of the times You have rekindled my hope, and use me to reignite Your flame in others' hearts.

NEVER TOO LATE TO REPENT

Read 2 Kings 23:19–25

KEY VERSES

Furthermore, Josiah got rid of the mediums and spiritists, the household gods, the idols and all the other detestable things seen in Judah and Jerusalem. This he did to fulfill the requirements of the law written in the book that Hilkiah the priest had discovered in the temple of the LORD. Neither before nor after Josiah was there a king like him who turned to the LORD as he did—with all his heart and with all his soul and with all his strength, in accordance with all the Law of Moses. 2 KINGS 23:24–25 NIV

UNDERSTAND

- *In today's scripture reading, what is most notable about the way that Josiah responded?*
- *How do you think the people in Judah and Jerusalem responded when Josiah began to make the changes he knew needed to be made?*
- *What were some of the risks Josiah took when he made reforms based on the books of the law discovered in the temple?*

APPLY

It's not easy to make a major change of direction in life. There are stubborn old habits to dislodge, and there may be fear of losses or mistakes. Family, friends, or colleagues may resist the changes you want to make. Yes, change can be hard—but Josiah shows that it is worth the effort to be single-minded and wholehearted in your pursuit of God.

Josiah could have given up in despair or shame when he discovered how far the people had strayed from God's commands. He surely wasn't popular with some people when he started removing household gods and other longstanding customs. But God honors those who turn toward obedience with their whole heart, mind, soul, and strength.

You have an invitation today to turn to God in the same way Josiah did. Consider the areas of your life where you may have strayed away from God's commands or even the places where you've been unaware of what He expected. You can turn to Him today and make changes, even drastic ones, that set you on the right course. But like Josiah, the best way forward is to make a clean break from disobedience and to follow God with all your heart, mind, soul, and strength.

PRAY

Lord, reveal the areas of my life where I have strayed from You, and help me to see a path forward through repentance and obedience. May I live in complete obedience to You throughout my day today. Amen.

HOW TO USE YOUR FREEDOM

Read 1 Corinthians 10:23-24

KEY VERSES

All things are permitted, but not all things are of benefit. All things are permitted, but not all things build people up. No one is to seek his own advantage, but rather that of his neighbor.
1 CORINTHIANS 10:23–24 NASB

UNDERSTAND

- *What has Christ set you free from, both generally and personally?*
- *When is it hardest to put others' needs ahead of your own? What makes it difficult?*

APPLY

John 8:36 (NLT) shows us that an effective witness begins with the liberation Christ purchased for us: "If the Son sets you free, you are truly free." Being set free from sin is all-encompassing: We are new creations in Christ, raised with Him from the dead spiritual state we were born into. Not only do we have His power in us to stop our bad habits, but we are also free from fitting into the world's mold.

That freedom, however, carries responsibility. God's grace reminds us to treat others the way He treats us, with respect for our free will and a relentless desire for our highest good. His Spirit in us inspires and strengthens us to obey out of love, from the same position of humility Jesus assumed with us.

After all, Jesus needed nothing when He came from heaven to rescue us. He did so because He wanted to please the Father and build a bridge to reunite God with His creation.

Stay mindful of how your choices in nonessential matters impact other believers. Err on the side of caution out of love, and as Paul said in 1 Corinthians 10:31 (NASB), "Whatever you do, do all things for the glory of God."

PRAY

Lord Jesus, the incredible cost You paid reminds me that true freedom isn't free, that it involves sacrificial love. Help me find the rhythm of enjoying the freedom You give me and respect the choices others make as they also seek to honor You.

DAY 96

WAITING ON JUSTICE, LIVING OUT MERCY

Read Psalm 9:1–10

KEY VERSE

Those who know Your name [who have experienced Your precious mercy] will put their confident trust in You, for You, O Lord, have not abandoned those who seek You.
Psalm 9:10 AMP

UNDERSTAND

- *How do you tend to see God's general attitude toward people—as one of wrath or grace?*
- *How does your view of God impact your heart toward people?*

APPLY

Compassion fatigue is real, and it can limit our desire for justice. The world is such a mess that it's easier not to care. The alternative—getting too deep in the weeds of daily headlines and the trials and problems of others—is no better. But there is more for the Christian than a seesaw between apathy and anger, and it starts with God.

Psalm 9 reminds us that God is paying attention to current events, as He has throughout history. He isn't blowing stuff off, and His temper isn't like ours—a cartoon thermometer boiling into the red with explosive fury. His anger at sin is righteous and just—and yet He is always good, just, and loving. He also has knowledge and perspective we don't, and our only real decision is whether we're going to trust Him to do what's right.

God will "judge the world in righteousness," but He is also "a refuge and a stronghold for the oppressed" (Psalm 9:8–9 AMP). He perfectly strikes the proper balance of truth and love at all times and in all situations. Neither the times you've been wronged nor the times you've wronged others escape His notice. And whenever He chooses to deal with those injustices is the right time, whether in this life or the next.

PRAY

Almighty God, Your mercies are overwhelming and Your grace is amazing. Your love demands both justice and mercy. Help me to be Your agent for both today in whatever situations You set before me.

DAY 97

LISTENING ONLY MATTERS IF YOU ACT

Read James 1:12–27

KEY VERSES

For if any are hearers of the word and not doers, they are like those who look at themselves in a mirror; for they look at themselves and, on going away, immediately forget what they were like. But those who look into the perfect law, the law of liberty, and persevere, being not hearers who forget but doers who act—they will be blessed in their doing.
JAMES 1:23–25 NRSV

UNDERSTAND

- *What kind of situation do you think James was addressing in this passage of scripture?*
- *Why does James compare only listening to the Word of scripture to forgetting what you look like in a mirror?*
- *What kind of looking does James describe in this passage?*

APPLY

A mirror offers a reality check. Whatever you may think about your appearance, a mirror always tells the truth. However, you can use a mirror to your benefit. A mirror may help you spot a problem so that you will be able to act. It also works that way as you look into the mirror of scripture.

What James describes is no passing glance at scripture. This is a very intent and deep look at the message of scripture that leads to liberty and freedom. What you see in scripture can change your life and lead to significant blessings and benefits. It may not be easy to obey scripture, but if you look at it closely and trust in the words that God has passed on to you, you'll be prepared to live an obedient life.

How you live your life today matters a great deal to God. He doesn't want you to be deceived about yourself. So look to the Bible for the truth about how to live. There are plenty of other mirrors available, but none is as clear and reliable.

PRAY

Help me, Lord, to trust in Your Word and in Your message for guidance in my life. May I take Your message to heart and translate it into obedient action that conveys my love for You and for others so that You gain the glory. Amen.

DAY 98

GETTING TO THE HEART OF WHAT MATTERS

Read Galatians 1:10–12

KEY VERSE

Am I now trying to win the favor and approval of men, or of God? Or am I seeking to please someone? If I were still trying to be popular with men, I would not be a bond-servant of Christ. GALATIANS 1:10 AMP

UNDERSTAND

- *What does putting God first look like?*
- *When have you put your desire to please people over your desire to please God?*

APPLY

Tests are God's way of making sure you understand that following Christ was never meant to be comfortable or undertaken without consideration for what it will cost you. Just as it cost God everything to save you, you must decide what you will give up to follow Him.

At the heart of every test is the issue of surrender. What is God asking you to surrender to Him? Questions of evil and injustice? Bitterness over the hypocrisy you see in your church? Is it the feeling of God's absence at a critical moment?

When Paul says, "If I were still trying to be popular with men, I would not be a bond-servant of Christ," it's clear that the heart of his conversion hinged on sorting out what mattered most to him. He was basically the same man, but his view of God changed. He reordered his priorities, putting God first instead of his own accomplishments, views, background, or questions.

Because Paul saw God differently, he saw himself differently, and he learned to see others with fresh eyes. When what matters most to God matters most to you, your heart will change, and so will your corner of the world.

PRAY

Lord Jesus, forgive me for the times I give more weight to other people's opinions than Yours. Show me anything about myself—any habits or ways of thinking about You or myself or others—that keeps me from putting You first in everything I am and do.

HOW BIG IS GOD?

Read Genesis 1:1–31

KEY VERSE

And God blessed them. And God said to them, "Be fruitful and multiply and fill the earth and subdue it, and have dominion over the fish of the sea and over the birds of the heavens and over every living thing that moves on the earth." GENESIS 1:28 ESV

UNDERSTAND

- *What does the first chapter of the Bible tell us about God?*
- *What does it tell us about mankind?*

APPLY

God's Word is relevant to all men, everywhere, every time. According to 2 Timothy 3:16–17, all scripture is inspired by God and is useful, profitable, beneficial, practical, and full of rewards for the person who studies it.

The Bible contains truths, commands, and examples that speak directly to your heart and life today. It's full of countless amazing truths about God, your life, and things to come.

Sometimes the trick, however, is determining how to study the Bible when you're in a particular situation. The problem? You're often in a hurry to know which way to turn! How much better to slow down and check your God-given map for life. Even better, why not plot your course ahead of time? After all, the road ahead isn't about to move!

You can't find ten words more powerful than the Bible's opening line: "In the beginning God created the heavens and the earth" (Genesis 1:1 NKJV). Talk about *great*! On the sixth day, He made man (Genesis 1:26–27). Yet miracles are only ripples of God's first words. He isn't finished speaking yet!

No matter what challenges you face between here and heaven, God is big enough to meet your needs. He'll never say, "Whoa! Now *that's* a problem. You're on your own this time."

PRAY

Yes, Lord, I want to say "Thank You!" again that You could but speak the word and create the entire universe. Yet You know and care about us. You love me. I'm humbled and amazed.

TAMING THE GREEN-EYED MONSTER

Read Deuteronomy 4:23–24

KEY VERSE

"The Lord your God is a consuming fire, a jealous God." Deuteronomy 4:24 NASB

UNDERSTAND

- *What is worth fighting for?*
- *What makes you jealous?*
- *What do you think of when God says He is jealous?*

APPLY

We get nervous when we read that God is jealous. It's one of mankind's worst traits, so how could it possibly be any part of God's character? But dozens of verses speak of Him this way.

Here's the difference: God is jealous for His good name and for His people's hearts. He is jealous because He is holy, loving what He loves and hating what He hates with a purity of purpose and passion we cannot imagine.

Human jealousy is driven by envy—the selfish lust for what someone else has because we want to be superior in things like material goods, relationships, or reputation. Sin warps our desire to love and be loved by someone else completely into envy.

How, then, do we identify and fight our jealousy? As 1 Corinthians 6:19–20 (NIV) says, if you call Jesus Lord and Savior, you are "not your own; you were bought at a price." Jesus thus reserves the right to burn away everything that keeps you from being fully unified with Him. Christ's sacrifice consumes all your old ways, including your envy.

God wants us to want Him more than anything or anyone else. When we do, His Spirit in us purifies our desires and intentions. Over time, we learn to distinguish between our harmful, futile envy and His relentless, jealous love. With His help, we practice putting others' needs ahead of our own, wanting God's best for them more than anything else.

PRAY

Forgive me, Father, for the times and ways I've been jealous. I turn my sin over to You to be burned away in Your consuming fire. If anything remains, I know it will be for the benefit of others and Your glory.

GOD HAS YOUR BACK

Read Hebrews 2:14–18

KEY VERSE

Because he himself suffered when he was tempted, he is able to help those who are being tempted. HEBREWS 2:18 NIV

UNDERSTAND

- *What temptations most often befall you? What keeps you from asking God for help?*
- *What is your expectation when you ask God to help you overcome temptation?*

APPLY

To be human is to be tempted—even Jesus was tempted by Satan, which tells us that temptation itself isn't a sin. Our response is what matters. We forget who God is and what He has done to help us overcome our struggles with our flesh, the world, and the devil.

God limits the strength of temptation so you can bear it, and He gives you a way out (1 Corinthians 10:13). Even so, expect a struggle. Jesus died to set you free, but He suffered to do it. Jesus didn't want the cup of God's wrath, but He knew God would provide the way through, and that the reward (which includes you) would be worth the pain.

Jesus knows what it's like to stare down temptation. Hebrews 4:15–16 (NLT) assures us "he faced all of the same testings we do, yet he did not sin. So let us come boldly to the throne of our gracious God. There we will receive his mercy, and we will find grace to help us when we need it most."

Come boldly means to cry out to God with expectation—that no matter how strong the impulse is, He will help you fight and overcome it. Pray, fast, read scripture, and keep seeking His face till the terrible moment passes. Like Jesus, you will have to suffer to conquer temptation—but you can.

PRAY

Lord Jesus, You know what it's like to be tempted to choose the easier path, to choose immediate gratification over holiness, but You chose the Father's will when it counted the most. Give me Your power to withstand temptation at each moment of truth.

GOD HEALS OUR PAIN

Read Isaiah 53:1–12

KEY VERSES

He was despised and rejected—a man of sorrows, acquainted with deepest grief. We turned our backs on him and looked the other way. He was despised, and we did not care. Yet it was our weaknesses he carried; it was our sorrows that weighed him down.

Isaiah 53:3–4 NLT

UNDERSTAND

- *Why is it so significant that God's servant (Christ) wasn't beautiful or attractive?*
- *What does it mean to you that God's servant was a man of sorrows who was acquainted with deepest grief?*
- *What is the result of God carrying our weaknesses and our sorrows?*

APPLY

God's starting point with His people is often their pain and suffering, as He seeks out those who are overlooked, neglected, and sorrowful so that they can be restored. Even God's own approach to our salvation came through the man of sorrows, who bore the sin, sadness, and weakness of the world.

This is a major difference from the approach of our world today, where suffering is avoided, overlooked, and even actively hidden. Pastors who promise blessings and prosperity have no trouble drawing a crowd, but the dark side of such approaches is an inability to speak into the pain and loss that is certain to come in this world.

Jesus bore your grief and sadness and offers the hope of renewal and restoration. That hope isn't an empty promise with glamour and comfort. Jesus went through the path of suffering and transformed it. You can bring your pain to God today and trust that you aren't bearing it alone. That pain is right where God plans to be. And if you see others who are suffering, remember that God is near to them as well, and you can imitate God's example by sharing in their sorrow. One day your joy will be all the greater when God's restoration comes.

PRAY

Help me, Father, to see my suffering as an opportunity to draw near to You and to remember that You see my sorrow. May I acknowledge my pain and remain aware of those who are enduring grief and loss so that I can imitate the example of Jesus. Amen.

DAY 103

TAKE TIME TO REMEMBER

Read Psalm 105:1–11

KEY VERSE

Search for the Lord *and for his strength; continually seek him.* Psalm 105:4 NLT

UNDERSTAND

- *You're a part of God's astonishing history with all mankind. How does that make you feel?*
- *When is the last time God did something significant in your life? How did you celebrate that?*

APPLY

Psalm 105 praises God by looking back at the first part of His history with Israel. We see the pattern God established at creation and continues through this very day in the church age: taking barren hearts and making something fruitful. God looked at formless chaos and spoke the world and everything in it into existence.

Then He built a nation out of an unlikely bunch of wanderers and called it His own, putting Israel at the center of redemptive history. Jesus chose to be born into poverty and assembled a motley crew to spread His good news, changing the world. That's where you come in. You are part of God's story—through His grace and love a saint and coheir with Christ—and He has important things for you to do.

Throughout God's dealings with us is the command to remember. When God-centered things happened to saints of old, they built monuments. They celebrated God's triumph, whether by building piles of stones, celebrating high holy days, or recalling God's deeds in worship.

What are the monuments marking your history with God? Part of pursuing God is recalling His faithfulness. Find ways to remind yourself to thank and praise Him. Whatever you do, remember Him on those dates.

PRAY

Thank You, Lord, that You have made me a part of Your story. Your love, care, and provision are evidence of how great You are. Forgive me for the times when I forget all You have done and all You are doing now. Let my life be a monument to Your love.

GRACE UPON GRACE

Read John 1:14–16

KEY VERSE

For out of His fullness [the superabundance of His grace and truth] we have all received grace upon grace [spiritual blessing upon spiritual blessing, favor upon favor, and gift heaped upon gift]. John 1:16 AMP

UNDERSTAND

- *How does God's love affect your behavior on a daily basis?*
- *How hard is it for you to accept things you haven't earned?*

APPLY

The wonder of Jesus' exchange on the cross is He got all the bad stuff our sinful natures and behavior deserve, while we receive everything He deserves. As Ephesians 2:8–9 says, salvation is an undeserved, unexpected gift given by grace.

But God's favor doesn't stop when you receive Christ; it's only beginning. Once you are under the power of grace instead of sin, you should expect a constant outpouring of what John called His "fullness." As James 4:6 (ESV) puts it, throughout our time with Jesus, "He gives more grace." Grace includes God seeing us through the lens of Jesus' righteousness.

If God pouring out grace upon grace on you makes you feel unworthy, remember that's how grace works. God sees what you're becoming and what you will become—the image of Christ. Let God bless you, cover you, favor you, and be delighted with you—because He wants you to share the overflow of His grace with others.

Imagine a heart so full of His grace that you bless your enemies, that you speak God's redeeming truth to someone who has spoken lies about you. You are His beloved son, and He is pleased with you. Let that truth encourage you to see others through that grace-filled lens.

PRAY

Lord Jesus, Your grace overwhelms me. I don't deserve it, but I need Your help to move past that attitude of unworthiness into a habit of grace. You saved me so You could love me relentlessly and lavishly, and so I could be a conduit of that love and grace to others.

GOD IS GREAT, GOOD, AND GRACIOUS

Read Ephesians 1:1–14

KEY VERSE

He predestined us for adoption to sonship through Jesus Christ, in accordance with his pleasure and will. EPHESIANS 1:5 NIV

UNDERSTAND

- *According to today's key verse, how long has God planned on adopting you?*
- *According to the same verse, why did God plan to do this?*

APPLY

It's good to remember that no matter what challenges you face, God in His infinite and eternal greatness is plenty big enough to meet your needs. Again, He'll never say, "Whoa, now *that's* a problem. You're on your own this time."

God is great *and* good. Forget about a second honeymoon on a remote South Pacific isle. You can't ask for anything better than the Garden of Eden (Genesis 2:8–25). Adam and Eve had it made. Yet Paradise is only God's first act. He's saving His best for last! From now until eternity, God will always do what is truly best for us. He'll never be tempted to say, "I'm tired of all this righteous stuff. I feel like changing all the rules today. Watch out, world!"

What's more, God is gracious. Forget getting out of jail free. You can't thank God enough for showing mercy and promising a redeemer (Genesis 3:14–21). The wages of man's sin was death (Romans 3:23). Yet forgiveness is only God's first gift. He's promised you so much more!

You can always count on the fact that God has much more than salvation in store for us. He will always be glad to say, "Can I tell you again how much I love you? I'm so glad you're My child."

PRAY

Yes, Lord, I want to say "Thank You!" for Your incredible love for me. It's astounding. I love You too.

NO MORE CAT-AND-MOUSE

Read Luke 11:1–13

KEY VERSE

"Don't bargain with God. Be direct. Ask for what you need. This is not a cat-and-mouse, hide-and-seek game we're in." Luke 11:10 MSG

UNDERSTAND

- *How hard is prayer for you? What makes it difficult?*
- *What do you think God's best for you is?*

APPLY

Prayer is challenging because it reminds us of our reliance on God. When things are going well, it's human nature to leave prayer for meal times, because hey, things are going well. When things are not going well, we often complain first, try to place blame somewhere, or work on fixing the issue—leaving prayer as a last resort: "Well, I guess the only thing we can do now is pray."

When we fail to pray as a first option—to avail ourselves of our Christ-bought access to God—we default to self-sufficiency. And then we blame God when we're not enough. That suggests we aren't really trusting God—at least, not more than we trust ourselves. We treat God like a good backup plan.

We end up trying to game God with our prayers—to make sure we're using the right-sounding words, to pester Him like creditors seeking payment. We fear an answer of *wait* or *no*, as if a *yes* means God is finally seeing things the way we think they should be.

But when Jesus taught His followers to pray, He encouraged the boldness and persistence that comes from a healthy relationship. We are sons, and God is our Father. Do we love Him for who He is or what He can do for us? Either way, our prayer life reflects that basic attitude.

PRAY

Jesus, teach me to pray the way You pray. Let Your way become my way. Like a son coming to a beloved Father, I will be humble and bold, hopeful and persistent, trusting that You know what's best.

WORSHIP ON MANUAL

Read 1 Chronicles 16:1–4, 8–12, 34–36

KEY VERSE

Boast in His holy name; let the heart of those who seek the Lord *be joyful.*

1 Chronicles 16:10 nasb

UNDERSTAND

- *Aside from church services, when do you usually make time to worship God?*
- *Do you ever find yourself worshipping on autopilot?*

APPLY

In 1 Chronicles 16, David brought the ark to Jerusalem for the first time, placed it in the tabernacle as the focal point of God's presence, and led a God-honoring celebration, ending with the people shouting *amen* and praising the Lord. God was front and center, and all hearts were focused on Him.

If only every time we gathered for worship could be like that! Too often, we get stuck on music style or song length, or we just get bored and go through the motions. Regardless of our feelings, we should always bear in mind that, as John 4:24 (nkjv) says, God is looking for those who worship Him in "spirit and truth."

Even David didn't just automatically get it right—in fact, he had messed up royally not too long before this glorious moment when Israel didn't follow God's specific instructions about bringing the ark back to Jerusalem and someone died.

First Chronicles 16 shows us that David did it right the second time. The hard lesson he learned is that God reserves the right to tell us how He wants to be worshipped. The next time you're feeling itchy about worship, engage your heart first. Are you seeking to worship Him His way? God deserves all your attention.

PRAY

Father God, I want to worship You in spirit and truth. Forgive me for the times I've gotten stuck on a nonessential issue, and help me to keep my eyes on You, Your truth as expressed in Your Word, and Your heart as expressed in Jesus Christ. You deserve my full attention.

CHOOSE TO CELEBRATE WITH GOD

Read Luke 15:11–32

KEY VERSES

"'But when this son of yours who has squandered your property with prostitutes comes home, you kill the fattened calf for him!' 'My son,' the father said, 'you are always with me, and everything I have is yours. But we had to celebrate and be glad, because this brother of yours was dead and is alive again; he was lost and is found.'" LUKE 15:30–32 NIV

UNDERSTAND

- *How do people typically respond when others are shown mercy and forgiveness?*
- *Why did the father in today's scripture reading assure his son who remained at home that everything he has also belongs to him?*
- *Why was celebrating so important at a time when some may expect punishment and discipline?*

APPLY

God's mercy is almost always larger and more extensive than people expect. Whether you feel that you've gone past the point of no return or that you've lived in meticulous obedience for as long as you can remember, there is a place for you in today's reading.

God's mercy will always win when someone repents of sin, but the welcome party can take on a sour note to those who reject God's mercy. There is a party you are invited to join either as the recipient of God's mercy or as a member of the party sharing in the joy of restoration. While the sulking son in the Parable of the Lost Son refused to join the party because of what had happened in the past, God (like the father in this story) invites everyone to look forward to the future together.

The celebration of repentance doesn't minimize or gloss over sin. This party recognizes the seriousness of the sin, but it also celebrates the movement from death into life. This is truly cause for great celebration.

PRAY

Thank You, Father, for Your mercy and kindness—for Your promises that I can always return to You and celebrate in Your mercy and hope of renewal. May I share Your grace and mercy with others who are also in need of restoration and a new chance to live in obedience to You. Amen.

THE DEEPEST CUT

Read Romans 2:25–29

KEY VERSE

True circumcision is not merely obeying the letter of the law; rather, it is a change of heart produced by the Spirit. And a person with a changed heart seeks praise from God, not from people. Romans 2:29 NLT

UNDERSTAND

- *What makes you want to obey God?*
- *How challenging is it for you to let the Holy Spirit do His work in you rather than trying to do His job yourself?*

APPLY

When God made His covenant with Abraham, circumcision was a serious part of the covenant: To go uncircumcised was to be cut off from the covenant, from God, and from His chosen people. This continued as a requirement in the Law of Moses.

Christians are not required to be circumcised, simply because, as Galatians 2:16 (NKJV) says, "By the works of the law no flesh shall be justified." God wants a deeper cut—one that goes straight to the heart, that does away with all the excuses, the secret agendas, the sense of superiority we get when we obey His commands. In Romans 2, Paul makes it clear that such a wound only comes from receiving Christ's saving work as a free gift. Jesus was wounded on our behalf so we would never have to be cut off from God.

True circumcision depends on the work of the Spirit in us. He creates the change of heart that wants what pleases God more than anything else. Our part is to learn what He wants, then let Him do His work in us. Don't let anything get in the way of that.

PRAY

Lord God, forgive me for the times I've let rule-keeping and the appearance of holiness keep me from loving You wholeheartedly. I acknowledge that I haven't loved You or others like You want me to. Help me obey You out of love and not performance.

ARE YOU COACHABLE?

Read 2 Timothy 3:10–17

KEY VERSES

All Scripture is inspired by God and is useful to teach us what is true and to make us realize what is wrong in our lives. It corrects us when we are wrong and teaches us to do what is right. God uses it to prepare and equip his people to do every good work.

2 Timothy 3:16–17 NLT

UNDERSTAND

- *When was the last time you trusted God and acted based on something you read in the Bible?*
- *Based on your decision-making process, how much of your confidence is in God, and how much is in yourself?*

APPLY

Thankfully, God's wisdom doesn't depend on our age or experience, but rather on our experience of Him. God is faithful to provide wake-up calls—to remind us He wants all of us at all times.

Those wake-up calls can be subtle redirections of the way we're thinking about something, or they can be devastating breakdowns of life as we knew it. However, they are all tests—to see if we truly put our faith in God and if we're committed to doing what the Bible teaches us.

God's Word is more than just a book. Its deeper truth changes lives. We pursue not a place but a Person—not blessings or heaven but Jesus Himself. But we need His help—and that's why He gave us the ultimate coach, His Spirit, and the ultimate playbook, the Bible.

Be coachable. Let God's patience inspire you to be humble when God redirects you. Remember, He is equipping you for every good work.

PRAY

Father, please show me the areas of my life that You want to work on. I know this is a dangerous prayer, but I also know You are faithful and that all You do is for my good and Your glory. Give me the wisdom I need to see areas of improvement and work on them.

DAY 111

PEACE WITH GOD, OTHERS, AND YOUR CIRCUMSTANCES

Read Philippians 4:1–23

KEY VERSE

Finally, brothers, whatever is true, whatever is honorable, whatever is just, whatever is pure, whatever is lovely, whatever is commendable, if there is any excellence, if there is anything worthy of praise, think about these things. PHILIPPIANS 4:8 ESV

UNDERSTAND

- *Where was the apostle Paul when he wrote his letter to the Philippian church?*
- *How often do you think Paul had practiced what he preached?*

APPLY

Surprisingly, the simplest questions are sometimes the most profound. This is especially true when you're considering what God has to say to you in His Word. Sadly, many Christian men feel that personalizing scripture has to be complicated. Nothing is further from the truth!

Here are six simple yet profound questions. They can quickly transform ordinary Bible study into a life-changing experience. As you read a phrase, verse, or short paragraph of scripture, ask yourself these three sets of questions:

What **T**ruths does this passage teach? Do you **A**ffirm them?

What **C**ommands does the Lord give? Do you **O**bey them?

What **E**xamples does this scripture present? Do you **H**eed them?

This is the **TA-CO, EH?** (Truths to Affirm, Commands to Obey, Examples to Heed) approach to personalized scripture reading. It works great no matter where you live (Mexico or Canada, in between, or overseas), how you prefer to talk (*si*, eh, or yes), or what you like to eat!

TA-CO, EH? is the secret sauce of Bible study for men. Think of this as a bottle of your favorite hot-pepper mixture. Over the next few days, get ready for spicier Bible studies!

PRAY

Yes, Lord, I want to say "Thank You!" for the memorable TA-CO, EH? acronym. Even better, thanks that three simple sets of questions quickly and readily show me how to apply Your Word to my life today.

THE MIRROR DOESN'T LIE

Read James 4:1-10

KEY VERSE

Come close to God, and God will come close to you. Wash your hands, you sinners; purify your hearts, for your loyalty is divided between God and the world. JAMES 4:8 NLT

UNDERSTAND

- *How has God shown His love and loyalty to you?*
- *What makes it hard for you to offer those virtues in return to Him?*

APPLY

James is great because he is so blunt and practical. You don't go to James for a spiritual hug, but for an unblinking look at how you're living out your faith. You read James expecting a little course correction—and he doesn't disappoint.

Look at his verbs in James 4:7–10 (NKJV): *submit, resist, draw near, cleanse, purify, lament* and *mourn* and *weep, humble yourselves.* These are strong verbs, demanding wholehearted action. It's no surprise, coming from the guy who told us to view trouble as an opportunity for joy (James 1:2), who warned us that our own ungodly desires eventually conceive and deliver death (James 1:13–15).

James is like an Old Testament prophet, a tough voice bringing hard words that remind us that God's grace saves us from hell. Works don't save us, but they do show our faith—our belief that in following Christ, we have found the best, most meaningful, and ultimately satisfying way to live.

If Jesus isn't making a difference in the choices you make, in the actions you take, then James says you need to take a hard look at your faith. Is your trust in God or in yourself?

PRAY

Father God, give me the strength to look at what I need to improve in my walk with You. I want Jesus' heart, desiring to please You above all else, knowing that Your love demonstrated the greatest humility and sacrifice. I can't do it without You, but with You I can do all things.

SEEKING A HEART OF FORGIVENESS

Read Hosea 3:1–5

KEY VERSES

Israel will go a long time without a king or prince, and without sacrifices, sacred pillars, priests, or even idols! But afterward the people will return and devote themselves to the LORD *their God and to David's descendant, their king. In the last days, they will tremble in awe of the* LORD *and of his goodness.* HOSEA 3:4–5 NLT

UNDERSTAND

- *What is the deepest relationship wound you've ever suffered?*
- *What's the worst sin you've ever committed? Did you seek forgiveness?*

APPLY

Hosea had one of the toughest assignments of all the Old Testament prophets: to marry a woman and have children, knowing she was going to cheat on him time and time again—the same way Israel kept stepping out on God by worshipping false deities.

Even though Hosea knew the pain was coming, he had a job to do. His ministry to Israel meant telling them about God's anger and coming punishment for their lack of faith.

When someone has wronged you, the first and hardest move is to forgive—whether or not you continue in relationship with that person. You can't do it alone. Invite trusted, godly men into your pain; ask them to listen, then to help pray you through it until you're ready to take that step of obedience and forgive that person.

If you're the causer of the pain, the pattern is similar: Seek to make things right, putting the power to forgive in the other person's hands. Sometimes that person won't want to make things right. Do all you can, and then trust God with the outcome.

PRAY

Merciful God, I have carried a wound for a long time and I'm struggling with it. I don't want to set myself up to be taken advantage of again, nor do I want to keep hurting others. Help me to see forgiveness the way You do, to trust in the healing You want for Your people.

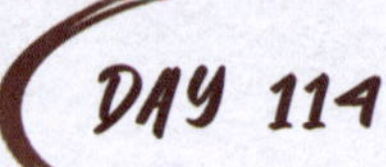

GOD REWARDS RIGHT ACTIONS AND JUST INTENTIONS

Read Jeremiah 17:9–18

KEY VERSES

"The heart is more deceitful than all else and is desperately sick; who can understand it? I, the LORD, search the heart, I test the mind, to give to each person according to his ways, according to the results of his deeds." JEREMIAH 17:9–10 NASB

UNDERSTAND

- *How does God's understanding of the human heart's deceptiveness bring assurance to you about God's justice and righteousness?*
- *How does the idea of the Lord understanding and searching your heart guide your thoughts about sin and obedience?*
- *What does the Lord's promise to reward or punish people according to their deeds imply about those who think they are sinning in secret?*

APPLY

The Lord assured Jeremiah that the people around him, even those who were prospering while disobeying God, would soon receive a just reward for their actions. There is no doubt that the choices you make today to follow God may feel like sacrifices and may even lead to some tension and difficulties. Yet the Lord will certainly make sure that your good deeds, honesty, and obedience will be rewarded.

God sees your purity of heart and intentions. Even when those around you fail to appreciate your faithfulness, God searches your heart and sees your commitments to justice and goodness. Those who act with duplicity or out of secretly selfish motives are also seen for what they are before God and will one day receive what they deserve.

It's tough to wait on God's reward in a culture immersed in instant gratification. How can you wait patiently for a reward you can't even quite imagine? You certainly don't even know when you'll be rewarded by God. The Lord invites you to take a leap of faith, trusting that your obedience and goodness today will not go to waste.

PRAY

Lord, You know my heart and mind before I can even speak. Thank You for Your mercy and compassion to forgive my sins and Your promise to reward my obedience. May I live today in dependence on You and Your provision. Amen.

THE GOD WHO WANTS TO KNOW YOU

Read Acts 17:22–31

KEY VERSES

"His purpose was for the nations to seek after God and perhaps feel their way toward him and find him—though he is not far from any one of us. For in him we live and move and exist." ACTS 17:27–28 NLT

UNDERSTAND

- *Looking back, how did God make Himself known to you?*
- *Are there areas of your life in which you tend to slip back into self-sufficiency instead of relying on God?*

APPLY

The goal of religion is to tell us how we can find God. But Christianity comes at it the opposite way, revealing a God who comes to find us. His approach goes against our nature—our default setting is self-sufficiency: We want to save ourselves and be free to determine our own purpose.

Even so, we grasp intuitively that things aren't the way they should be. The world's broken and unfixable, at least by us. Jesus is the fixer of all that is wrong with us and the world, and He wants to know you personally.

In Acts 17, Paul made it clear that the God the Greeks called *Unknown* is actually the God who made everything, who is bigger than any single set of beliefs, any idol, or any philosophy. And He is closer than we think, bestowing His common grace according to His good will to the just and unjust alike. He is a God of action and progress.

God's strange and wonderful purposes are fully displayed in Jesus Christ—God made flesh, who came to meet His own standards of righteousness and judgment, conquering the grave and sin so we could know Him personally. If that doesn't change the game for you, God remains unknown.

PRAY

Almighty, all-knowing God, thank You for making Yourself known to the world and to me. I want to live in the freedom and wisdom of being Your adopted son so I can know You more deeply and genuinely.

DAY 116

JOHN 3:16 TRUTHS TO AFFIRM

Read John 3:1–16

KEY VERSE

"For God so loved the world that He gave His only begotten Son, that whoever believes in Him should not perish but have everlasting life." JOHN 3:16 NKJV

UNDERSTAND

- *Imagine you could share one Bible verse with everyone you know. Why would John 3:16 be a good choice?*
- *What other single Bible verse would you share with everyone you know?*

APPLY

Let's begin by asking: What Truths to Affirm does today's famous key verse teach? Looking at the verse itself, you discover some important truths:

- *God loves the world.*
- *God loves you so much He sent His only Son.*
- *Whoever believes in Him will not perish.*
- *Whoever believes in Him will have everlasting life.*

These basic truths, however, don't tell you everything you want to know. If it's so important to believe in God's only Son, who is He? Where was He sent? And why? Thankfully, you can look at this same verse from an informed New Testament perspective, and then readily affirm four more truths:

- *God loves the world (everyone, including you).*
- *God loves you so much He sent His only Son (Jesus Christ, who died on a Roman cross in your place for your sins).*
- *Whoever believes in Him (Jesus Christ) will not perish (remain spiritually dead here on earth and afterward go to hell).*
- *Whoever believes in Him (Jesus Christ) will have everlasting life (enjoy spiritual life here on earth and afterward go to heaven).*

No wonder John 3:16 is the most loved verse in all scripture!

Caveat: Not all truths are created equal. Scripture accurately records outright lies, straightforward historical details, insights about how life works, and divinely revealed truths. The Bible itself places the most value on the latter.

PRAY

Yes, Lord, I want to say "Thank You!" for these rich and life-changing truths. No wonder John 3:16 is such a famous and memorable verse.

JOHN 3:16 COMMANDS TO OBEY

Read John 3:16–21

KEY VERSE

"For God so loved the world that he gave his one and only Son, that whoever believes in him shall not perish but have eternal life." John 3:16 NIV

UNDERSTAND

- *What verbs do you see in today's key verse?*
- *Who loved and gave? And who believes?*

APPLY

Now it's time to ask: What Commands to Obey does the Lord give in today's key verse?

The verse itself doesn't contain any commands, but it implies the most important command the Lord gives in all scripture. This is a command you find throughout the New Testament, and it is especially prevalent in John's writings. The implied command is this: *Believe in Jesus Christ.*

Again, John 3:16 doesn't state a direct command: "The Lord says to everyone, everywhere, for all of time, 'Believe in My only Son, Jesus Christ.'" But that imperative is embedded at the core of the verse in the phrase "believes in him."

Whenever you see a powerful verb in scripture, you want to ask yourself, *Does this verb imply a biblical command? If so, what is that command?*

If you're reading the Bible for the very first time, and you've read only snatches here and there, you may not be able to *see* the implied commands of scripture. With time, however, you'll see them on every page!

Caveat: Not all commands are created equal. Some commands are perpetual, other commands have clearly expired, and still others are for someone else—not for you.

PRAY

Yes, Lord, I want to say "Thank You!" for moving my heart months or years ago to believe in Your Son and my Lord and Savior, Jesus Christ. I still believe!

DAY 118

JOHN 3:16 EXAMPLES TO HEED

Read John 3:16–36

KEY VERSE

"For this is how God loved the world: He gave his one and only Son, so that everyone who believes in him will not perish but have eternal life." JOHN 3:16 NLT

UNDERSTAND

- *What are the best things about following God's examples?*
- *What are some of the hardest things about following God's examples?*

APPLY

Last but not least, it's time to ask: What Examples to Heed does this verse present?

In this single verse, you find two important examples:

- *God loves the world.*
- *God sent His only Son.*

What do these examples show us? The rest of John's Gospel communicates two more important truths:

- *Just as God loves the world, so you should love all people, whether or not they believe in Jesus Christ.*
- *Just as God sent His only Son, so you should give sacrificially so others can accept God's love, believe in Jesus Christ, and receive eternal life.*

After Jesus Christ's resurrection and ascension to heaven, the apostle John himself embraced both of these examples and faithfully lived them out for the rest of his life. They're worthy examples to imitate today and for the rest of your life.

Caveat: Not all examples are created equal. Some examples are positive, some are negative, and some don't apply to you.

PRAY

Yes, Lord, I want to say "Thank You!" for Your incredible demonstrations of sacrificial love. In return, I want to love You more. May I discover the secret of loving You with all my heart, soul, strength, and mind.

DAY 119

WHERE DO YOU FIND REFUGE?

Read Psalm 61

KEY VERSES

Hear my cry, O God; listen to my prayer. From the end of the earth I call to you, when my heart is faint. Lead me to the rock that is higher than I; for you are my refuge, a strong tower against the enemy. PSALM 61:1–3 NRSV

UNDERSTAND

- *What is the significance of calling out to God from the ends of the earth and expecting Him to hear your prayer?*
- *What does it mean that God is the "rock" that is higher than you? How is that image similar or different from God being a strong tower?*
- *Why does the psalmist ask to be led to the rock? Who do you think the psalmist is addressing with that question?*

APPLY

There are many places you can turn to for help during times of difficulty. But when you see challenges before you and trouble coming your way, you have a ready-made refuge in the Lord. You can approach God with confidence, knowing that He will hear your prayers and that He will take your well-being seriously.

But how can we cultivate that inner confidence in our God? We can look to the promises found in scripture, as well as to biblical examples of God answering prayer and caring for His people. We can also draw from the experiences of fellow Christians, as well as our own moments when God was present during difficult times.

The images of a high rock or strong tower may not be familiar to many today, but these things were used in scripture as illustrations of God's promise of protection and safety.

PRAY

Thank You, Father, that I am safe and secure in Your loving presence. You know my needs and hear me whenever I may pray to You. May I always find my safety and security in You, never settling for any other source of hope. Amen.

FIRST THOUGHTS

Read Psalm 5:1–3

KEY VERSE

In the morning, O Lord, You will hear my voice; in the morning I will prepare [a prayer and a sacrifice] for You and watch and wait [for You to speak to my heart]. Psalm 5:3 AMP

UNDERSTAND

- *How often do you praise God simply for being who He is?*
- *How does the thought of God waiting to hear from you in the morning make you feel?*

APPLY

Even if you're not a morning person, it's still a good idea to focus on God first thing. It doesn't have to be a full-on devotional or study (especially if you're no good pre-coffee). Just talk to God as soon as you can. A psalm of praise is a great way to offer God your first thoughts.

It helps to do a little prep work the night before. Find a Bible verse or passage you want to focus on, then bookmark it so you can grab it the next morning and read it to God. You can read the verse as a prayer or use it as a launching pad for what comes to mind.

Then take a moment of silence just to see if God impresses anything on your heart—a thought that you're reasonably sure came from Him and not you, a word of challenge or awareness, or even just a sense that it's good to seek God.

You can even do the same passage several days in a row to help fasten it onto your memory and into your heart. As a bonus, watch for ways in which God will repeat and confirm what you've read during the day or the week. He has His ways of letting you know His eye is on you and He sees what you're doing in faith each morning.

PRAY

Thank You, Lord, for Your Word. I want to develop David's habit of turning my first thoughts over to You each morning.

HOPE IN THE DARKNESS

Read Luke 22:39–46

KEY VERSES

"Father, if you are willing, remove this cup from me. Nevertheless, not my will, but yours, be done." And there appeared to him an angel from heaven, strengthening him.

Luke 22:42–43 ESV

UNDERSTAND

- *What is the hardest moment God has ever allowed you to face?*
- *How did He eventually bring you comfort?*

APPLY

At Gethsemane, Jesus looked down the barrel of God's wrath, the first and only time in His eternal existence He would be separated from the perfect community of the Trinity. He faced a darkness that we as Christians will never have to—the eternal, dissolving misery of getting what we deserve as sinners.

And as a setup for that unbearable event, Jesus couldn't even get His closest friends to pray with Him. Another would turn Him over to the authorities, and the crowds that lined His path with palm fronds a week earlier would be calling for His execution in a few hours.

If your heart aches thinking about that, let it ache. But then take comfort in knowing that Jesus understands darkness. Just as God sent an angel to comfort and strengthen Him, He will send comfort to you too in your darkest hours.

God asks us to do hard things at times and allows trials and troubles into our lives—not always because we've sinned but because He wants us to seek Him no matter what, to share in Christ's sufferings and then be strengthened with the hope He bought with His blood. The difference is that the separation from God we may feel is never actual distance. Jesus made sure of that.

PRAY

I am humbled and awestruck by what You did for me, Lord Jesus. Thank You that the darkness You faced means that the darkness I face never gets the last word. Hardship affects me but doesn't define me. You do. I choose to die to myself today so I can follow You more closely.

NEVER, NEVER GIVE UP

Read Psalm 27:7–14

KEY VERSE

I would have lost heart, unless I had believed that I would see the goodness of the Lord *in the land of the living.* Psalm 27:13 nkjv

UNDERSTAND

- *How do you feel when it seems like God is not answering your prayers?*
- *How do you usually look for God to work—in big ways or small ones?*

APPLY

People bail on Jesus when the going gets tough. It was true two-thousand years ago, and it's true today. When He doesn't meet our expectations, we often look for a savior who matches our expectations.

David saw the evil and cruelty in the world, recalled what he knew about God, and determined there was no one else worth trusting. He looked ahead to God's goodness in "the land of the living"—to the Messiah—and decided He was worth waiting on. At one point, in John 6:67–69 (esv), Jesus even asked the Twelve if they were leaving Him too, and Peter said, "Lord, to whom shall we go? You have the words of eternal life, and we have believed. . .that you are the Holy One of God."

Knowing that God is working, even if it's behind the scenes, provides an anchor, a hope for those who believe. God never wastes pain. Every hardship, trial, and tear has purpose and meaning. The Bible lauds those who look beyond their immediate environment and trust in a kingdom yet to come—a creation restored and ruled with justice and compassion by the one who made it and then redeemed it. Don't lose heart. He is coming back, and He is here now, in the land of the living.

PRAY

Sovereign God, I will wait on You. In this world of sin and suffering, I have still seen Your goodness and faithfulness. I will praise You, especially when I don't understand what You are doing. You are making all things new, and You will do what is right.

DAY 123

HOW DO YOU SPEND YOUR TIME?

Read Psalm 27:1–10

KEY VERSES

One thing I have asked from the Lord, *that I shall seek: that I may dwell in the house of the* Lord *all the days of my life, to behold the beauty of the* Lord *and to meditate in His temple. For on the day of trouble He will conceal me in His tabernacle; He will hide me in the secret place of His tent; He will lift me up on a rock.* Psalm 27:4–5 nasb

UNDERSTAND

- *Since it wasn't possible for the people of Israel to actually live in the temple, what does this psalm mean when it says to "dwell in the house of the* Lord*"?*
- *What are the psalm writer's goals as he is in the temple of the Lord?*
- *How does dwelling in the Lord's house change the direction of the psalmist's life? How does the psalmist benefit from these changes?*

APPLY

You can "dwell" at your home, at your workplace, at a friend's house, or at a store for part of your day. But the writer of Psalm 27 adopts a broader, deeper understanding of what it means to "dwell" as he describes both *where* you spend your time and *how* you spend your time. The time you spend in worship, alone with God or in a "church" setting, can serve as a catalyst for "dwelling" with the Lord.

As a recipient of the Holy Spirit, God's dwelling is now within you. And so the act of dwelling with God has much more to do with your awareness and intention each day.

Where you dwell and how you spend your time will significantly impact how you weather the storms of life and the challenges that may be coming today. You'll find stability and hope when you dwell with God and trust in His presence to carry you through whatever life here on earth may bring your way.

PRAY

Thank You, Lord, for Your comforting and empowering presence. Help me to remain in You so that I can be full of faith and hope in Your power and guidance. May I stay mindful of Your promise to never leave or forsake me as the difficulties of life increase. Amen.

TRUE PURPOSE

Read Ephesians 2:1–10

KEY VERSE

We are His workmanship, created in Christ Jesus for good works, which God prepared beforehand so that we would walk in them. EPHESIANS 2:10 NASB

UNDERSTAND

- *How would you describe your purpose?*
- *How quick are you to follow God's leading? What, if anything, holds you back from doing so as soon as possible?*

APPLY

The Greek word Paul used in Ephesians 2:10 for *workmanship* is *poiema*, meaning "something made." We get our English words *poem* and *poetry* from it. Paul used it one other time, in Romans 1:20 (ESV), when he noted that God's "invisible attributes, namely, his eternal power and divine nature, have been clearly perceived, ever since the creation of the world, in *the things that have been made*" (emphasis added).

When God created the world, He poured His eternal power and divine nature into all He made and called it good. You are an example of His finest work—the reason some translations of Ephesians 2:10 replace *workmanship* with *masterpiece*. Not only is God shaping and crafting you into a unique expression of His love and power, but He is brimming with purpose for you.

We are used to thinking of art as a result—a painting, a statue, a composition in words or music—that expresses something about the artist. And if God is the artist, the way He is sculpting you can only result in more than you can dream or imagine. You matter to your Maker, and nothing and no one can fulfill you like He can, and no one can delight Him the way you do. Listen for His calling, do everything for His glory, and enjoy all He has for you.

PRAY

God, You are the original artist, the great Creator. You are the source of all beauty, goodness, and truth, and Your purposes are higher and better than anything the world can offer or humans can imagine. Your glory resides in what's best for me.

PAIN'S HARVEST

Read Hebrews 12:5–13

KEY VERSE

No discipline is enjoyable while it is happening—it's painful! But afterward there will be a peaceful harvest of right living for those who are trained in this way. HEBREWS 12:11 NLT

UNDERSTAND

- *What qualities do you respect most in a mentor, coach, or teacher?*
- *What is your initial reaction to being redirected or challenged to improve?*

APPLY

The human capacity for endurance and pain tolerance is impressive, but it helps to have someone who's been there telling you what to expect, honing your skills, and encouraging you to press on. For the Christian, that's Jesus.

Jesus endured hostility and apathy, rejection and betrayal—culminating at the cross—because as Hebrews 12:2 (NKJV) says, He kept His eyes on the "joy that was set before Him": the goal of bringing as many people as would accept Him into the unity and harmony of relationship with God. He leaned into the brokenness of this world with the long-term goal of redeeming and restoring it, and He expects us to do the same. The pursuit of God revolves around letting Him teach us more about and guide us deeper into His truth, even and especially during painful times.

Hebrews 12:11 (NLT) offers a promise that God's chastening has a reward: "a peaceful harvest of right living for those who are trained in this way." Because of Jesus, we are part of the new covenant in His blood, bonded by His forgiveness and His promise to never leave nor forsake us. Because of this, we can endure pain, knowing it will pass and that His eternal purposes are in it.

PRAY

Father, I freely accepted Your gift of adoption through Jesus Christ. I also accept the responsibilities of being Your son, of enduring the trials of this sin-broken world and doing my best to keep Your ultimate goals of repentance, redemption, and restoration in mind. I trust You.

DAY 126

WHAT IS GOD ASKING YOU TO DO?

Read Isaiah 61

KEY VERSES

The Spirit of the Sovereign Lord *is upon me, for the* Lord *has anointed me to bring good news to the poor. He has sent me to comfort the brokenhearted and to proclaim that captives will be released and prisoners will be freed. He has sent me to tell those who mourn that the time of the* Lord*'s favor has come, and with it, the day of God's anger against their enemies.* Isaiah 61:1–2 NLT

UNDERSTAND

- *How would a message of future deliverance from a Messiah give hope to people living in exile in a foreign nation?*
- *How did the idea of being "anointed" by God give greater meaning to this calling to bring God's good news to the poor, brokenhearted, and captives?*
- *What do the different people groups listed in this passage reveal about God's concerns and priorities?*

APPLY

Much like in the times of Isaiah and Jesus, who based His ministry on this prophetic passage, God's Spirit may be guiding you or even prompting you to take specific actions. Today you can begin to look at the people around you who may be in need or who are suffering. Does God have something specific for you to do or to say in a particular situation?

You don't have to look at serving others as a solo venture. God is with you and will lead you. There are plenty of worthy ministries you could get involved in, but you only need to concern yourself with where the Spirit has led you and where the "anointing" of God rests.

Service under God's direction isn't flashy or high profile. It's often a simple loving presence that could include providing relief to the brokenhearted, sharing God's hope with those who mourn, and setting things right with those in need of restoration. Most importantly, when God calls you to serve others, God will go with you, lead you, and empower you to do what you didn't even think possible.

PRAY

Father, thank You for the ways You've guided and empowered Your people throughout history. Lead me forward today, and give me eyes to see and ears to hear Your calling so that I can serve those in the greatest need of Your healing touch and hopeful message. Amen.

A REDEEMED VIEW OF SEX

Read 1 Corinthians 6:12–20

KEY VERSE

Flee from sexual immorality. Every other sin a person commits is outside the body, but the sexually immoral person sins against his own body. 1 Corinthians 6:18 ESV

UNDERSTAND

- *What old ways and habits of thinking about sex has God delivered you from?*
- *Why do you think sex is a different kind of temptation than, say, food or drinking?*

APPLY

Sex is God's idea. It isn't inherently wrong or dirty. Whatever rules God set up for sex do need to be obeyed. His invention, His rules. When God established the boundaries for sex within the covenant of marriage, that's where He meant for it to happen—for unity, procreation, and pleasure.

In marriage, sex is the deepest expression of intimacy that is physically possible; it encompasses physical desire, but also emotional need and spiritual harmony. Marriage means that a man and a woman have committed to being unified in every way (Genesis 2:24), including being a model of the unity and intimacy Christ desires with His church (Ephesians 5:31–33).

So when we're told to flee sexual immorality, it's because it represents a unique threat to our unity with God. First Corinthians 6:17 (NLT) says if you belong to Christ, you're His, body and soul, "one spirit with him." Few things require more discipline than sexual self-control, but do whatever you have to—confession, accountability, counseling, cold showers, device filters—to glorify God with your body. The level of suffering can be high, but not higher than the price God paid to make you His.

PRAY

Heavenly Father, redeem my view of sex. Forgive me for the ways I've sinned sexually, treating my body as if it was mine alone. Give me the courage to do what I need to in this area, to bring all my thoughts into captivity to Christ.

SET YOUR HEART

Read 1 Chronicles 22:17–19

KEY VERSE

"Now set your heart and your soul to seek the LORD your God. Therefore arise and build the sanctuary of the LORD God, to bring the ark of the covenant of the LORD and the holy articles of God into the house that is to be built for the name of the LORD."

1 CHRONICLES 22:19 NKJV

UNDERSTAND

- *What does it look like to give yourself completely to God? Name a few ways you do so.*
- *How do Bible study and worship help you put God first?*

APPLY

What David did in arranging for the temple to be built foreshadowed what God is doing now in the church age. Instead of a single building and center of worship, however, God's presence and power are found in every individual who believes in the name of God's Son. Instead of drawing believers to a single place in Jerusalem, He is reaching the world through the gospel, so voices from all nations can be raised in worship.

The heart of worship, however, remains the same: "Set your heart and your soul to seek the LORD your God." *Set* in Hebrew means to give with a determined purpose in mind. In context, it points to David's instructions to honor God wholeheartedly, to put Him first, and to seek His help in building a place to honor Him above all else.

If you belong to Him body and soul, you're engaging in kingdom building. You're acting as His temple, bringing people to seek and worship God for themselves, some with refreshed hearts and others for the first time.

PRAY

Lord, come soon. In the meantime, strengthen me to be focused on kingdom business—knowing You better, representing You well to others through acts of love, forgiveness, and kindness. I rejoice in Your faithfulness and set my heart and soul on seeking You today.

DAY 129

GOD KNOWS WHAT YOU CAN HANDLE

Read 1 Kings 19:1–9

KEY VERSES

The angel of the Lord came back a second time and touched him and said, "Get up and eat, for the journey is too much for you." So he got up and ate and drank. Strengthened by that food, he traveled forty days and forty nights until he reached Horeb, the mountain of God. 1 Kings 19:7–8 NIV

UNDERSTAND

- *Elijah felt hopeless as he fled the threats from King Ahab and Queen Jezebel. Why is it important that the angel acknowledged the journey was too much for Elijah?*
- *Why was a retreat into the wilderness so important for Elijah after his confrontations with the prophets of Baal and the king and queen of Israel?*
- *What does today's scripture reading suggest about God's approach to His people when they are suffering through seasons of discouragement?*

APPLY

God knows better than you what you can handle—and when you've reached your limit, your own doubts and discouragement aren't going to scare Him away. In fact, it's when you feel most overwhelmed and burned out that God can support you the most. Yes, there are moments in life that are too much for you, but God will remain with you throughout them.

Taking a page from Elijah's story, the best step you can take when feeling overwhelmed is to retreat to a quiet, solitary place and speak honestly to God about how you're feeling. Then. . .just wait patiently. You may not hear exactly what you expect from God in that moment of retreat (remember, He gave Elijah more tasks to accomplish), but you will receive the mercy and provision you need to continue.

Your trials and struggles aren't a surprise to God. He will meet you in the pauses and solitary moments of your day to help you continue in faith and hope.

PRAY

Thank You, Lord, for Your presence and provision during difficult times. I ask that You lift me up and encourage me in the moments when I feel most overwhelmed and uncertain about what's next. May I find courage and hope in Your comforting presence. Amen.

DAY 130

DO YOU WANT TO BE HEALED?

Read John 5:2–9

KEY VERSE

When Jesus saw him lying there and knew that he had already been there a long time, he said to him, "Do you want to be healed?" John 5:6 ESV

UNDERSTAND

- *How did God answer the last big request you made of Him?*
- *When your prayers go unanswered or answered in a way you don't like, how do you respond?*
- *What does it mean to pray with expectation?*

APPLY

Jesus cut right to the heart of the matter with the sick man at the pool of Bethesda: "Do you want to be healed?" Excuses are all he offered in reply—someone always beat him to the pool, no one helped him, and so on. What did Jesus know about this man that we don't?

Sometimes we get so used to a bad situation—a chronic illness or depression or anxiety—that we think God has lost interest in us. Or we think maybe God's grace isn't actually enough. God can handle honest doubt, but it's a mistake to hang on to doubt because we think it's all we have.

When God brings something like that to your attention, deal with it. If you can accept His redirection, no matter what it is, He will give you the grace and strength to move on. Let the Spirit guide you, bearing in mind Paul's words in Romans 8:26 (NKJV): "We do not know what we should pray for as we ought, but the Spirit Himself makes intercession for us."

PRAY

Jesus, You know what's in my heart better than I do. You know why I slip up, especially in my attitude when I pray. Show me by Your Spirit why I'm struggling even to ask You for an answer. Give me the grace and strength to accept Your response, trusting who You are and what You know I need.

DON'T GIVE UP, QUIT, OR WALK AWAY

Read 2 Timothy 4:1–18

KEY VERSE

The Lord will rescue me from every evil attack and will bring me safely to his heavenly kingdom. To him be glory for ever and ever. Amen. 2 TIMOTHY 4:18 NIV

UNDERSTAND

- *In verse 5 of today's scripture reading, what does Paul encourage Timothy to do?*
- *In verse 7, what does Paul declare about his own life and ministry?*

APPLY

How important is all this? Here is one man's story:

During a profound time of crisis, I suddenly stopped reading and studying the Bible, after reading it daily since I was a young teenager. I couldn't even pray. After several shattering back-to-back trials, I had wrongly concluded that God's own hand was crushing me.

Days went by. Weeks. Finally, in desperation, I opened my Bible again. I knew I couldn't immediately read page after page, as had been my custom. So I simply read one verse, and then asked myself, *Do you believe this?*

Thankfully, my answer was yes. Not a *huge* yes, but a yes nevertheless. That gave me the courage to read another verse. And another. In time, God restored my faith in a remarkable way. I'll never be the same.

Today, I delight in opening God's Word and affirming what He says. And when crises come—and they always will—I'm more confident than ever that the Lord hasn't changed. He's still great. He's still good. And He's still graciously at work in my heart and life. I can't thank Him enough!

PRAY

Yes, Lord, I want to say "Thank You!" that the Bible is true to life. What an example Paul set for us! Like him, I want to finish well.

NO FAKING IT

Read Zephaniah 2:1–3

KEY VERSE

Seek the Lord, *all you humble of the land, you who do what he commands. Seek righteousness, seek humility; perhaps you will be sheltered on the day of the* Lord*'s anger.*
Zephaniah 2:3 niv

UNDERSTAND

- *How do you show God that He has your whole heart?*
- *Does the thought of God's wrath scare you? Why or why not?*

APPLY

Zephaniah's prophecies rained down hard, proclaiming "the day of the Lord" more than any other Old Testament prophet—God's wrath coming down through the ages on all who reject His ways. One particularly frightening warning comes in Zephaniah 2:3 (niv): that if God's people will humble themselves, do what God commands, and pursue righteousness, "perhaps [they] will be sheltered on the day of the Lord's anger." *Perhaps* they'll be sheltered? What's that about?

In Matthew 7:21–23, Jesus referred to people who call themselves Christians, and even behave like Christians, but will not be saved. They won't realize this until it's too late, when they are rejected by Jesus when He returns to judge the earth.

There's no room for *perhaps*, as Matthew 7:23 (msg) cautions us: "All you did was use me to make yourselves important. You don't impress me one bit. You're out of here." Some men go to church for a long time before they actually become Christians.

Unless a man gives himself fully to God, letting his Maker do as He wants in his heart, he builds his life on sand. You know you're His when you'll give up anything to become more like Jesus, including coming clean and enduring temporary shame because you want to get right with Him.

PRAY

Lord God, You are holy and righteous in all of Your ways. You want all of me because You gave me Your Son—Your highest and best—to save me. You held nothing back. Forgive me for the times and ways I haven't honored You by doing the same.

CHOSEN TO BE FRUITFUL

Read John 15:9–17

KEY VERSE

"You did not choose Me, but I chose you and appointed you that you should go and bear fruit, and that your fruit should remain, that whatever you ask the Father in My name He may give you." JOHN 15:16 NKJV

UNDERSTAND

- *How do you think God defines love? How is His definition distinct from the typical human understanding of love?*
- *What does loving God look like to you?*

APPLY

Jesus sets up His statement in John 15:16 by talking about vines and branches (John 15:1–8). The analogy establishes Jesus as the true vine, the source of eternal life, and the Father as the vinedresser, determining which grafted-on branches are fruitful and which aren't. Once we are connected to God through Jesus, our responsibility is to bear fruit—to obey God's commands with humility and compassion.

In John 15:9 (NKJV) Jesus said, "Abide in My love." Clearly, God doesn't force our obedience. In that sense, we must cooperate with Him to fully work out His will for our lives. He knows who is going to receive His offer of salvation, but we still have to choose Him.

Jesus chooses to invest Himself in us, wanting to see us grow in godly love, and He tells us how to do so. In response, we obey His call to spread the good news to disciple those who respond to Jesus by choosing Him and lovingly serve others. That's God's definition of fruitfulness. As we abide in Christ, we are able to pray correctly, asking God in Jesus' name for things that are within His will and will bring Him glory.

PRAY

God, You are love. It is out of the great and perfect love You have in the Trinity that You created people—so You could share it. You made us with free will so we could choose to love You, and You saved us from our warped, self-centered version of love by the blood of Christ.

DAY 134

FREE TO HONOR AND SERVE OTHERS

Read 1 Peter 2:11–25

KEY VERSES

For it is God's will that by doing right you should silence the ignorance of the foolish. As servants of God, live as free people, yet do not use your freedom as a pretext for evil.
1 PETER 2:15–16 NRSV

UNDERSTAND

- *It's implied in today's key verses that doing the right thing isn't necessarily the natural response to the ignorance of the foolish. What do you think Peter has in mind when he sets up this contrast?*
- *How does living in "freedom" make Christians more likely to be servants of God and others?*
- *What are some ways that Peter expects Christians to honor everyone?*

APPLY

It is likely that there will be times when others won't fully understand you or give you the benefit of the doubt. Others may even malign you at times. Yet the apostle Peter, who had a fiery temper at one point in his life, suggests that the best response is to simply do what's right. He even adds that you are free to honor everyone, even when you are mistreated.

Your restraint when you are mistreated is in keeping with God's will and ultimately silences those who are most provocative. That isn't an easy ask in the heat of the moment, but if reaching resolutions matters to you, then Peter's advice is sound.

Tied in with this calling to respond with grace to insults and misunderstandings is the greater mission to use your freedom in Christ well. Being free from the law doesn't mean anything goes. It's a greater responsibility to remain in Christ and to be even more aware of others. How you live before them will shape how they view Jesus, and if His life is present in you, then you'll help them see God's work with clarity.

PRAY

Thank You, Jesus, that You have set me free to be Your servant, a servant who is free to love others. When I am misunderstood or treated unfairly, help me to remember how You were mistreated and still showed mercy so that I can honor everyone and respond with Your same grace. Amen.

BRINGING GOD YOUR BROKEN HEART

Read Lamentations 3:17–26

KEY VERSE

The LORD *is good to those who wait [confidently] for Him, to those who seek Him [on the authority of God's word].* LAMENTATIONS 3:25 AMP

UNDERSTAND

- *When bad things happen to people who reject God, what's your first reaction? What about when bad things happen to people who love God?*
- *Think of a time when God brought healing to your heartbreak.*

APPLY

The prophet Jeremiah wrote Lamentations from a deep well of pain. God used him to warn Judah and Jerusalem for decades that judgment was coming if they didn't get right with the Lord. For his courage and faithfulness to his calling, he got utterly rejected.

But when his prophecies came true, Jeremiah didn't gloat. His heart broke, just like Jesus' did in Luke 19:41–44 when He wept upon His triumphal entry into Jerusalem, knowing His chosen people didn't recognize Him and were about to reject and execute Him.

So Jeremiah poured out his pain in a book. Lamentations is a brokenhearted cry after watching people suffer the consequence of rejecting God for so long that He eventually gave them what they wanted—to be left alone without His protection or comfort. It's like a preview of hell, and it should keep anyone who loves God from rejoicing in a sinner's downfall.

Yet even in his lament, Jeremiah recalled God's faithfulness and mercy. It's just a few verses, but the impact is stunning—a man reminding himself (and us) that because God is who He is, there is hope in the midst of heartache. No moment is so dark that God's light can't shine in it. God will never abandon us.

PRAY

Lord God, the sorrows of my life and the heartbreak of the world overwhelm me. You don't owe me answers; I owe You everything. So I wait for Your hope.

WHO'S LOST?

Read Luke 19:1–10

KEY VERSE

"The Son of Man came to seek and save those who are lost." LUKE 19:10 NLT

UNDERSTAND

- *What led you to give your life to Jesus?*
- *How often do you fall back into acting like you don't need Him? Do you recognize it when it happens?*

APPLY

There's a part of us that says we're the ones pursuing God—the ones who strive for holiness and righteousness—and that God is there to reward us when we do. But in reality, it's the other way around: God pursues us. If He didn't come after us, we'd wander off into our version of salvation, our own views of right behavior.

Remember who Jesus came to seek and save? The lost. But He operated on a different definition of *lost* than people were used to. Jesus was harshest with those who seemed to have their act together—the religious leaders of His day who felt they had no need for the ministrations of some wandering preacher. But the truly desperate, the down and out, the empty hearted, the poor and beaten down, knew real hope when they saw Him—and they latched on for dear life.

For some of us who, like Zacchaeus in Luke 19, think we've got it right most of the time, that awakening is sudden. But once Zacchaeus saw that Jesus knew him and still loved him, he wasted no time in trying to right his wrongs with others—and it started with God calling out to him. Own your lostness and Jesus will find you. Then leave your old futile days behind forever.

PRAY

I trust You, Father. Thank You for coming to save me and not giving up on me when I resisted. Forgive me for the times I still resist, when I slip into self-sufficiency, and thanks for being faithful to teach me that I can't do life well on my own.

EXAMPLES OF TRUTHS TO AFFIRM

Read 1 John 1:1–10

KEY VERSE

If we claim to be without sin, we deceive ourselves and the truth is not in us. 1 John 1:8 NIV

UNDERSTAND

- *What does today's key verse say about affirming or denying what's true?*
- *Why is affirming biblical truths important in your everyday life?*

APPLY

It isn't enough to mentally assent to the truths of scripture. To apply them to your life, you want to actively and wholeheartedly *affirm* them!

How does Truths to Affirm actually work? Let's consider a few examples from the opening pages of Genesis and 1 John.

In Genesis 1:27 (NIV), God's Word says, "So God created mankind in his own image; in the image of God he created them; male and female he created them." In response to this verse, you can readily affirm, "I believe that every person is created in the image of God." You also can affirm, "I believe that *I* am created in the image of God." The key is to silently ask, *Do I really believe this?* If you do, you begin to gain a clearer picture of God and of yourself.

First John 1:9 (NIV) says, "If we confess our sins, he [God] is faithful and just and will forgive us our sins and purify us from all unrighteousness." In response, you can affirm, "I believe that God truly forgives me when I confess my sins." The key is to affirm this in prayer to the Lord Himself and to honestly tell Him if you have any struggles or doubts.

PRAY

Yes, Lord, I want to say "Thank You!" for forgiving all of my sins—past, present, and future. Please forgive me for what I've done wrong over the past day.

SAMPLES OF COMMANDS TO OBEY

Read 2 Peter 3:1–18

KEY VERSE

But according to his promise we are waiting for new heavens and a new earth in which righteousness dwells. 2 PETER 3:13 ESV

UNDERSTAND

- *Do you know anyone who says he isn't a Christian anymore? If so, what reasons does he give?*
- *Which is easier: to believe the truths of scripture or obey its New Testament commands?*

APPLY

It isn't enough to *notice* the commands in the Bible. To apply them to your life, you want to gladly and consistently *obey* them.

How does Commands to Obey actually work? Let's consider a few examples from Exodus and 2 Peter.

In Exodus 20:12 (ESV; also in Leviticus 19:3, Deuteronomy 5:16, Matthew 15:4, Mark 7:10, Luke 18:20, and Ephesians 6:2), the Lord commands us, "Honor your father and your mother." The question isn't what you think of your parents. The question is whether you can honestly say, "I honor my parents in obedience to the Lord's command." Sometimes the answer is no. If that's the case, the point isn't to heap guilt upon yourself. God simply asks you to be honest with Him and invites you to claim His promises for wisdom and strength.

In 2 Peter 3:14 (NLT) you're told, "And so, dear friends, while you are waiting for these things [the new heavens and new earth] to happen, make every effort to be found living peaceful lives that are pure and blameless in [God's] sight." Your response shouldn't be to read past this verse and pretend you're already perfect. Instead, you should decide to conform your life to scripture so you can honestly say, "I am now making every effort to live a pure and blameless life and to be at peace with God." To do that, you first want to come clean with God, and then start obeying this particular command.

PRAY

Yes, Lord, I want to say "Thank You!" for compelling us to finish well, just like Peter and Paul and other heroes of the faith. You made it clear that they weren't perfect. Yet they made every effort to keep close to You. I want to do that too.

DAY 139

ILLUSTRATIONS OF EXAMPLES TO HEED

Read 1 Peter 2:1–25

KEY VERSE

For God is pleased when, conscious of his will, you patiently endure unjust treatment.
1 PETER 2:19 NLT

UNDERSTAND

- *In Matthew 20:25–28 and John 13:13–16, Jesus instructed His disciples to follow specific examples of His. Was it easy or difficult for them to do so?*
- *The apostles Peter (1 Peter 2:18–20), Paul (Ephesians 5:1–2 and Colossians 3:13), and John (1 John 2:6 and 3:15–16) instruct believers to follow other examples of Jesus. Which one is the hardest for you?*

APPLY

It isn't enough to ponder the examples in scripture. To apply them to your life, you want to willingly and readily *heed* them.

How does Examples to Heed actually work? Let's consider a couple of examples from Leviticus and 1 Peter.

In Leviticus 8:4 (NLT) you read, "So Moses followed the LORD's instructions, and the whole community assembled at the Tabernacle entrance." You can keep reading or you can stop, note Moses' positive example, and then affirm, "I too choose to do what the Lord commands."

In 1 Peter 2:21, the apostle Peter spelled out the example to heed when he wrote, "For God called you to do good, even if it means suffering, just as Christ suffered for you. He is your example, and you must follow in his steps." He was calling for an immediate response. Will you say, "I follow Jesus Christ's example and am willing to suffer for doing right"?

In Joshua 1, Psalm 1, Psalm 119, 2 Peter 1, and other scriptures, God promises that He will prosper those who delight in His Word, take it to heart, and apply its truths.

Imagine what God could do in and through you if you read and studied the Bible and responded as God desired. Wow!

PRAY

Yes, Lord, I want to say "Thank You!" for the many, many examples in scripture of what to do and what not to do. I want to heed each one.

THE GREAT PURSUIT

Read Isaiah 65:1

KEY VERSE

"I permitted Myself to be sought by those who did not ask for Me; I permitted Myself to be found by those who did not seek Me. I said, 'Here am I, here am I,' to a nation which did not call on My name." Isaiah 65:1 NASB

UNDERSTAND

- *How did God pursue you to bring you to faith in Christ? Who or what did He use?*
- *How should you respond, knowing how relentlessly God has sought to make you His?*

APPLY

Story after story recounts God's pursuit of people's hearts, especially when they rejected Him and His ways. The Old Testament is primarily the story of how God picked out one old pagan guy and from him made a nation for Himself, preserving a lineage against all conceivable odds through which He would bring the Messiah and save the world.

Jesus is the face of God's great pursuit. He went out of His way to visit Samaria because He had a divine appointment to bring hope and healing to a woman who had been rejected by her whole community. His parables contain images of shepherds leaving a whole flock to find one lost sheep, a woman scouring her entire house to find a lost coin, and a man selling everything to buy a single pearl worth everything to Him.

The theme? You matter to God. He reaches down to you so He can lift you up. You have purpose. God has prepared in advance good works for you to do, and as a Christian, you are now part of His chosen people. Surely His goodness, mercy, and unfailing love will follow you all the days of your life.

PRAY

Thank You, Father, for never giving up on me. I confess the times I've tried to run from You for whatever reason. I want to know You more, to connect with Your heart so You can use me to connect others with Your astonishing love in Jesus.

WHEN GOOD THINGS GO BAD

Read Luke 16:14–31

KEY VERSE

"Abraham said, 'Child, remember that you in your lifetime received your good things, and Lazarus in like manner bad things; but now he is comforted here, and you are in anguish.'"
LUKE 16:25 ESV

UNDERSTAND

- *How does the reality of heaven and hell affect the way you live?*
- *How often do you make time to check your priorities and make sure they line up with God's?*

APPLY

In Luke 16, Jesus goes right from interpreting the Mosaic Law regarding marriage and divorce to the story of a rich man in hell. There's no indication that He shifted to a parable. It reads like a historical account; it feels real.

The story is not about rich people being inherently wicked or the poor innately good. Even though the possible glimpse into the workings of the afterlife is intriguing, that's not the point either. Jesus was driving at the unique power of His mission regarding one of the greatest worldly challenges to it: wealth and the power that comes from having money.

The story of Lazarus and the rich man is a stark illustration of the blinding power of wealth. If we have enough money, we hope we'll be able to avoid life's biggest problems. And money does help; it provides our daily bread and can be an equalizer for many injustices. But when a good thing replaces the best thing in our hearts, it becomes by definition a bad thing.

Unless God is our greatest desire, and our driving ambition is to know and serve Him, nothing—not even someone rising from the dead—will convince us that money and power won't do as well.

PRAY

Almighty God, the riches of Your kingdom are love, grace, mercy, and truth. The fruit of Your Spirit will last into eternity, fulfilled in our relationship with You in Christ and with others whom we help to know You. Anything else is fool's gold.

PONDER YOUR LIFE'S DIRECTION

Read Psalm 119:57–72

KEY VERSES

Lord, you are mine! I promise to obey your words! With all my heart I want your blessings. Be merciful as you promised. I pondered the direction of my life, and I turned to follow your laws. I will hurry, without delay, to obey your commands. Psalm 119:57–60 NLT

UNDERSTAND

- *What is the benefit of making a promise of obedience to God?*
- *Why is it important to ponder the direction of your life? How did this pondering help the writer of today's scripture reading?*
- *Why is the writer of today's key verses in a hurry to obey God's commands without delay?*

APPLY

Taking time to really think about the direction of your life can yield a lot of insights and wisdom that lead to better decisions and choices each day. By viewing the big picture of your life and where you hope to end up, you can ensure that your choices line up with your goals—and with God's goals for you.

Obedience to God requires intention and determination to rely on God's power and hold on to His promises. If you don't know what God has promised you, you won't know what you can ask of Him or how you can rely on Him. The more you learn about God's promises, the more faith you can put in Him—and the less pressure you'll put on yourself.

Don't delay in obedience to God, and don't neglect your spiritual life. If you're running counter to God's Spirit and His purposes, you'll develop habits and patterns that make it harder to receive His blessings.

PRAY

Lord, help me to see the larger picture of disobedience and obedience so that I can keep in step with Your Spirit and stay within the direction of Your will. Amen.

LOVE NEVER QUITS

Read 1 John 4:15-21

KEY VERSE

We love, because He first loved us. 1 John 4:19 NASB

UNDERSTAND

- *What do you think it means to truly love someone?*
- *How has God shown His love for you?*

APPLY

Love originates with God; as 1 John 4:8 says, He is love. Father, Son, and Holy Spirit have always existed in perfect community and love—love so vital and abundant that God chose to create us to share in His love. There is nothing He could receive from us that would make Him greater, better, or more loving. In other words, He loves because it's who He is.

We are not born knowing how to love. In our natural, sinful condition, all we know is need. We need food, we need shelter, and we need love. More than anything, we want to be loved, and we learn to give love so we can get it. When we run into God's love—love that has everything to offer and nothing to gain from us—we don't know how to respond. It's not in us, but it can be taught as part of our new nature in Christ.

John gave us insight into loving like God loves. First, we have to accept what it cost for Him to love us—the cross. Once His Spirit is in us, though, His love begins to move in our hearts, pricking our conscience when we love in the old ways—selfishly, transactionally—and moves us to love others because we love Him.

PRAY

Thank You for loving me before I ever loved You, God. I know I've made it hard at times, but You have relentlessly pursued me until Your love won me over. I want to love people today the way You love me—with patience and kindness, looking out for their highest good, especially when they make it hard.

JESUS CAME TO HEAL

Read Luke 5:27–39

KEY VERSES

But the Pharisees and the teachers of the law who belonged to their sect complained to his disciples, "Why do you eat and drink with tax collectors and sinners?" Jesus answered them, "It is not the healthy who need a doctor, but the sick. I have not come to call the righteous, but sinners to repentance." LUKE 5:30–32 NIV

UNDERSTAND

- *What is the difference between the "job description" for the Pharisees and the teachers of the law and the one Jesus adopted for Himself?*
- *How can we liken Jesus' earthly ministry to the work of a physician?*
- *What was Jesus accomplishing by eating and drinking with notorious "sinners"?*

APPLY

Pause for a moment and consider how you see God. Do you see Him as a harsh judge who is eager to sentence you for your sins or as a heavenly doctor who is dedicated to your healing and restoration?

When you feel shame over something, maybe to the point that you feel unworthy of God, remember that Jesus has come to heal you and make you worthy. You can come to Jesus as you would a doctor—with complete honesty about what is wrong, not hiding anything. When you do, you'll find hope that Jesus will heal the parts of you that never seem to be sorted out.

When Jesus heals you and forgives you, He also gives you the liberating calling of bringing others to Him for healing. You don't have to worry about who others might see as worthy and unworthy. You only need to share the joyful news that Jesus has come to heal the sick and sinners—and that there is hope in repentance.

PRAY

Thank You, Jesus, for coming to heal me and restore me so that I no longer need to live in shame or struggle to obey You. May I enjoy the liberty and freedom that come from knowing You, and may I share that healing and hope with those I meet today. Amen.

THE MYSTERY REVEALED

Read Jeremiah 33:2-3, 14-16

KEY VERSE

"Call to me and I will answer you and tell you great and unsearchable things you do not know." JEREMIAH 33:3 NIV

UNDERSTAND

- *What has God done in your life that you never imagined was possible?*
- *When God allows something hard that you don't understand, what is your response?*

APPLY

In the Bible, Paul used *mystery* to describe something previously unrevealed—a matter of God waiting until the right time to let us in on His plans. Nothing mystical or self-contradictory, just a matter of God's sovereignty and omniscience.

The Bible has a strong through line, especially in the Old Testament, of God's mysterious plan to save humankind from sin. It unfolds gradually and spans history, beginning directly after the fall, when God predicted in Genesis 3:15 that a unique descendant of Eve—the Seed—would crush Satan's head.

God told Jeremiah that if His people would look to Him, He would tell them "great and unsearchable things," specifically the mind-boggling approach He was undertaking to deliver everyone—not just Jews but Gentiles too—from the just deserts of our sin. The Old Testament contains more than 450 prophecies about the Messiah, some 300 of which were fulfilled during His earthly ministry.

We live now in the time the prophets looked forward to—the historical *anno Domini*, the era of our Lord Jesus. But there's more to come—the time of His return, reign, and restoration of creation, and eternity in the new heaven and earth beyond that. In Ephesians 1:9 (NIV), Paul described this as God making "known to us the mystery of his will according to his good pleasure, which he purposed in Christ." That's some mystery, and some revelation—more than enough to keep waiting on God in faith as He works out the rest of the details.

PRAY

God, Your timing is always perfect. Thank You for letting us in on Your astounding, counterintuitive plan of salvation. Lead and guide me into Your truth.

DAY 146

LIFE AND DEATH ON THE TIP OF YOUR TONGUE

Read Proverbs 18:12–24

KEY VERSE

Words kill, words give life; they're either poison or fruit—you choose. PROVERBS 18:21 MSG

UNDERSTAND

- *Do you tend to say what's on your mind or do you think before you speak?*
- *How often do you ask God to help you find the right thing to say?*

APPLY

Words either build or destroy, heal or harm. Wise words satisfy like a good meal, but rash or foolish words crush the spirit. Side effects include believing lies about yourself and others and stuffing feelings until they explode from your mouth and damage hard-to-rebuild trust.

If you don't give authority over your tongue to God, your words will be in a constant state of contradiction. You will speak wisdom and foolishness and bring light and darkness—often in the same conversation. But one word from God can change everything. His words can tell you where your own speech is driven by the wrong motives—ambition, aggression (and passive aggression), and apathy. As Proverbs 4:23 (NIV) says, "Above all else, guard your heart, for everything you do flows from it."

It's hard to find the right things to say if you're not familiar with the Bible. There is no substitute for God's own words of mercy and grace. The time you spend reading it, praying, and studying it is time spent stocking your heart with the vocabulary you need to control your tongue, filter out ungodly voices, and bring God's favor into your relationships.

PRAY

Your Word is life, Lord God. You are the source of all wisdom and truth and the compassion and grace needed to deliver it so it lands well. May my words reflect a heart turned over to You, filled with Your Word. Make me quick to listen, slow to speak, and slow to anger. Holy Spirit, grow in me the fruit of self-control so I can master my tongue today.

HOPE IN GOD AFTER FAILURE

Read Psalm 39:7–13

KEY VERSES

"And now, Lord, for what do I wait? My hope is in You. Save me from all my wrongdoings; Do not make me an object of reproach for the foolish." PSALM 39:7–8 NASB

UNDERSTAND

- *Psalm 39 suggests that God has disciplined David the psalmist after a season of disobedience. How does that discipline coexist with grace and forgiveness?*
- *What else could David have waited for instead of God?*
- *How could this season of waiting become derailed? How could it become beneficial and fruitful?*

APPLY

Failure is a part of life, and everyone has willfully disobeyed God at certain moments. Psalm 39 notes an especially lonely and serious moment when the consequences of sin offer a painful but useful reminder of the fragility of mankind and the brief nature of life. It shows us that life is too short to waste on rebellion against God, for the suffering that comes from rebellion will drain your enjoyment quickly.

Today's scripture reading poses an important question: Are you willing to humble yourself before God in order to be restored?

Waiting on God sometimes means bearing the full brunt of the consequences of your actions—and even His hand of discipline. Adding to the challenge is the fact that an answer from God may not be forthcoming on your timetable, and the path to restoration may be difficult and uncomfortable. Yet no other source of hope will lift you from despair over your own failure like God.

PRAY

Help me, Lord, to recognize my failures and compromises so that I can confess them and be restored. May I remain near to You and aware that each careless sin can bring me more pain than I could ever intend or imagine. Help me to wait patiently for You and You alone. Amen.

DAY 148

WORTH EVERY LOSS TO GAIN

Read Matthew 13:44

KEY VERSE

"The kingdom of heaven is like treasure hidden in a field, which a man found and covered up. Then in his joy he goes and sells all that he has and buys that field." MATTHEW 13:44 ESV

UNDERSTAND

- *Is there anything you would lose everything else over to keep?*
- *What does it mean to you that God considers you worth dying for?*

APPLY

We often pass by God's kingdom without paying any attention to it. Maybe that's why many of Jesus' parables feature a field—in Matthew 13 alone, we have the sower, the wheat and tares, the mustard seed, and the hidden treasure.

We pass fields as we drive from city to city and from appointment to appointment. Unless we're farmers, we don't pause to think about what might be hidden beneath the ground. More immediate concerns command us, events and problems that reside in plain sight, and that's where our focus and energy go.

Jesus tells us in Matthew 6:33 to seek God's kingdom as the top priority in our lives. When we do that, He will provide everything we need to function well in life. Unfortunately, we can easily reverse our priorities, taking the kingdom for granted as we pursue our daily needs.

These parables also remind us of the joy of finding and being found. Jesus is the merchant looking for hidden treasure, keeping His plans a mystery until He sold Himself to accomplish His rescue mission. We are His treasure, His joy in giving all He has to win us.

Such love requires a response. Jesus gave up heaven to root in the dirt for us; what are we willing to lose to gain His kingdom?

PRAY

Forgive me, Jesus, for all the times and ways I take Your pursuit for granted. You gave everything for my redemption. Help me to live with kingdom values embedded in my heart, putting You first in everything.

GOD PROMISES MORE GREAT BLESSINGS!

Read James 1:1-27

KEY VERSE

But if you look carefully into the perfect law that sets you free, and if you do what it says and don't forget what you heard, then God will bless you for doing it. JAMES 1:25 NLT

UNDERSTAND

- *Do you ever worry that God's promises might be too good to be true?*
- *Then again, do you ever worry about God blessing you too much?*

APPLY

Again, God prospers those who delight in His Word, take it to heart, and apply it in every area of life. How do we know that? Here are four more reasons:

1. In Jeremiah 15:16–17 and Ezekiel 3:1–11, the prophets described God's Word as sweet as honey, despite the difficult mission God gave both of them. Scripture isn't just sweetness. It also contains the piercing light of God's holiness, righteousness, and purity—to keep us from sinning.
2. In Ezra 7:6–10 (KJV), we read that Ezra was well-versed in the scriptures and that the king "granted him all his request, according to the hand of the LORD His God upon Him." God's blessing was on him indeed! The same can be our experience today.
3. In John 13:17, Jesus said the path to God's blessing is knowing *and doing* what God says. All the blessings of the Beatitudes (Matthew 5:3–12 and Luke 6:20–23) are ours, if only we obey the Lord and heed His Word.
4. In James 1:16–25 (NKJV), James said the person who does what God's Word says "will be blessed in what he does" (verse 25). He accepts the Bible as God's inspired Word, repents of his sins, humbly accepts the Word, experiences salvation, and then intently and continually looks into scripture and doesn't forget what he reads. Instead, he does what it says—and is blessed!

PRAY

Yes, Lord, I want to say "Thank You!" for motivating me to understand and apply Your Word in each area of my life.

MORE INSIGHTS ON INSPIRATION

Read Jeremiah 36:1–19

KEY VERSE

So Jeremiah sent for Baruch son of Neriah, and as Jeremiah dictated all the prophecies that the LORD had given him, Baruch wrote them on a scroll. JEREMIAH 36:4 NLT

UNDERSTAND

- *What puzzles you about God-inspired scripture?*
- *What do you wish were different?*

APPLY

The book of Jeremiah offers more insights into God's inspiration of the Bible:

1. Inspiration begins the moment God reveals any portion of His truth to His prophets for His people (Jeremiah 36:1). Text is not inspired when it's recognized as canonical (accepted by the church). It's not even inspired when it's written. Instead, it's inspired the second God communicates it. The prophet knew immediately that he had received a new revelation from God. He didn't have to think twice about it!

2. Inspiration often begins as an oral message that the prophet or apostle dictates or pens. It's inspired whether it's written down immediately or after an extended period of time (Jeremiah 36:1–2, 32). In this way, inspiration continues. It doesn't evaporate after God stops talking to a prophet or apostle.

3. Inspired messages communicate God's words to humanity in an exact form. They become inspired scriptures (writings) the moment they are penned. Their value as God's Word does *not* increase, but their effectiveness does. People can reconsider recorded messages and read them along with other messages from other times (Jeremiah 36:3).

4. Inspiration is not dependent on the written scriptures. When you share portions of scripture orally, you are transmitting God's Word to others (Jeremiah 36:9–16). In that way, you've become one of the links that helps God's Word become part of people's thoughts and actions.

There's more!

PRAY

Yes, Lord, I want to say "Thank You!" for all the ways You inspired the scriptures. It wasn't a static or boring process. Instead, it was a dynamic, active, and varied process. You worked through several dozen men to bless billions. Wow, indeed!

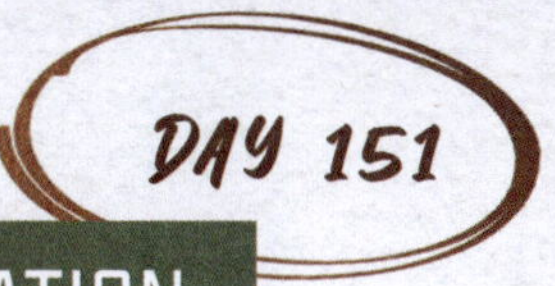

STILL MORE INSIGHTS ON INSPIRATION

Read Jeremiah 36:20–32

KEY VERSE

Even though [they] urged the king not to burn the scroll, he would not listen to them.
JEREMIAH 36:25 NIV

UNDERSTAND

- *How do you think Jeremiah and Baruch felt about writing down God-inspired messages?*
- *What must have felt the most frustrating to them?*

APPLY

The book of Jeremiah offers still more insights into God's inspiration of the Bible:

5. Verbal plenary inspiration does not depend on the actual existence of the originals today (Jeremiah 36:32). Jeremiah dictated "all the former words that were in the first scroll" (Jeremiah 26:38 ESV). He wrote a second scroll of newly inspired scripture that a wicked king had tried to destroy (36:22–23, 28).

6. Inspiration is progressive. Each book was inspired one thought at a time. Often long gaps separated sections (Jeremiah 36:2, 32).

7. Inspiration is exclusively God's message to humanity, through human instruments and their secretaries (Jeremiah 36:4; Romans 16:22).

8. Inspiration is always dependent on the Lord. Even though Jeremiah was a prophet of God, he couldn't prophesy whenever he felt like it. Sometimes the word of the Lord came to Jeremiah, compelling him to prophesy (Jeremiah 37:6). Sometimes the Lord gave Jeremiah a message as he spoke (37:17—this was essentially a message Jeremiah had delivered often before). Sometimes Jeremiah had to wait awhile until the Lord finally gave him a message (42:7).

9. Inspiration applies to the very choice of words. Jeremiah felt strongly that he had to deliver the whole message of the Lord, without omitting a word (Jeremiah 42:4; 43:1). Jeremiah also wrote down his own thoughts and the remarks of others, but the Holy Spirit directed every word he wrote.

PRAY

Yes, Lord, I want to say "Thank You!" that wicked men couldn't destroy even one passage of Your eternal Word.

DO YOU LOVE TO WORRY?

Read Matthew 6:25–34

KEY VERSE

"Seek first the kingdom of God and His righteousness, and all these things shall be added to you." MATTHEW 6:33 NKJV

UNDERSTAND

- *What worries you the most?*
- *How does worry affect your view of God?*

APPLY

Nobody loves to worry, any more than anyone loves to pay taxes or have a root canal or host their in-laws for a week. But those things need to be done, so we do them. Maybe the real question is *Do we love our stuff more than we love God?* The way we see God affects the way we do everything else, especially worry.

When we lean into our troubles instead of God, worry replaces worship; in effect, we're saying, "God, I don't think You've got this." We would rather trust our worry than His strength and provision. Worry impacts our witness: Who wants to listen to Christians who think their God isn't big enough to handle every problem?

Worry is a warning—a yellow light telling you that a choice is coming up fast. Choice one: Take your worry and turn your concerns over to God, trusting Him to help you get through them. Or choice two: Take your worry as a badge of honor, bravery in the face of God's apparent abandonment—a sign that you care more about your problems than God does.

Worry is a sign that you're paying attention, that you care about what's going on. That's good. But if you hang on to that worry, you risk making it an idol. So really, who do you love more, worry or God?

PRAY

Lord, I confess my worrying to You. You know my needs well, but I keep forgetting Your all-powerful, all-knowing love, care, and mercy. Forgive me and teach me to seek You first in every situation, especially the worrisome ones. I'll start by telling You what's on my mind today.

DAY 153

DON'T SELL YOURSELF SHORT

Read Titus 2:1–15

KEY VERSES

Say "No" to ungodliness and worldly passions, and. . .live self-controlled, upright and godly lives in this present age, while we wait for the blessed hope—the appearing of the glory of our great God and Savior, Jesus Christ. Titus 2:12–13 NIV

UNDERSTAND

- *Is it enough to know what not to do? Why or why not?*
- *Is past experience helpful? Again, why or why not?*

APPLY

Never forget: You can do a five-minute Bible study, nod your head throughout the scripture reading, and then jump out of your truck and never once stop to wonder, *What would Jesus have me do in this situation?*

Yet if you don't wholeheartedly obey the Lord's commands, you'll quickly go astray, risk your life in mad pursuit of the tempting and trivial, get terribly hurt in the process, and then have the audacity to point the finger at others—even God.

It's not enough to know the great Sunday school stories about Noah and Sarah, Joshua and Deborah, Ruth and Absalom, Elijah and Esther, Daniel and Mary, Nicodemus and Cornelius, John Mark and Timothy. True, the biblical narratives are intriguing. But what lessons can you learn from each character's faith and failings, victories and vices?

Experience truly is the best teacher—especially the experiences of others who have gone before us. So every time you study God's Word, you should seek to import lessons from the lives of both biblical scoundrels (1 Corinthians 10:1–13) and heroes of the faith (Hebrews 11:4–40).

Why hold back?

PRAY

Yes, Lord, I want to say "Thank You!" that I don't have to mess up my life. You call me to take the high road. It's steep. It's lonely sometimes. But the incredible vistas and rewards up ahead keep me going.

GOD'S LOVE WILL LEAD YOU

Read Psalm 5:1–8

KEY VERSES

But I, through the abundance of your steadfast love, will enter your house, I will bow down toward your holy temple in awe of you. Lead me, O Lord, in your righteousness because of my enemies; make your way straight before me. Psalm 5:7–8 NRSV

UNDERSTAND

- *Why was it so important for David, the writer of Psalm 5, to rely on the Lord's guidance for a straight path forward?*
- *According to Psalm 5, on what basis can we approach God's temple in worship? How is someone declared "worthy" before God?*
- *This psalm contrasts those who delight in evil and who are deceitful with those who rise early to make their requests known to God. How are these two approaches to problem-solving most different?*

APPLY

There are two paths you can travel today. One is a path of self-reliance that can sometimes turn into lying and cheating in order to get ahead; the other, a path that starts every day with requests to God and a complete reliance on Him to set a clear path for you.

Today's scripture reading assures us that God is not far from us when we are committed to His truth. If you fail to commit yourself to God's truth, you'll miss out on the opportunity to boldly step into His presence, which is where we receive mercy and guidance.

You don't have to worry today about finding the right path forward, simply because God, in His great love, will lead you—as long as you are open to His leading. God's presence will be with you, and that will be enough. Any other source of guidance or wisdom will let you down and lead you to a dead end, but that will never happen when you follow God's path for you.

PRAY

Thank You, Lord, for Your love, grace, and mercy—all of which You promise will meet me in my weakness and uncertainty today. May I find the time at the start of each day to share my requests with You and then trust that You will guide me in the correct path forward. Amen.

DAY 155

GETTING YOUR HEART STRAIGHT

Read 1 Chronicles 16:7–14

KEY VERSE

Look to the Lord and his strength; seek his face always. 1 Chronicles 16:11 NIV

UNDERSTAND

- *What generally happens when we forget who God is and what He has done?*
- *Do you make a regular habit of praising God?*

APPLY

First Chronicles 16 centers on a long psalm (verses 8–36) that David and Asaph wrote as a response to God's greatness and mercies. That's so David, right? The guy was a psalm machine, always ready to burst into song about the Lord. So cool. But David's greatness really lies in his willingness to turn to God and face the music when he messed up. That's when the praise really counts.

When you become aware that you've gotten it wrong in God's eyes, it's easy to try to avoid Him. You're embarrassed because you think you should know better, or you're mad because you think He is being too tough on you. Either way, you're not wrong. But don't let that keep you from coming to Him. And don't forget to start with praise.

Praising God is the only right move you have under every circumstance. Praise and worship are about Him, not you. He is the one who loves to forgive and reconcile and restore. He takes all your little brokenness and makes a straight path back to Him—but you can't see it until you acknowledge Him.

Sing with gratitude for His mercies and faithfulness; sing because He deserves it no matter how you feel, and watch how your feelings will catch up with your faithful actions.

PRAY

God, I am amazed by You. Please prepare my heart—the center of who I am, mind, body, and soul—to focus on You and let you know how great You are. Forgive me for my sin. Block out all my worries and thoughts so I'm only looking for You, only seeking to praise You.

OBEDIENCE OUTSIDE THE BUBBLE

Read Philippians 2:12–18

KEY VERSES

God is working in you, giving you the desire and the power to do what pleases him. Do everything without complaining and arguing, so that no one can criticize you. Live clean, innocent lives as children of God, shining like bright lights in a world full of crooked and perverse people. PHILIPPIANS 2:13–15 NLT

UNDERSTAND

- *What reasons, if any, make it difficult for you to share the good news?*
- *How mindful are you of God getting the glory for your words and actions?*

APPLY

How often are you outside the Christian bubble? In other words, how much of your week do you spend out in the world—away from church and like-minded folks—surrounded by people of different beliefs and backgrounds? What's your attitude toward them? How often do you catch yourself feeling superior to them? Do you let your standards slip because no other believers are around?

The key is obedience. Paul told the Christians in Philippi that it was even more important for them to obey God now that he, the founder of their church, wasn't among them. Philippians 2:12 (NLT) says we must "work hard to show the results of [our] salvation, obeying God with deep reverence and fear."

There's nothing passive about that work. We don't want to give people reason to think less of Him. People can be obnoxious about their objections to Jesus, the church, and Christians in general, but it does no good to respond in kind. When you humble yourself like Paul did, you find the rhythm needed to represent Jesus well.

PRAY

Jesus, if I just think about Your great love for me, demonstrated on the cross, I can see that there is a way to bring the truth to people outside my Christian sphere in a loving and respectful way. Help me to listen well and to speak with Your wisdom, insight, and compassion.

SCRIPTURE SPEAKS TO YOUR LIFE

Read Romans 12:1–21

KEY VERSE

If possible, so far as it depends on you, live peaceably with all. Romans 12:18 ESV

UNDERSTAND

- *When asked who you are, what's your best answer?*
- *Your life usually encompasses how many different areas?*

APPLY

Scripture speaks to every fiber of your being. It speaks to your looks and health, to your attitudes and actions, to your relationships with family and friends, to your use of time and money, to your employment and career options, to your educational and athletic pursuits, to your beliefs and convictions about God and the Bible.

Scripture also speaks to your interests in literature and movies, to your love of sports and music, to your hobbies and habits, to your Christian commitment and love for the Lord.

In other words, scripture speaks to *all of life*!

That's why it's crucial to read and study God's Word with a clear sense of *who you are.* How well do you understand your strengths and weaknesses, your current situation, your relationships with others, your relationship with God? Actively bring that understanding to the table when you study the Bible.

That's why it's also so important to *meditate on scripture.* It's not enough just to read the words on the page. You want to wash your mind with God's Word. Meditation involves any of these three actions:

- *Reflecting on the meaning of key words in a Bible phrase, verse, or paragraph*
- *Memorizing a verse, paragraph, or longer section of God's Word*
- *Rewriting a scripture passage in your own words*

PRAY

Yes, Lord, I want to say, "Thank You!" for today's key verse. It's such a great reminder that You know exactly what life is like here on earth. If I could ask for one miracle, I pray that I can be reconciled and at peace with one particular person.

VITAL NECESSITY

Read Jeremiah 29:10–14

KEY VERSE

"Then [with a deep longing] you will seek Me and require Me [as a vital necessity] and [you will] find Me when you search for Me with all your heart." JEREMIAH 29:13 AMP

UNDERSTAND

- *What comforts you most about God's promises in Jeremiah 29:10–14?*
- *What does it take to make you search for God with "deep longing" and "as a vital necessity"?*

APPLY

God's promises in Jeremiah 29 are familiar, but they go much deeper than the bumper-sticker context in which we normally see them. When Jeremiah passed these promises on to God's people, they were spiraling toward exile—the harsh, painful, uprooting consequences of their habitual hard-heartedness and spiritual infidelity. But even after seventy years as refugees, most of them got comfortable in Babylon and didn't want to go back to Jerusalem.

Only a few hardy, obedient souls returned, and no bed of roses awaited them. They were forced to rely on God as a vital necessity—to feed them, help them rebuild their broken city, and keep their families safe from the angry pagans who had moved in while they were in Babylon. It was literally do or die.

Today, hostility toward God and Christians is on the rise as the culture wins major battles for people's hearts. A time of "vital necessity" and "deep longing" is coming because God is both faithful to see us grow and jealous to make us fully His. Better to move from a bumper-sticker faith to a more deeply reliant one now—something you're doing every time you dig into His Word.

PRAY

Lord, will You make these well-known promises in Jeremiah 29 more real to me? I realize that's a dangerous prayer, one likely to push me out of my comfort zone, but I would rather have a deeper relationship with You in the trenches than a comfortable one with You at arm's length.

GOD STORIES

Read 2 Corinthians 5:14-21

KEY VERSE

He made Him who knew no sin to be sin for us, that we might become the righteousness of God in Him. 2 CORINTHIANS 5:21 NKJV

UNDERSTAND

- *What does God's grace mean to you in light of the worst thing you've ever done?*
- *What story would you tell someone of how God's grace personally impacted your life?*

APPLY

Because Jesus took on the ultimate pain of being cut off from God, you will never be cut off from Him. By His blood and with His strength, you can live the life God wants you to, drawing on His power, strength, and grace to be righteous, fully committed to knowing Him better and bringing Him glory.

Because Jesus did what He did in the way He did it, we should expect that anything is possible in this life, both good and bad. The good points to God's promise of life, but even the bad reminds us that God's light will eventually extinguish all darkness. That's the power of grace.

Human history is full of stories of God's grace. What makes these accounts so powerful and poignant is the light shining through in the darkest possible moments—of God pursuing people in POW camps, penitentiaries, and sickbeds and delivering them from despair to hope. God has turned ashes into beauty through failed suicide attempts, averted abortions, horrible sicknesses, and the healing of unimaginable wrongs and insurmountable losses.

Dramatic or not, your God stories are one of your best tools when it comes to sharing the good news. God doesn't waste a drop of pain or sorrow, and He will use yours. Your suffering in His hands supercharges your faith.

PRAY

Father God, I accept the hardship You allow in my life, knowing it strengthens my faith. Help me to learn what You're showing me and even to anticipate the impact it will have not just on me but on others who hear it and glorify You.

DAY 160

THE BIBLICAL HEROES MOSES AND JOSHUA

Read Joshua 8:30–35

KEY VERSE

There was not a word of all that Moses had commanded that Joshua did not read to the whole assembly of Israel, including the women and children, and the foreigners who lived among them. Joshua 8:35 niv

UNDERSTAND

- *Have you ever heard someone question the reliability of the Bible's first book, Genesis?*
- *What assumptions do such critics and skeptics make?*

APPLY

It's common to wonder, *Do we have all the right books in God's Word?* You can know for sure over these next few days of Bible study.

The first books of the Bible reveal the preservation of scripture from generation to generation.

The Books of Moses. The first five books of the Bible weren't put away in some obscure place after Moses wrote them. God gave Moses and the Israelites careful instructions during the latter part of Moses' life for the care and regular reading of the Law before "all Israel" (Deuteronomy 31:9–13, 24–29).

By the time Joshua found himself leading the Israelite nation, he recognized Genesis through Deuteronomy as written by Moses through God's direction (Joshua 1:8–9). Joshua probably had possession of the original writings.

Scribes made fastidious copies of the original autographs (with word-for-word precision), and God's people considered these equally authoritative (Joshua 8:32–35; Deuteronomy 27:3, 8). Verbal transmission was also authoritative (Joshua 8:34–35).

The Book of Joshua. Joshua wrote his book soon after the events recorded in it occurred. Records of what God told him suggest this. Specific historical references date the book to the time of Joshua, certainly much earlier than 1000 BC (see Joshua 15:63 and 16:10). Writers later added other authoritative material to Joshua's records. This includes material added soon after his death (Joshua 15:13–19; 24:29–33), when the records were being collected and probably copied in more permanent form.

PRAY

Yes, Lord, I want to say "Thank You!" that everything Moses and Joshua wrote in the first six books of the Bible is still in my hands today.

LESSER GODS

Read Romans 1:16–31

KEY VERSES

They knew God, but they wouldn't worship him as God or even give him thanks. And they began to think up foolish ideas of what God was like. As a result, their minds became dark and confused. Claiming to be wise, they instead became utter fools. And instead of worshipping the glorious, ever-living God, they worshipped idols. Romans 1:21–23 NLT

UNDERSTAND

- *Based on Romans 1:16–31, what qualifies something as an idol?*
- *How often do you pray for individuals or groups who really make you mad?*

APPLY

The second half of Romans 1 is an unflinching description of why the world is so messed up. Ultimately, idols exist because mankind has tried to embody a greater sense of things into single facets, individual representations of the divine that we can wrap our minds around. We try to put God in a box and bring Him down to our finite level, resulting in corrupt, confused minds. In trying to limit Him, we shackle ourselves.

Things that are by themselves good—work, ministry, government and politics, even family—become idols when we make them supreme. When good things become the most important things, we settle for lesser gods, and they fail us constantly. What results is everything wrong with the world—all the hot-button issues and every ugly sin in between.

It's easy to get angry at how badly we've broken what God made good. But being a new creation in Christ means we have to channel that anger into kingdom purposes. People are looking for ultimate meaning in their lives. You have it. Your role is to bring loving truth and truthful love into their day.

PRAY

Lord God, I will not be ashamed of the gospel of Jesus Christ. You are the world's only hope, just as You are mine. Let me be salt and light, preserving Your truth and making Your grace and love known through kind words and bold deeds.

THE SWEETNESS OF WISDOM

Read Proverbs 24:13–14

KEY VERSE

Know also that wisdom is like honey for you: If you find it, there is a future hope for you, and your hope will not be cut off. PROVERBS 24:14 NIV

UNDERSTAND

- *How often do you look to scripture when you need to make a decision?*
- *When has the wisdom of God's Word given you the same pleasure as a good meal?*

APPLY

Solomon's point in Proverbs 24:14 seems simple: Wisdom is sweet, just like honey. But there's more to this simple statement than meets the eye, and it starts with the sticky stuff. It helps to understand how honey was viewed in biblical times.

In ancient times, honey was considered to possess nearly magical qualities. It could be eaten raw or fermented into mead and honey wine, and was also commonly used as medicine. Egyptians offered it in sacrifices to their gods and used it in embalming their dead. Civilizations going back thousands of years employed it to treat infected wounds and intestinal maladies. Science has since confirmed that honey contains antibacterial and anti-inflammatory properties with modern applications.

So when God spoke of leading His people to a land flowing with milk and honey (Exodus 3:8), it suggests plentiful food but also a place of healing and well-being. God's desire to provide for us goes beyond meeting our basic needs; He also wants to draw us into the wonders of His wisdom.

That's what David meant when he wrote in Psalm 119:103 (NKJV), "How sweet are Your words to my taste, sweeter than honey to my mouth!" God's Word is the sweet treasure that enriches us, giving us wisdom and discernment to live as He intends.

PRAY

Almighty God, thank You for Your Word. You keep Your promises, and I can trust You. Help me take Your words to heart, to obey You through good times and bad so I can experience the sweetness of Your truth, goodness, and provision.

GOD IS GREATER THAN ANY CHALLENGE YOU FACE

Read 2 Chronicles 32:1–8

KEY VERSES

"Be strong and courageous, do not fear or be dismayed because of the king of Assyria nor because of all the horde that is with him; for the One with us is greater than the one with him. With him is only an arm of flesh, but with us is the LORD our God to help us and to fight our battles." And the people relied on the words of Hezekiah king of Judah.

2 CHRONICLES 32:7–8 NASB

UNDERSTAND

- *Hezekiah had been faithful to God before the Assyrian invasion of the land. Why did the author of Chronicles mention this detail at the start of today's reading?*
- *How did Hezekiah contrast the power of God with the power of the king of Assyria?*
- *What does this passage say about spiritual leadership and the impact a leader's encouraging words can have on the faith of others?*

APPLY

There's a good chance that you're facing some kind of challenge today. You may feel the weight of a difficult relationship, the uncertainty of a job, or the weary grind of many responsibilities stacked on top of each other. If there is no one in your life to encourage you and lift you up, those challenges can feel all-consuming, even crushing.

Today's scripture reading encourages you to shift your focus from your own difficulties to God's extensive power and resources, which can be unleashed in your life—if only you turn toward Him in faith. King Hezekiah and the people of Judah were an example of this truth. They had seen the Assyrians destroy one nation after another, but they took timely action and trusted in God to do the rest.

You may need to make some big, uncomfortable changes to your life in order to overcome the challenges before you. But the good news is that God is all-powerful and willing to remain with you through the highs and lows of today. If you remain in God, He will remain with you.

PRAY

Lord, You know better than I do what my challenges are and how I can best overcome them. Thank You for being near Your people in their times of challenge and struggle. May Your power be manifested on my behalf so that I am safe in Your presence. Amen.

FREE INDEED

Read John 8:31–36

KEY VERSE

"If the Son sets you free, you are truly free." JOHN 8:36 NLT

UNDERSTAND

- *What has Jesus set you free from?*
- *What things threaten to draw you back into captivity to the world?*

APPLY

Every discussion, argument, and protest about rights comes down to freedom, which is commonly interpreted as the right to do whatever you want, to live "your truth" without hindrance or restriction. Look past whatever group is currently bugging you with such protests and keep your eyes on the prize—living for Christ and filling and building the kingdom of God.

Only Jesus offers true freedom. What He has never offered, though, is an easy path to follow Him. He said in John 15:18 (NLT), "If the world hates you, remember that it hated me first." Luke 9:23 (ESV) says, "If anyone would come after me, let him deny himself and take up his cross daily and follow me." These are not statements of a trouble-free life. But then, the cross shows us that freedom isn't free.

Freedom carries responsibilities, primarily to honor and obey God. Psalm 119:45 (NLT) says, "I will walk in freedom, for I have devoted myself to your commandments." Pursuing God means obeying His Word, not because our salvation depends on it but because we are responding to His love and grace. That's freedom's path.

In Christ, you are free from the pressures and expectations of the world. Christians are no longer bound by the limited, materialistic, transactional view of relationships. Our value is based on Christ's love for us, not our accomplishments, networks, or net worth. Use your freedom to help set others free.

PRAY

Lord Jesus, You have set me free for freedom's sake (Galatians 5:1). I am not bound to my old habits, the ways of the world, or the devil's lies. Give me the wisdom and power to live a life liberated from these things.

DAY 165

EZRA PRESERVES THE HEBREW SCRIPTURES

Read Ezra 7:11–26

KEY VERSE

"And you, Ezra, according to the wisdom of your God that is in your hand, appoint magistrates and judges who may judge all the people in the province Beyond the River, all such as know the laws of your God. And those who do not know them, you shall teach."
Ezra 7:25 ESV

UNDERSTAND

- *Did you notice how the king described Ezra in verses 11, 12, and 21? Why is this significant?*
- *In verses 14 and 25, what does the king say is in Ezra's possession? Why is this so important?*

APPLY

When all is said and done, God's people have all the right books in the Old Testament. Tradition says Ezra wrote part of the Old Testament himself and helped confirm much of the Old Testament canon—the books the Jewish people believed God spoke through the prophets. This canon was started before 1400 BC (the books of Moses) and completed after 450 BC (Malachi).

According to first-century Jewish historian Josephus, the Jewish people divided the Old Testament into the following sections:

- *The Books of Moses: Genesis, Exodus, Leviticus, Numbers, Deuteronomy.*
- *The Prophets: Joshua, Ruth and Judges (considered one book), Samuel, Kings, Isaiah, Jeremiah and Lamentations (one book), Ezekiel, the twelve Minor Prophets (one book), Daniel, Job, Esther, Ezra and Nehemiah (one book), and Chronicles.*
- *The Writings: Psalms, Proverbs, Song of Solomon, and Ecclesiastes. Sometimes Job, Ruth and Judges, Lamentations, Esther, Daniel, Ezra and Nehemiah, and Chronicles were added to this third section of writings.*

Well over two millennia later, God's people still have every book of the Old Testament intact and in hand. That's amazing!

PRAY

Yes, Lord, I want to say "Thank You!" for making sure we have had every book of the Old Testament for thousands of years.

DO IT FOR LOVE

Read Colossians 3:17–25

KEY VERSES

Whatever you do, work at it with all your heart, as working for the Lord, not for human masters, since you know that you will receive an inheritance from the Lord as a reward. It is the Lord Christ you are serving. Colossians 3:23–24 NIV

UNDERSTAND

- *What motivates you in life? What gets you fired up?*
- *How do you decide if something is worth your effort?*

APPLY

In Colossians 3, Paul brings a serious challenge for Christian living, summed up in verse 17: Do everything in Jesus' name. We tend to add the phrase to the end of prayers like an automatic stamp of approval, the proper sign-off, instead of realizing that every time we talk to God, we are drawing on a seal of approval guaranteed by Jesus' blood.

Jesus' name is our salvation; we can only approach a holy God because He made it possible. But it should also remind us John 3:16-style that Jesus did what He did out of love—love for the Father and for the world.

It's only possible to obey the list of examples in Colossians 3:18–23 because of Jesus' love. When you're thankful you can call on His name, it helps you be a loving husband, an engaged father, a concerned friend, and a worker with integrity. Or as Paul asked in Romans 2:4 (NASB), "Do you think lightly of the riches of His kindness and restraint and patience, not knowing that the kindness of God leads you to repentance?"

God did it all for love. We should too.

PRAY

Thank You, Father, for Your patience with me. In my busyness, my ambition, my fear of missing out, I find myself forgetting that You are the one I'm doing it for—the one who makes any good thing worth doing, and worth doing Your way, with excellence in love, patience, and hard work. You gave Your best in Jesus Christ; You deserve my best in all I do.

TROUBLE'S ALWAYS KNOCKING

Read Job 5:6–16

KEY VERSES

"Trouble doesn't come from nowhere. It's human! Mortals are born and bred for trouble, as certainly as sparks fly upward. If I were in your shoes, I'd go straight to God, I'd throw myself on the mercy of God. After all, he's famous for great and unexpected acts; there's no end to his surprises." Job 5:6–9 MSG

UNDERSTAND

- *How has God delivered you from trouble most recently?*
- *When bad news gets you down, how quickly do you seek God?*

APPLY

Our natural state causes trouble. Without God intervening and making Himself known, we'd just keep going in the wrong direction. Even Christians. Our soul is redeemed, but our flesh isn't yet.

Thankfully, God is not content to just leave us to the mess we've made. Jesus came to make salvation possible, and Revelation 21:1–4 describes the coming day when He will return and fix all of it, creating the new heaven and earth and eliminating death, sorrow, and pain.

In the meantime, though, our natural state is born for trouble; if there weren't any, we'd make some. That's why Job noted that pursuing God is our only hope in this life. God has never been content to let us suffer the consequences of our actions without remedy.

We still find evidence of His goodness all around us if we're looking. All we do in this life involves risk—love, work, friendship, and obedience to God. But He is just and good, and He is making all things new, now and in the forever to come.

PRAY

Lord God, You have been incredibly merciful in light of our relentless drive to please ourselves rather than You. One day, You will make things right and good again, and our greatest pleasure and ambition will be pleasing You. Until then, I will seek to do so, with Your help. Trouble's always knocking, but I will let You answer.

ENCOURAGEMENT TO YIELD TO GOD'S PLANS

Read 1 Samuel 23:13–24

KEY VERSES

Jonathan went to find David and encouraged him to stay strong in his faith in God. "Don't be afraid," Jonathan reassured him. "My father will never find you! You are going to be the king of Israel, and I will be next to you, as my father, Saul, is well aware."

1 Samuel 23:16–17 NLT

UNDERSTAND

- *What does it say about Jonathan's faith in God that he gave up his rightful place as the king of Israel?*
- *Why did David need encouragement from Jonathan while King Saul was trying to kill him?*
- *What is the benefit of making a solemn pact before God with another person?*

APPLY

When someone reads God's promises in scripture, but they don't seem to make sense in light of their current circumstances, it may feel like they are on the ropes in their life of faith. In a situation where nothing seems to be going right or when someone feels like God has abandoned them, a timely word of encouragement can make the difference.

Faith and encouragement may require looking for things that are quite different from present circumstances. You may have to set aside your desires or how you think things should be in order to fully embrace the good things God has planned for those in need of encouragement.

Today, keep an eye out for those who are faltering or discouraged in their faith, and then consider how you can help them trust in God. You may be the person who keeps them on track to one day accomplish great things for God.

PRAY

Help me, Lord, to see the people around me who are discouraged, struggling with their faith, or facing adversity and uncertainty. May I support them with encouragement and intercession when they are most in need of compassionate, considerate assistance. Amen.

ABIDE

Read 2 Chronicles 15:1–7

KEY VERSES

"The Lord is with you when you are with Him. And if you seek Him, He will let you find Him; but if you abandon Him, He will abandon you. . . . Be strong and do not lose courage, for there is a reward for your work." 2 Chronicles 15:2, 7 NASB

UNDERSTAND

- *What evidence do you have that God is sticking with you?*
- *In what areas or situations do you find it hardest to stick with God?*

APPLY

In 2 Chronicles 15, God ensures His people that when they truly seek Him, they will find Him. It's a promise that is also a prophecy of Christianity. In Jesus, God lets Himself be found by us in an inclusive way that means He will never leave nor forsake us. Put another way, His desire has always been to abide with us.

To abide is to remain in place. Jesus used *abide* memorably when He said in John 15:4 (NKJV), "Abide in Me, and I in you." We are to stay true to Him, remaining unified with Him primarily by obeying His singular command in John 13:34–35 to love one another as He has loved us. But as John 15:6 (MSG) says, failing to abide that way means we're "deadwood, gathered up and thrown on the bonfire."

Abiding is our responsibility under the new covenant in Jesus' blood. We love others as He has loved us so we can draw the lost to God's kingdom. As you abide in Him, enjoy the deep sense of purpose God has given you and let it guide you in all you do.

PRAY

God Almighty, You are always faithful. I can trust You to stick with me no matter what. In response, I will abide with You, following Your commands to love out of love for You. Let Your purposes and ways fill me till I'm overflowing with them.

SCRIBES PRESERVED GOD'S WORD

Read Ezra 7:1–10

KEY VERSE

For Ezra had set his heart to study the Law of the Lord*, and to do it and to teach his statutes and rules in Israel.* Ezra 7:10 esv

UNDERSTAND

- *Do you remember the telephone game? If so, why was it sometimes humorous?*
- *How similar or different is the story of the Bible's transmission down through the ages?*

APPLY

It's common to ask, "Does every verse in scripture say what it's supposed to say?"

Thankfully, textual criticism plays an important role in confirming the inspiration of scripture.

Textual criticism is a careful science that uses thousands of ancient manuscripts to determine texts that are most like the original copies. None of the manuscripts considered are originals (since they have long since been lost or destroyed), so the reliability of the copies must be proved. God's people can be sure of the accuracy of the transmission of the original message to the copies in four ways.

First, after the Babylonian captivity, Ezra and other scribes carefully went to work to ensure that plenty of copies of God's Word would always exist. These scribes became known as "lawyers" because of their knowledge of the Old Testament law.

Second, the Talmudists (AD 100–450), the Masoretes (AD 450–900), and other such groups who copied under the strictest of rules, reproduced the Old Testament. Their high standards reflect the accuracy of their copying. Here are only two of the many rules they followed:

- *They could not correct the original if they felt it was wrong (they could only add notations in the margins).*
- *On each line they copied, they counted the number of letters and words, compared middle words, checked the frequency of each letter, and the like.*

There's more!

PRAY

Yes, Lord, I want to say "Thank You!" for the incredible work done by scribes to preserve the scriptures down through the ages. May I never take the Bible for granted again.

DAY 171

MORE ABOUT THE SCRIBES

Read Malachi 4:1–6

KEY VERSE

"Remember to obey the Law of Moses, my servant—all the decrees and regulations that I gave him on Mount Sinai for all Israel." MALACHI 4:4 NLT

UNDERSTAND

- *Some Bibles use the word* Savior *and some use* Saviour. *What are the differences in meaning?*
- *The original King James Version uses the word* let *in the sense of "hinder." What's changed in the past four hundred years? The accuracy of the Bible—or something else?*

APPLY

Here are several more rules that the Talmudists, Masoretes, and others followed when copying the Old Testament scriptures:

- *They could not copy from memory.*
- *They used the space of a hair between each letter. (Talk about precise!)*
- *They reverently burned or buried old, worn copies of scripture (to avoid profaning the Lord's name, should they become smudged or otherwise unreadable).*

How accurate were these scribes? Bible scholars familiar with their work confidently assert that the time gap doesn't mean the text has degenerated over the millennia. In his *Survey of the Bible,* William Hendriksen quotes one scholar who said, "If we had in our possession a first- or second-century manuscript, we would find it to have substantially the same text as those of much later date."

Only months after that statement was published, the Dead Sea Scrolls were discovered in a cave in Qumran. Among the findings were two copies of the book of Isaiah dating back to 150 BC. Hebrew scholars diligently compared the newly discovered manuscripts with much more recent manuscripts that had come from the Masoretic tradition and were dated from the medieval period. Their conclusion? Only a few insignificant changes (mostly spelling variations) had crept into the Isaiah text after more than a millennium!

Thanks to the careful work of the Jewish scribes, we can rest assured that the Old Testament has been passed on to us with a very high degree of accuracy. Wow, indeed!

PRAY

Yes, Lord, I want to say "Wow!" for the incredible accuracy of the Old Testament scriptures preserved for all of history.

DEPENDS ON HOW YOU ASK

Read James 1:1–8

KEY VERSE

If any of you lacks wisdom, let him ask of God, who gives to all liberally and without reproach, and it will be given to him. James 1:5 NKJV

UNDERSTAND

- *When was the last time you had no idea what to do in a hard situation?*
- *How difficult is it for you to seek advice? Why?*

APPLY

Have you ever been in a situation in which none of the standard decision-making protocols are working? Prayer isn't yielding a direction, listing the pros and cons reveals no clear option, the friends we consult are stumped, and our normal stress-reducing measures aren't helping. The fear of making the wrong choice paralyzes us.

Go back to prayer, though. What James makes clear is that the attitude with which we seek God makes all the difference. A tough choice is exactly the kind of trial that forces us to check our faith. Do we really believe what we say we believe about God, about prayer, about Him giving us what we need?

When you ask God for wisdom, don't hedge your bets—just think of what matters most to Him and then ask Him for help. James 1:5 assures you that God isn't going to look at you and say, "Dummy! It's about time." No, He is glad you're asking and will give you insight. Just make sure you're willing to line up your goals with His will.

The joy of seeking God doesn't come from having all the details sorted out but from remembering everything you know about your heavenly Father. He won't leave you hanging, but His response depends on your attitude about Him when you ask for His help.

PRAY

Father, Your Word says so much about Your character—that You are good, faithful, and righteous. When I need Your wisdom, I am going to ask You for it. Please give me ears to hear and eyes to see Your response.

TRUE CONFESSION

Read 2 Kings 22:11–20

KEY VERSE

"Go, inquire of the Lord for me, for the people and for all Judah, concerning the words of this book that has been found; for great is the wrath of the Lord that is aroused against us, because our fathers have not obeyed the words of this book, to do according to all that is written concerning us." 2 Kings 22:13 NKJV

UNDERSTAND

- *What is your response when a passage of scripture convicts you of something?*
- *Who is affected most by your sin? What does confessing a sin to God mean to you?*

APPLY

Today, some live as if the Bible were lost, but in King Josiah's day, it was literally true. It wasn't until he ordered repairs to the temple that a priest found a copy of the Bible. When the king heard what God's Word said, he tore his robes in dismay. Because of the king's humble response, God said He would hold back His just judgment until after Josiah's time.

Sometimes God's Word holds a hard message for us. We need reminders that our sin, first and foremost, is against Him. We break His heart when we go our way instead of His. Others may suffer because of our choices, but we hurt God the most.

That's why the Bible reminds us to read it and to pray regularly, so we can be attuned to God. Our awareness and sensitivity to sin will increase, along with our willingness to confess it—to agree with Him that we've messed up. When we do, we are assured that He will take us back, that He won't cut us off as long as we remember who is on the throne.

PRAY

Your mercies are humbling, Almighty Lord. You are justified in all Your judgments and correct in calling me out when I sin against You. I'm thankful that when I confess, You will wash me clean and restore me to right relationship with You.

REMEMBER GOD'S FAITHFULNESS

Read Deuteronomy 11:1–12

KEY VERSES

Observe therefore all the commands I am giving you today, so that you may have the strength to go in and take over the land that you are crossing the Jordan to possess, and so that you may live long in the land the LORD *swore to your ancestors to give to them and their descendants, a land flowing with milk and honey.* DEUTERONOMY 11:8–9 NIV

UNDERSTAND

- *Why was obedience so important for the Israelites as they entered the land God promised to them?*
- *God promised the land to the people of Israel and their descendants. Why did He remind them of this promise at this moment?*
- *How could it help the people of Israel to be reminded of how God had delivered them from the armies of Egypt in the past?*

APPLY

Consider the challenges you are facing today or this week—or the worries weighing on your mind. Take notice of them and how they are impacting you. As you see these challenges with clarity, you can also look at the ways God has been with you, the people in your family, or those in your immediate circles through difficult times.

Remembering God's past faithfulness as you think about your present challenges will help you realize both the stakes of your day and the hope He offers. Most importantly, obedience is a key part of remaining close to God throughout today and the rest of your week.

As you listen to God's commands and act obediently, you'll have the intimacy and access to Him you need to thrive in your difficulties. Obedience ensures that you see your life on God's terms and are prepared to depend on Him rather than on your own resources or plans. Drawing near to God in obedience will ensure that He is already near when you are in need.

PRAY

Thank You, Lord, for the ways You've been present for Your people, providing for their needs and delivering them from trouble. May I live today with an awareness of Your power and ability to save. And may my awareness of You help me to live in faithful obedience. Amen.

THE PARADIGM SHIFT

Read Romans 3:10–26

KEY VERSES

"None is righteous, no, not one; no one understands; no one seeks for God. All have turned aside; together they have become worthless; no one does good, not even one."
ROMANS 3:10–12 ESV

UNDERSTAND

- *Would you say that you are, generally speaking, a good person? Why or why not?*
- *How would you describe the differences between your goodness and God's?*

APPLY

To establish his claim in Romans 3:23 that we all sin and fall short of God's glory, Paul quoted Psalm 14, where David observed that no one is righteous or wise enough to seek God. Because of our sin, God is justified in His anger with the world and everyone in it. That shocks people who think that being good should be enough to get on God's good side.

Compared to God's holy standard of goodness, however, there is no such thing as a good person. Of course, we all know people who are kind, decent, upstanding citizens. But humanity's version of good isn't enough to save us from our sin. When we relinquish the notion that people are inherently good in favor of faith in the good God who wants to save us all from ourselves, we undergo a paradigm shift.

Once you've shifted, you can fully embrace your true identity in Christ. This is part of what the oft-used phrase *the fear of the Lord* means—the humbling, awe-inspiring acceptance that God alone is God, and we must respond to Him, not the other way around. Then He will help us love Him and others in ways that honor and please Him.

PRAY

I'm so grateful, God, that You have made Yourself known to me. Knowing You has changed my life for the better because Your love teaches me to love the right way—with Your glory and the good of others as my highest goals.

THE NEW TESTAMENT'S RELIABILITY

Read Luke 1:1–25

KEY VERSE

Having carefully investigated everything from the beginning, I also have decided to write an accurate account for you, most honorable Theophilus. LUKE 1:3 NLT

UNDERSTAND

- *Which do you think are more reliable: the writings of Plato, Aristotle, and Homer—or the New Testament's twenty-seven books?*
- *Is it even close?*

APPLY

There is an overwhelming amount of evidence for the accuracy of the New Testament. Men wrote its twenty-seven books between AD 40 and 100. The earliest known copy of part of the New Testament is dated only a few short decades after the completion of the original.

Also, there are 5,400 ancient copies of the New Testament in Greek, 10,000 more in Latin, and 9,300 more in other languages. From this wealth of sources, scholars and experts have made comparisons to accurately determine the original.

Sir Frederic George Kenyon, former director and principal librarian of the British Museum, said, "Thanks to these manuscripts, the ordinary reader of the Bible may feel comfortable about the soundness of the text. Apart from a few unimportant verbal alterations, natural in books transcribed by hand, the New Testament, we now feel assured, has come down intact."

What's more, almost the entire New Testament can be reproduced from the writings of the second- and third-century church fathers alone. All but eleven verses can be reconstructed from the verses they cited.

In sharp contrast, other classical writings are suspect at best. Scholars have only 7 copies of Plato's writings, dating 1,200 years after his death. They have only 5 copies of Aristotle's writings, dating 1,400 years after his death. They have 643 copies of Homer's writings, dating 1,800 years after his death, with errors prevalent in 5 percent of his 15,600 lines.

You can read every section of the New Testament with confidence!

PRAY

Yes, Lord, I want to say "Wow!" for the incredible accuracy of the New Testament scriptures. I can read and study Your Word with incredible confidence.

GETTING TO GIVE

Read Luke 6:27-42

KEY VERSE

"Give, and you will receive. Your gift will return to you in full—pressed down, shaken together to make room for more, running over, and poured into your lap. The amount you give will determine the amount you get back." LUKE 6:38 NLT

UNDERSTAND

- *What is your greatest challenge when it comes to giving?*
- *How does God demonstrate His attitude about giving?*

APPLY

Based on what Jesus is saying in Luke 6, it's clear that in God's economy, money isn't just about money. He was discussing the right *attitude* toward money—lending to those in need without expecting repayment and giving out of compassion, not just doing smart business. Jesus sets up His idea of giving by challenging us about our inherent judgmentalism and hypocrisy. Wait—what?

It's a brilliant setup because it reveals the ungodliness of our default setting about giving. We give to get. We give to the needy because it makes us feel good about ourselves, or it's a tax write-off, or it reinforces our sense of superiority. In other words, we judge ourselves and others based on how generous we are. Thankfully, God doesn't judge us based on what we can give Him. He just wants us.

The image in Luke 6:38 is of a measure of grain—a daily allotment—shaken and pressed into the measuring cup so that it can't hold a single grain more and runs over. That's how God has blessed you in Christ: giving you His very best so you couldn't possibly feel shortchanged by His blessing. And that's how He wants you to be in your giving—joyfully meeting others' needs because your cup is overflowing with His love, grace, and provision.

PRAY

Father God, I ask for Your wisdom in untangling my thoughts about money and giving and how closely they are related to judging others. Help me to see others the way You see them—as being worth the highest cost to seek and to save.

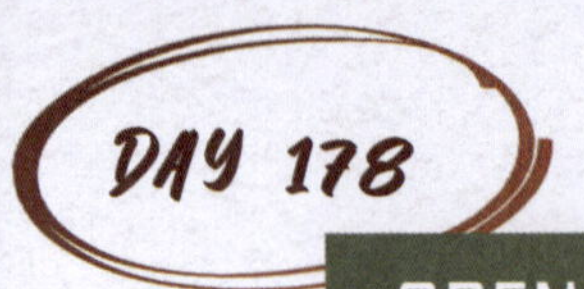

OPEN ARMS AND UNMERITED MERCIES

Read Psalm 51:1–6

KEY VERSES

You're the One I've violated, and you've seen it all, seen the full extent of my evil. You have all the facts before you; whatever you decide about me is fair. I've been out of step with you for a long time, in the wrong since before I was born. What you're after is truth from the inside out. Psalm 51:4–6 MSG

UNDERSTAND

- *How hard is it for you to seek God when you've sinned?*
- *How often do you condemn yourself instead of seeking God's forgiveness?*

APPLY

David wrote Psalm 51 after Nathan busted him for committing adultery with Bathsheba, then arranged for her husband, Uriah (one of his most loyal soldiers), to die at the frontlines of a battle at which David wasn't present. Once David saw his actions through God's eyes, his heart broke, and he penned this famous psalm of repentance.

How could David turn so wholeheartedly to God after messing up so badly? Rather than asking that question, we're better served to see something bigger and deeper than David's sin—we need to grasp his view of God.

God hates sin because it separates us from Him. He knows we can't repay the cost, but His perfect love demanded that He pay that painful price Himself. He is always standing nearby, wanting to pull you into a loving embrace of forgiveness and peace. The depth of your wretchedness can't match the greatness of His love.

Like David, you're worse than you can even imagine and more loved than you can ever dream. Forgiveness and restoration begin when you get out of your head and trust in His love for you.

PRAY

Holy and merciful Lord, I've too often ignored Your love, Your willingness to forgive and restore me. I'm so sorry. Please help me to see You not as my fear dictates but as You are—arms open, waiting for me to turn back to You.

REWARDS FOR GODLY LIVING

Read Matthew 5:1–11

KEY VERSES

"Blessed are the meek, for they will inherit the earth. Blessed are those who hunger and thirst for righteousness, for they will be filled. Blessed are the merciful, for they will be shown mercy. Blessed are the pure in heart, for they will see God." MATTHEW 5:5–8 NIV

UNDERSTAND

- *Why does Jesus make such an amazing promise to those who are "meek"?*
- *Why is mercy such an important quality in the Beatitudes?*
- *Why is purity of heart so instrumental in seeing God? What did Jesus mean when He said the pure in heart will "see God"?*

APPLY

The Beatitudes—Jesus' statements of blessings found in today's scripture reading—suggest a way of living that is in opposition to the "wisdom" of the world today. But these are Jesus' promises of joy and fulfillment for those who orient their lives and thinking according to God's wisdom. This is Jesus' invitation to keep ourselves in the right perspective so that we can be fully present for God and for others.

Some of these promises may come to fruition in the present, and some may be fulfilled when we are in the very presence of God. Either way, we can count on Him to keep these and every other promise He has made. He has said it, and He will do it!

Yet even with so many promises that will be fulfilled one day, the wisdom of Jesus remains especially true for you today. If you hope to receive mercy, then be merciful toward others. If you want things to be made right in this life, then you need to crave it like it's the food that sustains you. And as you align your desires with God's will, Jesus promises that you will find fulfillment.

PRAY

Jesus, help me to see the world through Your eyes and to value what You value. May I look ahead to the rewards You have promised me, and may I take actions that bring benefit to those around me. I ask that Your power and influence in my life would lead me to a pure heart and a greater awareness of You. Amen.

GETTING RIGHTEOUSNESS RIGHT

Read Matthew 5:3–10

KEY VERSE

"Blessed are those who hunger and thirst for righteousness, for they shall be filled."
MATTHEW 5:6 NKJV

UNDERSTAND

- *When you read the Sermon on the Mount, what challenges you?*
- *What is the difference between God's righteousness and the human version?*

APPLY

The challenge of hungering for righteousness is that we don't hunger for what we don't think we need. But over and over, the Bible talks about the importance of righteousness. We are to pursue it, practice it, do it, walk in it, and suffer for it. But before any of that, we must become it. All the right behavior in the world doesn't make us right with God.

The more we grasp our need for Jesus, the more we see the value of His righteousness: humbling Himself to do the dirty work required to save us and standing for what matters to God when it cost Him His reputation. Because Jesus had right standing with God, He wanted to obey, and He had the courage to do God's will. Thus, His suffering only strengthened His resolve.

Suffering can clarify your priorities—because it makes you desperate enough to see what really matters. On our own, we can't be humble or hungry or merciful enough, can't mourn our wretched state enough, can't think or speak or behave purely enough to get into God's kingdom.

But Jesus' righteousness is enough. The Beatitudes should lead you to the end of yourself, but when you get there, you'll see all that God has offered you in Jesus.

PRAY

Jesus, thank You for being perfect in righteousness so I could receive Your right standing with God. I'm asking You to show me anything in my life that threatens my knowing You better. Even when it hurts, I want to be more like You because I know You are the way, the truth, and the life.

THE CHURCH PRESERVES THE NEW TESTAMENT

Read Acts 1:1–26

KEY VERSE

In my former book, Theophilus, I wrote about all that Jesus began to do and to teach.
ACTS 1:1 NIV

UNDERSTAND

- *Tradition says Luke wrote the book of Acts in anticipation of Paul's trial before Caesar. What does Luke say in Acts that seems to confirm this?*
- *The name Theophilus means "friend of God." Do you think he was a real person? Why or why not?*

APPLY

Soon after the church began, the need for a second canon of accepted scripture writings developed. The New Testament canon formed much more quickly than the Old Testament because of the loss of the apostles and other witnesses, the expansion of Christianity beyond Israel, the need to protect the message from false teachings, and the missionary enterprise (they needed to know which books to translate and use in preaching).

The early church went through several steps to finalize the New Testament canon. Most of the books were widely recognized as canonical in the second and third centuries. Some seriously questioned only a few of the latter books in the New Testament. By AD 397, two official church councils had confirmed the canonical nature of the twenty-seven books of the New Testament.

Members of these councils asked specific questions to determine which books were canonical:

- *Is it written by or under the direction of an apostle?*
- *Is it inspired by the Holy Spirit?*
- *Is it circulated among the churches?*
- *Is it consistent with the rest of scripture?*

Some reliable books were left out of the canon, including a harmony of the four Gospels. It was widely read among the churches, but didn't measure up to the four rigid standards of canonicity. Many unreliable books were rejected out of hand.

How good to know that Christians have all the right books in the New Testament!

PRAY

Yes, Lord, I want to say "Thank You!" for inspiring Matthew, Mark, Luke, John, Peter, James, Jude, and Paul to write the New Testament scriptures.

SEEKING NEXT STEPS

Read Ezra 8:21–23

KEY VERSES

We had told the king, "The hand of our God is for good on all who seek him, and the power of his wrath is against all who forsake him." So we fasted and implored our God for this, and he listened to our entreaty. Ezra 8:22–23 esv

UNDERSTAND

- *What kind of situation compels you to fast as you seek God?*
- *Why does denying yourself help you to follow God more confidently?*

APPLY

Ezra was a priest who led a small group of courageous volunteers on a dangerous journey out of exile and back to Israel. The odds were against him, but he had made a stand—a strong statement of faith to the king that God would see them through. Realizing what a struggle lay before him and all those God had entrusted to him, he wisely turned to God with prayer and fasting.

The combination of prayer and fasting leads to powerful results. When you hunger for God more than for food, you can grasp what David experienced in Psalm 63:1, 3, 5 (niv): "You, God, are my God, earnestly I seek you; I thirst for you, my whole being longs for you. . . . My lips will glorify you. . . . I will be fully satisfied as with the richest of foods."

Trusting God to the extent that you deprive yourself helps you to see the situation through God's eyes, and that often leads to Him showing you what to do next. It's not usually a linear path, but it's the path God wants you to travel. Fasting and prayer have a humbling effect that put you in the right frame of mind to follow Him where He leads.

PRAY

Heavenly Father, I don't want to be on any path but the one You set before me. I trust You with the situation before me now, and I understand that fasting and prayer open my heart to receive my next step from You.

WHEN GRACE IS ALL YOU'VE GOT

Read 2 Corinthians 12:7–10

KEY VERSES

At first I didn't think of it as a gift, and begged God to remove it. Three times I did that, and then he told me, "My grace is enough; it's all you need. My strength comes into its own in your weakness." Once I heard that, I was glad to let it happen. I quit focusing on the handicap and began appreciating the gift. 2 Corinthians 12:8–9 MSG

UNDERSTAND

- *Has God allowed a recurring challenge in your life? What might He be doing through it?*
- *When has God shown up strong in a moment of weakness for you?*

APPLY

When Jesus brought Paul into the fold, the former Pharisee had some catching up to do. Paul had been a zealous legalist and Christian terminator, so, as 2 Corinthians 12:1–6 tells us, Jesus took him on personally, preparing him for service.

God used that unspecified physical/spiritual ailment to educate Paul about the sufficiency of His grace. When God refused to remove it, Paul surrendered any sense of entitlement, markers of status, or worldly success. As a result, God's grace—His abiding power and favor in the face of hardship—enabled Paul to endure a staggering checklist of missionary suffering (see 2 Corinthians 11—yikes!).

So when Paul said in 2 Corinthians 12:10 (MSG) that he had learned to "take limitations in stride," he meant it. Revisit your worst moments—the times when all seemed lost and none of your experience, talents, or skills were enough to fix the problem. Jesus was there, and by His grace you persevered.

PRAY

Lord Jesus, compared to Your strength, all else is feeble and small. That includes all the obstacles You allow into my path, all the valleys You walk me through, all the times I fail miserably—they don't get the final word. You do, and that is enough for me.

GOD HEARS THE PRAYERS OF THE DESTITUTE

Read Psalm 102:12–22

KEY VERSES

For the Lord *will build up Zion; he will appear in his glory. He will regard the prayer of the destitute, and will not despise their prayer. Let this be recorded for a generation to come, so that a people yet unborn may praise the* Lord. Psalm 102:16–18 NRSV

UNDERSTAND

- *How does Psalm 102 consider the praise and worship of today in light of the worship of future generations?*
- *As the people of Israel suffered the tragedy of exile, how did they find hope in the Lord?*
- *What is the significance of the Lord hearing the groans of prisoners and those condemned to die?*

APPLY

Each day you are surrounded by people who are suffering immensely today or who bear the wounds from past trauma. You may even be among them. Some are trapped in a mental prison of depression from past trauma, and some are dealing with real limitations that hold them back from personal freedom. But the Lord is aware of people's cries for relief and wants to have compassion on them.

Today's psalm encourages us to pray to God for relief—for ourselves or for others who are suffering. And when God acts on our behalf, we will be able to praise Him for what He has done for us.

Suffering may be temporary, but the Lord is enthroned in heaven forever. There is no limit to His power and compassion. One day God will appear in glory to right the wrongs of today. In the meantime, we should keep ourselves in a constant state of prayer as we wait for Him to act.

PRAY

Lord, You see my suffering and the suffering of others, and You desire to bring justice and relief to all who suffer. Help me to wait patiently for You, placing my faith in Your everlasting power and the hope that You will one day return to earth to rule. Amen.

GOD HAS THE FINAL WORD

Read Romans 8:28–39

KEY VERSES

[God's Spirit] knows us far better than we know ourselves, knows our pregnant condition, and keeps us present before God. That's why we can be so sure that every detail in our lives of love for God is worked into something good. Romans 8:27–28 msg

UNDERSTAND

- *What is the worst thing you can think of happening to you? Why might God allow it?*
- *Have you ever mistaken God's sovereign perspective for disinterest or even dislike?*

APPLY

Being a Christian means being persuaded of the joy, relief, and comfort that come from being right with God—to the extent that tribulation doesn't shake us. We receive His blessings as coheirs with Christ, along with the power to pass through the troubles that come with this world, rather than getting stuck in them.

Romans 8:28 is so well known that we can forget its power. God causes *everything* to work together. Take the proper view of God's role in your life. He is there at the beginning, waiting for you to respond to your calling in Christ, and He is there along the way, working all things together for good. And you can be sure He will be with you in the end.

When hard times come, let God have the final word, as Paul did in Romans 8:29–30 (nlt): "God knew his people in advance, and he chose them to become like his Son, so that his Son would be the firstborn among many brothers and sisters. And having chosen them, he called them to come to him. And having called them, he gave them right standing with himself. And having given them right standing, he gave them his glory."

PRAY

Father, I give You the final word in my life. I believe what You say about me—that I am Your son, that You are for me, and that You are changing me into the image of Jesus.

NOTHING LOST IN TRANSLATION

Read 2 Timothy 3:10–17

KEY VERSE

You have been taught the holy Scriptures from childhood, and they have given you the wisdom to receive the salvation that comes by trusting in Christ Jesus. 2 Timothy 3:15 NLT

UNDERSTAND

- *Have you ever found a typographical error in one of your Bibles? If so, what does it mean?*
- *And what does that typo not mean?*

APPLY

It's common to ask, "What about translations? What's lost in some of them?" Thankfully, the apostle Paul gave us the biblical perspective we should have toward copies and translations.

The scripture Paul referred to as "inspired by God" was not a collection of the original works. It was only one among thousands of copies of the Old Testament scriptures. Additionally, these scriptures were translated from Hebrew and Aramaic into Greek (a translation known as the Septuagint).

Without hesitation, Paul told Timothy that the sacred writings he had known from childhood were able to give him wisdom leading to salvation. Then he added: "All Scripture is God-breathed and is useful for teaching, rebuking, correcting and training in righteousness, so that the servant of God may be thoroughly equipped for every good work" (2 Timothy 3:16–17 NIV).

Because of this, we can see that copies and translated works are still inspired. They accurately reflect the original manuscripts and communicate God's intended meaning.

The verdict?

Our English Bibles truly *are* inspired. They are the Word of God communicated to us in a language we can read, understand, personalize, and apply to our lives.

PRAY

Yes, Lord, I want to say "Thank You!" again for motivating me to go through this book and learn so much about how to read and study and apply Your Word to my life.

DON'T GO WITH THE FLOW

Read 2 Chronicles 17:3–10

KEY VERSES

The Lord *was with Jehoshaphat, because he walked in the earlier ways of his father David. He did not seek the Baals, but sought the God of his father and walked in his commandments, and not according to the practices of Israel. Therefore the* Lord *established the kingdom in his hand.* 2 Chronicles 17:3–5 esv

UNDERSTAND

- *What is your natural tendency—to go along to get along or to risk offending people with God's truth?*
- *When have your feelings won out over your knowledge of God?*

APPLY

Israel's history is stained with the spiritual affairs God's people had with lesser gods and ways of living—telling Him repeatedly with their hard-hearted actions, "You aren't enough for me; You don't make me happy anymore."

Sadly, they forgot the fear of the Lord. Little by little, they stopped doing the things that promoted healthy respect and awe for God, His Word, and His ways. Infidelity, whether it's marital or spiritual, results from dozens of small decisions that break trust, mixed with all our indulged resentments. Eventually, we'll cross the line, one way or another. Spiritually, the only difference is that God is never at fault. We keep Him at arm's length, acting like we love better or know more about our needs than He does. In the name of pursuing happiness, we forsake righteousness.

To avoid slipping away from God, cultivate your relationship with Him. Consider how Jehoshaphat broke sin's cycle in 2 Chronicles 17: Fear the Lord, seek His ways in His Word, then do them. Don't chase your feelings or go with the flow; what's easy is seldom what's right.

PRAY

Lord, You know if there are any areas in my heart I'm setting aside from You for something lesser. I know that if I'm right with You, I will be able to resolve issues in my other relationships in ways that please and honor You.

IN IT FOR THE GLORY

Read John 17:1–10

KEY VERSES

"Father, the hour has come; glorify your Son that the Son may glorify you, since you have given him authority over all flesh, to give eternal life to all whom you have given him. And this is eternal life, that they know you, the only true God, and Jesus Christ whom you have sent." JOHN 17:1–3 ESV

UNDERSTAND

- *What does the word* glory *make you think of?*
- *Why do you think Jesus was so focused on bringing glory to God and Himself?*

APPLY

When Jesus asked the Father to restore Him to His proper place of glory, He was signaling more than the successful end of His mission on earth. He was also describing our path forward as believers: The Son glorified the Father through His obedience at the cross, and the Father glorified Him in return by raising Him from the dead and restoring Him to heaven. We who believe in Jesus will also be glorified.

Jesus did all He did so God would receive glory. When in John 11:4 (ESV) He raised Lazarus, it was for "the glory of God, so that the Son of God may be glorified through it." And Jesus signaled His own impending death by telling His disciples in John 12:23 (NASB), "The hour has come for the Son of Man to be glorified."

That same glory is ours now, fueling us to do our best to honor God in response to His grace and love. His glory includes the way we honor Him when we suffer, the same way Jesus honored His Father by taking the cup. Your perseverance in hard times and your gratitude in peaceful ones bring Him glory.

PRAY

Father, Son, and Holy Spirit, You alone deserve all glory and honor. It blows my mind that Your plan in saving me was so I could share in Your holy glory. Let everything I think, say, and do today be focused on making Your name great.

DAY 189

HANDLING COMPROMISE

Read 1 Kings 11:1–13

KEY VERSES

In Solomon's old age, they turned his heart to worship other gods instead of being completely faithful to the LORD his God, as his father, David, had been. Solomon worshipped Ashtoreth, the goddess of the Sidonians, and Molech, the detestable god of the Ammonites.

1 KINGS 11:4–5 NLT

UNDERSTAND

- *How do you think Solomon justified marrying women who worshipped false gods? Why did he tolerate their worship of these deities?*
- *How did the writer of 1 Kings characterize Solomon's faithfulness—or lack of faithfulness—to the Lord?*
- *What do the consequences of Solomon's unfaithfulness suggest about the high cost of compromise?*

APPLY

Compromise has a way of sneaking up on a man—one ungodly decision here, one corner cut there—and in time we can find ourselves living a life of repeated compromise over what God tells us is right. Any of us can find ourselves making excuses for our compromise, and we may even convince others that we are right or justified in compromising. But compromising our faithfulness to God will always wear us down over time, and the results may be far worse than we ever could have imagined or intended at the outset.

Complete, uncompromising faithfulness to God may feel like a high standard to hold. It's a commitment to examine yourself and find areas of compromise in your life. When you find areas of compromise, it's best that you confess them to God and ask Him to help you to do better.

You have an opportunity today to examine your life to ensure that you are completely faithful and committed to the Lord. If you've failed, you're in good company. God will be gracious to forgive you, just as He has forgiven so many of His people who have repented for falling into compromise. If you return to God, He will certainly return to you.

PRAY

Thank You, Lord, for Your mercy and forgiveness that lift me up whenever I fail. May You examine my heart and expose any places that are divided or not given wholly to You so that I can serve You and Your people with a single-minded commitment all the days of my life. Amen.

EVEN WHEN YOU DON'T GET IT

Read Isaiah 45:9–12

KEY VERSE

"What sorrow awaits those who argue with their Creator. Does a clay pot argue with its maker? Does the clay dispute with the one who shapes it, saying, 'Stop, you're doing it wrong!' Does the pot exclaim, 'How clumsy can you be?'" ISAIAH 45:9 NLT

UNDERSTAND

- *When have you felt like God let you down or seemed far away when you needed Him?*
- *What is your perspective on that time now? Did God teach you anything about Himself or yourself?*

APPLY

Sometimes we feel like God lets us down. A heartfelt prayer goes unanswered, or we don't like the answer we get—and we double down on what we want, feeling shortchanged, rather than asking if God might have something different for us. In those moments, we forget that faith is about trust.

When disappointed, our default reaction is to make it about us, thinking we know better than God. Even as Christians, our flesh still resists the idea of having a master. Jesus busted us when He asked in Luke 17:9–10 (NLT), "Does the master thank the servant for doing what he was told to do? Of course not. In the same way, when you obey me you should say, 'We are unworthy servants who have simply done our duty.'"

Pursuing God means that when God disappoints you, He is still God to you. No matter what you accomplish in this life, He will always be the boss, and you an unprofitable servant. But by His grace you are a beloved adopted son, freed from depending on worldly outcomes to make you secure and valued. Set your expectations accordingly.

PRAY

Lord God, I admit there are times when I just need to get over myself, especially when it comes to my attitude toward You. Forgive me for giving You lip service while I keep my heart closed to Your holiness. Thank You for being patient to finish what You started with me.

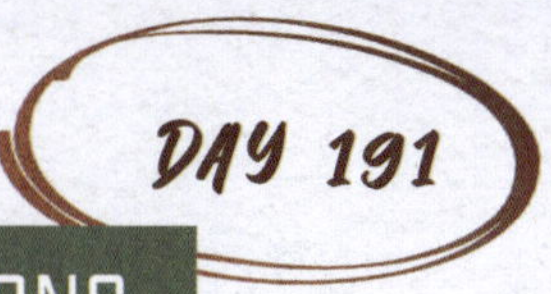

THE RELIABILITY OF TRANSLATIONS

Read 2 Timothy 2:1–15

KEY VERSE

Do your best to present yourself to God as one approved, a worker who has no need to be ashamed, rightly handling the word of truth. 2 TIMOTHY 2:15 ESV

UNDERSTAND

- *Do you think Jesus and the apostles ever read, studied, and memorized Bible verses translated from Hebrew into Greek?*
- *What would it mean if they had?*

APPLY

Throughout the ages, God's people have accepted, valued, created, and used Bible translations to reach the widest possible audiences.

How do you know that Bible translations are trustworthy? Here are four reasons:

1. The apostle Paul affirmed the inspiration of Bible translations (2 Timothy 3:14–17). Paul spoke Hebrew fluently. Still, to effectively communicate to his listeners and readers, he often quoted from the Greek translation of the Old Testament (Acts 13:34; Romans 9:12; 1 Corinthians 2:9).

2. The apostle Peter affirmed the inspiration of Bible translations (2 Peter 1:19–21). Peter probably spoke all three of the original languages of the Bible. Because the Greek translation of the Old Testament was popular in his day, he often quoted from it (Acts 2:17–21; 3:22).

3. Jesus Himself affirmed the eternal nature of the Bible (Matthew 5:17–18), exemplified God's great love for the whole world (John 3:16; 17:20), and often quoted from the Greek translation of the Old Testament (Matthew 9:13; Mark 14:27; Luke 4:12; John 15:25).

4. The apostle John affirmed the eternal nature of the Bible (Revelation 22:18–19), proclaimed God's great love for the whole world (1 John 2:2; Revelation 4:9–10), and often quoted from the Greek translation of the Old Testament (John 12:38; 19:36–37).

There's more!

PRAY

Yes, Lord, I want to say "Thank You!" that I don't have to be ashamed about how I rightly handle the Word of truth. May I sense Your blessing and approval today.

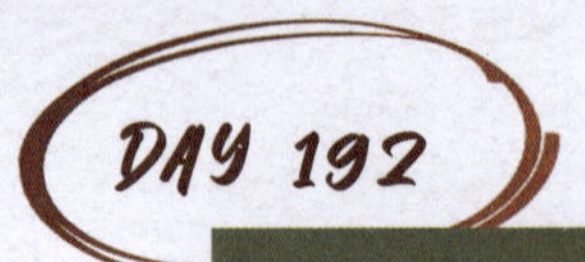

MORE ON THE RELIABILITY OF TRANSLATIONS

Read 2 Timothy 1:1–14

KEY VERSE

Through the power of the Holy Spirit who lives within us, carefully guard the precious truth that has been entrusted to you. 2 TIMOTHY 1:14 NLT

UNDERSTAND

- *Within your extended family tree, going back as far as you can, how many languages were spoken? One? Two? Three?*
- *Within your family today, how many languages are spoken?*

APPLY

Here are four more reasons you can be certain that Bible translations are trustworthy:

5. The apostle Matthew is the only New Testament writer who apparently didn't quote from the Greek translation of the Old Testament. That's because his original audience was predominately Jewish.

6. The early church produced a number of important translations of the Old and New Testaments during the first four centuries after Jesus Christ's ascension: Old Latin, Latin, Syriac, Coptic, Old Nubian, Armenian, Old Georgian, Ethiopic, and Gothic. They used these translations to reach as many people as possible with God's Word. New Christians weren't forced to learn the original Bible languages.

7. To help fulfill Jesus Christ's Great Commission, the church has now translated the Bible or portions of the Bible into more than 2,200 languages. Why? Because less than 0.00001 percent of the people alive today understand the three ancient biblical languages, and more than 85 percent don't understand English fluently. The scriptures are best understood when translated into the reader's (or listener's) native language.

8. Every significant English Bible published within the past generation or two has been translated by an interdenominational team of scores of scholars working from the Hebrew, Aramaic, and Greek texts. They're aided by contemporary literary consultants and by a library of scholarship compiled over the past few centuries.

PRAY

Yes, Lord, I want to say "Thank You!" that I can read my English Bible with confidence in its trustworthiness and sacred truths.

DAY 193

THE RULES OF TRANSLATION

Read John 19:17–22

KEY VERSE

Many of the Jews read this inscription, for the place where Jesus was crucified was near the city, and it was written in Aramaic, in Latin, and in Greek. JOHN 19:20 ESV

UNDERSTAND

- *Do some, many, or all of your favorite sports have carefully articulated rules?*
- *When it comes to Bible translation, why are rules even more important?*

APPLY

Again, almost all Bible translations are trustworthy. That's true in almost every language. Wycliffe Bible Translators has used the following rules for its work around the world:

Based on the best Hebrew and Greek texts. English isn't good enough.

Other than word-for-word. Martin Luther put it this way: "What do the Germans say in such a situation?" In other words, how would the man on the street say it in plain German?

Fastidious in meaning or form. One paraphrase of Revelation 18:22 says, "Never again will the sound of music be there—no more pianos, saxophones, and trumpets" (TLB). Many translators would agree that particular paraphrase crosses the line between biblical facts and sanctified imagination.

Structurally adapted to maintain accuracy. In a number of languages within the Philippines, for example, the phrase "verily, verily" or "truly, truly" is best translated as one word, not two.

Updated regularly as language changes. In the King James Version, 1 Thessalonians 4:15 uses an archaic form of the verb *prevent*. Instead, modern translations use the current form of the verb *precede* to ensure that readers know what Paul is really saying.

Free from any theological biases. The New World Translation twists John 1:1 to say—counter to all grammatical rules in Greek—that Jesus was merely "a god," not God Himself. That's a blatant mistranslation of a key verse in scripture. Thankfully, virtually all major English Bibles are free from such theological errors.

PRAY

Yes, Lord, I want to say "Thank You!" that the Bible or portions of the Bible have been translated into thousands of languages around the world. Almost everyone I know and meet can read Your Word in his mother tongue.

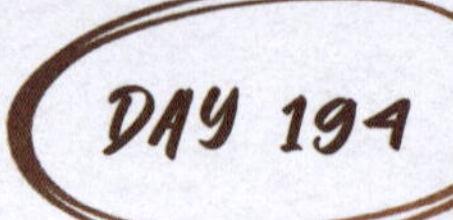

QUESTIONABLE TRANSLATIONS

Read 2 Peter 3:1–18

KEY VERSE

His [Paul's] letters contain some things that are hard to understand, which ignorant and unstable people distort, as they do the other Scriptures, to their own destruction.
2 PETER 3:16 NIV

UNDERSTAND

- *Imagine that two Mormons come to your door. You offer to read their literature if they read the letter to the Romans and then come back. How do you think they will respond?*
- *Imagine that two Jehovah's Witnesses come to your door. You want to study the Gospel of John with them. Which Bible translation do you think you should use?*

APPLY

We don't need to worry about questionable English Bible translations. This may sound counterintuitive, but it's true. Here are four reasons why:

1. They're often the product of an individual, small group, or cult.
2. They're rarely available for sale in Christian bookstores.
3. These questionable translations still contain God's Word. Except for verses in which the translators twisted scripture (say, John 1:1 in the New World Translation), you could read these translations with benefit. While that's not recommended, these translations are still well over 95 percent the inspired Word of God. However, this doesn't excuse the scripture-twisting the translators did in some places.
4. These translations are often highly revered but little read. Many members of these religious communities memorize specific scriptures and do their prescribed Bible studies each week, but they don't actually read the Bible like a book, cover to cover.

So the next time two cult members come knocking on your door, don't be afraid to discuss the scriptures with them. Ask them to open up their Bibles right on the spot. Don't be afraid to read over their shoulders, so to speak. Their questionable Bible translation isn't going to hurt you!

Pray that God will reveal Himself to these individuals through His Word, despite known translation errors.

PRAY

Yes, Lord, I want to say "Thank You!" for this new perspective on using Your Word to reach the men who knock on my door representing unorthodox groups.

DAY 195

THE ONLY RIGHT RESPONSE

Read Romans 11:33–12:2

KEY VERSES

Therefore, I urge you, brothers and sisters, in view of God's mercy, to offer your bodies as a living sacrifice, holy and pleasing to God—this is your true and proper worship. Do not conform to the pattern of this world, but be transformed by the renewing of your mind. Then you will be able to test and approve what God's will is—his good, pleasing and perfect will.
ROMANS 12:1–2 NIV

UNDERSTAND

- *What have you sacrificed to follow Jesus?*
- *How has knowing God transformed the way you think, speak, and act?*

APPLY

Paul opens Romans 12 with *therefore*, an invitation to view what he will say next through the lens of what he just established in Romans 11, where he detailed God's plan for Israel in light of the gospel. His point? God's knowledge and wisdom are deeper than the Mariana Trench. He made everything, holds it together with His will, and His creation sings His praises.

God is who He is: holy and majestic, all-knowing and all-powerful, fully present in every moment and place, good and loving and just. Therefore, the only proper response is to give ourselves completely to Him—to offer our bodies as a living sacrifice.

Knowing Him personally transforms us from death to life, selfish to selfless, judgmental to gracious. Any sacrifice we might make pales next to what He has done, particularly at the cross. And His reward for our total commitment to Him is life to the fullest, now and in eternity.

PRAY

Almighty God, You alone deserve all praise and glory. It is the honor of my life to lay down everything I am and have for Your sake. I forsake my rights, my accomplishments, my dreams so I can realize Your plans for me, which are part of a story that is greater and higher and more wonderful than I can even imagine.

TRUST FALL

Read Proverbs 3:3–6

KEY VERSES

Trust God *from the bottom of your heart; don't try to figure out everything on your own. Listen for* God's *voice in everything you do, everywhere you go; he's the one who will keep you on track.* Proverbs 3:5–6 msg

UNDERSTAND

- *Think of a time when God showed you the right path in His Word.*
- *How often do you seek God in His Word when you face a difficult challenge?*

APPLY

The most dominant philosophy today is this: What you think is true is what matters most. To refute another's claim to what's right or even to ask questions is the same as attacking that person's core identity. The idea of objective truth—facts, ideas, ethics—that holds true for every person in every culture is, to say the least, out of fashion. But God's words never lose their power or relevance, so He defines what matters most.

Trusting God means not leaning on your own understanding. If God made all your paths straight before you ever set out, you wouldn't need to trust Him. The bumps, twists, and turns, the dark alleys and flat tires—these are all chances for you to look to God for wisdom and help. And He will not let you down.

If you aren't regularly reading God's truth and applying it to how you live, the world's views will replace God's wisdom. Let His words change your default setting from self-sufficiency to God-dependency. Trade in the world's lesser gods for the wisdom and guidance of the one true God. Lean into Him; He won't let you fail.

PRAY

*Jesus, You are the Word of God. No one is greater than You. As Peter said in John 6:68 (*amp*), "Lord, to whom shall we go? You [alone] have the words of eternal life [you are our only hope]." I bring my praise, questions, and troubles to You. Lead me in the way I should go.*

CELEBRATING GOD'S POWER AND GOODNESS

Read Exodus 15:1–11

KEY VERSES

Then Moses and the Israelites sang this song to the LORD*: "I will sing to the* LORD*, for he is highly exalted. Both horse and driver he has hurled into the sea. The* LORD *is my strength and my defense; he has become my salvation. He is my God, and I will praise him, my father's God, and I will exalt him."* EXODUS 15:1–2 NIV

UNDERSTAND

- *What emotions do you think the Israelites felt after seeing God sweep away the Egyptian army in the sea?*
- *What details about God are mentioned in today's scripture reading?*
- *How did their view of God change after being delivered from slavery in Egypt and from the Egyptian soldiers on the far side of the sea?*

APPLY

There are moments in life when God shows up in ways that seem more obvious and apparent than others. Although you may have endured long seasons of distance from God, a sudden revelation of His power pulls back the veil between God and you. These are moments to celebrate and to remember.

A moment of revelation or awareness of God may not last forever. The Israelites' challenging years of slavery were soon followed by wandering in the wilderness. Their disobedience and fear prevented them from fully entering into God's rest in a new land.

One way to guard your heart in preparation for the challenging times is to praise God for the good things He has done. Such moments of praise and thanksgiving can make it easier to remember how the Lord has acted in your favor and helps you remain grounded when life becomes difficult. Celebration isn't a frivolous use of your time. It's a vital part of your worship and faith.

PRAY

Thank You, Lord, for the ways You have provided and cared for Your people throughout the years. . .and for the ways You have provided and cared for me. Today I will remember and rejoice in Your provision and kindness toward me, trusting that You will never fail me. Amen.

GOOD TROUBLE

Read John 5:24-30

KEY VERSE

"I can of Myself do nothing. As I hear, I judge; and My judgment is righteous, because I do not seek My own will but the will of the Father who sent Me." JOHN 5:30 NKJV

UNDERSTAND

- *Have you ever gotten in trouble for doing the right thing?*
- *Based on Jesus' interactions with people, what matters most to God?*

APPLY

Jesus made trouble. He tipped apple carts (and temple tables) regularly, rolling everyone's rotten fruit right out in their paths. He claimed that sin, evil, and hell were real, along with other divisive claims, and He owned it in Luke 12:51 (NKJV): "Do you suppose that I came to give peace on earth? I tell you, not at all, but rather division."

If we want to truly know Jesus, we must accept all of Him—not just the love and mercy but the unrelenting zeal for God's glory and the disquieting holiness of His words and claims. Jesus fully represents God, both the grace and the wrath, the stunning humility required to save us and the unswerving confidence that His judgment is just. We can't pick and choose with Jesus.

We want to live up to Jesus' high expectations because He saved us, not so we can be saved. That means we can do what's right, enjoying the fruits and enduring persecution because we know our salvation doesn't depend on it. We are free to speak truth lovingly and to love truthfully. That is God's will, expressed perfectly in Jesus. If we can limit our offenses to the gospel, we'll still get in trouble—but it will be the good kind.

PRAY

Jesus, You met Your own holy requirements—fully God and fully man, a perfect, spotless sacrifice—and gave Your life for mine. Thank You for showing God's gracious and patient heart through all You said and did. I hear Your voice and I am Yours. Help me to represent You well to others.

GOD HAS PROTECTED HIS WORD

Read Psalm 119:89–105

KEY VERSE

Forever, O Lord, your word is firmly fixed in the heavens. Psalm 119:89 ESV

UNDERSTAND

- *If the Lord could but speak and create the entire universe, is anything too hard for Him?*
- *What about safeguarding the Bible in human hands here on earth?*

APPLY

God has carefully protected the Bible. How do we know that? Here are eight reasons:

1. God Himself promises that scripture is completely true and trustworthy (Psalm 19:7; 33:4; 119:42). He wants us to take it seriously!
2. Today's key verse affirms that scripture is eternal (Psalm 119:89). Unlike the world's fads, which come and go, God's Word has endured the test of time.
3. The greatest Old Testament prophet after Moses and a leading apostle of Jesus Christ both affirmed that scripture stands forever (Isaiah 40:8; 1 Peter 1:23–25).
4. Jesus Himself promised that scripture will remain until its purpose is achieved (Matthew 5:18). Nothing will be lost before the end of time.
5. The first prophet and the last apostle both issued harsh warnings to anyone who dared tamper with scripture (Deuteronomy 4:2; Revelation 22:18–19; see also Proverbs 30:6).
6. The discovery of the Dead Sea Scrolls confirms the remarkable accuracy of the transmission of the Old Testament over thousands of years.
7. The wealth of manuscripts dating back to the first century AD confirms the text of the New Testament beyond any shadow of a doubt.
8. Every critic's claim to have found a supposed "error" in scripture has been discredited without exception for the past four centuries. That's a remarkable track record!

PRAY

Yes, Lord, I want to say "Thank You!" that You have protected Your Word and still use it with great power and effectiveness today.

PERFORMANCE ANXIETY

Read Isaiah 58:1–14

KEY VERSES

"This is the kind of fast day I'm after: to break the chains of injustice, get rid of exploitation in the workplace, free the oppressed, cancel debts. What I'm interested in seeing you do is: sharing your food with the hungry, inviting the homeless poor into your homes, putting clothes on the shivering ill-clad, being available to your own families." ISAIAH 58:6–7 MSG

UNDERSTAND

- *What do you think the purpose of fasting is?*
- *Do you ever catch yourself performing like a Bible-believing Christian instead of just being one?*

APPLY

God's message in Isaiah 58 criticizes those who act in ways that seem religious but completely miss the point. Fasting and praying, for instance, should lead to compassionate behavior toward others for their good, not "Hey, look how super holy I am, everyone!"

Performance is often a protective mechanism. Church can be the most judgmental place on earth. Everyone goes through hard times, but when we get to church, the masks go up. Any problems get back-burnered in the one place they should be safest to discuss, where grace and loving truth are supposed to be our calling cards. To love like Jesus does is to accept that everyone struggles, even us. We own our shortcomings, give them up to God, forgive and seek forgiveness, and then show His grace to others.

Then when we pursue God through fasting and prayer, we'll hear God clarify who He is, which helps us know what we should do and how we should love others. When what He thinks matters most, then we will find our joy in Him and He will guide, protect, provide, and prepare us for His good work—no faking required.

PRAY

Lord, I want to honor You in everything I do. Forgive me for the times I've slipped into acting like a good Christian instead of just being one. I want to use everything You have given me for Your glory, not mine.

DAY 201

KNOW YOUR END-TIMES STUFF

Read Luke 21:5–38

KEY VERSES

"Watch out! Don't let your hearts be dulled by carousing and drunkenness, and by the worries of this life. Don't let that day catch you unaware, like a trap. For that day will come upon everyone living on the earth. Keep alert at all times. And pray that you might be strong enough to escape these coming horrors and stand before the Son of Man."

LUKE 21:34–36 NLT

UNDERSTAND

- *How well do you understand the biblical conditions for the end times?*
- *Does waiting for Jesus to return make you want to check out and wait or engage more fully in His work?*

APPLY

The end times are always a hot topic, both in and out of the church. We know Jesus is coming back and will fix everything when He does—pause for a hallelujah!—but when? How long, Lord?

In Luke 21, Jesus offers a number of predictions about the end times. Some of them have already been fulfilled, and others describe pre-fulfillments—wars, uprisings, false messiahs, persecution for believers—that are only signs of similar, greater-scale conflicts that will come at the end of days.

The details Jesus spoke of are well worth studying if only because He told us to in Revelation 1:3. Every generation has had reason to believe the last days are at hand. This one is no different—although, seriously, this could be it! But just as important as knowing about the last days is living in light of them. Make each day count while this age of grace lasts.

PRAY

Father, as I look at the madness of the world, help me fight the desire to check out. I want to be able to speak Your truth in a world where people are losing hope. Give me the strength to stay engaged and involved in the sphere of influence You have given me. Come soon, Lord Jesus!

JOY AND MOURNING CAN COEXIST

Read Ezra 3:8–13

KEY VERSES

When the builders laid the foundation of the temple of the Lord, *the priests in their vestments were stationed to praise the* Lord *with trumpets, and the Levites, the sons of Asaph, with cymbals, according to the directions of King David of Israel; and they sang responsively, praising and giving thanks to the* Lord, *"For he is good, for his steadfast love endures forever toward Israel."* Ezra 3:10–11 NRSV

UNDERSTAND

- *What was the significance of rebuilding the temple after the people began returning from the Babylonian exile?*
- *What do you think it was like to sing praises to God while standing around the rubble of the former temple and former city walls?*
- *Why do you think it was so important for the people to praise God at the beginning of the temple work?*

APPLY

Ezra records that the people shouted both for joy and in mourning when they saw the second temple's foundation. Mourning and joy often go together—like when a joyous family gathering reminds you of a lost loved one. . .or when the start of a new venture also means the end of a previous task that felt like the perfect fit. You can both thank God and mourn your losses at the same time—in fact, your spiritual and emotional health may depend on it!

A simple examination of what you're thankful for and what's causing you to struggle can help you take stock of the emotions at play in the present moment. Perhaps you're in a season of thankfulness and healing, seeing many struggles come to a happy resolution.

Then again, you may be facing a lot of pain and uncertainty, which makes it hard to rejoice. You can still mourn what has been lost while appreciating the good things you have in the present. In fact, the longer you deny the pain that weighs on your mind, the harder it will be to fully enjoy the good things coming in your life.

PRAY

Thank You, Lord, that You have compassion on those who mourn and that You want to turn our mourning into gladness. I ask for comfort for my own sorrow—and for the sorrows of others—and thank You for Your provision for those who seek You with thankful hearts. Amen.

PEACE IN TROUBLED TIMES

Read Habakkuk 3:17–19

KEY VERSES

Though the fig tree may not blossom, nor fruit be on the vines; though the labor of the olive may fail, and the fields yield no food; though the flock may be cut off from the fold, and there be no herd in the stalls—yet I will rejoice in the Lord*, I will joy in the God of my salvation.* Habakkuk 3:17–18 nkjv

UNDERSTAND

- *What are your hardest struggles today?*
- *Think of God's track record with you. How has He delivered you in the past?*

APPLY

When you read Habakkuk's description of his hard times, try to put it in terms of the challenges you're facing—with your marriage, job, or kids, for example. How do you say that last line and mean it? When nothing good is happening in your life, how do you get in touch with God's goodness?

In Habakkuk 3:2 (amp), the prophet said, "O Lord, I have heard the report about You and I fear. O Lord, revive Your work in the midst of the years." He remembered what God had done in His history with Israel, bringing blessing and, when needed, judgment to bring repentance and restoration. God doesn't forget or abandon His people, no matter how bleak their outlook seems. You are not alone, and you never will be.

When Jesus said He is the bread of life, He meant that He alone could satisfy our deepest needs—deeper than job satisfaction, than fulfilling human relationships, than hunger itself. Though your situation may be dire, He will lift your head in expectation of what He will do.

PRAY

God, I confess that I often expect You to answer my prayers my way. Help me to leave room for You to answer them Your way. You know everything, You are faithful, and You are working all things together for my good and Your glory. I trust You with my troubles.

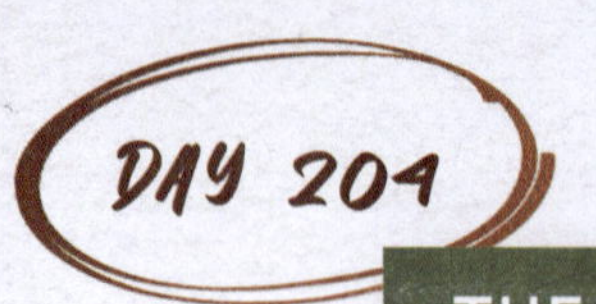

THE BIBLE'S SELECTIVE REPORTING

Read John 20:30–21:25

KEY VERSE

Jesus performed many other signs in the presence of his disciples, which are not recorded in this book. John 20:30 NIV

UNDERSTAND

- *Imagine that the Yankees and Red Sox just split a doubleheader. How similarly or differently will the games be reported in Boston and New York?*
- *Imagine the Seahawks just beat the 49ers with a last-second field goal. How will the news differ up and down the West Coast?*

APPLY

When it comes to addressing apparent Bible contradictions, perhaps it would be best to start with the basic principles of journalism. These include seeking answers to six key journalism questions: *Who? What? When? Where? Why?* and *How?*

Any journalist worth his salt will compile far more facts than can be reported in an article and then use the principle of selectivity to report only the facts deemed most relevant to the intended readers. As a result, a news story about an NBA game will sound far different in the guest team's hometown than in the home team's. Same game, same hundreds or thousands of facts—but a different audience!

The same principle of selectivity applies to scripture. Moses didn't write down everything that happened in Adam's life. Far from it. He recorded only what God said was relevant.

The same is true when John wrote his Gospel. He wasn't trying to write *The Exhaustive Life of Jesus Christ.* Instead, he admitted, "Jesus did many other things as well. If every one of them were written down, I suppose that even the whole world would not have room for the books that would be written" (John 21:25 NIV).

In other words, John selected only those events, miracles, interviews, teachings, prayers, persecutions, and sufferings that best communicated the gospel message to his intended audience. The other three Gospel writers did the same. All the better for us!

PRAY

Yes, Lord, I want to say "Thank You!" for how professional sports help me better understand the selective reporting of the biblical writers.

WHEN THE CRITICS COME

Read 1 John 1:5–10

KEY VERSE

If we confess our sins, He is faithful and just to forgive us our sins and to cleanse us from all unrighteousness. 1 JOHN 1:9 NKJV

UNDERSTAND

- *What is your typical first reaction to criticism?*
- *Reread 1 John 1:8–10. What do you have in common with all critics, regardless of their intention or accuracy?*

APPLY

It's hard to admit you're wrong. No one likes being criticized. Whether the comment has merit or not, it feels unfair and unjust. You're busy enough trying to do your best without these stings and arrows. So how do you deal with criticism?

First, you have to ask the right question—which isn't *Why am I being attacked?* but *Why does this attack bug me so much?* Whenever those irritable feelings crop up and make you mad, you are reacting out of pride, as 1 John 1:8 suggests. You can't control the other person's attack, but you can mind your response. And the best way to do that is to go plank-eye with the criticism (Matthew 7:3), checking yourself to see if there's even a sliver of truth. You might, for instance, have been criticized because you made a good point with a graceless tone.

It's also possible, especially with a critic who doesn't know you, that you're being criticized for a view you don't hold. But even if the critic is totally wrong, you have to go back to times you've spoken imperfectly, carelessly, and hastily and let that humble you toward grace and prayer. Remember, confession and forgiveness apply to you first.

PRAY

Father, forgive me for bristling at criticism and resorting to counterproductive reactions. Help me to seek to convince others without condemning them, to build them up instead of knocking them down. I am so grateful that when I confess my sins, You are faithful to forgive me and set me back on Your path of righteousness.

LIFTED UP IN THE CHAOS

Read Isaiah 40:27–31

KEY VERSES

Even youths shall faint and be weary, and young men shall fall exhausted; but they who wait for the Lord *shall renew their strength; they shall mount up with wings like eagles; they shall run and not be weary; they shall walk and not faint.* Isaiah 40:30–31 ESV

UNDERSTAND

- *What do you do when you feel worn out by the world?*
- *When you read Isaiah 40, what stands out to you about God?*

APPLY

The first thirty-nine chapters of Isaiah center on God confronting Israel for trusting in kings and nations rather than their true King, God Himself. So it's a refreshing surprise when Isaiah 40:1 (NKJV) shifts gears: "'Comfort, yes, comfort My people!' says your God." He chastens His people for their own good, but He also redeems His people from their trouble.

In verse 3 (NKJV), Isaiah predicts the coming of Christ—the focal point of redemptive history, heralded by John the Baptist: "The voice of one crying in the wilderness: 'Prepare the way of the Lord; make straight in the desert a highway for our God.'" And in verse 4, God's healing methods are poetically described—valleys lifted up, mountains brought low, crooked places straightened, and rough ground leveled—forecasting the miraculous work Jesus did in His ministry to bring redemption, restoration, and holiness.

In this chaotic, selfish world, we must not lose hope. God is aware of the injustices we have done and those done to us, and He is setting them right. When the world exhausts you, when you're sick of the sin still evident in you, don't give up. God has more than enough power to lift you up.

PRAY

Almighty God, faithful and true, You deserve all the praise and thanks. The world surrounds me, overwhelms me with cruelty and chaos and conflict—but You are making all things new, starting with me. You are my strength and shield, my hope, and all I truly want or need.

DAY 207

OBEDIENCE REQUIRES RISK

Read Psalm 106:24–31

KEY VERSES

The people refused to enter the pleasant land, for they wouldn't believe his promise to care for them. Instead, they grumbled in their tents and refused to obey the LORD.
PSALM 106:24–25 NLT

UNDERSTAND

- *If the Promised Land was such a "pleasant" place, why did the Israelites resist entering the land?*
- *How did the Israelites' thoughts about God prompt them to grumble?*
- *What does this passage suggest about the challenges of obeying God's commands?*

APPLY

God can lead you on many paths toward blessings and joy, but it's often likely that the paths toward those blessings and joy will be difficult—and some may even appear dangerous. Receiving God's blessings often requires risk and sacrifice, and it may mean leaving the comfort of what you know behind and reaching out for His next new thing with open hands.

When you resist the high risks and high rewards of seeking God's blessings, you place yourself in opposition to Him. The more you grumble and complain against God's direction in your life, the more you alienate yourself from Him.

In the case of the Israelites in the wilderness, it took the courageous intervention of the priest Phinehas going against the trends of the time. Such advocates and spiritual guides will be essential for your own perseverance. Look for people who are both dedicated to God's will and capable of speaking the truth courageously.

PRAY

Thank You, Lord, for Your kindness to provide for Your people, just as You once led Your people to the Promised Land. May I look to You in faith and take courage to obey Your commands. The risks are numerous, but reaching Your blessings is well worth the challenge. Amen.

ON EQUAL FOOTING

Read Galatians 3:26–29

KEY VERSE

There is neither Jew nor Greek, there is neither slave nor free, there is neither male nor female; for you are all one in Christ Jesus. GALATIANS 3:28 NKJV

UNDERSTAND

- *What types of people or situations tempt you to have an attitude of superiority?*
- *How does the knowledge that all people stand equally before God affect your treatment of others?*

APPLY

Everyone longs to be loved and highly valued. We have these desires because we're made in God's image; therefore, only He can meet them. Our sinful tendency is to think we know better than our Maker what is best for us. But our best thoughts should turn us toward God, not from Him.

When we reject God, we can no longer see His truth, beauty, or goodness. Without His protective boundaries and limits, anything is possible—and that's not good. Any earthly minded institution or philosophy moves us not toward freedom from what truly shackles us—sin and its consequences—but *from* accountability *to* a power higher than ourselves.

Both religion and secular humanism give false context and misinterpreted facts to justify judgmentalism and segregation. The horrors that result from putting this belief into action—racism, genocide, terrorism, war, and eugenics, among others—offer a foretaste of hell.

Before God, we are all equal. Nothing distinguishes us from each other or makes us worthy of His presence—not race, religion, or sex; not social class, cultural status, or political power. We have no justification to think we're better than anyone else. The true freedom that Christ brings is about relationship, and it is for all of us, as is His command to love others as He loves us.

PRAY

Lord Jesus, You have set us all on equal footing before the cross. Help me to embrace all who want to receive You as brothers and sisters, and give me Your heart's desire to make our family as big as possible.

DAY 209

THE BIBLE IS ROOTED IN HISTORY

Read Acts 2:14–41

KEY VERSE

"Let all the house of Israel therefore know for certain that God has made him both Lord and Christ, this Jesus whom you crucified." Acts 2:36 ESV

UNDERSTAND

- *After His resurrection, Jesus appeared to His disciples for forty days and then ascended back to heaven. Their initial fear gave way to boldness and courage rarely seen in human history. These men were ready to give their lives. What made such a radical change in their hearts and minds?*
- *Ten days after Jesus ascended, Peter boldly preached the gospel to thousands of people. To what did he appeal? To the Hebrew scriptures, yes. What else?*

APPLY

The biblical writers often took the time to describe the historical accuracy of their writings. Here are a few brief examples from the New Testament:

- *Luke anchored the main narrative section of his Gospel on a solid group of authenticating historical reference points (Luke 3:1–2).*
- *John verified the actual physical death of Jesus Christ by reminding his readers that he was an eyewitness of Jesus' final moments on the cross (John 19:34–35).*
- *Peter appealed to the knowledge of the crowd when he talked about Jesus Christ on the Day of Pentecost (Acts 2:22). If he had been fabricating a story, he would have received a far different response at the end of his sermon.*
- *Paul appealed to the knowledge of King Agrippa as he talked about Jesus Christ (Acts 26:26). Jesus Christ and His disciples hadn't performed miracles in some obscure corner—everyone knew about them.*
- *Paul said that to deny the possibility of someone's rising from the dead was to deny the obvious historical fact of Jesus Christ's resurrection (1 Corinthians 15:1–8).*
- *Peter rightfully claimed to have been an eyewitness of one of Jesus Christ's most glorious miracles—the Transfiguration (2 Peter 1:16–18).*
- *John reminded the early Christians toward the end of the first century that he and others had repeatedly touched Jesus Christ (1 John 1:1–3). Think elbow and fist bumps, hands on the shoulder, and slaps on the back.*

PRAY

Yes, Lord, I want to say "Thank You!" that Judaism and Christianity are rooted in history. That's so different from other world religions.

THE BIBLE AND SCIENCE

Read Romans 1:16–23

KEY VERSE

For since the creation of the world God's invisible qualities—his eternal power and divine nature—have been clearly seen, being understood from what has been made, so that people are without excuse. ROMANS 1:20 NIV

UNDERSTAND

- *Did you know that the ancient Chinese, Indians, Mesopotamians, Babylonians, Egyptians, Greeks, and Romans celebrated (and sometimes weaponized) scientific discoveries?*
- *Did you know these ancient civilizations developed the empirical (scientific) method, geometry, advanced mathematics, astronomy, atomism, deductive reasoning, physics, and much more?*

APPLY

Some critics have argued that the Bible contains scientific errors. They claim scripture incorrectly speaks of the sun "going down" (see Ephesians 4:26). They gleefully point out that Galileo discredited this concept centuries ago. Despite the critics' claims, however, the idea of the sun "going down" is still part of the English language. Almost everyone loves to watch a spectacular sunrise or sunset. Every day news agencies across the country list the times for the sun to come up and go down.

Other scientific "problems" include these two false ideas:

1. *The Bible can't be proven scientifically.* The problem is a matter of confusion on the part of the critics. The scientific method is a very limited test. It can't prove historical facts (Abraham Lincoln was president of the United States), musical standards (Mozart was a brilliant composer), tenets of faith (Jesus Christ is God's Son), or matters of the heart (you love your family).

2. *The uniformity of nature makes supernatural intervention (miracles) impossible.* Of course these critics are leaving God out of their picture! If God *is* God, He can do whatever He wants—even supersede the principles governing His creation. Besides, the scientific theory of the universe as an absolutely uniform system is more than half a century out of date.

PRAY

Yes, Lord, I want to say "Thank You!" that the Bible's supposed scientific errors are themselves in error. Yes, I know the Bible isn't a science textbook. I know it uses figures of speech. Still, I can trust it cover to cover.

THE BIBLE'S HARMONY WITH SCIENCE

Read Psalm 19:1–6

KEY VERSE

The heavens declare the glory of God, and the sky above proclaims his handiwork.
PSALM 19:1 ESV

UNDERSTAND

- *Scientific discoveries birth more discoveries. Sometimes new discoveries correct faulty ideas. Is this good or bad?*
- *We still don't know how many hundreds of billions of stars are in our galaxy alone. Estimates vary by up to a third of a trillion stars. Is this good or bad?*

APPLY

Even though the Bible isn't a science textbook, its scientific descriptions contain no real problems. In fact, many of its statements, though contrary to scientific thought at the time, have long since been proven true. Here are four examples:

1. Many hundreds of years before the theory of the circulation of blood within the body was even proposed, the Bible proclaimed that life is in our blood (Genesis 9:4).
2. Ancient civilizations commonly believed the Earth was held in place by some support such as a large reptile's back or a set of pillars. But Job 26:7 (NKJV) declares, "He [God] stretches out the north over empty space; He hangs the earth on nothing."
3. The Greek astronomer Hipparchus (c. 190–120 BC) confidently stated, "There are only 1,056 stars in the heavens. I have counted them." In the second century AD, Ptolemy counted 1,056 and agreed that no others existed. Yet Jeremiah 33:22 (NKJV) insists, "The host [stars] of heaven cannot be numbered." Not until AD 1610 did Galileo look through a telescope and prove the Bible right.
4. On a clear night, many of the stars that appear in the sky look alike. Modern astronomers have photographed millions, however, and found that no two are identical. Paul spoke about this nearly two thousand years ago: "One star differs from another star in glory" (1 Corinthians 15:41 NKJV).

PRAY

Yes, Lord, I want to say "Thank You!" for reminding me that the Bible is in harmony with important scientific truths.

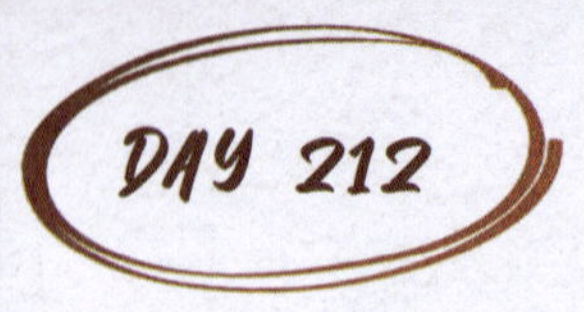

THE PROBLEM OF EVIL

Read Isaiah 59:1–3, 16–21

KEY VERSES

The Lord's hand is not shortened, that it cannot save; nor His ear heavy, that it cannot hear. But your iniquities have separated you from your God; and your sins have hidden His face from you, so that He will not hear. Isaiah 59:1–2 NKJV

UNDERSTAND

- *How would you answer this question: "If God is good, all-powerful, and all-knowing, why does evil exist?"*
- *When you're facing hard times, what are your go-to Bible verses for comfort and strength?*

APPLY

Isaiah 59 touches on one of the biggest problems in theology: the problem of evil. If God is good, all-powerful, and all-knowing, how can human suffering exist? Because the level of human suffering remains as high as it's ever been, many people respond by reasoning that God must not be everything the Bible says He is.

The result is thinking that while God is all-loving, He is not all-powerful (or vice-versa); He wants to help us when we're in trouble, but He can't. Isaiah 59:1 (NLT) responds to such an idea, "The Lord's arm is not too weak to save you." And to the suggestion that God isn't aware of or interested in our troubles, Isaiah 59:1 (NASB) says, "Nor is His ear so dull that it cannot hear." God permitting evil isn't the same as God producing evil. In fact, His permission must mean He has some purpose in allowing it.

Only in Jesus Christ do we have a chance of understanding that purpose. While His crucifixion was the greatest moral evil ever committed (a truly perfect, innocent man unjustly condemned), His resurrection made the greatest moral good possible: deliverance from evil for all who believe in Him.

PRAY

Heavenly Father and Almighty God, in Jesus Christ, You have solved the problem of evil by breaking sin's hold on my heart. You have overcome the world, and Your peace and strength steady me in these wicked days.

READY FOR WAR

Read Ephesians 6:10–18

KEY VERSE

A final word: Be strong in the Lord and in his mighty power. EPHESIANS 6:10 NLT

UNDERSTAND

- *What is your attitude about spiritual warfare? Who is it for? What is the nature of it?*
- *What is your tendency regarding Satan—to make too little of him or too much?*

APPLY

Start with the biblical facts: Satan is a real, personal spirit, evil and intent on ruining your life because God loves you. Spiritual warfare is just as real as physical battle. Paul made no bones about it in Ephesians 6:10–18, clearly defining both the nature of spiritual warfare and the protection God has provided so we can fight.

Jesus blesses you because you are unified with Him. Naturally (and supernaturally), Satan attacks you at that point of unity, seeking to disrupt your connection to those blessings—the power of redemption, forgiveness, kindness, and the other fruit of the Spirit. He wants to cut you off from a full view of Jesus, and he wins when he neutralizes you through ignorance and apathy.

God has won the war against Satan, but spiritual battles continue for your growth and God's glory. When you claim the name of Christ, you enter the fray, but He has given you all you need to resist the devil and stand.

Your tour of duty will end someday, so spend your shift on alert for the enemy's movements. Like Paul in 2 Timothy 4:7 (ESV), your goal is to be able to say "I have fought the good fight, I have finished the race, I have kept the faith."

PRAY

Lord Jesus, Almighty God, You are my commander in chief, the general of heaven's armies, and the victor over sin, death, and hell. I have entrusted myself to You: spirit, body, and soul. Arm me with Your power to withstand the devil's fiery darts so that I can grow to be more like You and bring glory to Your name.

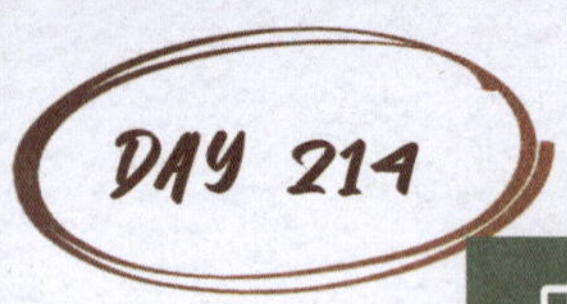

GOD LONGS FOR YOUR RETURN

Read Zechariah 1:1–6

KEY VERSES

"Therefore tell the people: This is what the LORD Almighty says: 'Return to me,' declares the LORD Almighty, 'and I will return to you,' says the LORD Almighty. Do not be like your ancestors, to whom the earlier prophets proclaimed: This is what the LORD Almighty says: 'Turn from your evil ways and your evil practices.' But they would not listen or pay attention to me, declares the LORD." ZECHARIAH 1:3–4 NIV

UNDERSTAND

- *What is the significance of this passage in light of God's people being exiled?*
- *What does God want His people to learn from past generations?*
- *Why is it so important for the people to make the first step toward returning to God?*

APPLY

Take a moment today to think about how your failures or bad life choices have come between you and God. These could be in your distant past, or they could have happened yesterday. Think of the burdens you have carried that have led to feelings of shame and isolation from God.

Much like God sought out Adam and Eve hiding in the garden, He sought out the people of Judah while they were in exile in Babylon. He reaches out to you today in the same way. The choice you make to return to God is all that you need to do in order to start again.

God is ready and willing to extend forgiveness and restoration to you, and He invites you to take that first step by returning to Him. Past generations have missed out on God's mercy and offer of restoration, but you have an opportunity today to reunite yourself with a merciful and kind God who longs for your return.

PRAY

Thank You, Lord, that Your mercy and forgiveness overcome my greatest failures and deepest shame. Help me to learn from the mistakes of past generations who rejected Your mercy. May I make a definitive choice to return to You with an open heart and a teachable mind. Amen.

ENGAGING THE PSALMS

Read Psalm 1

KEY VERSES

Blessed is the person who does not walk in the counsel of the wicked, nor stand in the path of sinners, nor sit in the seat of scoffers! But his delight is in the Law of the Lord, *and on His Law he meditates day and night.* Psalm 1:1–2 NASB

UNDERSTAND

- *What are the three things a person needs to avoid to be blessed?*
- *What does a wise person choose to focus on?*
- *What habit arises from delighting in God's Word?*

APPLY

The middle of the Old Testament contains what is called "wisdom literature." Job is an epic poem about suffering and God's sovereignty. Proverbs is a collection of sayings of and about wisdom. Ecclesiastes is a memoir of the meaninglessness of life apart from God. And then there's the book of Psalms—literally a catalog of songs that cover virtually every human emotion possible. Joyful? Terrified? Hopeful? Angry? Confused? Thankful? You'll find it in Psalms.

Songs (and poetry) have always been a way to express the range of the human experience, putting feelings into words that resonate with the listener. King David was a prolific psalmist, but about half the book is authored by others—the sons of Korah, Asaph, and even Moses.

Why is a song catalog *wisdom* literature? Because the wise man expresses himself honestly. He takes his complaints and troubles to a God who loves him since He is the source of hope and rescue. He trumpets his thanks and praise to the one who deserves adoration. And in being open about his own life, the psalmist teaches others to walk in wisdom, not to be influenced by the *wicked*, the *sinner*, or the *scoffer*. The Psalms confirm God's goodness, love, and sovereign wisdom without dismissing the hardships, sin, and injustice of this world.

PRAY

I will sing of Your goodness, O God, and confess what's on my heart to You. You are my life and my hope.

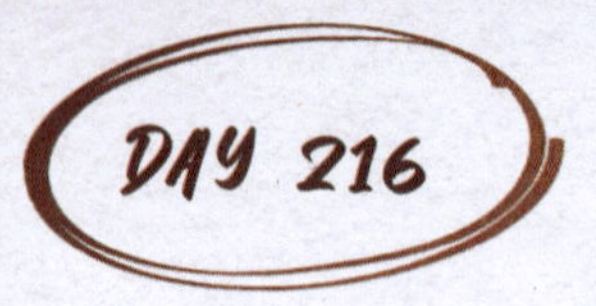

MEDITATING

Read Psalm 119:9–16

KEY VERSES

I rejoice in following your statutes as one rejoices in great riches. I meditate on your precepts and consider your ways. I delight in your decrees; I will not neglect your word.
Psalm 119:14–16 NIV

UNDERSTAND

- *What three words does the psalmist use to describe God's Word?*
- *What does the psalmist declare he will do with God's Word?*

APPLY

As believers, we are right to rejoice that we are "not under law, but under grace" (Romans 6:14 NIV). But being *under law* didn't mean that the precepts and statutes of God were bad. On the contrary, Paul said, "For we know that the law is spiritual, but I am of the flesh, sold under sin" (Romans 7:14 ESV). The problem lies with us, and the law's purpose was to make that clear. The longest psalm in the Bible is an acrostic poem (each section of eight lines begins with the same letter of the Hebrew alphabet) that praises God for His *statutes*, *precepts*, and *decrees*.

As we've seen, the blessed man "meditates" on God's law day and night (Psalm 1:2). Deeper Bible study requires meditation—not the kind that empties the mind, but the opposite. After Moses' death, God commanded Joshua, "Keep this Book of the Law always on your lips; *meditate on it day and night*, so that you may be careful to do everything written in it" (Joshua 1:8 NIV, emphasis added). Meditating means chewing on a verse or passage thoughtfully, like you might savor a bite of steak. It means camping out on a passage for a while, perhaps committing it to memory. Maybe a verse from this study keeps coming to mind, or the Spirit had impressed you with something Paul wrote. Just like that steak, start with one bite at a time, and see what God shows you as you chew on it.

PRAY

With the psalmist, I rejoice in the riches of Your Word, O Lord my God!

THE BIBLE'S CLEAR MORALITY

Read Jude 1–25

KEY VERSE

But these people scoff at things they do not understand. Like unthinking animals, they do whatever their instincts tell them, and so they bring about their own destruction.
JUDE 10 NLT

UNDERSTAND

- *Early Christians were often martyred for their unbending faith in Jesus Christ. Was this good or bad?*
- *Then again, few early Christians were willing to be martyred in protest of infanticide, let alone gladiator fights to the death and other gruesome blood sports. Was this good or bad?*

APPLY

Some critics have argued that the Bible contains moral errors. They claim that Jesus and His disciples violated one of the Ten Commandments by working on the Sabbath. Did they? In Matthew 12:1–2, the Pharisees emphatically said yes. According to their list of rules, someone was "working" if he walked through a field when the heads of grain were mature. Yet their rule went far beyond anything the Old Testament actually said. In fact, Deuteronomy 23:25 says someone could pick grain from someone else's field if he was hungry. Jesus said He came to fulfill the law (Matthew 5:17), but He had little patience for those who oppressed the multitudes with all their man-made regulations.

Other moral "problems" include these two dubious criticisms:

1. *The Bible is full of sex and violence.* It's true that the Bible doesn't gloss over the violent and sometimes lustful lives of the people it mentions. Yet the Bible's purpose isn't to provide crude entertainment but to provide clear examples of what honors God—and what doesn't.
2. *The Bible is often offensive.* It's true that the Bible speaks of God's ultimate judgment against wrongdoers and provides many examples of His judgment here on earth. The real moral problem, however, resides not with the Lord or His Word but with those who would set themselves up as judges of either.

PRAY

Yes, Lord, I want to say "Thank You!" for the intrinsic, bedrock morality of Your Word, which reminds me daily of Your absolute holiness, righteousness, and justice.

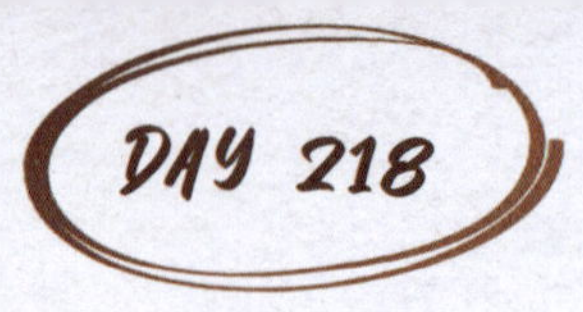

WILLING OBEDIENCE

Read Psalm 32

KEY VERSES

I will instruct you and teach you in the way which you should go; I will advise you with My eye upon you. Do not be like the horse or like the mule, which have no understanding, whose trappings include bit and bridle to hold them in check, otherwise they will not come near to you. PSALM 32:8–9 NASB

UNDERSTAND

- *What promises does God make in this verse?*
- *What does He warn us about?*
- *What characterizes a horse or mule that might apply to us?*

APPLY

A student of scripture is only as wise as his willingness to take what he learns to heart. As we've seen, wisdom abides in the inner man, which leads to right living because we are growing in our knowledge of God as we are "conformed to the image of His Son" (Romans 8:29 NASB). Sounds simple, right? But we all know from experience that we sometimes resist God.

The beginning of Psalm 32 points to one possible problem: unconfessed sin. We can't harbor known iniquity without creating conflict with a God who has a different plan for us: "When I kept silent, my bones wasted away. . . . Day and night your hand was heavy on me" (Psalm 32:3–4 NIV).

But what if there's truly nothing to confess? Perhaps there's a different heart issue. James instructed some believers to "purify your hearts, for your loyalty is divided between God and the world" (James 4:8 NLT). Growing in wisdom means we face choices—but we're not alone. God Himself is the one instructing us *with His eye upon us*—not to catch us in wrongdoing, but to strengthen us to draw near. We are to participate willingly, not require "bit and bridle" to pull us along like a horse or mule. What good would that be to us or our Father?

PRAY

Patient Father, thank You for drawing me closer; teach me to cooperate!

THE DAYS WE ARE GRANTED

Read Psalm 90

KEY VERSE

So teach us to number our days, that we may present to You a heart of wisdom.
Psalm 90:12 NASB

UNDERSTAND

- *How many days have you already lived?*
- *How many more days do you hope to live?*
- *What is the goal of seeing ourselves as finite creatures?*

APPLY

Accounting for race, ethnicity, and lifestyle decisions, the average lifespan of an American male is about seventy-six years, or 27,758 days. Psalm 90, the only psalm directly attributed to Moses, describes a similar average lifespan: "The years of our life are seventy, or even by reason of strength eighty; yet their span is but toil and trouble; they are soon gone, and we fly away" (Psalm 90:10 ESV).

Moses, who himself lived to 120, was making a pointed statement: No matter how long we live, compared to the Ancient of Days, for whom a thousand years are "as yesterday when it is past, or as a watch in the night" (Psalm 90:4 ESV), our days are obviously limited.

James expressed a similar sentiment when he warned those who presumed upon the future, saying, "You do not know what tomorrow will bring. What is your life? For you are a mist that appears for a little time and then vanishes" (James 4:14 ESV). James wasn't trying to be pessimistic about life, just realistic, and he followed with this admonition: "Instead you ought to say, 'If the Lord wills, we will live and do this or that'" (James 4:15 ESV).

Moses and James both suggested the same perspective: The brevity of life gives us reason to choose carefully how we invest the days we've been granted. Not just to gain a heart of wisdom for ourselves, but when the time comes, to present that heart as faithful stewards to the Creator.

PRAY

Teach me to number my remaining days rightly, Father, that I may invest them in Your kingdom.

TRUST IN GOD ALONE

Read Psalm 33:13–22

KEY VERSES

A horse is a false hope for victory; nor does it rescue anyone by its great strength. Behold, the eye of the LORD is on those who fear Him, on those who wait for His faithfulness.
PSALM 33:17–18 NASB

UNDERSTAND

- *What does today's passage tell us about those who depend on something other than God for their strength and victory?*
- *How does the writer of Psalm 33 offer assurance to those who wait on the Lord?*
- *Today's scripture reading begins with God looking down from heaven on all of humanity (verse 13). How does that image shape the promises that follow?*

APPLY

Consider for a moment the sources of stress, uncertainty, and fear in your life. Look at the areas where you wish you had more control and influence. Consider how you go about trying to solve or address these challenges each day.

There are many people, organizations, possessions, and financial resources on which you rely and place your trust today to solve your problems. But today's psalm makes God's place in this world unmistakable and supreme over everything else. It guarantees that even the best man-made solutions, though they may work for a time, will eventually let you down.

The only sure bet is the God who looks down from heaven and sees everything unfolding on earth below. You may need to wait a while to see your hope in God fulfilled, but there is certainly no safer bet than trusting in God.

PRAY

Thank You, Lord, for Your deep love and concern for Your people. You hear my cries when I call out to You, and You promise to care for me in difficult times. May I leave behind my hope in anything else that promises security and learn to wait patiently for Your help. Amen.

PERSONAL HISTORY

Read Psalm 107

KEY VERSES

Give thanks to the LORD, for he is good! His faithful love endures forever. . . . Those who are wise will take all this to heart; they will see in our history the faithful love of the LORD.
PSALM 107:1, 43 NLT

UNDERSTAND

- *Thinking back over your history with God, what eventful moments stand out to you?*
- *Do you feel confident that you have a "story" to tell others about God's faithfulness?*

APPLY

Psalm 107 is a song about how God rescues His people over and over from all manner of troubles, with the repeated refrain: " 'LORD, help!' they cried in their trouble, and he rescued them from their distress" (Psalm 107:6, 13, 19, 28 NLT). God's history with Israel as a nation illustrates how He deals with us as individuals, with enduring and faithful love.

God calls some men to become theologians or apologists to defend the faith in erudite ways and to "exalt [God] publicly before the congregation and before the leaders of the nation" (Psalm 107:32 NLT). That may apply to you, but *all believers* are called to testify to God's faithfulness in their own lives. Your experience with Him is meant to be shared in a way that's real, providing a unique testimony that no one else has. "Has the LORD redeemed you? Then speak out! Tell others he has redeemed you from your enemies" (Psalm 107:2 NLT).

Even if you're young in the Lord, His history with you goes much further back than yours with Him! In fact, long before you were born, "Your eyes saw my unformed body; all the days ordained for me were written in your book before one of them came to be" (Psalm 139:16 NIV).

Think about the history of your life, and consider documenting the things that celebrate God's faithfulness so you can share them with others.

PRAY

You are good and loving to me, O God! I proclaim Your faithfulness to the world!

LEGACY

Read Matthew 2:1–12

KEY VERSES

Now after Jesus was born in Bethlehem of Judea in the days of Herod the king, behold, wise men from the east came to Jerusalem, saying, "Where is he who has been born king of the Jews? For we saw his star when it rose and have come to worship him."

MATTHEW 2:1–2 ESV

UNDERSTAND

- *What were these wise men seeking?*
- *How did they know to look for this "king of the Jews"?*
- *What sign did they claim identified this new king?*

APPLY

Some Bible stories take a bit of "unlearning." Manger scenes often feature Jesus, His parents, some shepherds and animals. . .and three wise men. Feels good, but it's inaccurate. The number *three* is an assumption based on the gifts presented (Matthew 2:11), and their arrival may have been a year or two *after* Jesus was born (Matthew 2:16).

The more traditional rendering of "magi from the east," however, is very accurate. This word traces its roots to the Persian Empire, which conquered the Babylonians, where Daniel had been taken into captivity and distinguished himself. "[Daniel] was found to have insight and intelligence and wisdom like that of the gods. . . . King Nebuchadnezzar. . .appointed him chief of the magicians, enchanters, astrologers and diviners" (Daniel 5:11 NIV). "Then at Belshazzar's command, Daniel. . .was proclaimed the third highest ruler in the kingdom" (Daniel 5:29 NIV). "Daniel so distinguished himself among the administrators and the satraps by his exceptional qualities that the king [Darius] planned to set him over the whole kingdom" (Daniel 6:3 NIV).

The magi visited Jesus because of Daniel's legacy. His faithful testimony to a divine King lasted hundreds of years, despite being in the extreme minority.

No one can ensure his own legacy, but God builds on faithfulness. A life of wisdom that points to Christ is the seed God uses in the lives that come after us.

PRAY

Father, by Your Spirit I want to remain faithful and allow You to use me as You see fit.

HOW TO HANDLE DOUBTS

Read 1 John 2:1–3:3

KEY VERSE

I write to you, not because you do not know the truth, but because you know it, and because no lie is of the truth. 1 JOHN 2:21 ESV

UNDERSTAND

- *Jesus and the apostles recognized that men naturally have doubts. What is the opposite of doubt?*
- *What else is the opposite of doubt?*

APPLY

If left unaddressed, doubts will fester in your soul and can lead to a lack of faith or outright unbelief. So whatever you do, you can't ignore doubts!

Instead, here's how to handle them:

Revelation. You have to get back to the question *How do you know what you believe?* The answer is that God has revealed His message in a book called the Bible. In this book you find all the answers you need for life and godliness. You don't find answers to all of life's tough questions. But most of them are answered with far greater authority and clarity than thousands of years of philosophy have provided.

Authority. You have to address the question *Who decides what is true?* Ultimately, the answer is God. He has stated His position quite clearly in the scriptures. God's Word is our absolute authority for faith and practice.

Inspiration. You have to tackle the question *Is scripture inspired by God?* Scripture itself says yes. The early church fathers agreed. They also believed that the Bible contained a unified message and story.

Doctrine. You have to wrestle with the question *What do you believe?* The answer is in the teachings of your particular denomination or church. To the degree that they're based solidly on scripture, you can bank on them. The answer is also found in your own beliefs and convictions—and questions and doubts.

PRAY

Yes, Lord, I want to say "Thank You!" for this new perspective on doubts. I'm glad that having doubts is a good thing. Thanks too for showing me how to handle them.

DAY 224

DOUBTS ABOUND IN A FALLEN WORLD

Read Mark 9:14–32

KEY VERSE

Immediately the boy's father exclaimed, "I do believe; help me overcome my unbelief!"
MARK 9:24 NIV

UNDERSTAND

- *What happens when you try to bury your doubts?*
- *What else happens?*

APPLY

Even the godliest Christian men struggle with doubts. Doubts are a natural by-product of taking God's Word seriously while living in a fallen world.

You need to bring your toughest questions to the Lord. Scripture makes it clear that Jesus can remove people's doubts (Matthew 14:25–31; Luke 24:36–45).

Where do doubts come from? Here are five possibilities:

- *Life has been very painful for you.*
- *You wonder if something scripture says is too good to be true.*
- *You have an incorrect perception of God or scripture.*
- *You have been introduced to false ideas.*
- *You are struggling with depression.*

How do you get rid of doubts? Here are seven possibilities:

- *Tell God about what has happened.*
- *Ask God to search your heart.*
- *Read scripture and study what it says.*
- *Affirm what you believe, obey, and heed.*
- *Ask the Lord to speak to your heart as you read and pray.*
- *Ask God to fill you with the Holy Spirit and teach you.*
- *Talk with someone you respect for his faith.*

It's not a sin to have doubts—everyone has them. Don't pretend you don't. And whatever you do, don't hide them. Instead, deal with your doubts head-on. Address each one that comes up. In the end, your faith will be stronger!

PRAY

Yes, Lord, I want to say "Thank You!" for relieving my concerns about the doubts I have had. Please help me address and remove any doubts I have in the days ahead.

EXPECTING A KINGDOM

Read Matthew 5:1–12

KEY VERSES

And he opened his mouth and taught them, saying: "Blessed are. . ." MATTHEW 5:2–3 ESV

UNDERSTAND

- *What are the types of people that Jesus called "blessed" in Matthew 5?*
- *What are the promises He makes to each of these people?*

APPLY

Matthew 5–7 records the Sermon on the Mount—Jesus' longest teaching in scripture. And it was so extraordinary that "when Jesus finished these sayings, the crowds were astonished at his teaching, for he was teaching them as one who had authority, and not as their scribes" (Matthew 7:28–29 ESV). Jesus' authority was evident because He spoke with wisdom from above—that is, from the perspective of the kingdom of heaven. And that turned more than a few expectations upside down.

Matthew 5 begins with a series of proclamations (called the Beatitudes) for the types of people Jesus described as "blessed" (happy or to be envied)—if you were in one of these categories, you were fortunate "for/because" of the reasons that followed. Interestingly, the first (the poor in spirit, Matthew 5:3) and last (those persecuted for righteousness' sake, Matthew 5:10) have identical reasons to be happy—"for theirs *is* the kingdom of heaven"—while the others are all promised they *shall* receive a corresponding reward. The list highlights the tension of the kingdom for all believers: It exists between *already have* and *will inherit*.

The Promised Land provides a metaphor for the kingdom. God commanded, "And you *shall take* possession of the land and settle in it, for I *have given* the land to you to possess it" (Numbers 33:53 ESV, emphasis added). Like those Israelites, we *have* and *will have* an inheritance from God. But if our expectations aren't based on both the present gift of the kingdom *and* the future promise of heaven, then we will never walk in the fullness of wisdom.

PRAY

Heavenly Father, teach me to walk in the reality of Your present and future kingdom.

THE RETURN OF CHRIST

Read Luke 12:35–48

KEY VERSES

Peter said, "Lord, are you telling this parable for us or for all?" And the Lord said, "Who then is the faithful and wise manager, whom his master will set over his household, to give them their portion of food at the proper time? Blessed is that servant whom his master will find so doing when he comes." LUKE 12:41–43 ESV

UNDERSTAND

- *What two qualities describe the kind of manager the Lord is talking about?*
- *What is the responsibility of the manager?*

APPLY

Scripture is filled with various styles of communication, from the poetic language of prophets to the matter-of-fact reporting in Judges. Even the Son of God had a distinct manner of speaking. Two of Jesus' patterns come together in today's passage—His use of metaphors and His habit of answering a question with a question.

Jesus shared several parables about being ready for His return. Sometimes He appears as a bridegroom, sometimes a nobleman, or as in today's passage, a master on a journey—in each case the theme is always *Be wise! Don't be caught unaware!*

At first, Jesus appears to ignore Peter's question about whether the parable includes inside information or not. Instead of a straight answer, He pushed Peter to think. Did Peter see himself as a "faithful and wise manager" of what God had entrusted to him? Did he really want the responsibility, because "from the one who has been entrusted with much, much more will be asked" (Luke 12:48 NIV)? But being ready for Christ also comes with rewards: "[The master] will dress himself to serve, will have [the servants] recline at the table and will come and wait on them" (Luke 12:37 NIV). As with so much in scripture, there's a choice to be made. "Whoever has ears to hear, let them hear" (Luke 14:35 NIV).

PRAY

Eternal Father, help me to live wisely and faithfully as I await the return of Jesus!

GUIDELINES FOR GREAT LEADERSHIP

Read 2 Timothy 2:15–26

KEY VERSES

Work hard so you can present yourself to God and receive his approval. Be a good worker, one who does not need to be ashamed and who correctly explains the word of truth. Avoid worthless, foolish talk that only leads to more godless behavior. 2 TIMOTHY 2:15–16 NLT

UNDERSTAND

- *Timothy had to keep himself prepared for God's work. How are obedience and purity key parts of being ready to do that work?*
- *How did the idea of presenting himself to God influence the way Timothy pursued his ministry?*
- *What is the danger of foolish talk for a Christian leader like Timothy?*

APPLY

The Bible holds church leaders to higher standards. Whether you are a leader or simply trying to discern whether a leader is reliable enough to follow, today's passage is instructive because it tells us to look for leaders—and to be leaders—who don't engage in worthless arguments, foolish talk, or vain quarrels. Such actions undermine both leaders' and followers' work in spreading the gospel.

Ideal leaders—those who can help unlock the wider potential of the church to serve God and others—are those who patiently and gently instruct others. They lead and teach even the most difficult and argumentative of people with kindness and humility that doesn't alienate them and still hopes for their redemption.

Leaders who allow themselves to become distracted or combative most often cause those who follow them to also become distracted and combative. But those who follow the advice Paul gave to Timothy benefit both individuals and their communities simply because they are focused on opportunities for growth and on the worthiest of goals.

PRAY

Jesus, send Your church leaders who are humble servants and capable teachers who can discern between what is worthwhile and what is a distraction. May these leaders help me to remain true to Your teachings and help draw me nearer to You. Help me to be that kind of leader. Amen.

BUILDING A FIRM FOUNDATION

Read Psalm 111

KEY VERSE

The fear of the LORD *is the beginning of wisdom; all those who follow His commandments have a good understanding; His praise endures forever.* PSALM 111:10 NASB

UNDERSTAND

- *What is the meaning of "fear" in this context?*
- *Why is this kind of fear necessary for wisdom?*
- *What promises are made to the one who obeys?*

APPLY

To continue building on a firm biblical foundation and truly grasp the wisdom of God and how it applies to our lives, we have to consider what some may think of as an odd component. The psalmist declares that "the fear of the LORD"—the awe, wonder, and respect of the Creator of all things—is our starting point for a proper understanding. The fear of the Lord is not the same as being scared of Him, though He can and should be terrifying to those who embrace wickedness and love sin. For His children, fearing their Father-King is the beginning of seeing His creation as it really is, His authority as it really is, and our lives in this world as they really are.

Once we begin exercising the proper perspective by applying the fear of the Lord to our daily lives, we start seeing things differently. That's where we begin to grow in wisdom, but there's more. Throughout the Bible, wisdom is not merely insight or an intellectual experience. It's bound together with right actions and right living. As today's key verse points out, "those who follow His commandments" are the ones who gain understanding. It's similar to playing a sport or musical instrument: You gain understanding as you practice.

PRAY

Lord, God of all creation, bless me with a heart that fears You in holiness and reverence that I may gain wisdom. And help me to obey Your commandments that I may grow in my understanding of You.

THE HOME OF WISDOM

Read Psalm 51

KEY VERSE

Behold, You desire truth in the innermost being, and in secret You will make wisdom known to me. PSALM 51:6 NASB

UNDERSTAND

- *What does God desire that we possess?*
- *How does God choose to reveal wisdom to us?*

APPLY

One of the recurring themes in the Bible is the importance of our "innermost being." Sometimes words like *heart, soul,* or *mind* are used to describe this inner part of us. When Moses commanded the people to love the Lord "with all your heart and with all your soul and with all your strength" (Deuteronomy 6:5 NIV), he wasn't describing individual parts but rather was emphasizing that the whole inner man is to be involved.

Our innermost being is the source of our thoughts and our values, thus making it the seat of our choices and actions. In Psalm 51, David confessed his outward sin of adultery with Bathsheba but knew his failing originated from within and cried out, "Create in me a pure *heart*, O God, and renew a steadfast spirit within me" (Psalm 51:10 NIV, emphasis added). If the inner man changes, the outer man must follow.

In Christ, we experience even more than David asked for. Jesus said that if anyone loved and obeyed Him, He *and* the Father would "come to him and make [their] home with him" (John 14:23 ESV) through the Holy Spirit. That inner fact, Jesus claimed, produces an outward effect: "The one who believes in Me, as the Scripture said, 'From his innermost being will flow rivers of living water'" (John 7:38 NASB).

Jesus *is* truth and wisdom, and as He lives in us, our lives *will* reflect His presence. "Whoever says 'I know him' but does not keep his commandments is a liar, and the truth is not in him" (1 John 2:4 ESV).

PRAY

Author of all truth, help me to listen to Your voice in the secret place where You give me life.

THE LORD LOVES QUESTIONS

Read Luke 2:39–52

KEY VERSE

Three days later they finally discovered him [Jesus] in the Temple, sitting among the religious teachers, listening to them and asking questions. Luke 2:46 NLT

UNDERSTAND

- *What are the benefits of asking questions?*
- *What are the benefits of getting solid answers to our questions?*

APPLY

When you study the Bible, you want to be fully engaged—mind, will, and emotions. Bible study doesn't mean blind or passive acceptance of what scripture says. Just the opposite! Whatever you do, you have to keep asking questions.

Five fast facts about asking questions:

1. The world's smartest people ask lots of questions.
2. The man who doesn't ask questions doesn't care or is afraid.
3. The man who is afraid to ask questions doesn't know who to ask, is worried about sounding dumb, or is afraid of the answer.
4. The man who is afraid of the answer wants to believe something is true no matter what—even if it's not true—or is more afraid of the answerer's rebuke than of the answer itself.
5. Fortunately, God doesn't rebuke you when you ask honest questions.
   a. Is it okay to ask questions when praying to God? (See Habakkuk 1:12–13.)
   b. Is it okay to ask God, "Why did You let this happen?" (See Malachi 3:13–15.)
   c. Is it okay to ask questions about God's Word? (See Acts 8:30–35.)
   d. Is it okay to ask questions in church? (See Acts 15:1–11.)

PRAY

Yes, Lord, I want to say "Thank You!" for encouraging me to ask questions. That's helpful and motivating to me. I want to love You with all my heart, soul, strength, and mind.

WISDOM'S PURPOSE

Read Ephesians 1:15–22

KEY VERSES

For this reason, ever since I heard about your faith in the Lord Jesus and your love for all God's people, I have not stopped giving thanks for you, remembering you in my prayers. I keep asking that the God of our Lord Jesus Christ, the glorious Father, may give you the Spirit of wisdom and revelation, so that you may know him better. Ephesians 1:15–17 NIV

UNDERSTAND

- *What kind of believers was Paul addressing?*
- *What was Paul's response to the testimony of the Ephesians?*
- *What did he ask God for and why?*

APPLY

As we study the Word, we'll employ various Bible study techniques, one of which is to simply compare different translations. Good translations attempt a *word-for-word* rendering; however, there are many occasions when scholars must use a *meaning-for-meaning* approach. For example, in today's reading, the phrase "give you the Spirit of wisdom" can also be expressed "give you a spirit of wisdom" (NASB) or "give you spiritual wisdom" (NLT). These options help clarify that Paul wasn't asking for the Holy Spirit to come again to these believers but for something very specific—a unique kind of wisdom and insight. And for a specific purpose.

For God's children, there's nothing better than to grow up in faith and mature in Christ. That growth, Paul prayed, would encompass three things: "I pray that the eyes of your heart may be enlightened in order that you may know the hope to which he has called you, the riches of his glorious inheritance in his holy people, and his incomparably great power for us who believe" (Ephesians 1:18–19 NIV). These three things were on Paul's heart for all believers. He prayed constantly for them to *know*, not just *believe*. Next we'll see why Paul considered these so important for us.

PRAY

Glorious Father, I want to receive the wisdom Paul prayed for so earnestly and know You more!

WISDOM'S PURPOSE: HOPE

Read Ephesians 1:15–22

KEY VERSES

Having the eyes of your hearts enlightened, that you may know what is the hope to which he has called you, what are the riches of his glorious inheritance in the saints, and what is the immeasurable greatness of his power toward us who believe, according to the working of his great might. EPHESIANS 1:18–19 ESV

UNDERSTAND

- *How is spiritual hope different from worldly hope?*
- *Where does the hope of a believer come from?*

APPLY

Certain elements will be repeated as we study wisdom since they're tied closely to the subject. As we've seen, *heart, soul,* and *mind* are all used to describe our innermost being. While often interchangeable, the nuances of language can add special emphasis. Paul's phrase "eyes of your hearts" points us to the center and deepest part of our being. This is where the "spirit of wisdom and revelation" begins to move us beyond believing to knowing the truth in our hearts, starting with our hope in Christ.

The hope we are called to is, simply put, eternal life. Certainly, we experience hope in Christ in daily life, but "If we have hoped in Christ *only in this life*, we are of all people most to be pitied. But the fact is, Christ has been raised from the dead" (1 Corinthians 15:19–20 NASB, emphasis added). Paul was looking ahead "with eager hope for the day when God will give us our full rights as his adopted children, including the new bodies he has promised us. We were given this hope when we were saved" (Romans 8:23–24 NLT).

Peter also emphasized that God "caused us to be born again to a living hope through the resurrection of Jesus Christ from the dead" (1 Peter 1:3 NASB). Our hope of eternal life only exists because of the fact of His resurrection.

PRAY

God of hope, may I know and live out the truth of the eternal life You've promised.

TRUST IN GOD, NOT IN YOUR OWN POWER

Read Matthew 26:47-56

KEY VERSES

Then Jesus said to him, "Put your sword back into its place; for all who take the sword will perish by the sword. Do you think that I cannot appeal to my Father, and he will at once send me more than twelve legions of angels?" MATTHEW 26:52–53 NRSV

UNDERSTAND

- *Why did Jesus hold back on the legions of angels God could have sent to rescue Him?*
- *What did Peter need to learn about relying on violence to advance God's cause?*
- *How does this passage help you understand God's power and restraint in using that power?*

APPLY

Even though Peter had spent three years with Jesus, his response to the men who had come to arrest his Lord showed that he still had a lot to learn about Jesus, the power of God, and the place of force in advancing God's cause. It's simple enough to understand that God's kingdom can't be advanced by the edge of a sword, but the deeper meaning of Jesus' teaching about living by the sword and dying by the sword is that mere human effort can't do what He came to earth to accomplish.

Jesus asks you to trust God today with even the most challenging moments of your life and to know that He will have the final say one day as the all-powerful judge. Your own power is limited, and the consequence of relying on your own strength and efforts may be far worse than you can imagine.

God is both merciful and all-powerful, but our fallen human nature can tempt us to believe that we need to depend on our own power and might. Yet even when life proves daunting, we can rest in the presence of a God who is never overwhelmed or overpowered.

PRAY

Jesus, thank You for Your power and patience, both of which guide our world and give many an opportunity to know You personally. May I imitate Your mercy and restraint with others while also trusting in Your all-powerful rule over the earth. Amen.

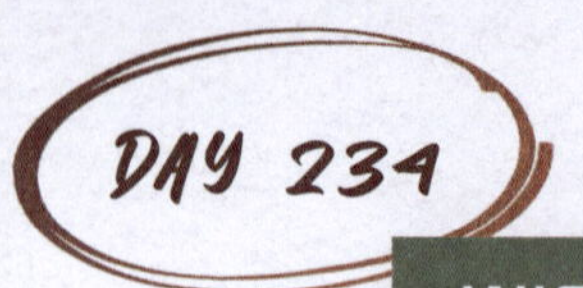

WISDOM'S PURPOSE: INHERITANCE

Read Ephesians 1:15–22

KEY VERSES

I pray that the eyes of your heart may be enlightened in order that you may know the hope to which he has called you, the riches of his glorious inheritance in his holy people, and his incomparably great power for us who believe. EPHESIANS 1:18–19 NIV

UNDERSTAND

- *What kind of inheritance is Paul talking about?*
- *Who gets this inheritance?*

APPLY

Part of the covenant with Abraham included the promise of a homeland that would be passed down to future generations: "And I will give to you and to your offspring after you the land of your sojournings, all the land of Canaan" (Genesis 17:8 ESV). Though the patriarchs occupied some areas of Canaan, it took more than four centuries for Israel to begin settling the Promised Land. Therefore being new to land ownership, Moses provided laws concerning its use and how it would be passed to the next generation.

The Hebrew root for "inheritance" (*nachal*) means "stream" or "river," so an inheritance was a blessing flowing to the recipients. We have every reason to get excited about our eternal blessing in Christ—"an inheritance that is imperishable, undefiled, and unfading, kept in heaven for you" (1 Peter 1:4 ESV). But we're not the only ones looking forward to that day!

God is eager for "his glorious inheritance in his holy people." God created Israel, "the people of [His] inheritance, whom [He] redeemed" (Psalm 74:2 NIV), from Abraham to be His own. David sang, "Blessed is the nation whose God is the LORD, the people he chose for his inheritance" (Psalm 33:12 NIV). Through the faith-based covenant begun with Abraham and fulfilled in Christ, the Father sought "to purify for Himself a people for His own possession" (Titus 2:14 NASB). Imagine. . .God is excited about what He's going to get one day in us!

PRAY

Lord, I am humbled to be Your own possession. Help me to live that truth every day.

WISDOM'S PURPOSE: POWER

Read Ephesians 1:15–22

KEY VERSES

I pray that the eyes of your heart may be enlightened, so that you will know what is the hope of His calling, what are the riches of the glory of His inheritance in the saints, and what is the boundless greatness of His power toward us who believe. EPHESIANS 1:18–19 NASB

UNDERSTAND

- *What characterizes God's power?*
- *Who benefits from this power?*

APPLY

Our final day with this passage shows just how much can be packed into a few lines of scripture! St. Jerome, the scholar behind the Latin *Vulgate* (the Bible of Western Europe for a thousand years), captured this feeling well: "The scriptures are shallow enough for a babe to come and drink without fear of drowning and deep enough for theologians to swim in without ever touching the bottom."

Comparing translations as we have before, we find "the boundless greatness of His power," also rendered "incomparably great power" (NIV) and "immeasurable greatness of his power" (ESV). The Amplified Bible, which attempts to express the fullest meaning of each phrase, says: "the immeasurable and unlimited and surpassing greatness of His [active, spiritual] power." In any reading, it's big!

Paul goes on to explain how this power benefits us: "This is the same mighty power that raised Christ from the dead and seated him in the place of honor at God's right hand in the heavenly realms" (Ephesians 1:19–20 NLT) where we will join Him one day. Everything we hope for in Christ and everything God hopes for in us rests on the risen Messiah.

With Paul, we should pray for the gift of the "Spirit of wisdom and of revelation" (Ephesians 1:17 ESV) to know God more and believe His Word, thus avoiding Jesus' rebuke of the skeptics of the resurrection: "You are mistaken, since you do not understand the Scriptures nor the power of God" (Matthew 22:29 NASB).

PRAY

Open the eyes of my heart, O Lord, to embrace all that You have promised.

DAY 236

SEEING THE REALLY BIG PICTURE

Read Luke 24:13–53

KEY VERSE

He said to them, "This is what I told you while I was still with you: Everything must be fulfilled that is written about me in the Law of Moses, the Prophets and the Psalms."
LUKE 24:44 NIV

UNDERSTAND

- *How well did Jesus (and later the disciples) know the Old Testament scriptures?*
- *How important is it for you to know the Bible cover to cover?*

APPLY

Once you see the big picture, you'll always be able to see the Bible's design!

One Author, Forty Writers

Unlike other books, the Bible doesn't list any author on the cover or title page. Then again, the Bible isn't any book! God is the author. He inspired a diverse group of forty individuals to write the Bible over the course of sixteen hundred years. The first writer was Moses, who penned the first five books. Other important writers include David, Solomon, Isaiah, Jeremiah, Ezekiel, Daniel, Hosea, Matthew, Mark, Luke, Paul, James, and Peter. The last writer was John, who wrote the fourth Gospel, three letters, and the book of Revelation. The Holy Spirit guided all of these individuals to write what they did.

Sixty-Six Books, One Story

The Bible contains a total of sixty-six books. Because God inspired all the writers, the Bible contains a unified message from beginning to end. In fact, the opening page talks about the beginning of time. The last page talks about the end of time as you know it. In between, the story of the Bible unfolds in all its drama, conflict, violence, irony, and glory. The hero of the Bible is Jesus Christ. The enemies of Jesus Christ are Satan, evil people, and death. Everything and everybody in the first three-fourths of the Bible foreshadow the life, death, burial, and resurrection of Jesus Christ (or the ultimately futile opposition of His enemies).

There's more!

PRAY

Yes, Lord, I want to say "Thank You!" that I'm reading and studying the Bible. I want to keep doing it long after I finish this book.

SEEING MORE OF THE REALLY BIG PICTURE

Read Acts 6:1–7

KEY VERSE

And the word of God continued to increase, and the number of the disciples multiplied greatly in Jerusalem, and a great many of the priests became obedient to the faith.
Acts 6:7 ESV

UNDERSTAND

- *How much of the Bible have you already read?*
- *How much would you like to read over the next ten or twelve months?*

APPLY

Over time, be sure you make it a goal to read all sixty-six books of the Bible. True, when you finish, you may think, *Wow, I didn't get all of that!* That's why it's great to make it a priority to read the whole Bible every year.

To do that, make it a practice to buy Barbour Publishing's bestselling *Daily Wisdom for Men* every autumn. Then use its "Read Thru the Bible in a Year Plan" in the back of every annual edition.

Once you see the really big picture, reading through the Bible makes a lot more sense.

One Work, Two Testaments

Like some books, the Bible is divided into two parts (called *testaments,* which is another word for *covenants*). The following lists clearly show how each testament is divided into four distinct, logical sections:

Old Testament

1. Pentateuch: Genesis–Deuteronomy (five books written by Moses)
2. History: Joshua–Esther (mostly anonymous authors)
3. Literature: Job–Song of Solomon (primarily by David and Solomon)
4. Prophets: Isaiah–Malachi (by more than fifteen authors)

New Testament

1. Gospels: Matthew–John (by four writers)
2. Acts (by Luke)
3. Letters: Romans–Jude (by Paul, James, Peter, John, and Jude)
4. Revelation (by John)

PRAY

Yes, Lord, I want to say "Thank You!" for challenging me to read the entire Bible.

DAY 238

YEARS DO NOT ALWAYS MATTER

Read Job 32

KEY VERSES

Now Elihu had waited before speaking to Job because they were older than he. . . . "I am young in years, and you are old; that is why I was fearful, not daring to tell you what I know. I thought, 'Age should speak; advanced years should teach wisdom.' But it is the spirit in a person, the breath of the Almighty, that gives them understanding. It is not only the old who are wise, not only the aged who understand what is right." Job 32:4, 6–9 NIV

UNDERSTAND

- *Is there a relationship between age and wisdom?*
- *Where does wisdom come from?*

APPLY

Job famously experienced tremendous suffering as part of God's eternal and often mysterious plan. One thing is clear from the first chapter: Job was not being punished for any sin. But three close friends still tried to persuade him that his predicament was somehow his fault. Their counsel was based on worldly arguments and theological assumptions that missed the mark. Then a younger man named Elihu appeared, taking Job to task "for justifying himself rather than God" (Job 32:2 NIV). Job's situation was not caused by his sin, but it did lead him to demand the Almighty to explain Himself to a man.

Elihu was slow to join the conversation out of respect for his elders. But seeing that they lacked real insight, he spoke up to correct their error. Elihu demonstrated that age doesn't guarantee wisdom. The only source of wisdom is "the breath of the Almighty" (Job 32:8 NIV). Paul echoes this belief in his advice to Timothy: "Don't let anyone look down on you because you are young, but set an example for the believers in speech, in conduct, in love, in faith and in purity" (1 Timothy 4:12 NIV).

PRAY

Breath of life, fill me with wisdom through Your Holy Spirit. Teach me when to listen to others and when to speak words of sound counsel.

ASKING FOR WISDOM

Read James 1:1–8

KEY VERSES

If any of you lacks wisdom, you should ask God, who gives generously to all without finding fault, and it will be given to you. But when you ask, you must believe and not doubt, because the one who doubts is like a wave of the sea, blown and tossed by the wind. That person should not expect to receive anything from the Lord. Such a person is double-minded and unstable in all they do. JAMES 1:5–8 NIV

UNDERSTAND

- *Can anyone ask for wisdom?*
- *How are we to approach God when seeking wisdom?*
- *How does God respond to those who seek Him?*

APPLY

For those of us who feel a deficit of wisdom, it's encouraging to hear James say God gives it generously. . .even if there's a small catch.

God is a generous Father to His children. In fact, He's so generous by nature that He even provides for those who ignore Him. When Jesus commanded His disciples to love their enemies, He tied it directly to acting like their Father in heaven, who "causes His sun to rise on the evil and the good, and sends rain on the righteous and the unrighteous" (Matthew 5:45 NASB).

As sons, we have a unique relationship with our gracious Father, and thus we never face conditional love; we don't have every shortcoming pointed out before receiving His blessing. But we do face one condition when asking for wisdom: We must believe. Our doubt creates an obstacle even for our generous Father. In fact, belief is fundamental to receiving any of God's gifts, starting with salvation. "If you declare with your mouth, 'Jesus is Lord,' and believe in your heart that God raised him from the dead, you will be saved" (Romans 10:9 NIV). James says a "double-minded" man shouldn't expect to receive anything from the Lord.

PRAY

Gracious Father, I happily accept the wisdom You want me to have!

FINDING HOPE WHEN THE WORST HAPPENS

Read Genesis 39:10–23

KEY VERSES

But the Lord *was with Joseph in the prison and showed him his faithful love. And the* Lord *made Joseph a favorite with the prison warden. Before long, the warden put Joseph in charge of all the other prisoners and over everything that happened in the prison.*
Genesis 39:21–22 NLT

UNDERSTAND

- *How did Joseph respond to the false accusation against him?*
- *Joseph certainly didn't look very blessed when he ended up in prison. How does this story challenge assumptions today about God's blessings?*
- *What does this passage teach about faithfulness and obedience to God?*

APPLY

There's a good chance that you haven't been treated as unfairly as Joseph was, but small and large slights and mistreatments are bound to happen. Joseph's story suggests that even under the threat of a false accusation or unjust judgment against you, God will remain with you and even continue to bless you.

This calls for humility, as you will certainly need to sometimes swallow the bitter medicine of injustice. Yet if you trust in God, you will find that He can work with even the least desirable raw materials. What can be worse than being locked away in an ancient prison?

Even if there is pain and discomfort today in what you endure, you also can't imagine how God will shape and form you for future service to others. The worst thing that happens to you may be the key to unlocking what God has destined you to accomplish.

PRAY

Lord, thank You for the many models of Your faithfulness and love to those who have suffered unfairly. May I seek You in faith and hope without demanding specific outcomes as the sure sign of Your blessing. May I see each challenge as an opportunity to be shaped and formed into Your servant who is ready to serve others. Amen.

WISDOM FROM ABOVE

Read James 3

KEY VERSES

Who is wise and understanding among you? Let them show it by their good life, by deeds done in the humility that comes from wisdom. But if you harbor bitter envy and selfish ambition in your hearts, do not boast about it or deny the truth. Such "wisdom" does not come down from heaven but is earthly, unspiritual, demonic. For where you have envy and selfish ambition, there you find disorder and every evil practice. JAMES 3:13–16 NIV

UNDERSTAND

- *How is wisdom recognized?*
- *What characterizes wisdom that is not from heaven?*
- *What is the root of "earthly" wisdom?*

APPLY

Wisdom from God is a way of life. In the books of the Bible known as "wisdom literature" is recorded helpful, practical advice. Those books are always concerned about us living wisely before God and man. James, whose entire letter is about actions speaking louder than words, echoes their sentiment.

What we really believe and cherish comes out in our lives for all to witness. This is the principle Jesus described when rebuking the Pharisees: "A good man brings good things out of the good stored up in him, and an evil man brings evil things out of the evil stored up in him" (Matthew 12:35 NIV). Whether we "harbor bitter envy and selfish ambition" in our hearts or desire to honor the Lord, the evidence is found in our day-to-day walk. For people in love with this world, an "earthly, unspiritual, demonic" approach to life passes for a type of wisdom. Some write bestselling business books while others just brag to their friends. But as children of the Almighty, we are to reflect something grander—the "wisdom from above" (James 3:17 ESV).

PRAY

Father, fill my heart and mind with Your Word and lead me to live according to the humility of heavenly wisdom.

THE OLD TESTAMENT'S FIRST FIVE BOOKS

Read Genesis 15:1–6

KEY VERSE

And Abram believed the LORD, and the LORD counted him as righteous because of his faith.
GENESIS 15:6 NLT

UNDERSTAND

- *What does Moses have to teach us 3,500 years later?*
- *Who taught Moses?*

APPLY

Before you read the whole Bible, it's wise to look at each section of the Bible in more depth, starting with its first five books, also called the Pentateuch. Moses, one of the earliest and greatest prophets of God's people, wrote these books. God clearly chose Moses, called him to service, and revealed to him what to write in each of these five foundational books of the Bible.

Moses wrote these books in a straightforward, selective narrative format. (This means that he provides only selected narratives, not all the stories that could possibly be told about Adam and Eve, Noah, Abraham, etc.) His narratives of creation are breathtaking. Moses went on to record important epic stories of early human history. Then he recorded the stories of God at work to create a nation that would be His witness to the world. Sadly, this nation (Israel) often turned from God, with disastrous results.

In these five books, Moses also included quite a bit of discourse (by God and Moses), several beautiful poetic sections (by God, Moses, and possibly Moses' sister, Miriam), and a few important genealogical records (we'll see the value of those records later in scripture).

Expectations of a coming Messiah (Jesus Christ) appear throughout the books of Moses, from Genesis (3:15) to Deuteronomy (18:15).

PRAY

Yes, Lord, I want to say "Thank You!" for promising to bless the world through Abraham, the father of all who believe and trust in You.

THE OLD TESTAMENT'S NEXT TWELVE BOOKS

Read Joshua 1:1–18

KEY VERSE

"This Book of the Law shall not depart from your mouth, but you shall meditate on it day and night, so that you may be careful to do according to all that is written in it. For then you will make your way prosperous, and then you will have good success." JOSHUA 1:8 ESV

UNDERSTAND

- *True or False? "Experience is the best teacher—especially the experiences of others who have gone before us."*
- *In Romans 15:4, what did Paul say about the value of the Hebrew scriptures?*

APPLY

Before you read the Old Testament, it's wise to look at the second section in more depth. That section is the history books, and it contains twelve books. Joshua, Ezra, and others wrote these books. They tell the story of God's people, the Israelite nation, for a thousand years from the death of Moses (around 1400 BC) until the completion of the Old Testament (after 450 BC). Like Moses did, Joshua, Ezra, and the other authors wrote these books in a straightforward, selective narrative format.

The narratives of Joshua's early exploits are riveting. Joshua then recorded how the Israelites divided up and settled the Promised Land. Sadly, the Israelites often rebelled against the Lord, fought against each other, and—after a period of great prosperity—ultimately fought again and split into two kingdoms. The Northern Kingdom, Israel (ten Israelite tribes), never turned back to the Lord, and eventually the Assyrian Empire conquered it (722 BC). The Southern Kingdom, Judah (two tribes), turned back to the Lord on several occasions, but eventually the newly dominant Babylonian Empire conquered it (586 BC).

After the seventy years of Babylonian captivity, a remnant of the people from Judah (and Israel) returned to the former Promised Land, eventually rebuilt Jerusalem, and sought to start over. In these twelve books of history, you'll find not just narrative but also discourse, poetry, prayers, and genealogies.

PRAY

Yes, Lord, I want to say "Thank You!" for the way You challenged, strengthened, and blessed Joshua. Please do all three in my life as well.

THE OLD TESTAMENT'S SECOND HALF

Read Psalm 1:1–6

KEY VERSE

He is like a tree planted by streams of water that yields its fruit in its season, and its leaf does not wither. In all that he does, he prospers. PSALM 1:3 ESV

UNDERSTAND

- *God richly blesses the man who does what?*
- *Do you want to be a God-blessed man? If so, when?*

APPLY

The rest of the Hebrew scriptures offers a lot of variety in style, tone, and content. This second half of the Hebrew scriptures includes the two following sections:

Literature. This section contains five books. David and Solomon wrote most of them, but they also include writings by Moses and many other contributors. These five books present the best of five kinds of Hebrew literature written between 1450 BC (Psalm 90 by Moses, probably before the Lord called him to deliver the Israelites from slavery in Egypt) and 450 BC (Psalm 137 by Jeremiah, according to ancient Jewish tradition). The types of literature include drama, worship lyrics, wise sayings, a sermon, and a love song.

The anticipation of the coming of Jesus Christ is especially evident in more than a dozen psalms that include detailed messianic prophecies.

Prophets. This section contains seventeen books, written by Isaiah, Jeremiah, Ezekiel, and Daniel (known as the *major prophets*) and twelve other prophets (known as the *minor prophets*—but "minor" only in the sense that they wrote shorter books). Isaiah and the others wrote these books in the prophetic genre, largely in poetic form with some narrative interludes. These books contain a series of messages from God dating from 850 BC to sometime after 450 BC.

Many of these prophetic messages call the Israelites to repent of their sins and turn back to the Lord. Other messages foretell future events, including God's coming judgment on the kingdoms of Israel and Judah and surrounding nations.

The expectation of the coming Messiah is also strongly apparent throughout these prophetic writings.

PRAY

Yes, Lord, I want to say "Thank You!" for promising to bless the man who meditates on Your Word day and night. I want to start by taking today's key verse to heart.

THE SILENT YEARS

Read Daniel 9:1–27

KEY VERSE

"Know and understand this: From the time the word goes out to restore and rebuild Jerusalem until the Anointed One, the ruler, comes, there will be seven 'sevens,' and sixty-two 'sevens.' " DANIEL 9:25 NIV

UNDERSTAND

- *If Jesus had been born fifty years earlier or fifty years later, would it have mattered? Why or why not?*
- *True or False? "In His wisdom, God orchestrated Christmas and Calvary at just the right time." If true, why does it matter?*

APPLY

After the close of the Old Testament, it appears that God was silent for more than four hundred years. Why did God wait so long before sending Jesus Christ to earth?

A prophecy in the book of Daniel holds part of the key to the answer. In Daniel 9:24–27, the prophet foretold that more than four hundred years must pass from the return from captivity until the Messiah would come and be "cut off." That time was drawing near when Jesus began His public ministry among a people longing for and anticipating the Messiah's coming.

The cultural and political situation in Israel during the first century also explains God's purpose in waiting so long. Three different peoples had a tremendous influence on the times of the life of Jesus Christ and His newborn church.

1. *The Greeks.* The Greeks had ruled the world, and their culture influenced the Romans. The Greeks passed from the scene politically, but their language survived as the universal world language for many years. This was the language in which the New Testament was written. Greek culture, particularly philosophy, influenced much thinking in the first century.

There's more!

PRAY

Yes, Lord, I want to say "Thank You!" for Your sovereignty and providence. Your plan from all eternity has been unfolding exactly as You decreed.

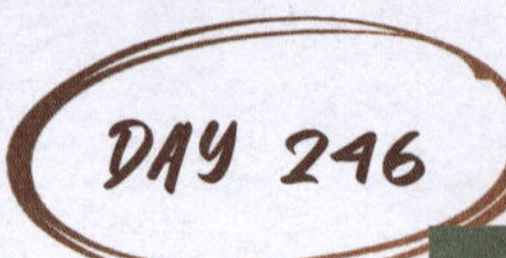

MORE ABOUT THE SILENT YEARS

Read Malachi 3:1–18

KEY VERSE

"Ever since the time of your ancestors you have turned away from my decrees and have not kept them. Return to me, and I will return to you," says the Lord *Almighty. "But you ask, 'How are we to return?'"* Malachi 3:7 niv

UNDERSTAND

- *What does Paul say in Galatians 4:4 about God's timing for sending His Son?*
- *How did God orchestrate everything? Mostly using good angels or mostly using unbelieving men?*

APPLY

Two more peoples had a tremendous influence on the times of the life of Jesus Christ and His newborn church:

2. *The Romans.* Some sixty years before the birth of Jesus Christ, the Roman Empire (the last great world empire) arose. The Romans ruled all of the Mediterranean area and the rest of the known world at that time. The Caesars brought world peace under one government, which aided the early church as it began to spread from Israel. Also, the vastly improved transportation systems the Romans developed gave the first missionaries the opportunity to carry the gospel of Jesus Christ to new areas. It wasn't until after AD 60 that local persecution against Christians started engulfing the empire.
3. *The Jews.* The Jewish people had lived in Israel for nearly fourteen hundred years. Then they found themselves under the yoke of Rome, and most found it unpleasant. The Jewish people's hope was deliverance from Roman domination. Sadly, Judaism had degenerated from a religion based on faith into a weighty compilation of human laws and traditions. The leadership and masses no longer worshipped God, and soon Jerusalem and Israeli Judaism were destroyed (AD 70).

Into this world situation Jesus Christ came to redirect people (all people, Jewish and Gentile) back to God. The Lord waited until the right time!

PRAY

Yes, Lord, I want to say "Thank You!" for Your right and perfect timing. The ancient empires didn't know that You orchestrated their rise and fall. Your ways are so much higher than man's.

WISDOM IS. . .PURE

Read James 3:13–18

KEY VERSE

But the wisdom from above is first pure, then peaceable, gentle, open to reason, full of mercy and good fruits, impartial and sincere. James 3:17 ESV

UNDERSTAND

- *What does "pure" mean in this context?*
- *Why would James list it first here?*

APPLY

Bible study begins with simple observations. That means trying to discover what a passage would have meant to the original reader rather than making assumptions or introducing a modern, or even theological, bias. Sound observations make interpretation and application much easier.

Basic observations include knowing who's speaking, who the audience is, and what cultural and political situations might be in play. It also includes defining words to the best of our ability both in English and in the original Hebrew or Greek. And with today's online resources, there's no easier time in history to dig deeper!

The Greek word translated as "pure" is *hagnē,* which includes the concepts of undivided or clean, much in the same way English would describe gold or silver being uncontaminated by other elements. But there's one other interesting meaning to this word found in *Thayer's Greek Lexicon*—"exciting reverence." The wisdom from above is not only completely uncontaminated, it also causes reverence and awe. It's motivating because of its purity.

We've all seen old westerns where the grizzled prospector works his claim on some lonely mountain, then takes his find to the assayer in town to test it. The question wasn't *Did he find gold* but *How* pure *was the gold?* The less contaminated, the more exciting his find. Likewise, since Jesus Himself is our wisdom from above, we can have utter confidence that His commands are uncontaminated and trustworthy.

In the next few studies, we'll see how each of the characteristics James uses to describe wisdom is embodied in Christ.

PRAY

Lord God, thank You for the purity of Your commands and how trustworthy everything You say is!

WISDOM IS. . .PEACEABLE

Read James 3:13–18

KEY VERSE

But the wisdom from above is first pure, then peaceable, gentle, open to reason, full of mercy and good fruits, impartial and sincere. JAMES 3:17 ESV

UNDERSTAND

- *What does "peaceable" mean in this context?*
- *How would a peaceable person behave?*
- *How does seeking peace demonstrate wisdom?*

APPLY

To continue our observations in James 3:17, let's look at the Greek word for *peaceable (eirēnikē),* sometimes translated as "peace-loving." Either of those work well in English, but the root word also implies an additional idea beyond simply avoiding strife or conflict—reconciliation.

Reconciliation was at the very heart of Jesus' purpose for coming into the world. The gospel itself is "the good news of peace through Jesus Christ" (Acts 10:36 NIV). And not just between man and God, but between Jew and Gentile:

> *For [Jesus] himself is our peace, who has made the two groups one and has destroyed the barrier, the dividing wall of hostility, by setting aside in his flesh the law with its commands and regulations. His purpose was to create in himself one new humanity out of the two, thus making peace, and in one body to reconcile both of them to God through the cross, by which he put to death their hostility. He came and preached peace to you who were far away and peace to those who were near. For through him we both have access to the Father by one Spirit.* (Ephesians 2:14–18 NIV)

In the miraculous solution of the cross, God offered salvation to those under the Law *and* to those outside the covenant equally since both needed Jesus. "But to those called by God to salvation, both Jews and Gentiles, Christ is the power of God and the wisdom of God" (1 Corinthians 1:24 NLT). The wisdom from above seeks the peace of reconciliation.

PRAY

Father, how awesome is the reconciliation You planned for us in Your Son at the cross!

WISDOM IS. . .GENTLE

Read James 3:13–18

KEY VERSE

But the wisdom from above is first pure, then peaceable, gentle, open to reason, full of mercy and good fruits, impartial and sincere. JAMES 3:17 ESV

UNDERSTAND

- *What does "gentle" mean in this context?*
- *How would a gentle person behave?*
- *How does seeking to be gentle demonstrate wisdom?*

APPLY

This passage is so rich that we need to park on it for a while! It will help lay the foundation for later studies as we follow one of the most important rules of Bible study: allowing scripture to interpret scripture. By using one passage as a tool to understand another, we gain a fuller understanding and become "like the owner of a house who brings out of his storeroom new treasures as well as old" (Matthew 13:52 NIV).

This principle is demonstrated well in three passages about the gentle Messiah who was to come rather than a conquering king. In the first, Jesus says, "Take My yoke upon you and learn from Me, for I am *gentle* and humble in heart, and you will find rest for your souls" (Matthew 11:29 NASB, emphasis added). Jesus applies Jeremiah 6:16 to Himself, claiming to be the salvation Jeremiah rebuked Israel for rejecting.

Likewise, a gentle Messiah was promised by Isaiah: "Here is my servant whom I have chosen, the one I love, in whom I delight. . . . A bruised reed he will not break, and a smoldering wick he will not snuff out" (Matthew 12:18–20 NIV).

And when Jesus rode into Jerusalem, He fulfilled Zechariah 9:9. "See, your king comes to you, gentle and riding on a donkey" (Matthew 21:5 NIV). In wisdom, God sent a gentle King to a hurting and lost world and spoke of it over and over through His prophets, though many did not see it.

PRAY

Gentle Savior, You humbled Yourself to bring salvation and life. I give You thanks!

WISDOM IS. . .OPEN TO REASON

Read James 3:13–18

KEY VERSE

But the wisdom from above is first pure, then peaceable, gentle, open to reason, full of mercy and good fruits, impartial and sincere. JAMES 3:17 ESV

UNDERSTAND

- *What does being "open to reason" mean?*
- *How would a reasonable person speak to those who disagree with him?*

APPLY

A quick way to get a better understanding of a verse if you don't have time to research the Hebrew or Greek is by comparing various English translations. Some websites and apps will actually display multiple translations side by side to see how scholars render the meaning. Using this method, we see that "open to reason" can also be translated as "reasonable," "willing to listen," "approachable," "sensible."

From the beginning, God has been more than willing to listen to and engage His people for their benefit. Just after Adam and Eve sinned, God approached them in the garden and asked four questions: "Where are you?" "Who told you that you were naked?" "Have you eaten of the tree. . .?" and "What is this that you have done?" (Genesis 3:9–13 ESV). It's not for His benefit that an omniscient Creator asked questions but for theirs.

Similarly, Jesus asked questions He already knew the answers to. "And behold, a lawyer stood up to put him to the test, saying, 'Teacher, what shall I do to inherit eternal life?' He said to him, 'What is written in the Law? How do you read it?'" (Luke 10:25–26 ESV). Jesus certainly didn't need a lesson in the Law! Likewise, Paul "reasoned in the synagogue with the Jews and the devout persons, and in the marketplace every day with those who happened to be there" (Acts 17:17 ESV).

Wisdom from above doesn't debate to win an argument; it reasons to open people's eyes.

PRAY

Father in heaven, help me to listen to others and engage them with Your truth for their good.

WISDOM IS. . .FULL OF MERCY

Read James 3:13–18

KEY VERSE

But the wisdom from above is first pure, then peaceable, gentle, open to reason, full of mercy and good fruits, impartial and sincere. JAMES 3:17 ESV

UNDERSTAND

- *Why does being full of something indicate, good or bad?*
- *How is showing mercy wise?*
- *How have you experienced mercy from God?*

APPLY

This is the first of two traits to which James adds an interesting descriptor—"full of." This is the same term used to describe a net full of fish (John 21:8) or the Pharisees' hypocrisy (Matthew 23:28). There's no room for more.

Nothing characterizes divinity more than mercy. *Merriam-Webster* defines mercy as "compassion or forbearance shown especially to an offender or to one subject to one's power." What could better describe God's dealings with humankind from the beginning than mercy? Adam and Eve experienced it from the very moment they sinned, as God "made garments of skin for Adam and his wife, and clothed them" (Genesis 3:21 NASB). Despite mischaracterizations of the "God of the Old Testament" as harsh and judgmental, there are far more instances of His mercy. Noah, all the patriarchs, and Moses knew Him as "a God merciful and gracious, slow to anger, and abounding in steadfast love and faithfulness" (Exodus 34:6 ESV).

Jesus is the fulfillment of God's promise, as His mother Mary understood when she sang, "He has helped his servant Israel, in remembrance of his mercy, as he spoke to our fathers, to Abraham and to his offspring forever" (Luke 1:54–55 ESV). In Christ, we avoid the judgment we deserved, since "according to his great mercy, he has caused us to be born again to a living hope through the resurrection of Jesus Christ from the dead" (1 Peter 1:3 ESV). As James declared: "Mercy triumphs over judgment" (James 2:13 NASB).

PRAY

Merciful Father, compassionate Savior, I thank You for the mystery of the cross and the mercy found in Jesus.

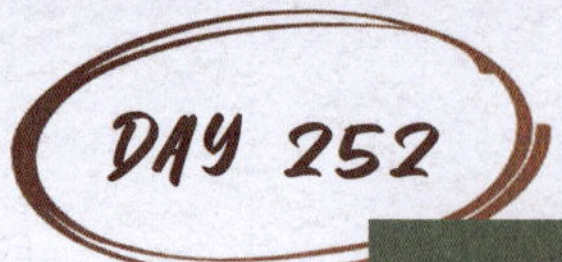

WISDOM IS. . .FULL OF GOOD FRUITS

Read James 3:13–18

KEY VERSE

But the wisdom from above is first pure, then peaceable, gentle, open to reason, full of mercy and good fruits, impartial and sincere. JAMES 3:17 ESV

UNDERSTAND

- *What does the figure of speech "good fruits" refer to?*
- *What is the relationship between wisdom and actions?*

APPLY

The figurative use of "fruits" in English is the same in the Greek—the result of one's choices and actions, whether good or bad. "A healthy tree cannot bear bad fruit, nor can a diseased tree bear good fruit" (Matthew 7:18 ESV). The tree determines the produce.

We begin to bear good fruit when we sink our roots deep into God: "Blessed is the man who trusts in the LORD, whose trust is the LORD. He is like a tree planted by water, that sends out its roots by the stream, and does not fear when heat comes, for its leaves remain green, and is not anxious in the year of drought, for it does not cease to bear fruit" (Jeremiah 17:7–8 ESV).

The Bible speaks of two kinds of fruit—inner and outer. Paul lists the inner fruit we bear when walking with Jesus: "The fruit of the Spirit is love, joy, peace, patience, kindness, goodness, faithfulness, gentleness, self-control" (Galatians 5:22–23 ESV). Likewise, walking in the wisdom from above leads also to outward fruit. Jesus told His disciples shortly before His crucifixion, "You did not choose Me but I chose you, and appointed you that you would go and bear fruit, and that your fruit would remain" (John 15:16 NASB). Their calling and assignment were to bring others into the kingdom.

Godly wisdom always leads to godly actions and to God's results.

PRAY

Lord, You have given me a path that bears fruit inside and out; help me to trust in You for the strength to always walk in Christ's wisdom.

WISDOM IS. . .IMPARTIAL AND SINCERE

Read James 3:13–18

KEY VERSE

But the wisdom from above is first pure, then peaceable, gentle, open to reason, full of mercy and good fruits, impartial and sincere. JAMES 3:17 ESV

UNDERSTAND

- *How does an impartial person behave?*
- *How important is sincerity when we share our faith?*
- *What common elements do these two traits share?*

APPLY

Our last look at James 3:17 is a good opportunity to again compare other English translations for clarity. Many versions, such as the King James, phrase it negatively: "without partiality, and without hypocrisy." Remember that "wisdom from above is *first* pure." Without impartiality and sincerity, wisdom couldn't be pure—it would be suspect to contamination. In fact, if either of these traits were missing, then the other characteristics wouldn't matter because you could never trust this kind of wisdom.

Being impartial and sincere both have to do with trustworthiness. An impartial person shows no favoritism and treats people equally. James condemns favoritism when treating the rich better than the poor in the church: "Doesn't this discrimination show that your judgments are guided by evil motives?" (James 2:4 NLT). It may seem "wise" to treat big donors better than poorer members, but not in God's eyes!

Similarly, a sincere person can be trusted since he has no hidden agenda. You don't have to wonder what he really means. You can take him at his word. Paul elegantly connected wisdom, sincerity, and integrity in a single statement: "Now this is our boast: Our conscience testifies that we have conducted ourselves in the world, and especially in our relations with you, with integrity and godly sincerity. We have done so, relying not on worldly wisdom but on God's grace" (2 Corinthians 1:12 NIV).

Impartiality and sincerity are crucial to wisdom because they produce trust.

PRAY

Heavenly Father, teach me to be honest, sincere, and fair in all my ways to honor You before all men.

YOUR PRIMARY MISSION

Read 2 Timothy 2:1–13

KEY VERSES

Share in suffering like a good soldier of Christ Jesus. No one serving in the army gets entangled in everyday affairs; the soldier's aim is to please the enlisting officer. And in the case of an athlete, no one is crowned without competing according to the rules.

2 Timothy 2:3–5 NRSV

UNDERSTAND

- *How did Paul's mission to reach more people with the gospel inform his view of suffering and hardship?*
- *How can comparing your commitment to Christ with the commitment of a soldier to a commanding officer help you think about your priorities today?*
- *In what ways can comparing the Christian life to an athletic competition help you think about setting goals and enduring difficulty?*

APPLY

You have a holy calling: to participate in the new life of Christ and to share that life with others. Just as Timothy had to be resourceful and determined in passing that message along and enduring suffering, you should think about the ways that God's message will be a part of your day. There are plenty of things to juggle each day, but as a soldier who serves Christ, you should never allow the life of God to be lost in the shuffle.

Perhaps a key word from today's scripture verses to consider is *entangled*. You can't avoid being involved in the affairs of this life, and everyone has basic needs to meet. But what about when are you entangled in something that isn't your concern? When something ties you up to the point that you can't find time to share the life of God with others, then you will know you'll need to make adjustments.

To be certain, there are endless entanglements. There are sports teams, political parties, technology designers, app makers, and entertainers all vying for your attention. Your commitment to Christ is a calling to be involved in His new life without becoming entangled in the distractions of today.

PRAY

Jesus, thank You for including me in Your new life and for giving me the promise of overcoming suffering and death as I will one day be raised with You. Help me to see the entanglements that have kept me from serving You by sharing Your gospel message with others. Help me to avoid distractions from my primary mission in this life. Amen.

THE NEW TESTAMENT'S FIRST FIVE BOOKS

Read John 1:1–18

KEY VERSE

For the law was given through Moses; grace and truth came through Jesus Christ.
JOHN 1:17 ESV

UNDERSTAND

- *What does God want you to do as you read the four Gospels?*
- *What does He want you to do as you read Acts?*

APPLY

Before you read the New Testament, it's wise to look at each section in more depth. The first two sections are:

The Gospels. This section contains four books, written by Matthew, Mark, Luke, and John. These four men tell us about the significance of the divinity, birth, life, ministry, teachings, miracles, suffering, death, burial, resurrection, ascension, heavenly reign, and future return of Jesus Christ. Matthew and the others wrote these books in the gospel genre, mostly in narrative style with a number of sections of discourse, some poetic passages and prayers, and two genealogies.

The key period of time the Gospels cover stretches from about 6 BC to about AD 30, which represents the years Jesus lived here on earth. The expectation of the coming Messiah is realized—and the Lord offers the good news (the gospel) of salvation to everyone.

Acts. This section contains one book, written by Luke. It picks up the narrative at the end of Jesus' time here on earth, records the birth of the church, and shows how the church spread from Jerusalem and Judah to Samaria, and then to many regions throughout the Roman Empire, from about AD 30 to AD 61. The church's message is clear: Believe in Jesus Christ, the Savior of the world. Some met that good news with open arms—many others with much resistance. The theme of Jesus Christ as the Messiah is strongly emphasized in this book.

PRAY

Yes, Lord, I want to say "Thank You!" for the Gospels and Acts. It's incredible to read about Your Son and our Lord and Savior, Jesus Christ, and His work through the apostles and early church.

THE NEW TESTAMENT'S SECOND HALF

Read Romans 1:1–17

KEY VERSE

For I am not ashamed of this Good News about Christ. It is the power of God at work, saving everyone who believes—the Jew first and also the Gentile. ROMANS 1:16 NLT

UNDERSTAND

- *Is it surprising to you that a lot of the New Testament is written to problem-filled churches?*
- *If that isn't surprising to you, why is that?*

APPLY

Before you read the New Testament, it's wise to look at the longest and shortest sections in more depth:

Letters. This section contains twenty-one books, written by Paul, James, Peter, John, and Jude. These twenty-one books present what the life, ministry, and message of the church should (and shouldn't) look like. Most of the books address problems in the early churches. Many sections, however, provide positive explanations of Christian teachings and practices. Paul and the other authors wrote these books in the epistle genre, mostly as discourse with some poetry and prayers. Most of these books were written between AD 45 and AD 70, but John may have written his several shorter letters after AD 85. The theme of Jesus Christ as Messiah is clearly proclaimed throughout these letters.

Revelation. This section contains one book, written by the apostle John about AD 95. John wrote this book in an apocalyptic manner, enfolding poetry and discourse in a narrative framework. In many ways, this book echoes the passion and some of the themes of the Old Testament prophets: Turn from your sins, turn back to God, and get ready for the Lord's pending judgments on the whole earth.

Interestingly, the theme of Revelation isn't so much *how the world ends* but rather *how will your life end—with you staying true to the Lord or not?* The Lord Jesus Christ is clearly worshipped as God's Son, the Messiah, and the Savior of the world.

PRAY

Yes, Lord, I want to say "Thank You!" for the good news about Jesus Christ. It's Your power at work, saving everyone who trusts You. I am one of Yours—I believe.

STILL MORE SILENT YEARS

Read Revelation 22:1–21

KEY VERSE

Then the angel said to me, "Everything you have heard and seen is trustworthy and true."
REVELATION 22:6 NLT

UNDERSTAND

- *In 2 Peter 3:8, the apostle told us to not forget something. What are we not to forget?*
- *In Psalm 90:4, the prophet Moses said something similar. Why has this truth been so important to remember all throughout history?*

APPLY

After the close of the New Testament, it appears that God has been silent for almost two thousand years. In reality, God has been speaking powerfully through the Bible's sixty-six books, which easily fill a thousand pages in most Bibles.

During the past two millennia, God has been using scripture to build His church around the world. Today, more than 2.5 billion people call themselves Christians. Even in the remotest corners of the world, despite intense persecution, people of every nation, people, and tongue are starting to believe.

Part of the key to the expansion of the church has been the translation, publication, reading, and teaching of the Bible among thousands of groups. That expansion has accelerated at a phenomenal rate over the past two generations.

Bible reading and studying isn't a luxury. It's the way the Christian faith takes root in your heart and is shared with others.

Start making a mental list. Include two, three, or four Christian friends you'd like to invite to study this book with you. Yes, you'll be all set to go. Still, there's nothing better than taking a few friends along to see the vistas of scripture with you!

PRAY

Yes, Lord, I want to say "Thank You!" that You live outside and far beyond what I see and know and think of as reality. All that I see, hear, smell, taste, and feel will one day pass away. I can't wait to be with You, in Your presence, in the new heaven and new earth.

FIND HOPE IN THE IMPOSSIBLE

Read Isaiah 40:21–31

KEY VERSES

Do you not know? Have you not heard? The LORD is the everlasting God, the Creator of the ends of the earth. He will not grow tired or weary, and his understanding no one can fathom. He gives strength to the weary and increases the power of the weak. Even youths grow tired and weary, and young men stumble and fall; but those who hope in the LORD will renew their strength. ISAIAH 40:28–31 NIV

UNDERSTAND

- *What did the people of Israel know of God after the tragedy of the exile and the promise of being restored to the land? What did they still need to learn?*
- *Why does today's passage compare the everlasting power of God, the Creator, with the fleeting power of earthly authorities and government?*
- *How is the promise to those who "hope in the LORD" counterintuitive to how some think of waiting?*

APPLY

Waiting well often involves letting go of your expectations for a desired resolution delivered when you want it. You may feel weary in a season of waiting, but you have an everlasting resource. God, who created the heavens and outlasts every person in power and authority, seeks those who will wait, who can look ahead in faith.

Letting go of your plans and hopes doesn't feel great. You may be in a situation where you want to know that things will get better right away. But hope in God doesn't always work like that—even if God promises to renew your strength as you wait.

Just as Israel had to look to God in faith despite the seemingly impossible odds of the exile and the power of its captors, you may need to find hope in God while facing the impossible. What you know of God and His power will go a long way in determining how long you can wait and whether your hope in God will sustain you.

PRAY

I praise You, Lord, for being mighty and all-powerful. You have created all things on earth, and nothing is outside Your influence. I ask for Your mercy and healing in the places of suffering and grief in my life and in the lives of those around me. May I find hope in Your everlasting promises and renewal in Your loving presence. Amen.

REASON ISN'T ENOUGH

Read Acts 17:16–34

KEY VERSES

Now while Paul was waiting for them at Athens, his spirit was provoked within him as he saw that the city was full of idols. So he reasoned in the synagogue with the Jews and the devout persons, and in the marketplace every day with those who happened to be there. ACTS 17:16–17 ESV

UNDERSTAND

- *What was Paul provoked by in the city of Athens?*
- *What did he do in response to a city filled with idols?*

APPLY

Paul, a Hellenistic Jew from Tarsus, had an impressive lineage—"a Hebrew of Hebrews; in regard to the law, a Pharisee" (Philippians 3:5 NIV). He was also well-educated in Greek philosophy and poetry, which he sometimes referenced. Knowing Paul's background adds context to our studies.

On his second missionary journey, Paul visited Athens, the birthplace of Socrates and Plato, whose inhabitants had a reputation: "Now all the Athenians and the foreigners who lived there would spend their time in nothing except telling or hearing something new" (Acts 17:21 ESV). Eventually some philosophers invited him to address the elite body of thinkers called the Areopagus, where he included quotes from two Greek philosophers in his presentation of the gospel. There were three reactions: "When they heard about the resurrection of the dead, some of them *sneered*, but others said, '*We want to hear you again* on this subject.' At that, Paul left the Council. Some of the people became followers of Paul and *believed*" (Acts 17:32–34 NIV, emphasis added). Shortly after this, Paul left for Corinth, where he spent a year and a half.

Why is this part of Paul's story important? Though Paul communicated wisely, he did not put his trust in his own powers of communication.

PRAY

Father, give me insight and wisdom to present clearly the importance of the cross of Jesus.

THE KEYS TO CONTINUAL WORSHIP

Read Psalm 105:1-7

KEY VERSES

Give thanks to the Lord, *call upon His name; make His deeds known among the peoples. Sing to Him, sing praises to Him; tell of all His wonders. Boast in His holy name; may the heart of those who seek the* Lord *be joyful. Seek the* Lord *and His strength; seek His face continually.* Psalm 105:1–4 NASB

UNDERSTAND

- *Which practices mentioned in today's psalm (give thanks to the Lord, make His deeds known, sing to Him, etc.) are the most natural for you to practice? How can you invest more time today in the ones that are a stretch for you?*
- *What does seeking the Lord's face look like in your life? What are some ways you could make this practice something you do "continually"?*
- *How could seeking the Lord lead to a joyful heart?*

APPLY

Thanksgiving and singing have long been essential aspects of worship that will help you focus on the blessings God has given to you—and to offer praise to God for His goodness and generosity. Singing praise of God could be in the form of a hymn, a praise song, a chant, or simply reciting a psalm to a simple melody. These practices can draw your attention away from the distractions of today and shift your gaze to God's presence.

Yet there are many other ways to offer praise to God today. As you grow in your awareness of God's goodness in your life and the ways His power has been at work in you and in others, your worship can spill over into boasting to others about God's goodness. You could say that what is often classified as "missionary" or "evangelistic" work gets merged with the practices of praise and thanksgiving.

While there are private elements to your worship, your praises for God shouldn't be limited to your own mind or prayer journal. As you seek God continually and grow in your awareness of Him, your blessings are the very things to talk about with others.

PRAY

Thank You, Father, for revealing Yourself to me this day and for being present in these quiet moments of study and prayer before You. Help me to recognize the many ways You've blessed me, and help me to take delight in boasting of Your goodness before others. Amen.

DAY 261

GROWING WITH THE WORD, PART 1

Read 2 Timothy 3:10–17

KEY VERSE

From childhood you have known the sacred writings which are able to give you the wisdom that leads to salvation through faith which is in Christ Jesus. 2 TIMOTHY 3:15 NASB

UNDERSTAND

- *What are "the sacred writings" Paul refers to in today's key verse?*
- *What is the point of these sacred writings?*
- *When did Timothy begin learning from these sacred writings?*

APPLY

Today's focus comes from Paul's exhortation to his "beloved son" in the faith, Timothy (2 Timothy 1:2 NASB). Acts 16 records their meeting during Paul's second missionary journey in Asia Minor. Timothy, a believer with a Jewish mother but a Greek father, had a strong spiritual lineage: "For I am mindful of the sincere faith within you, which first dwelled in your grandmother Lois and your mother Eunice, and I am sure that it is in you as well" (2 Timothy 1:5 NASB).

Timothy's mother raised him to know the "sacred writings"—today's Old Testament. That was no easy task in a time when literate women were rare and a household copy of the scriptures even more so. It's unlikely that Timothy's Greek father helped (Timothy was uncircumcised according to Acts 16:3, indicating that the family did not have a Jewish identity). Scholars suggest that Eunice made sure Timothy had a tutor or recited what she herself had been taught. In any case, she was intentional about teaching her son God's Word because those writings would prepare him for the message of the Messiah.

Today, parents have the benefit of the New Testament and its commentary and explanation of the words Timothy would have read. Wise parents will "bring [their children] up in the training and instruction of the Lord" (Ephesians 6:4 NIV) by using the entire handbook He has provided.

PRAY

Author of life, thank You for the full message of salvation in Jesus that has been recorded for us and future generations!

GROWING WITH THE WORD, PART 2

Read 2 Timothy 3:10–17

KEY VERSE

All Scripture is inspired by God and beneficial for teaching, for rebuke, for correction, for training in righteousness. 2 Timothy 3:16 NASB

UNDERSTAND

- *What is the source of all scripture?*
- *How are each of scripture's four uses different?*
- *Is it still useful for our spiritual growth today even though it's thousands of years old?*

APPLY

Some modern writers have suggested that the Old Testament's relevance has been lost and that we should just focus on the New Testament. But in today's key verse we see a different view about "the sacred writings" (2 Timothy 3:15 NASB). Paul declares the scripture to be useful in four ways, all of which are for our spiritual growth. His conviction lay in the fact of the origin of the writing—namely, the breath of God. The author made it authoritative.

Similarly, Jesus looked to the Old Testament as trustworthy and inspired. Not only did He quote it extensively, but after His resurrection, two followers had the privilege of the greatest Bible study imaginable: "Then beginning with Moses and with all the Prophets, He explained to them the things written about Himself in all the Scriptures" (Luke 24:27 NASB). The Old Testament is filled with Jesus!

But what of the Law, from which believers are set free (Romans 7:4)? It also plays a part in the plan of salvation, as Paul explained: "The Law has become our guardian [or tutor] to lead us to Christ" (Galatians 3:24 NASB) by revealing the truth about ourselves. "So the trouble is not with the law, for it is spiritual and good. The trouble is with me, for I am all too human, a slave to sin" (Romans 7:14 NLT). The Law's purpose was to point to a Savior, not become a means of salvation without Him. The same is true still.

PRAY

Gracious Lord, I rejoice in the handbook You have created for us to draw closer to You!

GROWING WITH THE WORD, PART 3

Read Colossians 3:12–17

KEY VERSE

Let the word of Christ dwell in you richly, teaching and admonishing one another in all wisdom, singing psalms and hymns and spiritual songs, with thankfulness in your hearts to God. Colossians 3:16 ESV

UNDERSTAND

- *What does Paul desire about "the word of Christ" for the Colossians?*
- *What kinds of activities does "the word of Christ" lead to?*

APPLY

As we've seen, the Old Testament was filled with the message of the coming Messiah, though often obscured. And that the scriptures are still useful for "training in righteousness" (2 Timothy 3:16 NASB) because "the Lord gives wisdom; from his mouth come knowledge and understanding" (Proverbs 2:6 ESV).

In the New Testament, the wisdom of God becomes clearer; the mystery of salvation is revealed, and we gain an understanding of "things into which angels long to look" (1 Peter 1:12 ESV).

As sons of God, we are designed to grow spiritually by "the word of Christ." Paul said, "Faith comes from hearing, and hearing through the word of Christ" (Romans 10:17 ESV). That's not only *saving* faith but also *growing* faith.

Jesus made it plain how we can go deeper with Him: "Whoever has my commands and keeps them is the one who loves me. The one who loves me will be loved by my Father, and I too will love them and show myself to them" (John 14:21 NIV). In His wisdom, He'll add trials, challenges, and other training tools, but the foundation of our lives must be built on His Word first. If you've ever tried to put together furniture without the manual, you understand the idea.

We can only become the sons that God called us to be through the teachings, instructions, and explanations we have collected in His manual!

PRAY

Lord, my God, You have called me and also provided for me in Your written Word. Thank You with all my heart!

GOD WANTS YOU TO ASK!

Read Matthew 7:7–11

KEY VERSE

"Ask, and it will be given to you; seek, and you will find; knock, and it will be opened to you." MATTHEW 7:7 ESV

UNDERSTAND

- *How would you feel if you had actively and repeatedly encouraged a loved one to tell you whenever that person has a specific need, but he never does?*
- *How would you feel if a long-forgotten second cousin showed up unannounced, says he hears you've done well for yourself, and then tells you exactly what he wants from you?*

APPLY

Throughout His three years of public ministry, Jesus modeled the substantive value of prayer. Not just prayer in the air, but prayer to God our Father. And not just prayer for something good, but detailed and specific prayers.

What's the most specific prayer you have ever prayed? How earnest were your prayers? Did you know you absolutely *needed* the Lord, and the Lord alone, to come through?

Sometimes the poor have an advantage. They know exactly what they need and when they need it. And they know exactly how to respond when the Lord answers such prayers. Yes, they cheer and thank God with all their heart, soul, strength, and mind.

If only we could capture a bit more of their deep trust and dependence on God's guidance, goodness, and outright miracles, it would do something wonderful. It would increase our love, faith, and trust in Jesus—just as it did for the disciples nearly two thousand years ago.

PRAY

Thank You, Lord, for Your providential work and for Your answers to my specific prayers, which increase my faith and trust in You. I'm so glad You want me to turn to You always.

A STUMBLING BLOCK

Read 1 Corinthians 1:17–25

KEY VERSES

For Jews demand signs and Greeks seek wisdom, but we preach Christ crucified, a stumbling block to Jews and folly to Gentiles. 1 CORINTHIANS 1:22–23 ESV

UNDERSTAND

- *Why did Jews insist on seeing signs from heaven?*
- *How accustomed were the Jews to seeing many signs in the Old Testament?*
- *How accustomed were those who lived during Jesus' ministry to seeing signs?*

APPLY

Paul criticized the Jews' insistence on "signs" not because God doesn't grant them, but because the Jews were never satisfied. The prophets performed miracles for centuries, and still many died at the hands of their own people.

Jesus rebuked the Jews of His day for following the pattern of their forefathers: "You consent to the deeds of your fathers, for they killed [the prophets], and you build their tombs" (Luke 11:48 ESV). When they demanded a sign of His own authority, He answered, "A wicked and adulterous generation asks for a sign! But none will be given it except the sign of the prophet Jonah" (Matthew 12:39 NIV), meaning His death and resurrection. Even when He provided that very sign, the Jews demanded more: "Let him come down now from the cross, and we will believe in him" (Matthew 27:42 ESV).

The irony is that if He had come down, they would have had nothing to believe in. He would not have been their Messiah without the cross, and they couldn't see it. The Old Testament clearly promised a Savior who would suffer and die, but the Jews stubbornly relied on their own intellect, which blinded them to it.

Even His closest followers were slow to grasp the resurrection until He "opened their minds so they could understand the Scriptures. He told them, 'This is what is written: The Messiah will suffer and rise from the dead on the third day'" (Luke 24:45–46 NIV).

PRAY

Thank You, Father in heaven, for giving me the only sign that really matters!

FOOLISH AND WEAK

Read 1 Corinthians 1:26–31

KEY VERSE

But God chose the foolish things of the world to shame the wise; God chose the weak things of the world to shame the strong. 1 Corinthians 1:27 NIV

UNDERSTAND

- *Why would God have any interest in shaming the wise or choosing the weak?*
- *The Greeks valued wisdom: How can that be an impediment to knowing God?*

APPLY

Not many people would enjoy being called "foolish" and "weak" (verse 27 NIV), not to mention "lowly" and "despised" (verse 28 NIV). There's not much point in doing a deeper word study either—it doesn't get any better! But in today's passage, Paul argues that it's a blessing and an important part of God's plan for all humankind as announced in the scriptures: "As the Scriptures say, 'I will destroy the wisdom of the wise and discard the intelligence of the intelligent'" (1 Corinthians 1:19 NLT, quoting Isaiah 29:14). God "opposes the proud but gives grace to the humble" (1 Peter 5:5 ESV, quoting Proverb 3:34).

In the gospel, God turns "the world upside down" (Acts 17:6 ESV) for those who deny Him, but He hits the Reset button for all who believe. After the fall, humankind "did not see fit to acknowledge God" (Romans 1:28 NASB) and hit the accelerator to create a world without Him: "For although they knew God, they neither glorified him as God nor gave thanks to him, but their thinking became futile and their foolish hearts were darkened. Although they claimed to be wise, they became fools" (Romans 1:21–22 NIV). Thus, God chose the "things counted as nothing at all, and used them to bring to nothing what the world considers important" (1 Corinthians 1:28 NLT). He's shaming the wise and the strong of this world by using the worst He can find: you and me!

PRAY

I praise You, holy Father, because I'm happy to be a fool who brings You glory!

THE SOURCE OF COURAGE

Read Acts 4:8–14

KEY VERSES

When they saw the courage of Peter and John and realized that they were unschooled, ordinary men, they were astonished and they took note that these men had been with Jesus. But since they could see the man who had been healed standing there with them, there was nothing they could say. Acts 4:13–14 NIV

UNDERSTAND

- *What gave Peter and John the courage to speak up as they did?*
- *What did Jesus pass on to Peter and John that helped when confronted by the religious authorities?*
- *Based on the wider context of this passage, what didn't Peter and John say in this passage and why is that significant?*

APPLY

Courage doesn't just happen on its own, so if you're gearing up for a challenging situation today or if you want to be prepared for future challenges, Peter and John demonstrated a path you can follow. They learned how to speak and act courageously by being with Jesus, who had warned them on many occasions that they would face adversity. Acting courageously starts with learning from Jesus—by being with Him.

In the midst of adversity, you can also follow the example of Peter and John when they focused on the healing God had done and the benefit brought to the lame man. When you move forward in the face of criticism, you will find strength in the importance and benefit of your mission.

It's notable that Peter and John simply being with Jesus spoke volumes to others, and perhaps that is the greatest challenge for you today. The time you are with Jesus and in conversation with Him throughout your day, even if you're driving around town or working on a project at home, will produce unmistakable fruit.

PRAY

Jesus, help me to slow down and to take notice of You throughout my day. I ask for Your wisdom and power so that I can see those in need around me and then intervene for their benefit. May I always do what is right through the courage You provide. Amen.

WISDOM FOR THE MATURE

Read 1 Corinthians 2:1–11

KEY VERSES

We do, however, speak a message of wisdom among the mature, but not the wisdom of this age or of the rulers of this age, who are coming to nothing. No, we declare God's wisdom, a mystery that has been hidden and that God destined for our glory before time began.
1 CORINTHIANS 2:6–7 NIV

UNDERSTAND

- *What is the "mystery" of God Paul is referring to in this passage?*
- *Who does Paul look for to share the deeper things of God?*

APPLY

If you've ever been asked by a child where babies come from, you'll understand something of Paul's dilemma among the Corinthians. He wanted to impart so much about the mystery of God revealed in Christ, but he was held back by their spiritual immaturity.

Although salvation through Jesus had been "made known through the prophetic writings by the command of the eternal God" (Romans 16:26 NIV), people could still not comprehend it. Some were hardened, some found it foolish, and some, like the Corinthian church, were stubbornly immature in their faith. They weren't growing up, and for Paul, that was frustrating: "When I was with you I couldn't talk to you as I would to spiritual people. I had to talk as though you belonged to this world or as though you were infants in Christ" (1 Corinthians 3:1 NLT). Being a baby isn't wrong, but remaining one is a problem: "like newborn babies, long for the pure milk of the word, so that by it you may grow in respect to salvation" (1 Peter 2:2 NASB).

For Paul, preaching the gospel wasn't merely about evangelism. "[Jesus] we proclaim, warning everyone and teaching everyone with all wisdom, that we may present everyone mature in Christ" (Colossians 1:28 ESV). Maturity is the hope of all good parents for their children.

PRAY

Sovereign Lord, forgive me for my immaturity either through stubbornness or complacency!

LEARNING TO SPEAK SPIRITUAL WORDS

Read 1 Corinthians 2:12–16

KEY VERSES

Now we have not received the spirit of the world, but the Spirit who is from God, so that we may know the things freely given to us by God. We also speak these things, not in words taught by human wisdom, but in those taught by the Spirit, combining spiritual thoughts with spiritual words. 1 Corinthians 2:12–13 NASB

UNDERSTAND

- *What characteristics would you expect of "the spirit of the world"?*
- *What has God freely given us?*
- *Who teaches us to communicate spiritual ideas?*

APPLY

Think about Paul's experience in Athens and how he proclaimed the gospel before the leading philosophers—only a few believed although Paul's presentation was one of the most profound recorded in the Bible. That experience framed his time in Corinth and also gives us insight into today's passage.

Paul wrote 1 Corinthians to a growing, though immature congregation. And although he did speak a message of wisdom, he emphasized that it was not something he or any other man had invented, unlike the Greek philosophers who built up human reason alone. Paul drew from another source entirely. Like Paul, we are connected to that source and can experience the promise of Jesus to His followers: "I will give you words and wisdom that none of your adversaries will be able to resist or contradict" (Luke 21:15 NIV).

Being "taught by the Spirit" means both a learning process *and* divine inspiration. Jesus combined these two ideas when He promised, "The Holy Spirit, whom the Father will send in my name, will teach you all things and will remind you of everything I have said to you" (John 14:26 NIV). Paul knew the scriptures well and the teaching of Jesus, but he also knew that to speak spiritually, he had to listen and learn from the Spirit.

PRAY

Keep me ever attentive to the voice of Your Holy Spirit, O Lord, as I study Your living Word.

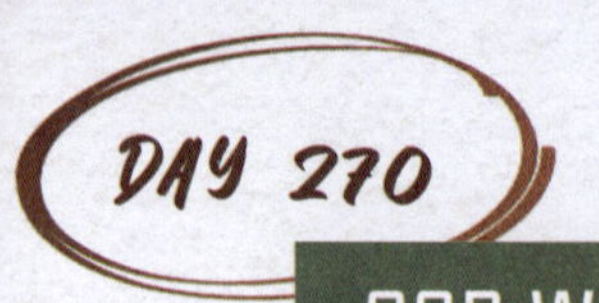

GOD WANTS TO MAKE YOU MORE LOVING

Read 1 Corinthians 12:31–13:13

KEY VERSE

But earnestly desire the higher gifts. And I will show you a still more excellent way.
1 Corinthians 12:31 esv

UNDERSTAND

- *What if your closest friend or loved one suddenly became 25 percent more loving to you? How long do you think it would take before you figured it out?*
- *What if you could become 10 percent more loving to your closest friends and loved ones? What would it take to make that happen?*

APPLY

What's the longest period of time that you and your wife or closest loved one have been apart? A week? A month? A year? Several years? Career-dominated jobs abound in the military, firefighting, professional sports, and many other fields of endeavor.

It was no different for the Twelve. Jesus called Peter and Andrew, James and John, and each of the other apostles to follow Him—and didn't wait around for an answer. It was either instant yes or automatic no.

What was Jesus trying to teach them during those three years of life together? A lot! But mostly, He showed them what the marvelous, amazing mercy, grace, and love of God look like in flesh and blood.

As we read the Gospels, we sometimes miss the elbow and fist pumps, laughter and ribbing, humor and sarcasm of Jesus. Sometimes we miss the bone-tiring walks, the leisurely meals, the beachside BBQs. Everything, *everything*, Jesus said and did was done 100 percent in love.

PRAY

Lord, I can't spend most of my time today with You, but You already know that. Still, I want to walk in step with Your will. Please infuse my heart with more of Your love.

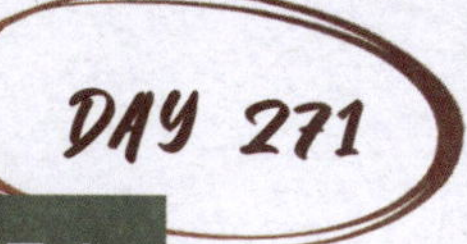

THE MYSTERY OF THE CHURCH, PART 1

Read Ephesians 3:1–13

KEY VERSE

This mystery is that through the gospel the Gentiles are heirs together with Israel, members together of one body, and sharers together in the promise in Christ Jesus. Ephesians 3:6 niv

UNDERSTAND

- *What was the mystery Paul says God had revealed to him?*
- *Why would including Gentiles in the offer of salvation be such a big deal?*

APPLY

As we've discussed, knowing the context of a passage can make all the difference. What seems obvious to us today—the availability of the gospel to all humankind—was a mystery to the Jews of Jesus' and Paul's day.

From the fall of man to the Tower of Babel, humankind repeatedly rejected God. Then the Bible concentrates on a nation that God created from one man—Abraham—to whom He promised: "I will make you into a great nation, and I will bless you" (Genesis 12:2 niv). His descendants were chosen "to be the people of [God's] inheritance" (Deuteronomy 4:20 niv). It's important to note that God *created* a nation for Himself; He did not select one from those that existed. Thus, everyone outside of Abraham's lineage (the Gentiles) were "excluded from the people of Israel, and strangers to the covenants of the promise, having no hope and without God in the world" (Ephesians 2:12 nasb), and that a "wall of hostility" (Ephesians 2:14 nlt) separated Jew and Gentile.

But in mercy, God had also promised Abraham, "Through your offspring all nations on earth will be blessed" (Genesis 22:18 niv). Jesus fulfilled that promise. "You will do more than restore the people of Israel to me. I will make you a light to the Gentiles, and you will bring my salvation to the ends of the earth" (Isaiah 49:6 nlt). In Christ, we all become full heirs of God's covenant and promises.

PRAY

I thank You, merciful Father, for including me in Your covenant through Jesus!

THE MYSTERY OF THE CHURCH, PART 2

Read Ephesians 3:1–13

KEY VERSES

I was chosen to explain to everyone this mysterious plan that God, the Creator of all things, had kept secret from the beginning. God's purpose in all this was to use the church to display his wisdom in its rich variety to all the unseen rulers and authorities in the heavenly places. This was his eternal plan, which he carried out through Christ Jesus our Lord.
EPHESIANS 3:9–11 NLT

UNDERSTAND

- *Who does Paul say he was called to preach to?*
- *Regarding the mystery of the church, what is God's purpose?*
- *What are "rulers and authorities in the heavenly places"?*

APPLY

The Bible is a history of the natural and supernatural worlds and their relationship. The natural world is what we experience through our senses, and the "heavenly places" are an unseen realm of spiritual beings (*elohim*), of whom God is supreme (*Elohim*). Not all people follow God, and likewise not all *elohim* are on His side. Paul faced human opposition but emphasized that "we do not wrestle against flesh and blood, but against the rulers, against the authorities, against the cosmic powers over this present darkness, against the spiritual forces of evil in the heavenly places" (Ephesians 6:12 ESV).

Commonly called "spiritual warfare," we need to be aware of its reality, though not afraid since Jesus "disarmed the powers and authorities" and "made a public spectacle of them, *triumphing* over them by the cross" (Colossians 2:15 NIV, emphasis added). In addition, God "raised [Jesus] from the dead and seated him at his right hand in the heavenly places, far above all rule and authority and power and dominion" (Ephesians 1:20–21 ESV). As the body of Christ, we were created to "display [God's] wisdom in its rich variety" not just on earth, but in the "heavenly places" too.

PRAY

I praise You, Lord, for Your victory over all things that would separate us from You.

A CONTINUOUS FOUNDATION

Read Matthew 7:21–29

KEY VERSES

"Therefore everyone who hears these words of mine and puts them into practice is like a wise man who built his house on the rock. The rain came down, the streams rose, and the winds blew and beat against that house; yet it did not fall, because it had its foundation on the rock." MATTHEW 7:24–25 NIV

UNDERSTAND

- *What does Jesus say qualifies us to be called wise?*
- *In this parable, does the wise man face less trouble than the foolish man?*
- *What was the foolish man's outcome in this parable?*

APPLY

Some parables can be tough to grasp when looking at them from a modern perspective. Today's reading is not one of those! And you don't have to be in the construction industry to get the point Jesus is making. A solid foundation for a house is just common sense. Even if you live along the coast where houses are built on pilings, the goal is to hit rock by going deep. The same is true for our spiritual lives.

There is, however, an interesting grammatical usage in today's passage. Jesus uses the present tense to qualify the subject—"everyone who *hears* these words of mine and *puts* them into practice"—then He equates those people to a man who "*built* his house on the rock," which is past tense. How can someone who *does* something be like someone who *did* something?

A building's foundation is a continuous thing. Our houses only work because the foundation keeps doing its job, providing ongoing stability. Obedience works in a similar way, allowing us to expect ongoing spiritual stability in the face of the inevitable tests of life. While God will never abandon His children, last year's obedience isn't a guarantee for today's walk of faith.

PRAY

God, keep me ever laying the solid foundation of a life of obedience in Christ.

WORSHIP IS A CHOICE

Read Joshua 24:14–27

KEY VERSES

"Now therefore revere the LORD, and serve him in sincerity and in faithfulness; put away the gods that your ancestors served beyond the River and in Egypt, and serve the LORD. Now if you are unwilling to serve the LORD, choose this day whom you will serve, whether the gods your ancestors served in the region beyond the River or the gods of the Amorites in whose land you are living; but as for me and my household, we will serve the LORD."

JOSHUA 24:14–15 NRSV

UNDERSTAND

- *How does today's passage address the spiritual danger of a divided heart?*
- *Why was the example of Joshua so important for the people of Israel?*
- *Why did Joshua give the people of Israel a choice?*

APPLY

Autopilot doesn't work when it comes to your spiritual allegiance. If you let the tyranny of the urgent determine your priorities today, there's a good chance that other activities and other values will take over God's rightful place in your life. Just sliding by with the status quo of the popular culture won't serve you well.

You can start (or end) today with a simple choice about whom you will serve. The answer may not be as obvious as some think it should be. There are so many other competing priorities and values that can send you off course. A simple choice that sets your course for today and determines what you'll cherish above all else can prove to be a powerful catalyst for a life devoted to God.

If you find yourself slipping off course, consider which spiritual leaders, whether in your church or in Christian books, can help you make a better choice. Sometimes the clarity of a healthy spiritual leader or guide can make your choice of allegiance much easier to settle.

PRAY

Father, thank You for the grace and patience You've shown me, and thank You as well for the spiritual leaders who have helped set a path ahead of me. May I serve You with an undivided heart by choosing to make You my focus for today, tomorrow, and the days that follow. Amen.

A POSITIVE LOOP

Read Colossians 1:1–14

KEY VERSES

We continually ask God to fill you with the knowledge of his will through all the wisdom and understanding that the Spirit gives, so that you may live a life worthy of the Lord and please him in every way: bearing fruit in every good work, growing in the knowledge of God.
COLOSSIANS 1:9–10 NIV

UNDERSTAND

- *What was on Paul's heart for these believers?*
- *Where do wisdom and understanding come from?*
- *What does a life "worthy of the Lord" look like?*

APPLY

As we saw in our last study, it's the practice or habit of living by the Word of God that demonstrates wisdom, not simply the collection of insights. While the wisdom from above does enlighten our minds, its goal is to change our lives. We see that combination in today's key verses: Knowledge and understanding of God's will lead to a life that pleases Him. That in turn produces fruit that leads back to knowing more about God. It's a positive loop of knowing, doing, and knowing more.

Even Jesus—the embodiment of wisdom—experienced this loop. At twelve years old, Jesus accompanied His family on their annual trip to Jerusalem. When they left, He stayed behind. Three days later, His alarmed parents "found Him in the temple, sitting in the midst of the teachers, both listening to them and asking them questions. And all who heard Him were amazed at His understanding and His answers" (Luke 2:46–47 NASB). The remainder of Jesus' youth is described in a single fascinating comment: "And Jesus kept increasing in wisdom and stature, and in favor with God and people" (Luke 2:52 NASB).

Jesus increased in wisdom, even as God in the flesh set an eternal example for all believers.

PRAY

Open my eyes, Lord, that I may see and understand and obey Your will and draw closer to You.

THE HAIRS ON YOUR HEAD

Read Acts 27:9–37

KEY VERSE

"Please eat something now for your own good. For not a hair of your heads will perish."
ACTS 27:34 NLT

UNDERSTAND

- *When Paul added that last statement, what kind of promise was he making?*
- *Was Paul's phrase meant to be understood literally or metaphorically?*

APPLY

After surviving the shipwreck, none of Paul's shipmates double-checked to make sure he hadn't lost any hair. Instead, they were deeply moved that his God-ordained promise came true. Not a man was lost!

To understand Paul's use of the phrase "Not a hair of your heads will perish," it's helpful to see how it was used in biblical times. The phrase, it turns out, had a long history.

The use of this phrase as a biblical metaphor dates back before 1000 BC and the start of the united Israelite monarchy under Saul, David, and Solomon. Metaphors included "safety" (1 Samuel 14:45; 2 Samuel 14:11; 1 Kings 1:52) and "huge number" (Psalm 40:12; 69:4, both attributed to David).

Centuries later, both during and after the Babylonian captivity, use of this phrase became literal. Its literal meanings included "safety" (Daniel 3:27) and "extreme grief" (Ezra 9:3).

During His public ministry here on earth, Jesus used this phrase literally and as metaphor. Its literal meanings included "humanly impossible" (Matthew 5:36) and "divinely known in exact detail" (Matthew 10:30; Luke 12:7). Its metaphorical meaning included "safety" (Luke 21:18).

During his apostolic ministry, Paul used this phrase with the metaphorical meaning of "safety" (Acts 27:34). Again, not a man was lost!

PRAY

Yes, Lord, I want to say "Thank You!" that You kept Your promise to Paul and his shipmates. It reminds me to trust Your promises about forgiving my sins, giving me eternal life, and so much more.

DAY 277

LOOK TOWARD THE UNSEEN

Read 2 Corinthians 4:11–18

KEY VERSES

For our present troubles are small and won't last very long. Yet they produce for us a glory that vastly outweighs them and will last forever! So we don't look at the troubles we can see now; rather, we fix our gaze on things that cannot be seen. For the things we see now will soon be gone, but the things we cannot see will last forever. 2 CORINTHIANS 4:17–18 NLT

UNDERSTAND

- *How do you typically evaluate the size of the troubles you are facing right now? What kind of shift does Paul suggest in today's verses?*
- *What is the challenge of focusing on the things that you can't see right now?*
- *How can you strike a balance between an awareness of God's rewards for today's faithfulness and being present in the challenges of the present moment?*

APPLY

You are right to take the troubles you face today seriously, and you should give them your full consideration. The pain and exhaustion of challenges and suffering can take a very real toll. You should also respond with empathy and care to the difficulties others face.

Yet when you step back from the immediacy of the moment and read today's scripture verses, you'll see that Paul offers another viewpoint. You can look at today through God's eternal lens, seeing how each small choice and action impacts your enjoyment of the new life. The more you learn to value the things of God's kingdom today, the more you'll find contentment in Him.

This is a moment for encouragement and hope even in dark, uncertain times. God hasn't forgotten you. Persevering today and remaining present in His will has far-reaching ramifications that you can only imagine on this side of heaven.

PRAY

Father, thank You for Your generous comfort and hope that can carry me through the difficulties of today. May I never become so preoccupied with the things of the present moment that I can't see how You've prepared a place for me that will overshadow the pain of today. Amen.

OUTSIDERS

Read Colossians 4:1–6

KEY VERSES

Walk in wisdom toward outsiders, making the best use of the time. Let your speech always be gracious, seasoned with salt, so that you may know how you ought to answer each person.
Colossians 4:5–6 ESV

UNDERSTAND

- *Who or what is an outsider?*
- *In what ways are we to make the best use of our opportunities with outsiders?*
- *How should we talk to those who are not of the same Christian worldview?*

APPLY

In New Testament times there weren't churches on every corner. There may have been various congregations that met in homes (1 Corinthians 16:19; Philemon 2), but "the church" in most cities viewed itself, and functioned, as one body. Christians were obviously in the minority among Greek pagans but sometimes also among large Jewish communities. Believers had to be wise in how they navigated the society that surrounded them.

Sometimes the church enjoyed "having favor with all the people," as in Jerusalem after Pentecost, when "the Lord added to their number day by day those who were being saved" (Acts 2:47 ESV). But often it was the opposite, as in Thessalonica: "The Jews were jealous, and taking some wicked men of the rabble, they formed a mob, set the city in an uproar, and attacked the house of Jason, seeking to bring them out to the crowd" (Acts 17:5 ESV).

Despite the danger of persecution, Paul's instruction to be wise toward outsiders wasn't primarily about avoiding trouble; it was about making the gospel credible by our example. Peter similarly reminded his audience, "Always be prepared to give an answer to everyone who asks you to give the reason for the hope that you have. But do this with gentleness and respect, keeping a clear conscience" (1 Peter 3:15–16 NIV). The world has the right to judge our message by our behavior.

PRAY

Father, grant me wisdom to live and to speak wisely so unbelievers will see Your Spirit working.

NO GOOD THING IS HELD BACK

Read Psalm 84:5–12

KEY VERSES

For a day in Your courtyards is better than a thousand elsewhere. I would rather stand at the threshold of the house of my God than live in the tents of wickedness. For the LORD God is a sun and shield; the LORD gives grace and glory; he withholds no good thing from those who walk with integrity. PSALM 84:10–11 NASB

UNDERSTAND

- *What benefit does the writer of Psalm 84 seek to gain by dwelling at the entrance to God's house?*
- *What does it mean for God to be a sun and a shield for His people?*
- *Why is walking with integrity so important for those who want God to withhold "no good thing" from them?*

APPLY

You're likely immersed in a culture that is always on the lookout for one more good thing—and then one more good thing. . .and then another. Yet God promises to withhold no good thing from you if you walk with integrity. As you look ahead to your day, you have an opportunity to trust God to generously supply everything you need.

It's possible that you may believe you need more than what God has given to you. But instead of focusing on what you don't have, you can shift your priorities and spend more time in God's presence and among God's people. When you do that, you'll find more peace and contentment than you could living "in the tents of wickedness."

Contentment isn't easy to find today. But where you spend your time today may prove to be one of the most important factors in determining whether or not you feel content and at peace with God.

PRAY

Father, thank You for the promise to care for the needs of those who walk with integrity and seek You first by dwelling in Your house. May I find what I need in You and forever leave behind the empty promises found among those who seek only their own satisfaction. Amen.

OPPORTUNITIES

Read Ephesians 5:1–21

KEY VERSES

So then, be careful how you walk, not as unwise people but as wise, making the most of your time, because the days are evil. Therefore do not be foolish, but understand what the will of the Lord is. EPHESIANS 5:15–17 NASB

UNDERSTAND

- *What does Paul point to as the reason to live wisely?*
- *What are we to avoid or pursue?*

APPLY

Paul had similar concerns for all the churches he shepherded. Today's passage is similar to his directions to the Colossians, whom he had not met, but with a darker tone, likely from his own experience in Ephesus.

As was his custom, Paul entered the local synagogue on his first visit to Ephesus, "and for three months spoke boldly, reasoning and persuading them about the kingdom of God" (Acts 19:8 ESV). Some believed, but others began to malign the gospel. So Paul "withdrew from them and took the disciples with him, reasoning daily in the hall of Tyrannus. This continued for two years, so that all the residents of Asia heard the word of the Lord, both Jews and Greeks" (Acts 19:9–10 ESV). Paul turned the Jews' rejection into a unique opportunity.

During those two years, many were converted as "fear fell upon them all, and the name of the Lord Jesus was extolled" (Acts 19:17 ESV). But fierce opposition grew from a silversmith named Demetrius, "who had a large business manufacturing silver shrines of the Greek goddess Artemis" (Acts 19:24 NLT). As the gospel threatened his income, he stirred up a mob that could have ended badly if a coolheaded city official hadn't intervened. Knowing his opportunity in Ephesus had come to a close, Paul left for Macedonia.

Like the Ephesians, as our "days are evil," we need to be wise about every opportunity for the gospel.

PRAY

Lord, I want to know Your will, making the most of the opportunities You give me for the gospel.

WHAT SHOULD YOU THINK ABOUT?

Read Philippians 4:8–13

KEY VERSE

Whatever is true, whatever is noble, whatever is right, whatever is pure, whatever is lovely, whatever is admirable—if anything is excellent or praiseworthy—think about such things. PHILIPPIANS 4:8 NIV

UNDERSTAND

- *How many minutes per day (outside of work) do you actively choose what you're going to think about?*
- *Do you tend to actively choose based on intentional plans or the spur of the moment?*

APPLY

One of men's greatest fears is someone figuring out what they think about. Yet what you think about defines almost everything else about you. So why the deep fear? And how do you overcome it?

The apostle Paul provided the answer in the verse quoted above. The verse's eight terms describe the Lord and His Word and fill its pages from Genesis 1 to Revelation 22. As well, the eight terms describe a number of biblical heroes. Best of all? They can describe you too!

The biggest surprise? How many of the biblical heroes are *women*, both ideal and real. *Ideal* women like Wisdom and the Virtuous Woman. *Real* women like Ruth, Rebekah, Rachel, and many others. Yes, it's good to think about them (instead of ignore them, which we guys are prone to do).

The last of the eight terms—*praiseworthy* and its synonyms—describes Abel (Hebrews 11:4), Enoch (Hebrews 11:5), Job (Job 29:11), Paul and Silas (Acts 15:40), Phoebe (Romans 16:1), and local church elders (Titus 1:7). Like the other seven terms, it describes both someone's character and what he thinks about. Each day, may you be a praiseworthy thinker.

Like Paul, you can actively choose to think about what is true, noble, right, pure, lovely, admirable, excellent, and praiseworthy. If so, what you say and do will eventually reveal your Christlike character to a watching world.

PRAY

Yes, Lord, I want to say "Thank You!" that You and Your Word can fill my thoughts with all that is true, noble, right, pure, lovely, admirable, excellent, and praiseworthy.

PERSECUTION

Read Matthew 10:5–20

KEY VERSE

"Behold, I am sending you out as sheep in the midst of wolves, so be wise as serpents and innocent as doves." MATTHEW 10:16 ESV

UNDERSTAND

- *What characteristics do the four animals in this verse personify?*
- *How is a "serpent" a metaphor for wisdom?*

APPLY

Animal metaphors have always been part of human language and appear throughout the Bible: Lions are strong, heifers are stubborn, and eagles are swift. In today's key verse, Jesus used four animals symbolically to emphasize His meaning.

At a key point in His ministry, Jesus sent out His twelve disciples to proclaim a simple message: "The kingdom of heaven is at hand" (Matthew 10:7 ESV). And despite being given the authority to heal the sick and even raise the dead, they would still be like "sheep in the midst of wolves" (Matthew 10:16 ESV). They would attract opposition from both religious and secular sources and be "dragged before" courts, governors, and kings (Matthew 10:18–19 ESV).

Because they would be so vulnerable, these situations would require the disciples to be wise. In Greek, *phronimos* means "practically wise" or "discerning." Ironically, the serpent personified those things even in the garden of Eden! "Now the serpent was more crafty than any other beast" (Genesis 3:1 ESV). The Hebrew for *crafty* is elsewhere translated as "shrewd" or "sensible." For good or ill, the serpent was a thinker, and Jesus wanted His disciples to take note.

But in a possible counterbalance to the historically problematic serpent, Jesus invoked the dove, which is "innocent" (*akeraios*) or *unmixed with contaminants* and *without guile*. No matter how shrewd they must become, the disciples could not afford to play the world's game if their message was to be true to the one who sent them.

PRAY

Wise Father, teach me to be practical and discerning but also gentle and innocent for the sake of Your gospel.

SOLOMON'S REPUTATION

Read 1 Kings 3:16–28

KEY VERSES

Then [Solomon] said, "Cut the living child in two, and give half to one woman and half to the other!" Then the woman who was the real mother of the living child, and who loved him very much, cried out, "Oh no, my lord! Give her the child—please do not kill him!" But the other woman said, "All right, he will be neither yours nor mine; divide him between us!" Then the king said, "Do not kill the child, but give him to the woman who wants him to live, for she is his mother!" When all Israel heard the king's decision, the people were in awe of the king, for they saw the wisdom God had given him for rendering justice. 1 Kings 3:25–28 NLT

UNDERSTAND

- *How did Solomon know what the mother's reaction would be?*
- *What was the nation's reaction to his judgment?*

APPLY

The first story of Solomon's God-given wisdom was as dramatic as it was unlikely. How did two prostitutes even get an audience with the king? Apparently, the case was so puzzling to the lower courts that it ended up in front of the king, as Moses' father-in-law had intended: "And [trusted men] judged the people at all times. Any hard case they brought to Moses, but any small matter they decided themselves" (Exodus 18:26 ESV). This case wasn't hard—it was impossible. Imagine the murmurs as the women argued and the breathlessness when Solomon asked for a sword! Was he going to be an unpredictable and violent king like Saul rather than a shepherd like his father?

But "wisdom is proved right by her deeds" (Matthew 11:19 NIV), and the results of this case established Solomon's reputation before the entire kingdom. That was just the beginning. Other nations would soon hear of this wise king.

PRAY

Father, grant me wisdom when faced with tough choices so that Your reputation spreads, not mine.

OBEDIENCE CALLS FOR COURAGE

Read 2 Chronicles 15:1–9

KEY VERSE

When Asa heard these words and the prophecy of Azariah son of Oded the prophet, he took courage. He removed the detestable idols from the whole land of Judah and Benjamin and from the towns he had captured in the hills of Ephraim. He repaired the altar of the Lord *that was in front of the portico of the* Lord*'s temple.* 2 Chronicles 15:8 niv

UNDERSTAND

- *King Asa faced a lot of adversity in restoring the people of Israel. While he received a clear prophetic message about continuing his reform work, why do you think he needed to be courageous?*
- *What is the significance of the Lord's altar being in disrepair and then fixing it?*
- *After his repair work, Asa gathered the people together. What was at stake in this kind of public gathering?*

APPLY

God may not have given you a clear message about what He wants you to do next, but He has given you plenty of teachings and commands in scripture to guide you. Removing any false gods or sources of comfort and control could be a very practical place to begin. Or you may need to consider the places where you worship Him and ask yourself if they are in need of repair.

Whatever your next step is in response to God's teachings or direction in your life, you may need to make some hard choices. You may need to run against the accepted wisdom of the day or even in your community. Making big shifts always requires courage and vision as you look ahead to a promising future that others may not be able to imagine.

Others in your community may not recognize you for your faithfulness, and that's where courage will surely come in handy. If you have a clear vision from God, then you are free to take risks and to see how God's blessings unfold.

PRAY

Father, help me to listen to Your voice in my life and to make the hard choices that remove the obstacles from knowing and loving You as You are worthy. May I repair what is broken down in my worship of You, and may I never give in to the pressure of others but instead remain wholly devoted to You. Amen.

AUTHORITY, PART 1

Read Titus 2

KEY VERSES

Teach slaves to be subject to their masters in everything, to try to please them, not to talk back to them, and not to steal from them, but to show that they can be fully trusted, so that in every way they will make the teaching about God our Savior attractive. TITUS 2:9–10 NIV

UNDERSTAND

- *What was the historical context of Paul's instruction to Titus?*
- *What's the point Paul is making about wise behavior toward authority?*

APPLY

Historical context is critical in today's passage since it touches on a subject that has changed drastically since ancient times. We need to look for the principles that will be useful today.

Thankfully, legal slavery does not exist in the West anymore, but for thousands of years indebted servitude was an economic fact of life. The scriptures taught the fair treatment of slaves (Exodus 21:26–27) and encouraged obtaining freedom when possible (1 Corinthians 7:21). But what if you were stuck under someone else's authority? As always, Paul's main concern was the gospel. He commanded that slaves show "they can be fully trusted" because it would make "the teaching about God our Savior attractive." Paul wasn't unsympathetic to the "yoke of slavery" (1 Timothy 6:1 NIV), but his point was that even from a position of weakness, we can serve God.

Joseph was sold into slavery by his own brothers but honored God, and "Potiphar put him in charge of his household, and he entrusted to his care everything he owned" (Genesis 39:4 NIV). Later, Pharaoh said, "There is no one so discerning and wise as you. You shall be in charge of my palace, and all my people are to submit to your orders" (Genesis 41:39–41 NIV). Joseph never sought advancement; he simply acted faithfully, and the God of Israel was made known to an entire nation.

PRAY

Faithful Father, teach me to be faithful and trustworthy in my work, for Your name's sake.

AUTHORITY, PART 2

Read Ephesians 6:1–9

KEY VERSE

And masters, do the same things to them, and give up threatening, knowing that both their Master and yours is in heaven, and there is no partiality with Him. Ephesians 6:9 NASB

UNDERSTAND

- *How are those who are in authority over people to act toward those they direct?*
- *Is there any room for abusive or threatening behavior in a Christian leader?*
- *What should be the motivation of a believer who is in authority?*

APPLY

The epistles of the New Testament explain both *how* and *why* we should act as "ambassadors for Christ" (2 Corinthians 5:20 ESV), addressing both sides of human relationships—husbands and wives, children and parents, slave and free. While instructions to bondservants may not completely translate to modern-day employment, the warning to those in authority over people is still applicable.

Those who are given authority, whether in the marketplace, the military, or the church, have clear responsibilities. When Paul tells masters to treat slaves "in the same way" (Ephesians 6:9 NLT), he's emphasizing that it's not just the slave who is "working for the Lord" (Ephesians 6:7 NLT). These two have a mutual Master in heaven who "will reward each one of us for the good we do, whether we are slaves or free" (Ephesians 6:8 NLT).

Jesus went so far as to redefine authority: "You know that the rulers in this world *lord it* over their people, and officials flaunt their authority over those under them. But among you it will be different" (Mark 10:42–43 NLT, emphasis added). Your position may put you over people, but it doesn't make you superior; it makes you more accountable! Those who are in authority should take to heart what the psalmist said: "Now therefore, O kings, be wise; be warned, O rulers of the earth. Serve the LORD with fear, and rejoice with trembling" (Psalm 2:10–11 ESV).

PRAY

Sovereign Lord, in whatever position You place me, may I be a faithful witness to Your great salvation.

WHAT YOU CAN LEARN FROM A BIBLICAL WOMAN

Read Mark 12:41–44

KEY VERSE

"They all gave out of their wealth; but she, out of her poverty, put in everything—all she had to live on." MARK 12:44 NIV

UNDERSTAND

- *When you filled out your latest tax returns, were you surprised by how little or by how much charitable giving you had done this past year?*
- *Are you willing to consider heeding the poor widow's example?*

APPLY

The poor widow in today's reading walks into the Women's Court in front of the temple. You can imagine her rehearsing God's promises—and what she has prayerfully decided to do. As Jesus watches, she stops in front of a funnel-shaped offering receptacle. She reaches out her hand and drops in her last two small bronze coins.

Jesus knew this widow well. Yes, it's true, He knows all widows. And He knew this poor woman had no property and no close family to take care of her. Therefore, since a big part of Jesus' ministry was caring for the poor, it's likely that Jesus motioned for one of His disciples to follow after her and quietly give her several silver coins.

Still, think about this poor widow's example.

First, she showed that no gift is too large. Jesus said she put in more than all the other contributors. She put in all she had to live on. Now, of course, she could do this because she wasn't obligated to care for anyone else. Scripture teaches that your obligation to care for your family's real needs supersedes any gift you desire to give. Giving isn't a way to shirk our God-given responsibilities at home.

Second, this poor widow showed that no gift is too small. Her two small coins couldn't even buy the smallest bird to sacrifice or eat. How in the world could her miniscule donation make any difference? To Jesus, though, it made all the difference. That small donation proved that this poor widow was fully and wholly dedicated to the Lord her God. Her love, trust, and sheer bravery were moving. It clearly moved Jesus, who honored her here and in Luke 21:1–4.

PRAY

Yes, Lord, I want to say "Thank You!" for all of the Bible's heroes, both men and women. May I follow the poor widow's example in the ways I give in coming days and weeks.

A PROPER SELF VIEW, PART 1

Read Romans 12

KEY VERSE

Live in harmony with one another. Do not be haughty, but associate with the lowly. Never be wise in your own sight. ROMANS 12:16 ESV

UNDERSTAND

- *Why is harmony between believers important?*
- *Who qualifies as "the lowly" today? Do you know any "lowly" people?*
- *How would you paraphrase being "wise in your own sight"?*

APPLY

Sometimes verses speak for themselves, making them great to memorize and share. But even those verses need context from the fuller passage.

Most of the New Testament comes to us as letters, which would have been read aloud to a congregation. As part of your Bible study approach, try listening to a passage being read in a Bible app and see if it offers a different perspective than reading silently.

Romans 12 is a turning point in Paul's letter, moving from a theological, explanatory tone to an impassioned plea for godly living. It implores believers to offer themselves as a "living sacrifice" (verse 1) to God, not to earn salvation, but because of it, and to not conform to this world. Paul warns the mature in Christ "not to think more highly of himself than he ought to think; but to think so as to have sound judgment" (Romans 12:3 NASB). Be self-aware, just not puffed up. Paul knew that a clear indication of an exaggerated self-opinion is disassociation with the "lowly"—those who can't offer anything in return for attention. We make a serious mistake when we don't regard those at the "bottom" as worth serving, as Jesus made clear: "I tell you the truth, when you refused to help the *least of these my brothers and sisters*, you were refusing to help me" (Matthew 25:45 NLT, emphasis added).

PRAY

Open my eyes, Father, to see those who are in need and to serve You through them.

A PROPER SELF VIEW, PART 2

Read 2 Corinthians 10

KEY VERSES

We do not dare to classify or compare ourselves with some who commend themselves. When they measure themselves by themselves and compare themselves with themselves, they are not wise. We, however, will not boast beyond proper limits, but will confine our boasting to the sphere of service God himself has assigned to us, a sphere that also includes you. 2 Corinthians 10:12–13 niv

UNDERSTAND

- *What does it mean for someone to "commend" himself?*
- *What did Paul do in contrast to those who boasted about themselves?*
- *What "sphere of service" has God assigned to you?*

APPLY

Paul spent a fair amount of energy defending his flocks. He told the Ephesian church, "I know that after I leave, savage wolves will come in among you and will not spare the flock. Even from your own number men will arise and distort the truth in order to draw away disciples after them" (Acts 20:29–30 niv). Self-centered and greedy false teachers were just as rampant in Paul's day as they are in ours.

Often, the tone of a letter can help clarify a passage. Paul begins this section ironically: "We do not dare to classify or compare ourselves. . ." and then goes ahead and does it! He's answering fools according to their folly (Proverbs 26:5) to highlight their absurd mutual admiration society. They were "not wise" for exchanging pats on the back and calling it credibility.

Paul had real credibility, but he wasn't interested in self-promotion. He took his own advice "not to think more highly of himself than he ought to think" (Romans 12:3 nasb). That meant simply being honest with what God had called him to do and letting "someone else praise you, and not your own mouth; an outsider, and not your own lips" (Proverbs 27:2 niv).

PRAY

Father, Your opinion alone matters. Help me to simply be faithful to Your calling.

REMEMBER WHAT YOU'VE SEEN

Read Deuteronomy 4:9–14

KEY VERSES

But take care and watch yourselves closely, so as neither to forget the things that your eyes have seen nor to let them slip from your mind all the days of your life; make them known to your children and your children's children—how you once stood before the Lord *your God at Horeb, when the* Lord *said to me, "Assemble the people for me, and I will let them hear my words, so that they may learn to fear me as long as they live on the earth, and may teach their children so."* Deuteronomy 4:9–10 nrsv

UNDERSTAND

- *What do you think Moses specifically meant when he told the Israelites to "take care and watch yourselves closely"?*
- *What was at stake when the Israelites heard the words of God and repeated them to their children and grandchildren?*
- *What does this passage teach about passing along spiritual experiences and lessons to younger generations?*

APPLY

What you experience with God and what you learn about Him today isn't just for your own benefit in the present moment. When you have a significant experience or learn an insight that shapes how you live, you have a holy calling to remember that moment and to pass it along to future generations.

God's teachings are meant to be taken seriously and obeyed. Even the moment of receiving those teachings for the first time is a significant step toward passing them along in the future. Each major step forward or epiphany of God's grace in your life can become an opportunity to pass something vital along to others, including future generations.

Whether or not you have children or grandchildren, you have a calling that extends far beyond today. Future generations can benefit from your faithfulness and commitment to the Lord and to His Word.

PRAY

Father, help me to notice what is most important and to remember what You have passed along to me both in my spiritual experiences with You and in my knowledge of Your Word. May I invest in the spiritual health of future generations so that they will never forget how You have revealed Yourself. Amen.

FAME GROWS

Read 1 Kings 10

KEY VERSES

When the queen of Sheba heard about the fame of Solomon and his relationship to the Lord, she came to test Solomon with hard questions. . . . Solomon answered all her questions; nothing was too hard for the king to explain to her. When the queen of Sheba saw all the wisdom of Solomon and the palace he had built, the food on his table, the seating of his officials, the attending servants in their robes, his cupbearers, and the burnt offerings he made at the temple of the Lord, she was overwhelmed. 1 Kings 10:1, 3–5 NIV

UNDERSTAND

- *What was the queen's purpose in visiting Solomon?*
- *What was her response to what she heard and saw?*

APPLY

Many years into his reign, Solomon received a visit from the queen of Sheba (or "Queen of the South," Matthew 12:42; most likely southern Arabia). Monarchs had come before, but this visit made front-page news! Her gifts were unheard of. In addition to mountains of gold and jewels, "Never again were so many spices brought in as those the queen of Sheba gave to King Solomon" (1 Kings 10:10 NIV). But she got more than she gave and was "overwhelmed." Her reaction?

"How happy your people must be! How happy your officials, who continually stand before you and hear your wisdom! Praise be to the Lord your God, who has delighted in you and placed you on the throne of Israel. Because of the Lord's eternal love for Israel, he has made you king to maintain justice and righteousness" (1 Kings 10:8–9 NIV).

Solomon had become a testimony to the world of God's love and a gift to Israel to "maintain justice and righteousness." But the wisdom Solomon shared with others, he did not always apply to himself.

PRAY

May my words and my life point always to Your loving-kindness and goodness, O Lord.

DAY 292

THE APOSTLES WROTE WITH THE OLD TESTAMENT IN MIND

Read Philippians 2:5–11

KEY VERSES

At the name of Jesus every knee should bow, in heaven and on earth and under the earth, and every tongue acknowledge that Jesus Christ is Lord, to the glory of God the Father.
PHILIPPIANS 2:10–11 NIV

UNDERSTAND

- *What does it mean that one day every knee will bow at the name of Jesus?*
- *What does it mean that every tongue will acknowledge that Jesus Christ is Lord?*

APPLY

God the Father has given Jesus Christ the greatest honor in the universe. One day, everyone "in heaven and on earth and under the earth" (Philippians 2:10 NIV) will do two things. First, "every knee [will] bow" (verse 10) in submission to Jesus Christ. Second, everyone will audibly "acknowledge that Jesus Christ is Lord, to the glory of God the Father" (verse 11).

These words take us back to 700 BC. In a majestic passage, Isaiah 45:18–24, the LORD (*Yahweh*) spoke to the nations. He described Himself as Creator of the heavens and earth (verse 18), as the one and only LORD God (verses 18, 21, 22), as one who speaks only truth (verses 9, 23), as the only one who knows the future (verse 21), and as "a righteous God and a Savior" (verse 21).

Then the Lord issued these words through the prophet Isaiah: "Turn to me and be saved, all you ends of the earth; for I am God, and there is no other. By myself I have sworn, my mouth has uttered in all integrity a word that will not be revoked: Before me every knee will bow; by me every tongue will swear" (verses 22–23 NIV).

When Paul wrote to the Philippian believers, he was clearly applying this stirring prophecy to Jesus Christ. What's more, he was saying that Jesus is the LORD (*Yahweh*). (Paul wrote the book of Philippians in ancient Greek, which had no equivalent to "*Yahweh*." But we know he meant that Jesus is *Yahweh* because Isaiah explicitly used that name for God five times in the passage Paul references.)

In the end, the question isn't *Is Jesus LORD?* He *is*, now and for eternity. Instead, the question is *Have you acknowledged that fact in your own life?* How good it is to gladly acknowledge His place in the universe and in your life, here and now.

PRAY

Yes, Lord, I want to say "Thank You!" that the New Testament wasn't written divorced from the Old Testament. Instead, it proclaims the fruition of all that the prophets wrote.

SOLOMON'S DOWNFALL

Read 1 Kings 11:1–15

KEY VERSES

King Solomon, however, loved many foreign women besides Pharaoh's daughter—Moabites, Ammonites, Edomites, Sidonians and Hittites. They were from nations about which the LORD had told the Israelites, "You must not intermarry with them, because they will surely turn your hearts after their gods." Nevertheless, Solomon held fast to them in love.

1 KINGS 11:1–2 NIV

UNDERSTAND

- *What caused Solomon's spiritual and political downfall?*
- *How would a man of such great wisdom ignore the direct commandment of God?*

APPLY

By all human accounts, King Solomon was a success. "Solomon's wisdom was greater than the wisdom of all the people of the East, and greater than all the wisdom of Egypt. He was wiser than anyone else. . . . And his fame spread to all the surrounding nations" (1 Kings 4:30–31 NIV).

His forty-year reign brought peace and made Israel rich. But there's no real wisdom without obedience to God's Word. Israelites were forbidden to intermarry with people from foreign nations because it would lead to idolatry (Deuteronomy 7:3–5). Pretty simple.

But Moses went further: "The king must not take many wives for himself, because they will turn his heart away from the LORD" (Deuteronomy 17:17 NLT). Israel wouldn't even have their first king for 360 years, but just to remove any excuses by those future kings, Moses commanded: "When he sits on the throne as king, he must copy for himself this body of instruction on a scroll in the presence of the Levitical priests. He must always keep that copy with him and read it daily as long as he lives. That way he will learn to fear the LORD his God by obeying all the terms of these instructions and decrees" (Deuteronomy 17:18–19 NLT).

Solomon was granted wisdom by God, but in the end, he abandoned the wisest thing of all: obedience to the written Word.

PRAY

Gracious God, grant me wisdom, but with it teach me obedience to Your Word.

A LESSON FOR ALL

Read 1 Kings 11:1–15

KEY VERSES

For when Solomon was old, his wives turned his heart away to follow other gods; and his heart was not wholly devoted to the LORD his God, as the heart of his father David had been. . . . So Solomon did what was evil in the sight of the LORD, and did not follow the LORD fully, as his father David had done. 1 KINGS 11:4, 6 NASB

UNDERSTAND

- *When did Solomon begin to falter in his relationship to God?*
- *Who does God compare Solomon to in these verses?*

APPLY

As we've seen in our previous studies, Solomon had a great start but a poor finish. Most scholars believe Solomon repented of his idolatry before his death and wrote Ecclesiastes as his final testimony: "The words of the Preacher, the son of David, king in Jerusalem" (Ecclesiastes 1:1 NASB). Regardless of Solomon's personal relationship with God, the impact of his sin changed history. As punishment, God raised up two previously defeated enemies outside Israel, and a new one from inside—Jeroboam, an official in Solomon's own court. Solomon's sin set the kingdom on a path to war.

Solomon, for all his God-given wisdom, made poor choices. He did not remember his own words: "Guard your heart above all else, for it determines the course of your life" (Proverbs 4:23 NLT). Rather, he allowed his heart to become divided. The wives certainly played their part in Solomon's sin, just as temptations come to all of us. But as a descendent of his, who was "greater than Solomon" (Luke 11:31 NIV), said, "Where your treasure is, there will your heart be also" (Luke 12:34 ESV). Solomon lost sight of this critical fact.

We don't need Solomon's wisdom to please God. We just need to guard our hearts according to His Word.

PRAY

Wise King, show me where I may be making the same mistakes as Solomon, and correct me!

GOD LOVED YOU FIRST

Read 1 John 4:16–21

KEY VERSES

There is no fear in love, but perfect love drives out fear, because fear involves punishment, and the one who fears is not perfected in love. We love, because He first loved us.
1 John 4:18–19 NASB

UNDERSTAND

- *How do you reconcile the concept of "the fear of the Lord" with perfect love driving out fear?*
- *Why is it so significant that God loved you first? What is the result of that love for you?*
- *Why are loving God and loving others so closely connected?*

APPLY

How would your outlook for today change if, before you even got out of bed, you remembered that God loves you deeply and passionately, that He loved you before you could possibly love Him in return?

God's love is a transformational kind of love, and it puts you in a place of security from where you can be freed from the fear of judgment and enabled to imagine new ways of relating to others. If God loves you so much, that also means that He loves the people you encounter each day. God's love may not have shaped every person you meet, and many may have rejected it outright, but each person holds tremendous possibility in God.

John saw loving God as a compelling commandment that requires His beloved people to love their neighbors. As you prepare to face your day, ask God how you can show His love to the people in your sphere of influence.

PRAY

Father, help me to see with clarity the love that You have so generously shown me. May I live free from fear and approach You in prayer with confidence that Your love has come to me before I could do anything for You in return. May I show Your perfect love to those I meet today. Amen.

UNDERSTANDING PROVERBS

Read Proverbs 1:1–7

KEY VERSES

Let the wise hear and increase in learning, and the one who understands obtain guidance, to understand a proverb and a saying, the words of the wise and their riddles.
PROVERBS 1:5–6 ESV

UNDERSTAND

- *What is the point of a proverb?*
- *Do proverbs need to be "spiritual" to be true?*
- *How can proverbs be used in daily life?*

APPLY

When we dig deeper into the "proverbs of Solomon, son of David, king of Israel" (Proverbs 1:1 ESV), we need to understand what a proverb is and what it isn't. The book of Proverbs belongs to a type of biblical writing known as wisdom literature (along with Job, Psalms, Ecclesiastes, and Song of Solomon). These books are designed to teach God's perspective through a number of literary vehicles—including sayings, songs, poetry, and dialogues; they may employ metaphors, allegories, or even sarcasm!

Most of the sayings we call proverbs were designed to encapsulate a single truth in a memorable way. Collectively, they provide an inspired set of guidelines for wise living that pleases God, explains much about the world, and protects the man who lives by them. They communicate principles rather than promises; general guidance rather than absolute formulas. Sometimes they sound like plain old common sense, and other times they can be esoteric and obscure.

Think of the book of Proverbs as an enormous tool store with aisle after aisle of shiny gadgets and finely crafted utensils. The purpose (meaning) of many will be obvious, but others will need to be explained and demonstrated. But in every case, a tool must be used to increase in skill.

Today's key verses admonish those who are wise to learn and become skillful in the tools Solomon left us!

PRAY

Eternal God, teach me how to apply the proverbs in my own life, as well as how to share them with others.

WHAT YOU CAN LEARN FROM THE VIRTUOUS WOMAN

Read Proverbs 31:10–31

KEY VERSE

Who can find a virtuous and capable wife? She is more precious than rubies.
PROVERBS 31:10 NLT

UNDERSTAND

- *Do the women in your life tend to enjoy or get annoyed at today's scripture passage?*
- *If you don't know, ask!*

APPLY

Only the Lord Himself knows how many women's articles, women's Bible studies, women's talks, and women's retreats have extolled the Virtuous Woman described in today's reading. The only problem is they usually ignore the fact that the entire book of Proverbs was written to *men*.

In other words, today's reading is a challenge to *men*. It's for you. That changes things up, doesn't it? But it's all good. This scripture passage explains four specific ways a good husband can encourage his wife to beautifully and actively flourish in every area of her life.

Cherishing. The good husband recognizes the true value of his wife as a person (31:10). He sees her as God's priceless, one-of-a-kind masterpiece. He knows that her worth is far above precious jewels.

Supporting. The good husband believes in the potential of his wife (31:11). He doesn't put her in a box called home only to let her lie there dormant. Instead, he allows her to be productive and fulfilled both in and out of the home (31:16, 20).

Listening. The good husband realizes the importance of listening to (and learning from) the wisdom of his wife (31:26). He is spared from many rash and foolish actions when he respects her faithful love and wisdom.

Praising. The good husband praises the virtues and accomplishments of his wife (31:29). He doesn't flatter her but praises his wife for her fear of God (31:30) and her successful endeavors (31:31). He lets others know how much he cherishes her.

PRAY

Yes, Lord, I want to say "Wow!" I don't know how I missed this all these years. Okay, maybe I do. May I cherish, support, listen to, and praise the godly women in my life.

FREE TO BLESS OTHERS

Read Romans 12:14–21

KEY VERSES

Bless those who persecute you. Don't curse them; pray that God will bless them. Be happy with those who are happy, and weep with those who weep. Romans 12:14–15 NLT

UNDERSTAND

- *How is treating your enemies or opponents with compassion and understanding an act of faith in God?*
- *How would it benefit you to bless those who mistreat you?*
- *In what ways could your day change if you were more aware of the happiness and sadness of others?*

APPLY

You could begin today feeling defensive and even combative toward those you perceive as enemies or opponents, or you could begin today by praying for them and resolving to treat them well. How you view and act toward those who are most opposed to you may determine the outcome of the rest of your day!

As long as you are withdrawn from others out of fear, anger, or other negative emotions, you'll never reach them with God's redeeming love—instead, you'll be preoccupied with negative thoughts of them. The path Paul lays out in today's scripture verses is a more constructive and hopeful way forward that frees you from fear and anger and opens up new possibilities for healing and improved relationships.

This is a liberating opportunity to look beyond your own concerns and worries. You can share the joy and sorrow of others, celebrating when appropriate and mourning when difficulties abound. It's possible that those with whom you celebrate and mourn today will do the same for you in the future.

PRAY

Jesus, help me to see all people as made in Your image and to treat opponents and enemies with compassion and consideration. I surrender my fears and distrust of others to You so that I can serve them and treat them with the same kindness I would hope to receive for myself. Amen.

A CALL IGNORED, PART 1

Read Proverbs 1:20–33

KEY VERSES

Wisdom shouts in the streets. She cries out in the public square. She calls to the crowds along the main street, to those gathered in front of the city gate: "How long, you simpletons, will you insist on being simpleminded? How long will you mockers relish your mocking? How long will you fools hate knowledge? Come and listen to my counsel. I'll share my heart with you and make you wise." PROVERBS 1:20–23 NLT

UNDERSTAND

- *What efforts has wisdom made to be heard?*
- *What kinds of people ignore wisdom's call?*

APPLY

This passage needs a bit of clarification since English has neither feminine nor masculine nouns like Hebrew. English assigns pronouns based on the physical gender of the subject, unless speaking metaphorically, like "She's a fine ship." But in this passage, there's no metaphor, just a grammatical agreement. The Hebrew word for wisdom, *chokhmah,* is a feminine noun requiring a feminine pronoun. The passage is not characterizing wisdom as a woman, unlike Proverbs 9:13 (NLT), which states "the woman named Folly" to alert the reader to the metaphor that follows. In Hebrew, *folly* is also a feminine noun, but that would have been insufficient to bring a woman to mind. Nonetheless, wisdom is personified. . .and pretty active!

Unlike cartoons of a wise man atop a mountain, God's wisdom is not far off. We often talk about pursuing wisdom, when in fact it's the other way around. Wisdom cries out, shouts, even cajoles. Wisdom is looking for us—sadly, to little avail. Why? The passage doesn't mince words: *Simpletons* "insist on being simpleminded," *mockers* "relish" in their mocking, and *fools* "hate knowledge"—they don't value wisdom or the God who offers it. In part two of this study, we'll see what happens when these folks get their own way!

PRAY

Father God, whether wisdom shouts, cries out, or whispers, don't let me fail to hear her voice!

A CALL IGNORED, PART 2

Read Proverbs 1:20–33

KEY VERSES

"They rejected my advice and paid no attention when I corrected them. Therefore they must eat the bitter fruit of living their own way, choking on their own schemes. For simpletons turn away from me—to death. Fools are destroyed by their own complacency. But all who listen to me will live in peace, untroubled by fear of harm." PROVERBS 1:30–33 NLT

UNDERSTAND

- *What is the consequence of ignoring wisdom?*
- *Where do the consequences come from?*
- *What is the promise to those who embrace wisdom?*

APPLY

There's a pattern in scripture of people who ignore wisdom and pay the price, starting with Adam and Eve, followed by their son Cain and many, many others. It's all recorded for our benefit, if we will listen. Actually, if we listen soon enough. Part of today's longer reading describes a sort of built-in time frame for wisdom to be advantageous to us: "When they cry for help, I will not answer. Though they anxiously search for me, they will not find me. For they hated knowledge and chose not to fear the LORD" (Proverbs 1:28–29 NLT).

These anxious cries for help are not about repentance or change, just regret when faced with the consequences of foolish choices. In that respect, wisdom's hands are essentially tied. Like a man who jumps from the top of a tall building and regrets it on the way to the pavement, sometimes it's too late to avoid "the bitter fruit" of bad choices.

Paul repeated this principle: "A man reaps what he sows. Whoever sows to please their flesh, from the flesh will reap destruction; whoever sows to please the Spirit, from the Spirit will reap eternal life" (Galatians 6:7–8 NIV). Consequences come from choices made—accepting wisdom's invitation leads to a life of peace that fools will never know.

PRAY

Good Father, let me never be among those who rejected wisdom's calling.

FOOLISH WANDERING

Read Proverbs 7

KEY VERSES

I saw among the simple, I noticed among the young men, a youth who had no sense. He was going down the street near her corner, walking along in the direction of her house at twilight, as the day was fading, as the dark of night set in. PROVERBS 7:7–9 NIV

UNDERSTAND

- *What kind of young man is the proverb describing?*
- *Who is the woman mentioned in the verse?*
- *Why might the time of day matter?*

APPLY

Different translations try to capture the main thought of a passage in headers that do not appear in the original manuscripts. But like the chapter and verse numbers added many centuries later, these can be useful. The cautionary poem in Proverbs 7 is variously labeled, "Warning Against the Adulteress," "The Lures of the Prostitute," or "Avoid Loose Women." You get the picture.

In a detailed story like this, we can make bullet-point observations of the characters' attributes and actions. For example, the man is young and not very bright; he's going down the street of a notorious woman, and he's doing it at twilight. In the following verses, we see the woman confront him, dressed seductively; she's cunning, restless, loud, wayward, brazen, and persuasive. He is no match for her. "All at once he follows her, as an ox goes to the slaughter" (Proverbs 7:22 ESV). The writer's advice: "Let not your heart turn aside to her ways; do not stray into her paths" (Proverbs 7:25 ESV). The folly of the young man lay in not avoiding a temptation he most certainly knew existed.

This story might sound like an unlikely scenario today, with one serious exception: the internet. There are illicit websites seeking to entice the foolish. Wise men do *not* wander past notorious places—they plan another route!

PRAY

Father, watch over me, and rebuke me if my carelessness might lead me astray!

WHAT TIME IS IT, ABRAHAM?

Read Genesis 15:1–21

KEY VERSES

He took him outside and said, "Look up at the sky and count the stars—if indeed you can count them." Then he said to him, "So shall your offspring be." Abram believed the Lord, *and he credited it to him as righteousness.* Genesis 15:5–6 niv

UNDERSTAND

- *How does Abraham's way of counting differ from the Lord's way of counting?*
- *Did you notice the phrase "if indeed you can"? Ancient astronomers confidently said there were 1,056 stars. So why did the Lord remark, "if indeed you can"?*

APPLY

So many questions come to mind when you carefully read and study today's scripture passage. One of the biggest questions: Does this chapter cover one rather full day or two separate occasions? Literary and biblical scholars wisely and rightly contend that it was a single day. Then comes the showstopper question: When today's key verse took place, what time of day was it?

At first, the answer seems obvious. It's the middle of the night, right? Abraham was in his tent praying. The Lord spoke to Abram (as he was called at that point). The two had a little chat. The Lord reinforced His promise and took Abram outside. They were no longer in Abram's tent. Before the Lord further reinforced His promise, He instructed Abram to do something. All is well with the world, it seems, until the Lord added that pesky phrase "if indeed you can."

Why would the Lord say that? Well, why not? After all, verse 12 talks about the sun going down, and verse 17 talks about after the sun had set and darkness settled over everything. If this is the same day, how can it be the middle of the night in verse 5?

As we see in Genesis 18:1—and as we see throughout that region and across southern Europe, southern Asia, and Latin America—many people rest during the hottest part of the day. It turns out that's the best explanation for what time of day it was in verse 5.

In other words, the Lord was saying, in effect: "Abram, I'm asking you to do something that you can't see now, but you'll be able to see it tonight, just like almost every other night."

Then the Lord added, "So shall your offspring be."

In response, Abram "believed the Lord."

PRAY

Thank You, Lord, for creating such a dramatic picture of faith. Faith isn't about what I can see now. It's believing You and taking You at Your Word. Help my unbelief.

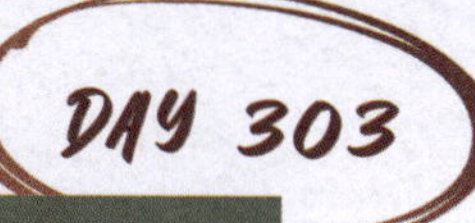

GOD USES THE EVIL DONE TO US FOR GOOD

Read Genesis 50:15–21

KEY VERSES

But Joseph said to them, "Do not be afraid, for am I in God's place? As for you, you meant evil against me, but God meant it for good in order to bring about this present result, to keep many people alive." GENESIS 50:19–20 NASB

UNDERSTAND

- *Joseph's brothers had dealt treacherously with him in the past, and even here they lied about his father's dying wishes in order to spare their own lives. What does this story show about the long-term impact of sin?*
- *How did Joseph view the evil brought against him?*
- *Why was the bigger picture of God's work so important for Joseph?*

APPLY

It may be difficult to look at the injustices or challenges of your life the way Joseph did. But God has invited you today to entrust yourself to Him and to seek ways He can use even your greatest losses for the benefit of others.

Seeking God at work in a bigger picture, one you may not fully understand until much later, helps you put less emphasis on the losses, suffering, and mistreatment of today. You will be less likely to hold grudges, because God so often uses even your worst losses for your benefit—and for the benefit of others. There surely will be pain and uncertainty along the way, but when you trust that God is with you, today's circumstances can shift in their significance.

Showing mercy to others is also easier when you recognize that you, like Joseph, aren't God. You have received mercy from the Lord, and it is up to Him alone to judge others. That means you are free from the burden of judgment on others, and you can share the grace and forgiveness you have received.

PRAY

Father, may I always remember the grace and mercy You have shown to me so that I will never hold grudges against others or set myself as a judge over them. May I see Your power at work in my life and respond with faith and hope when challenges surface. Amen.

THE WICKED

Read Proverbs 23:17–35

KEY VERSES

Do not let your heart envy sinners, but live in the fear of the Lord *always. Certainly there is a future, and your hope will not be cut off. Listen, my son, and be wise, and direct your heart in the way.* Proverbs 23:17–19 nasb

UNDERSTAND

- *What is there to envy about the wicked?*
- *What are believers to set their hearts on?*
- *What is the promise for those who live in "the fear of the* Lord*"?*

APPLY

Sometimes studying the Bible means rethinking the meanings of words we assume we know. Today's proverb offers us that opportunity.

We don't use the word *sinner* much, and even in religious settings, it's often used in a generic way like "Jesus came to save sinners." Of course, we "all have sinned and fall short of the glory of God" (Romans 3:23 nasb), but that's not really what the term denotes in the scriptures. The biblical usage of *sinner* refers not to merely imperfect or flawed people but to the ungodly who embrace rebellion as a lifestyle.

And sometimes sinners are very successful people! Frankly, it can be discouraging, as the psalmist confessed: "Truly God is good to Israel, to those whose hearts are pure. But as for me, I almost lost my footing. My feet were slipping, and I was almost gone. For I envied the proud when I saw them prosper despite their wickedness" (Psalm 73:1–3 nlt). Thankfully, Asaph stuck to the path of wisdom, regained hope, and saw the future that today's reading promises. "You guide me with your counsel, and afterward you will take me into glory. Whom have I in heaven but you? And earth has nothing I desire besides you" (Psalm 73:24–25 niv).

Nothing sinners gain on earth can compare to what awaits the faithful.

PRAY

Gracious Lord, keep my heart from envying those who reject You. May my hope rest solely on Christ.

THE NEXT GENERATION

Read Proverbs 22:1–16

KEY VERSE

Train up a child in the way he should go; even when he is old he will not depart from it.
PROVERBS 22:6 ESV

UNDERSTAND

- *What does it mean to "train up a child"?*
- *Does this verse promise that all godly parents will produce godly children?*

APPLY

It's God's design that we grow and mature. In His wisdom He created a process—a journey—integral to the human experience. Even Jesus, though God in the flesh, "grew in wisdom and stature, and in favor with God and man" (Luke 2:52 NIV).

The Hebrew word for "train up" (*chanak*) occurs five times in the Bible, normally translated as "dedicate" (referring to houses or Solomon's temple). That adds an interesting take on today's verse. Parents are to dedicate, or *offer up,* their children to the Lord by giving them the right start on their journey. Of course, it's not a guarantee of a righteous life since each man makes his own choices, but those who do follow "in the way he *should* go" will always look back gratefully to the training he received as a child.

That training process isn't always easy. Sometimes we have to exercise tough love. "Folly is bound up in the heart of a child, but the rod of discipline will drive it far away" (Proverbs 22:15 NIV). The scriptures do not advocate abuse, but they clearly teach that disciplining a child is better than allowing him to get his own way. The same is true for us as God's children. "Endure hardship as discipline; God is treating you as his children. For what children are not disciplined by their father? If you are not disciplined—and everyone undergoes discipline—then you are not legitimate, not true sons and daughters at all" (Hebrews 12:7–8 NIV).

PRAY

Good Father, help me to raise up the next generation in wisdom and to accept Your discipline as a child myself.

THE UNCERTAINTY OF RICHES

Read Proverbs 18:10–12

KEY VERSES

The name of the Lord *is a strong tower; the righteous man runs into it and is safe. A rich man's wealth is his strong city, and like a high wall in his imagination.*

Proverbs 18:10–11 ESV

UNDERSTAND

- *Where do the righteous take refuge?*
- *What is the mistake of the "rich man"?*
- *What is the point of wealth?*

APPLY

We know that the Lord is sympathetic to the poor and the vulnerable. Conversely, He has abundant warnings for "the rich" who trust in money rather than in the Lord, since riches remain here. "For when they die, they take nothing with them. Their wealth will not follow them into the grave" (Psalm 49:17 NLT).

The lure of riches can be exhausting. "Do not weary yourself to gain wealth; stop dwelling on it. When you set your eyes on it, it is gone" (Proverbs 23:4–5 NASB). Money can quickly disappear! And even if our wealth doesn't leave us, *we* might leave it, as Jesus pointed out in the parable of a rich man who presumed upon the future:

> *"'And I'll sit back and say to myself, "My friend, you have enough stored away for years to come. Now take it easy! Eat, drink, and be merry!"'*
>
> *"But God said to him, 'You fool! You will die this very night. Then who will get everything you worked for?'*
>
> *"Yes, a person is a fool to store up earthly wealth but not have a rich relationship with God."* (Luke 12:19–21 NLT)

There's nothing inherently wrong with wealth as long as we heed Paul's command: "Instruct those who are rich in this present world not to be conceited or to set their hope on the uncertainty of riches, but on God, who richly supplies us with all things to enjoy" (1 Timothy 6:17 NASB).

PRAY

Your name, O Lord, is my sanctuary and my sufficiency; keep me from trusting in the wealth of this world.

HOW OLD ARE YOU, MOSES?

Read Psalm 90:1–17

KEY VERSE

Our days may come to seventy years, or eighty, if our strength endures. PSALM 90:10 NIV

UNDERSTAND

- *It's clearly understood that Moses wrote Genesis through Deuteronomy during the latter part of his life. Deuteronomy 31:2 and 34:7 specifically say that Moses finished writing his fifth book shortly before he died at age 120.*
- *So how old do you think Moses was when he wrote Psalm 90?*

APPLY

Using the internal historical and literary evidence within Genesis, Exodus, Leviticus, Numbers, and Deuteronomy, it's safe to say that Moses wrote all five books after age 80 (when God called him) and no later than age 120 (when he died).

So it's often assumed that Moses wrote Psalm 90 during that same span of time (again, after God called him but before he died forty years later). Using the internal evidence within Psalm 90, however, can we get a better idea how old Moses was? Thankfully, the answer is yes!

First, you want to notice the allusions Moses made in Psalm 90 to the basic facts about Creation and the Flood accounts and Israel's early history. With the word *our* (verse 1), Moses identified with his people. With the phrase "all generations" (verse 1), Moses hinted at the literary structure of Genesis. With his poetic references to Creation (verse 2), Moses foreshadowed Genesis 1–2. With the word *dust* (verse 3), Moses foreshadowed Genesis 2:7 and 3:19. With the phrase "thousand years" (verse 4), Moses foreshadowed Genesis 5:27. With the word *flood* (verse 5 NKJV), Moses foreshadowed Genesis chapters 6 to 9.

Second, you want to ponder what Moses said in verse 13. With his pleading question, "How long will it be?" (verse 13), Moses foreshadowed Genesis 15:13 and Exodus 1, and implied that the Lord hadn't yet stepped in to free His people from their terrible bondage in Egypt. Then, in today's key verse, Moses directly suggested that he's somewhere near that stage of life.

Bottom line: Moses probably was about eighty years old when he wrote Psalm 90. Finally, his heart was ready. The Lord then appeared to Moses in the burning bush (Exodus 3–5), and the rest is history!

PRAY

Yes, Lord, I see that You're waiting for me to have a ready heart before You call me into a new stage of life and possibly into my greatest purpose here on earth. I'm ready.

WORK, PART 1

Read Proverbs 24:30–34

KEY VERSES

I passed by the field of a sluggard, by the vineyard of a man lacking sense, and behold, it was all overgrown with thorns; the ground was covered with nettles, and its stone wall was broken down. PROVERBS 24:30–31 ESV

UNDERSTAND

- *What is the result of laziness and neglect?*
- *What lesson does the writer draw from his observations?*

APPLY

Work is foundational to all existence. It only turned into labor after man sinned. Part of the consequences of the fall specifically included "cursed is the ground because of you; in pain you shall eat of it all the days of your life; thorns and thistles it shall bring forth for you; and you shall eat the plants of the field" (Genesis 3:17–18 ESV). The satisfying days of the garden were gone; from now on the world would push back on man's efforts.

There's a funny meme that captures the grind that work can be: The first five days after the weekend are always the hardest. But the consequences of "a little sleep, a little slumber, a little folding of the hands to rest" (Proverbs 24:33 NIV) can be disastrous. The man "lacking sense" had a vineyard—a God-given opportunity—that he squandered. Like one of the men in the parable Jesus told of a master who gave three servants a sum of money to invest "each according to his own ability" (Matthew 25:15 NASB). Two worked to produce a return by investing, but the third buried the money and took no risks, even though that was the entire point of being entrusted with the money. The master pronounced the first two "good and faithful" and the third "wicked" and "lazy" (Matthew 25:23, 26 NIV).

The wise man sees the opportunity to work as a blessing but also a responsibility.

PRAY

Lord, strengthen me to take responsibility and be more intentional in all the work You've assigned me.

WORK, PART 2

Read Proverbs 6:6–11

KEY VERSES

Go to the ant, you sluggard; consider its ways and be wise! It has no commander, no overseer or ruler, yet it stores its provisions in summer and gathers its food at harvest.
PROVERBS 6:6–8 NIV

UNDERSTAND

- *What characteristics does the ant display that serves as an example of wisdom?*
- *Who tells the ant what to do and when?*

APPLY

In yesterday's study we saw how work became labor after the fall and that man was destined to face opposition to his efforts ever after. Work would still be a part of the man's identity, but its increased difficulty would present the temptation to avoid responsibility—to become lax, to become a sluggard. So Solomon directs our attention to the lowly ant.

The ant is "wise" because it needs no one to cause it to take responsibility—it's a self-starter! The ant looks ahead and makes plans. Like the ant, the wise make no excuses to provide for themselves and their family. Whether you're in a profession, a career, a trade, or still trying to find the right job, wisdom tells us to look to the ant for the basic lesson about taking responsibility.

The workplace isn't the only arena where men can grow slack. Family, church, and community all require taking responsibility. Marriages do not thrive without effort, children do not develop without care and energy, and a congregation falters without those who serve diligently. Is taking responsibility and being intentional easy? Of course not! But through the Holy Spirit we are to "work willingly at whatever [we] do, as though [we] were working for the Lord rather than for people" (Colossians 3:23 NLT).

PRAY

Gracious Father, may the work of my hands be a testimony of my faith in You.

THE ULTIMATE CHOICE IN LIFE

Read Luke 9:21–27

KEY VERSES

"If you try to hang on to your life, you will lose it. But if you give up your life for my sake, you will save it. And what do you benefit if you gain the whole world but are yourself lost or destroyed?" LUKE 9:24–25 NLT

UNDERSTAND

- *Why did Jesus challenge His followers to give up their own lives right after telling them about His own imminent crucifixion and resurrection?*
- *What do you think it means to "gain the whole world"?*
- *What does it look like to "give up your life" for the sake of Jesus?*

APPLY

As Jesus prepared Himself and His disciples for His upcoming death on a wooden cross, He taught them that they too needed to stop hanging on to their own lives. They had a choice to make—between devoting themselves to an uncertain world that leaves their souls in peril or devoting themselves to God and placing their souls in His care.

This is an invitation to look at the direction of your life. Each little choice you make every day will contribute to where you end up in life's journey. Where can you let go of your own desires and priorities and entrust them to God? This calls for ongoing examination and awareness of what goes into your choices each day.

Most importantly, remember that surrendering your life to the Lord comes with a no-doubt-about-it reward. While there are no guarantees regarding your own safety and security here on earth, your soul is safe with God, and no one can touch the reward He has promised you.

PRAY

Jesus, help me to see the areas of my life where I've sought control or failed to entrust myself to You. May I enjoy the rewards of faith and obedience as I choose life in You over anything else this world may offer. Amen.

SAUL'S FOLLY

Read 1 Samuel 15

KEY VERSE

And Samuel said, "Has the Lord as great delight in burnt offerings and sacrifices, as in obeying the voice of the Lord? Behold, to obey is better than sacrifice, and to listen than the fat of rams." 1 SAMUEL 15:22 ESV

UNDERSTAND

- *Why is obedience so important to the Lord?*
- *Is it possible to honor God but not obey Him?*

APPLY

Though God had created Israel as a unique people for Himself, after entering the Promised Land, they insisted on having a king to "be like all the nations" (1 Samuel 8:20 ESV). Samuel the prophet was rightly upset. But God said, "They have not rejected you, but they have rejected me from being king over them" (1 Samuel 8:7 ESV). So God gave them Saul, "as handsome a young man as could be found anywhere in Israel, and he was a head taller than anyone else" (1 Samuel 9:2 NIV).

But despite his early successes, Saul was not "a man after [God's] own heart" (1 Samuel 13:14 ESV). Instead of destroying the Amalekites and their livestock per God's sovereign judgment, Saul allowed his men to take the best animals, and he himself enslaved their king as a trophy. When confronted, Saul excused his disobedience, saying that they took "the best of the things devoted to destruction, to sacrifice to the Lord your God in Gilgal" (1 Samuel 15:21 ESV). Saul actually tried to cover up his sin in the name of religious fervor! And his foolishness cost him everything: "Because you have rejected the word of the Lord, he has also rejected you from being king" (1 Samuel 15:23 ESV).

Solomon may have had Saul in mind when he said, "To draw near [to God] to listen is better than to offer the sacrifice of fools" (Ecclesiastes 5:1 ESV).

PRAY

Almighty God, teach me to listen, and humble me to obey without making excuses!

SAMSON'S FOLLY

Read Judges 16

KEY VERSES

[Delilah] said to him, "How can you say, 'I love you,' when you won't confide in me? This is the third time you have made a fool of me and haven't told me the secret of your great strength." With such nagging she prodded him day after day until he was sick to death of it. So he told her everything. JUDGES 16:15–17 NIV

UNDERSTAND

- *What was Samson famous for?*
- *What did Delilah accuse Samson of?*
- *Why did Samson eventually give in?*

APPLY

Samson had a great start. An angel promised his barren mother, "You will become pregnant and have a son whose head is never to be touched by a razor because the boy is to be a Nazirite, dedicated to God from the womb. He will take the lead in delivering Israel from the hands of the Philistines" (Judges 13:5 NIV). A person could become a Nazarite for a period of time by taking certain vows, including letting his hair grow. When "the hair of his consecration" (Numbers 6:19 ESV) was shaved off, it signaled the end of the vow and release from God's special service.

But Samson was called "from the womb" to be a Nazarite, blessed with great strength, which led to outstanding victories and a fearful reputation for twenty years. Despite God's blessing, Samson had a mixed record. Alongside his successes, he chose a foreign wife, slept with a prostitute, beat and robbed men, and ultimately chose a lover from among Israel's enemies—who famously became his downfall.

Samson never learned the lesson Paul stressed: "Do not be misled: 'Bad company corrupts good character'" (1 Corinthians 15:33 NIV). He presumed on God's blessing, grew complacent, and ultimately chose this world over his calling. Though he repented in the end, his presumption cost him his life.

PRAY

God, my Father, humble me always to hold Your calling sacred so I am not deceived by my own success.

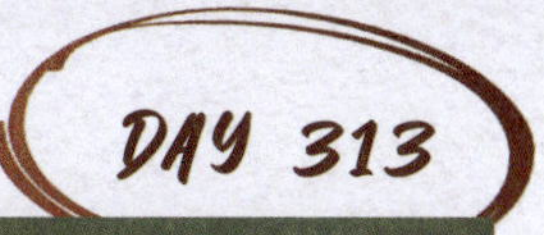

WHEN DID GOD'S PEOPLE KNOW "ALL HAVE SINNED"?

Read Romans 3:9–23

KEY VERSE

For all have sinned and fall short of the glory of God. Romans 3:23 NKJV

UNDERSTAND

- *What scriptures did Paul know forward and backward?*
- *How often did he draw on those scriptures in his New Testament letters?*

APPLY

It's natural for most Christian men to read the New Testament and think it's all fresh new revelation inspired by God. It is! That is, unless you think "fresh new" means divorced from what God revealed in the Old Testament.

Today's Bible reading ends with one of Paul's most famous, most memorized, and most quoted verses. It's today's key verse for good reason! But is it a brand-new Christian teaching?

If your study Bible offers cross-references, you'll quickly see that Paul was echoing the truth found in the very first verse in today's scripture reading. In turn, that verse is a quotation from Psalm 14:1 and Psalm 53:1.

Furthermore, additional cross-references will take you to 1 Kings 8:46; 2 Chronicles 6:36; Psalm 143:2; Proverbs 20:9; Ecclesiastes 7:20; Micah 7:2; and Jeremiah 2:9, 5:1–9, and 6:28.

And that doesn't count New Testament cross-references to James 3:2 (probably written before Romans) and 1 John 3:8 and 3:10 (likely written later).

So did Paul coin the idea that all have sinned? Hardly!

The reality is that most New Testament gospel truths are firmly embedded in Old Testament teachings and prophecies.

That's good news, indeed!

PRAY

Yes, Lord, I want to say "Thank You!" that the apostles and early church fathers weren't trying to invent a new religion. Instead, Your Holy Spirit helped them understand the fulfillment of the Hebrew scriptures in Jesus Christ and His gospel. I believe!

UNDERSTANDING ECCLESIASTES

Read Ecclesiastes 1

KEY VERSES

I, the Teacher, was king over Israel in Jerusalem. I applied my mind to study and to explore by wisdom all that is done under the heavens. What a heavy burden God has laid on mankind! I have seen all the things that are done under the sun; all of them are meaningless, a chasing after the wind. ECCLESIASTES 1:12–14 NIV

UNDERSTAND

- *Who is this teacher who was also king over Israel?*
- *How would you describe his tone in this personal introduction?*

APPLY

As we discussed previously, Ecclesiastes is part of the wisdom literature of the scripture and must be approached uniquely. Unlike the book of Proverbs with its memorable sayings, Ecclesiastes must be taken in its entirety like a memoir that unfolds chapter by chapter, only complete at the end.

"The words of the Teacher, son of David, king in Jerusalem" (Ecclesiastes 1:1 NIV) tells us that this is Solomon's work. His breadth of understanding was unparalleled, as were his wealth, power, and reputation. If anyone had the opportunity to explore "all that is done under the heavens," it was Solomon. He undertook great projects—homes, gardens, vineyards, and reservoirs; he amassed great wealth, herds, flocks, male and female slaves (Ecclesiastes 2:4-8); and "had 700 wives of royal birth and 300 concubines" (1 Kings 11:3 NLT). And as we've seen, that did not help his spiritual life at all!

As Solomon himself put it: "I denied myself nothing my eyes desired; I refused my heart no pleasure" (Ecclesiastes 2:10 NIV). Sounds like a dream, but for Solomon it was all "chasing after the wind"—a disappointing cycle of toil "under the heavens." Solomon learned how burdensome and unfair life can be. You might say the tone of Ecclesiastes is world-weary—but not without hope.

PRAY

Thank You, O Lord, that I don't have to test this life to know You are my only hope.

LISTENING

Read Ecclesiastes 5:1–7

KEY VERSES

Guard your steps when you go to the house of God. To draw near to listen is better than to offer the sacrifice of fools, for they do not know that they are doing evil. Be not rash with your mouth, nor let your heart be hasty to utter a word before God, for God is in heaven and you are on earth. Therefore let your words be few. ECCLESIASTES 5:1–2 ESV

UNDERSTAND

- *Why would a sacrifice to God ever be foolish?*
- *How should we approach the Almighty?*

APPLY

The temple Solomon built was referred to as the "house of God" (*bethel*). Of course, no one thought the Almighty was *only* in the temple because, as today's verse notes, "God is in heaven." Solomon emphasized this during the temple's dedication: "But will God really dwell on earth with humans? The heavens, even the highest heavens, cannot contain you. How much less this temple I have built!" (2 Chronicles 6:18 NIV). But the living God did intend to use the temple in a unique way. "I have chosen and consecrated this temple so that my Name may be there forever. My eyes and my heart will always be there" (2 Chronicles 7:16 NIV). Only fools would treat that lightly!

It was wise to seek out God and listen to Him since He intentionally placed Himself within reach. As the psalmist declared, "Now that you have made me listen, I finally understand—you don't require burnt offerings or sin offerings" (Psalm 40:6 NLT). The fool believes he can "game the system" with sacrifices that pay for his sin and allow him to go about his way. And even sincere people should pause—God doesn't need rash promises or excuses any more than burnt offerings. He needs (if you can say God needs anything) us to listen.

PRAY

Sovereign Lord, put a guard over my mouth and teach me to listen.

HEALED THROUGH INTERCESSION

Read 2 Chronicles 30:13–20

KEY VERSES

Hezekiah prayed for them, saying, "May the LORD, who is good, pardon everyone who sets their heart on seeking God—the LORD, the God of their ancestors—even if they are not clean according to the rules of the sanctuary." And the LORD heard Hezekiah and healed the people. 2 CHRONICLES 30:18–20 NIV

UNDERSTAND

- *The people of Israel were starting over with God after making many mistakes along the way. How have guilt and shame over your past sins kept you away from God, and what can you do about it?*
- *Today's scripture passage records Hezekiah's intercessory prayer for people who were sincerely seeking God but still breaking the rules. What does this show you about imperfect men seeking a perfect God?*
- *Why is intercession so important for God's people?*

APPLY

You are never too far from God that you can't start over by repenting and seeking to make things right. If you're dealing with guilt, shame, or the consequences of your past failures—even if they happened in the past twenty-four hours—God gives you the opportunity to begin anew with Him. The Lord longs to pardon the sins of His people when they humble themselves before Him.

The key here is that you need to make changes when you repent. The people of Israel did that when they got rid of the idols and other objects that had tripped them up. The status quo won't cut it, but if you're willing to reach out to God in sincere devotion, He welcomes even your imperfect prayers.

King Hezekiah modeled a pure spirit of intercession when he asked God to show mercy on His people rather than smugly dismissing those who failed to observe purity laws. In doing that, he showed that God will honor the prayers of His people on behalf of others and that His mercy will triumph when we pray.

PRAY

Father, reveal the shame and failures in my life that have kept me from You so that I can worship You without fear, discouragement, or self-condemnation. May I be a voice of encouragement and grace to those in need of healing and restoration, showing mercy even as You have shown mercy to me. Amen.

BOUNDARIES

Read Proverbs 23:9–11

KEY VERSE

Do not move an ancient boundary stone or encroach on the fields of the fatherless.
PROVERBS 23:10 NIV

UNDERSTAND

- *What were boundary stones used for in ancient times?*
- *What reason would anyone have to move one?*
- *Is there a modern equivalent to boundary stones?*

APPLY

For almost as long as humans have owned land, they've had to mark the boundaries. Historical markers exist all across the world, from Egypt to Ireland and from China to Greece.

The people of Israel did not know what it was like to occupy their own land for over 440 years. So naturally, there needed to be rules set up to avoid conflicts between neighbors. The boundary stone represented ownership, but more than that, it ensured stability for the entire society, generation after generation. "Do not move your neighbor's boundary stone set up by your predecessors in the inheritance you receive in the land the LORD your God is giving you to possess" (Deuteronomy 19:14 NIV). Moving a boundary stone equated to the theft of land assigned to each family by God Himself; most often it meant the oppression of the weak by the strong.

As physical boundary stones existed to create stability from one generation to the next, so there are faith boundaries set up for our stability that have been passed down to us: the divinity of Christ and His substitutionary death that allows for salvation; the call to repentance and a holy life by the power of the Spirit; participation in the body of Christ and bearing witness to the world of Jesus; the authority of all scripture. These are among the "boundary stones" that must not be moved, or else we risk robbing the faith from the next generation.

PRAY

Good Father, You have made Yourself known from generation to generation through Your Word. Teach me to handle the truth in a way that safeguards the next generation of believers.

HONOR

Read Proverbs 15:32–33 & Daniel 2

KEY VERSE

Wisdom's instruction is to fear the Lord, and humility comes before honor.
Proverbs 15:33 NIV

UNDERSTAND

- *What does it look like to be honored by the Lord?*
- *What is the prerequisite for being honored by the Father?*

APPLY

One way of allowing scripture to explain scripture is by finding a story that demonstrates the idea of a particular verse.

About two hundred years after civil war divided the Jews, Israel fell to the Assyrians, and eventually Judah fell to the Babylonians, who took captives "of the nobility, youths without blemish, of good appearance and skillful in all wisdom, endowed with knowledge, understanding learning, and competent to stand in the king's palace" (Daniel 1:3–4 ESV), including Daniel and three of his friends. Even in captivity they feared the Lord and refused unclean foods according to Jewish law. God so blessed them that "in every matter of wisdom and understanding about which the king inquired of them, he found them ten times better than all the magicians and enchanters that were in all his kingdom" (Daniel 1:20 ESV).

A year later King Nebuchadnezzar had a disturbing dream. Not trusting his wise men, he demanded, "Tell me the dream, and then I'll know that you can tell me what it means" (Daniel 2:9 NLT). Infuriated by their inability to describe the dream, the king commanded the death of all the wise men in Babylon! But Daniel, in a last-minute audience with Nebuchadnezzar, saved the lives of hundreds by revealing both the dream and its interpretation. Daniel could have taken credit but rather made it clear: "It is not because I am wiser than anyone else that I know the secret of your dream, but because God wants you to understand" (Daniel 2:30 NLT).

The king was ecstatic, honoring both Daniel *and* his God.

PRAY

Wise Father, may I always fear You so I can make You known in this generation.

YOU CAN OBEY THIS COMMAND!

Read Ephesians 6:10–18

KEY VERSE

Pray in the Spirit at all times and on every occasion. Stay alert and be persistent in your prayers for all believers everywhere. Ephesians 6:18 NLT

UNDERSTAND

- *Which of God's commands do you find easiest to obey? "Do not murder"? Any others?*
- *Which of God's commands do you find hardest to obey? "Do not covet"? Any others?*

APPLY

When it comes to commands, Paul really packed them into today's Bible reading. Seven of the nine verses are bold commands for you to obey. Most have to do with taking on the power and armor of God. Duly noted! The last one, however, has to do with prayer. It's a doubleheader found in today's key verse.

The first half of the verse says, "Pray in the Spirit at all times and on every occasion." In other words, Paul wanted Christian men to confess their sins and ask to be filled with the Holy Spirit. That way, you can pray with a clean, filled, and bold heart—with the Holy Spirit leading and guiding you.

The second half of the verse says, "Stay alert and be persistent in your prayers for all believers everywhere." The first eight words make sense. The last four words make many guys cringe. They think, *How in the world would it be possible to do that even once?*

In Paul's day, he did it by cities and regions.

In our day, it's done by nations and continents.

How? See below.

PRAY

Yes, Lord, I want to say "Thank You!" for commanding Christian men to pray "for all believers everywhere." I want to do that very thing right now. Lord, I pray for Your protection and for the spiritual growth, endurance, maturity, and love of Christians in Muslim, Hindu, and Buddhist nations, and in other countries where Christians are at risk.

CORRECTION

Read Proverbs 15:30–32

KEY VERSE

Whoever heeds life-giving correction will be at home among the wise. PROVERBS 15:31 NIV

UNDERSTAND

- *Why is correction so hard to take?*
- *Does it matter where correction comes from?*
- *What does it feel like to offer correction to another?*

APPLY

One of the themes repeated in wisdom literature is humility and the critical need to heed correction for our own benefit.

Maturity is voluntary; we don't have to change. Man is allowed to remain ignorant and face the consequences. "Whoever ignores instruction despises himself, but he who listens to reproof gains intelligence" (Proverbs 15:32 ESV).

King David has one of the most famous stories of correction and redemption in the Bible. After hiding his adultery and subsequent pregnancy of Bathsheba by setting up her husband to be killed in a military campaign, the king openly took her as a wife without any hint of remorse. This was the same David who as a young man was chosen by God to be king and described by God as "a man after my heart, who will do all my will" (Acts 13:22 ESV). When rebuked by Nathan the prophet, David responded in repentance (2 Samuel 12; Psalm 51).

Being corrected isn't pleasant, but correcting others can be just as hard. Nathan could have been punished for speaking the truth to a king, as John the Baptist was by the adulterous King Herod (Matthew 14:3–4). You can tell a lot about a man's character by his reaction to rebuke. "Do not reprove a scoffer, or he will hate you; reprove a wise man, and he will love you" (Proverbs 9:8 ESV). Whether we are corrected gently by a friend or harshly by an adversary, we should bear in mind that "a rebuke goes deeper into a man of understanding than a hundred blows into a fool" (Proverbs 17:10 ESV).

PRAY

Correct me often, O God, in any way that helps me become more like Christ.

THE TEST OF PRAISE

Read Proverbs 27:17–22

KEY VERSE

The crucible is for silver and the furnace for gold, and each is tested by the praise accorded him. PROVERBS 27:21 NASB

UNDERSTAND

- *What is the point of a crucible in refining silver or a furnace for gold?*
- *How do praise and honor test a man?*

APPLY

Most of us would probably think of testing as hardship, affliction, or persecution. Those certainly do test what we are made of the way a crucible shows the quality of a metal by bringing the dross to the surface. But there's a more subtle test of our inner qualities.

Take the example of Herod Agrippa, the Roman-raised grandson of Herod the Great (the king when Jesus was born) who ruled after his uncle Herod Antipas (the king during Jesus' life). Herod Agrippa was overseeing a political event, surrounded by people begging for his help, when his time of testing came: "On an appointed day Herod put on his royal robes, took his seat upon the throne, and delivered an oration to them. And the people were shouting, 'The voice of a god, and not of a man!' Immediately an angel of the Lord struck him down, because he did not give God the glory, and he was eaten by worms and breathed his last" (Acts 12:21–23 ESV).

Herod, a Jew by birth, allowed himself to be praised as a god (apparently Roman thinking had rubbed off) and paid a heavy price. Conversely, when the pagans of Lystra attempted to sacrifice offerings to Paul and Barnabas for healing a crippled man in Acts 14:14 (ESV), the apostles "tore their garments and rushed out into the crowd" to stop them. They are examples to us that we can pass the test of success too because "a person with a changed heart seeks praise from God, not from people" (Romans 2:29 NLT).

PRAY

Guard me, O God, from the temptation to seek the useless praise of this world.

REMEMBERING GOD'S PROMISES

Read 1 Kings 8:25–32

KEY VERSES

"May you watch over this Temple night and day, this place where you have said, 'My name will be there.' May you always hear the prayers I make toward this place. May you hear the humble and earnest requests from me and your people Israel when we pray toward this place. Yes, hear us from heaven where you live, and when you hear, forgive."

1 Kings 8:29–30 NLT

UNDERSTAND

- *Consider the promises Solomon brought to people's minds when he began the prayer to God recorded in today's scripture reading. What is the value of including a "reminder" of God's past promises while praying?*
- *Solomon asked God to watch over the temple day and night. Why would he make a point of asking Him to do that even if Israel could claim to be God's people?*
- *What did Solomon's prayer anticipate about God's people in the future? In light of that, how should God's people respond?*

APPLY

As you begin your day, Solomon's approach to prayer in today's scripture reading offers some practical guidance for your prayers: claiming God's promises for you, trusting in God's faithfulness and watchfulness, and then relying on God's mercy to restore you after failure. You may have moments of failure or struggle today, but you can follow Solomon's example by humbly praying for restoration.

Wrapped up in this prayer is the possibility of doubt. You may enter this day with lingering doubts about God's care for you, or you may worry that God will disown you if you fall into sin. It should offer you comfort that Solomon fully expected the people of Israel to fail and to need God's restoration. By relying on God's promises, he models a way to pray with faith and boldness.

Don't miss the fact that this was a public prayer in front of the whole nation—a prayer that was recorded for future generations. It may not be comfortable to admit that you or your own people will have failures to confess in the future, but this corporate humility was surely appropriate and is worth imitating.

PRAY

Father, You know that I may fail and struggle today, but I will trust in Your mercy and kindness and rely on the promises You have given me in Jesus. May I remain humble as I seek Your forgiveness and restoration. Amen.

DEBT

Read Proverbs 22:7–9

KEY VERSE

The rich rules over the poor, and the borrower is the slave of the lender. PROVERBS 22:7 ESV

UNDERSTAND

- *How does debt equate to "slavery"?*
- *Is borrowing money something the Bible frowns upon?*
- *Is it even possible to live in a modern world without debt?*

APPLY

Often the sayings of the wise are formulated as simple observations—*A penny saved is a penny earned*—rather than directives—*Don't take any wooden nickels.* Today's verse is just such an observation. It functions as a road sign warning of what's ahead. How you utilize that information is up to you.

In the Old Testament, lending was not forbidden but charging interest of fellow Israelites was. "Do not charge a fellow Israelite interest, whether on money or food or anything else that may earn interest. You may charge a foreigner interest, but not a fellow Israelite" (Deuteronomy 23:19–20 NIV). If there's a lender, there must be a borrower.

While the Bible does not forbid debt, it certainly doesn't encourage it. Debt may not mean literal slavery these days, but it's a form of obligation that can interfere with our legitimate obligations to God. Therefore, debt shouldn't be entered into lightly or, to be very specific, with thoughts of not repaying. "The wicked borrow and do not repay" (Psalm 37:21 NIV). Paul commanded us, "Give to everyone what you owe them: If you owe taxes, pay taxes; if revenue, then revenue; if respect, then respect; if honor, then honor. Let no debt remain outstanding" (Romans 13:7–8 NIV).

Today, the easiest way to get in over your head is through credit cards. The wise will handle them with extreme caution or, better yet, not at all! Enter contract purchases like houses and cars remembering today's verse. While theoretically they could be sold to repay an outstanding balance, they still involve risk.

PRAY

O Lord, keep me from enslaving myself for things that do not last!

SOWING AND REAPING

Read Proverbs 3:7-12

KEY VERSES

Honor the Lord *with your wealth, with the firstfruits of all your crops; then your barns will be filled to overflowing, and your vats will brim over with new wine.* Proverbs 3:9–10 niv

UNDERSTAND

- *How do we honor the Lord with our wealth?*
- *What are "firstfruits"?*
- *What happens to the one who puts God first in his financial practices?*

APPLY

As you know, proverbs do not provide rigid formulas; they highlight principles. What they underscore should be considered in light of the full teaching of the Bible. Today's proverb isn't a guarantee of increasing one's bank account; it's about putting the Lord first in our finances and trusting Him to take care of us in a cycle He designed known as *sowing and reaping*. He provides, we invest, and we gain a return so we can reinvest.

When the Corinthian church was preparing a donation for the needy in Jerusalem, Paul said, "Remember this: Whoever sows sparingly will also reap sparingly, and whoever sows generously will also reap generously" (2 Corinthians 9:6 niv). Paul echoes Solomon's observation that "a generous person will prosper; whoever refreshes others will be refreshed" (Proverbs 11:25 niv). The *reaping* or *refreshing* we receive may or may not be financial, though it could be. Paul didn't readily distinguish between material and spiritual blessings since in either case the point was to reinvest. Paul was perfectly confident that "he who supplies seed to the sower and bread for food will also supply and increase your store of seed and will enlarge the harvest of your righteousness" (2 Corinthians 9:10 niv), so the cycle of blessing others would continue.

And happily, giving isn't about the amount, "For if the willingness is there, the gift is acceptable according to what one has, not according to what one does not have" (2 Corinthians 8:12 niv). We can all participate!

PRAY

Giver of all things, may I always put You first in my finances, trusting You to provide.

WHY ARE R-RATED STORIES IN THE BIBLE?

Read Judges 19:16–30

KEY VERSES

He said, "Get up! Let's go!" But there was no answer. So he put her body on his donkey and took her home. When he got home, he took a knife and cut his concubine's body into twelve pieces. Then he sent one piece to each tribe throughout all the territory of Israel.
JUDGES 19:28–29 NLT

UNDERSTAND

- *Does the Bible usually whitewash or sanitize the stories it tells? Why or why not?*
- *Does the Bible usually tell us the moral of the story? Why or why not?*

APPLY

The first seven books of the Bible all contain stories that make good men wince. Murder. Rape. Slaughter. Incest. Pillaging. Prostitution. Annihilation. Gang rape. The short book of Ruth is the first Bible book that's only PG-13. Then it's back to more sex and violence at every turn from 1 Samuel to 2 Chronicles. The next two short books dial it back to PG-13, but Esther. . .well, you get the idea. Sex and violence and more sex and violence.

One of the Bible's most disturbing stories is found in today's reading. The book of Judges repeatedly shocks, and the appendices drive home the utter terror of these bookends: "In those days Israel had no king; all the people did whatever seemed right in their own eyes" (Judges 17:6; 21:25 NLT).

In this case, the ancient moral of the story is obvious. The contemporary moral is no less terrifying: If you do whatever seems right in your own eyes, there is no limit to how depraved you can be.

In a world hell-bent on the opiates of pick-and-choose reality, you have to fight hard to stay grounded in God and His Word.

If you let down your guard. . .if you forget that bad company corrupts good morals . . .if you give in to the world's blatant lies. . .if you shake your fist at God and decide to do whatever you want. . .your own life story soon will be R-rated.

Week in and week out, you see the tragic stories of other men played out in real life. In their wake? Sex and violence and broken lives and God's judgment.

Why is the Bible so honest? For very good reasons, indeed.

PRAY

Yes, Lord, I didn't enjoy today's Bible study. Maybe that was the point. I've already let down my guard. I repent. I turn from the errors of my way. I turn back to You. Cleanse me, fill me, and lead me in Your paths, I pray.

THE SOURCE OF PEACE WITH GOD

Read Romans 5:1–11

KEY VERSES

For if while we were enemies we were reconciled to God through the death of His Son, much more, having been reconciled, we shall be saved by His life. And not only this, but we also celebrate in God through our Lord Jesus Christ, through whom we have now received the reconciliation. ROMANS 5:10–11 NASB

UNDERSTAND

- *Do you feel "worthy" of God today? What does today's scripture passage say about your standing before God?*
- *Think about a time when you've been reconciled with someone after a failure or dispute. According to this passage, what does reconciliation with God look like?*
- *Paul describes being transformed from being an enemy against God to celebrating reconciliation with Him. Which do you relate to more right now? How can this passage help you shift your understanding?*

APPLY

Today you can fully enjoy and celebrate reconciliation with God. Many generations ago, Paul wrote today's passage and made it clear that God wants to be reconciled with you.

God's love is with you because He sent His Son, Jesus, to earth in order to bring about reconciliation between Himself and humanity. You can't undermine God's mercy because Jesus arrived while you and every other human who had lived or would ever live here on earth were still sinners. If you understand that you are a sinner right now, the good news is that you qualify for God's reconciling work.

Your only action right now is to have faith in Jesus, trusting God to change you in ways you could never change yourself. This was a calling you were never able to fulfill on your own. Yet God's love and mercy has lifted you out of conflict with Him and restored you to a place of peace and blessing.

PRAY

Jesus, thank You for Your love, mercy, and kindness, which You put on display in Your life, death, and resurrection here on earth. I am grateful to be healed, restored, and forgiven for my sins, grateful that I can trust in You without fear or reservation. May I fully live in the love You have poured out in my heart through Your Holy Spirit. Amen.

THE POOR

Read Proverbs 19:16–18

KEY VERSE

Whoever is kind to the poor lends to the LORD, and he will reward them for what they have done. PROVERBS 19:17 NIV

UNDERSTAND

- *Why would God consider kindness to the poor as a "loan" to Himself?*
- *Who are the poor today?*
- *What is promised to those who are kind to the poor?*

APPLY

In the scriptures, the Lord consistently aligns Himself with the underdog: the widow, the orphan, and the poor. "I know that the LORD secures justice for the poor and upholds the cause of the needy" (Psalm 140:12 NIV). "A father to the fatherless, a defender of widows, is God in his holy dwelling" (Psalm 68:5 NIV). His concern for those who are the lowest is part of His pattern of revealing Himself to the humble and shaming the proud. As we've studied earlier, "God chose things despised by the world, things counted as nothing at all, and used them to bring to nothing what the world considers important" (1 Corinthians 1:28 NLT).

The "poor" are those whose lot in life is one of weakness and vulnerability—a group to be helped, not ignored or used. But there's another kind of "poor" we need to be discerning about—the sluggard. God gave many laws to protect the poor, but to the slacker He gave only warnings: "A slack hand causes poverty" (Proverbs 10:4 ESV); "Mere talk tends only to poverty" (Proverbs 14:23 ESV); "Love not sleep, lest you come to poverty" (Proverbs 20:13 ESV). The sluggard needs to face the consequences of his choices, as Paul, who loved "the poor," commanded: "If anyone is not willing to work, then he is not to eat, either" (2 Thessalonians 3:10 NASB). We are called to be generous to the poor, not support the lazy.

PRAY

Father, give me a tender heart to the poor and a discerning heart toward those who need a different kind of help.

GOD'S ECONOMY

Read Proverbs 11:23-28

KEY VERSES

One person gives freely, yet gains even more; another withholds unduly, but comes to poverty. A generous person will prosper; whoever refreshes others will be refreshed.
PROVERBS 11:24–25 NIV

UNDERSTAND

- *What principles of generosity do you see in today's reading?*
- *What seems contradictory about this approach to wealth?*

APPLY

It's not surprising that the way the world sees things is often at odds with heaven. Perhaps no subject so clearly demonstrates that than money. Jesus pointedly said, "No one can serve two masters. . . . You cannot serve both God and money" (Matthew 6:24 NIV).

Today's verse is about living contrary to the world's approach to wealth and its purpose. The world says to store up all the wealth you can and use it for your own satisfaction. But God's path leads to being open handed in faith, knowing where wealth comes from to begin with.

Moses warned the people, who because of their enslavement in Egypt had never owned land for themselves, "Beware lest you say in your heart, 'My power and the might of my hand have gotten me this wealth.' You shall remember the LORD your God, for it is he who gives you power to get wealth" (Deuteronomy 8:17–18 ESV). From the Bible's perspective, you and I have never gotten a paycheck that wasn't a gift from God.

When King David collected money for his son Solomon to build God's temple, everyone gave "freely and wholeheartedly to the LORD" (1 Chronicles 29:9 NIV). But the king didn't take credit for such generosity: "But who am I, and who are my people, that we should be able to give as generously as this? Everything comes from you, and we have given you only what comes from your hand" (1 Chronicles 29:14 NIV). Really, you can only ever give back to God.

PRAY

Generous Father, show me how to give more and more, trusting You to supply all my needs.

LIKE FAMILY

Read 1 Timothy 5:1–16

KEY VERSES

Never speak harshly to an older man, but appeal to him respectfully as you would to your own father. Talk to younger men as you would to your own brothers. Treat older women as you would your mother, and treat younger women with all purity as you would your own sisters. 1 TIMOTHY 5:1–2 NLT

UNDERSTAND

- *How should a man relate to other men, both older and younger?*
- *How are older women to be treated?*
- *What additional instruction applies to young women?*

APPLY

The scriptures record all manner of dysfunctional families—from Cain, who murdered his brother, Abel, out of jealousy. . .to Noah, who cursed one of his sons. . .to Joseph, who was sold into slavery by his brothers. . .to David, whose son Absalom tried to usurp the throne. But despite the failings of any particular family, the family was God's design to fill the earth, and through His Son to redeem it as He promised Abraham: "In you and your offspring [Jesus] shall all the families of the earth be blessed" (Genesis 28:14 ESV).

Family was also the Father's design for the church to follow. Paul said, "I write so that you will know how one should act in the household of God" (1 Timothy 3:15 NASB). Paul even tied an elder's qualification to his own family's experience: "For if a man cannot manage his own household, how can he take care of God's church?" (1 Timothy 3:5 NLT).

To act wisely, we need to envision a healthy family dynamic, not treating older men disrespectfully, encouraging younger men as brothers, serving older women like our own mom, and behaving toward younger women as sisters, without any hint of impropriety. In other words, "In your relationships with one another, have the same mindset as Christ Jesus" (Philippians 2:5 NIV).

PRAY

Perfect Father, give me wisdom toward those I serve so I may be useful in Your household.

WHY DOES MARK 16 HAVE ALTERNATE ENDINGS?

Read Mark 16:1–20

KEY VERSE

Trembling and bewildered, the women went out and fled from the tomb. They said nothing to anyone, because they were afraid. Mark 16:8 NIV

UNDERSTAND

- *If today's key verse were the last verse in Mark's Gospel, why might Mark have stopped right in the middle of the action?*
- *Why else might Mark have stopped so abruptly in the middle of the resurrection story?*

APPLY

Virtually all modern English Bible translations include notes within the text itself and in footnotes indicating uncertainties about the last chapter in Mark's Gospel.

What is certain is that Mark 16 ends abruptly at today's key verse in the two oldest extant codices of the New Testament.

The first, *Codex Vaticanus*, includes small symbols to indicate where the scribes knew that variants existed in some of the biblical manuscripts within their scriptorium's library. These match up with what Greek New Testament scholars know today, even though the meaning of the small symbols weren't deciphered until 1995.

In that first codex, however, no small symbols appear at Mark 16:8. Instead, the scribes left nearly half of that particular page blank. That happens nowhere else. They wanted to leave no uncertainty about the fact that ancient manuscripts included alternate endings, and many included what we call Mark 16:9–20.

We have good reasons to believe that from the get-go multiple copies of some New Testament books were sent to a variety of churches throughout a given region of the Roman Empire. It's very possible that Mark did the same. It's also possible that the Holy Spirit inspired Mark to create versions with alternate endings.

If Mark intentionally ended some manuscripts at today's key verse, he likely hoped that Christians would read them to their households, provoking not-yet Christians to ask, "What? Why does he end the story so abruptly? What happened?"

PRAY

Yes, Lord, I want to say "Thank You!" for preserving the scriptures down through the ages. Before now, I didn't realize that the abrupt ending of Mark might have been intentional. Please keep using this Gospel to win millions more to faith in Your Son and our Savior, Jesus Christ.

DAY 331

WHAT ARE YOU ASKING GOD FOR?

Read James 4:1–10

KEY VERSES

You desire but do not have, so you kill. You covet but you cannot get what you want, so you quarrel and fight. You do not have because you do not ask God. When you ask, you do not receive, because you ask with wrong motives, that you may spend what you get on your pleasures. James 4:2–3 NIV

UNDERSTAND

- *What types of desires is James addressing in this passage? How can desires become positive—and how can they become destructive?*
- *James is concerned both with what you ask God to do and how you ask Him to do it. What does the right kind of asking look like in your life?*
- *James wrote of the importance of humility and submission to God. What do you need to submit to God today?*

APPLY

James invites you to examine your desires and the way you approach getting what you want. Your desires can be the catalyst for conflict that alienates you from others and prevents you from enjoying true intimacy with God.

Those who resist God leave themselves vulnerable to other influences that can send their lives into conflict. Humble submission means that you are no longer holding on to what you demand, and that frees you to receive from God. As you draw near to God, you'll have fewer conflicts with others.

Submission to God isn't easy. James describes it as a battle for good reason. It may be a lifelong process rather than a quick fix you enact today. Yet as you pray today, tomorrow, and the rest of this week, you can ask God whether you have laid down your desires to Him—and whether your motives in prayer are in line with God's best for you.

As you go about your day, examine what you desire and whether you have placed your desires in God's care.

PRAY

Father, examine my heart and reveal my inner motives and desires with Your light so that I can seek what is best for You, for myself, and for others. May I see the ways my heart can become divided, and may I become a person of peace who can release his own desires to You. Amen.

FATHERS AND MENTORS

Read Proverbs 4

KEY VERSES

Listen, my sons, to the instruction of a father, and pay attention so that you may gain understanding, for I give you good teaching; do not abandon my instruction. When I was a son to my father, tender and the only son in the sight of my mother, he taught me and said to me, "Let your heart take hold of my words; keep my commandments and live; acquire wisdom! Acquire understanding!" Proverbs 4:1–5 NASB

UNDERSTAND

- *Who is responsible for passing wisdom on to the next generation?*
- *Why is an older man's teaching so important?*

APPLY

Fatherhood can be a complicated subject. Some of us have (or had) highly engaged dads, some absent dads, and some no dads. No matter your situation, today's proverb speaks to all men—even if you're not a father.

God doesn't expect fathers to pass along all wisdom to their children, but each father can pass along the love of wisdom. No man has all the answers, but each man is responsible to equip the next generation to embrace the wisdom of a godly life, to mentor as God gives him the chance.

We all need mentors in addition to our own fathers or, if necessary, in place of them. And each of us can become a mentor. Paul referred to both Timothy and Titus as his "son in the faith" (1 Timothy 1:2; Titus 1:4), and he dealt with his congregations "as a father deals with his own children, encouraging, comforting and urging [them] to live lives worthy of God" (1 Thessalonians 2:11–12 NIV). Paul's mentoring covered four generations: "What you have heard from me in the presence of many witnesses entrust to faithful men, who will be able to teach others also" (2 Timothy 2:2 ESV).

All men can embrace the role of mentor whether they have children or not.

PRAY

Perfect Father, grant me the ability to pass wisdom on to the next generation.

THE TONGUE OF THE WISE

Read Proverbs 12:13–19

KEY VERSE

There is one who speaks rashly like the thrusts of a sword, but the tongue of the wise brings healing. PROVERBS 12:18 NASB

UNDERSTAND

- *Why do words have such potential to harm people?*
- *How do words bring healing?*

APPLY

Sometimes ancient figurative language lines up neatly with our own. In the scriptures, the words *tongue* or *mouth* mean speech or language, like we would say his "native tongue" or "a foul mouth." Figurative language is a powerful way to communicate and was used often throughout the book of Proverbs.

There's an old children's ditty that goes "Sticks and stones may break my bones, but words will never hurt me." It makes a good retort on the playground when you're six, but it's not always true. We've all felt the stab of hurtful words, and we're all guilty of wounding someone else. Taming the tongue is an ongoing challenge. James wrote, "With the tongue we praise our Lord and Father, and with it we curse human beings, who have been made in God's likeness. Out of the same mouth come praise and cursing. My brothers and sisters, this should not be" (James 3:9–10 NIV).

Since we know that "out of the abundance of the heart the mouth speaks" (Matthew 12:34 ESV), we have to start with our inner man, meditating on the Word with praise and thanksgiving. Only by filling our hearts with God will we have a chance to bring healing words and follow Paul's instruction: "Do not let any unwholesome talk come out of your mouths, but only what is helpful for building others up according to their needs, that it may benefit those who listen" (Ephesians 4:29 NIV).

Words are powerful, and the wise man will use them to bring healing.

PRAY

Lord, You spoke the heavens and earth into existence; teach me to speak healing to those who need it.

WHY IS ECCLESIASTES IN THE BIBLE?

Read Ecclesiastes 1:1–18

KEY VERSES

The words of the Teacher, son of David, king in Jerusalem: "Meaningless! Meaningless!" says the Teacher. "Utterly meaningless! Everything is meaningless." ECCLESIASTES 1:1–2 NIV

UNDERSTAND

- *Have you read all twelve chapters of Ecclesiastes at some point in the past?*
- *If so, what did you think of this one-of-a-kind book?*

APPLY

This fourth book of Hebrew literature explores a nagging age-old question: What is the meaning of life? This poetic essay or sermon, probably written by Solomon ponders the *apparent* meaninglessness of life "under the sun."

The phrase "under the sun" aptly describes Solomon's earthbound perspective through this book. He wasn't looking at life as the Lord in heaven sees it, but from the perspective of an immensely wise, fabulously wealthy, and politically powerful individual here on earth. From his famed vantage point, Solomon bookended Ecclesiastes by saying, "Everything is meaningless" (1:2 and 12:8 NIV).

Nevertheless, throughout this book Solomon alludes to basic beliefs in God's justice, graciousness, sovereignty, omniscience, transcendence, revelation, mystery, creative power, and eternal nature. Solomon wrapped up the book by saying: "Here is the conclusion of the matter: Fear God and keep his commandments, for this is the duty of all mankind. For God will bring every deed into judgment, including every hidden thing, whether it is good or evil" (12:13–14 NIV).

Solomon left it up to the reader to decide who God is (the Lord?) and how He reveals His commands (scripture?). It's quite likely that Solomon simply assumed his readers already were well versed in the commands the Lord God in heaven had revealed to Moses and other prophets.

It's also possible that Solomon may have distributed copies of this book to foreign visitors as a means of provoking their interest in the God of Israel.

PRAY

Yes, Lord, I want to say "Thank You!" for the book of Ecclesiastes. I'm still not quite sure what to make of it. Then again, this might be a good book to read with one of my more philosophical and not-yet-Christian friends.

OPINIONS AND BOASTING

Read Proverbs 18:1–8

KEY VERSE

Fools find no pleasure in understanding but delight in airing their own opinions.
Proverbs 18:2 NIV

UNDERSTAND

- *What is the common trait of all biblical "fools"?*
- *What does a fool find pleasure in when he speaks?*

APPLY

Today's verse is a form of Hebrew poetry known as *antithetic parallelism*, meaning the first and second parts of the verse highlight a contrast between two things. In this case, between what a fool does and does not enjoy.

The fool has no patience to listen or discover something new if it means he might be contradicted in his opinions. Grasping the truth about a subject isn't his goal, preferring to be the center of attention. As the old saying goes, he loves to hear himself talk.

The first cousin of this habit, so to speak, is boasting about himself and his life. Fools are self-aggrandizing—sharpest-guy-in-the-room syndrome—though they are warned, "Do not boast about tomorrow, for you do not know what a day may bring" (Proverbs 27:1 ESV). James expands on this cautionary proverb: "Come now, you who say, 'Today or tomorrow we will go into such and such a town and spend a year there and trade and make a profit'—yet you do not know what tomorrow will bring. What is your life? For you are a mist that appears for a little time and then vanishes" (James 4:13–14 ESV).

The common theme for us who desire to walk in wisdom is just to avoid talking too much. "When there are many words, wrongdoing is unavoidable, but one who restrains his lips is wise" (Proverbs 10:19 NASB). Wisdom is always consistently restrained, not self-asserting, quick to respond, or braggadocious. "Even fools are thought wise if they keep silent, and discerning if they hold their tongues" (Proverbs 17:28 NIV).

PRAY

Father, set a guard over my mouth and open my ears to listen and my heart to understand.

LIFELONG LEARNER

Read Proverbs 9:1–9

KEY VERSE

Give instruction to a wise person and he will become still wiser; teach a righteous person and he will increase his insight. PROVERBS 9:9 NASB

UNDERSTAND

- *What characterizes a wise man in today's verse?*
- *Is there ever a reason to stop learning?*

APPLY

There's an ancient proverb that's not in the Bible but nonetheless rings true: When the student is ready, the teacher will appear. A heart that is humble and a mind that is prepared to learn is like the good soil in Jesus' parable. Good soil is the condition of the heart of the "one who hears the word and understands it. He indeed bears fruit and yields, in one case a hundredfold, in another sixty, and in another thirty" (Matthew 13:23 ESV). Good soil produces results over many, many years.

The connection in today's verse between wisdom and righteousness is often found in the Bible. As you know, real wisdom is about a life that reflects godly character, not simply accumulating knowledge. In the Bible, wisdom is a means to an end, not an achievement in and of itself. "Let not the wise man boast in his wisdom, let not the mighty man boast in his might, let not the rich man boast in his riches, but let him who boasts boast in this, that he *understands and knows me*" (Jeremiah 9:23–24 ESV, emphasis added).

Jesus calls us to be His disciples. The word *disciple* means "learner"—one who "will become still wiser." And there's no expectation of plateauing since His resources are limitless: "In Him all the fullness of Deity dwells in bodily form" (Colossians 2:9 NASB). We'll never run out of things to learn—not in this life or the next: "This is eternal life, that they *know* you, the only true God, and Jesus Christ whom you have sent" (John 17:3 ESV, emphasis added).

PRAY

Lord of Righteousness, open my heart to learn from You and know You more every day.

SEEKING COUNSEL

Read Proverbs 15:21–23

KEY VERSE

Plans fail for lack of counsel, but with many advisers they succeed. PROVERBS 15:22 NIV

UNDERSTAND

- *What is the point of seeking counsel?*
- *What qualifies someone to speak into our lives?*
- *Who in your own life can offer wise counsel?*

APPLY

If you've ever taken on a home project that you've never attempted before (such as building a deck or remodeling a bathroom), then today's proverb will resonate immediately! Even if your handyman projects are limited to the occasional piece of IKEA furniture, it's far easier to succeed with the input of someone who's "been there, done that." Or maybe you just plowed ahead and tried to figure it out as you went, only to discover that you left out a foundational step that threatened everything. You learned the hard way that "enthusiasm without knowledge is no good; haste makes mistakes" (Proverbs 19:2 NLT).

Most men's lives are filled with complex issues that are too valuable to be left to trial and error: marriage, children, buying a home, navigating a career. Seeking outside counsel can make a difference in almost every aspect of our lives. "Where there is no guidance, a people falls, but in an abundance of counselors there is safety" (Proverbs 11:14 ESV), and "in an abundance of counselors there is victory" (Proverbs 24:6 NASB).

Of course, the quality of the counsel is based on the quality of the source. Paul warned, "The time is coming when people will not endure sound teaching, but having itching ears they will accumulate for themselves teachers to suit their own passions, and will turn away from listening to the truth and wander off into myths" (2 Timothy 4:3–4 ESV). We need to seek out qualified counselors whose input comes from a solid foundation in the Word of God and a life that demonstrates wisdom.

PRAY

Help me, Father, to humble myself and ask for guidance from those whom You approve.

HUMILITY IS TIED TO GOD'S PROVISION

Read Deuteronomy 8:1–10

KEY VERSE

"Yes, he humbled you by letting you go hungry and then feeding you with manna, a food previously unknown to you and your ancestors. He did it to teach you that people do not live by bread alone; rather, we live by every word that comes from the mouth of the LORD."
DEUTERONOMY 8:3 NLT

UNDERSTAND

- *Why is humility so important for those who want to receive God's provision?*
- *While everyone needs a source of income in order to eat, what does it mean to you that people don't live by "bread alone"?*
- *What would it look like today for you to more completely depend on every word from the mouth of God?*

APPLY

No one enjoys being humbled or disciplined, but today's scripture reading shares how God taught the people of Israel to depend more completely on Him. The process wasn't easy or pleasant—in fact, it involved a lot of fear and uncertainty in a hostile wilderness. God's method of provision was a complete unknown—a new kind of bread they had never before tasted, delivered in a most unusual way.

Yet on the other side of that difficult, humbling experience, the people of Israel started to learn to depend on God and to examine their hearts so that they turned only to Him and to no one else.

You may be in the midst of some uncertainty or an unfamiliar situation in which you don't know how things are going to turn out. This gives you an opportunity to humble yourself before God and to grow in your dependence and obedience.

The outcome of humbling experiences, or of God's discipline, may not be what you prefer in the moment, but you can be assured that depending on Him for your daily provision and care will lead to praise and gratitude. There is hope for you on the other side of life's lowest moments—if you can learn to seek God alone when all else remains uncertain.

PRAY

Father, You have promised to both humble me and to be present for me in life's challenges. May I learn to depend on You for my daily provision and care rather than relying on what I can control and what I can do on my own. I trust that You can provide for my needs in the most unlikely and unexpected ways. Amen.

WHO'S TO BLAME?

Read Proverbs 19:1–3

KEY VERSE

A person's own folly leads to their ruin, yet their heart rages against the Lord.
Proverbs 19:3 NIV

UNDERSTAND

- *Why is it so easy to blame God when we ruin our own lives?*
- *What does the Bible say about folly and the consequences of our own actions?*

APPLY

Facing the consequences of our own actions is a theme that repeats over and over in the stories of the Bible—as does man's tendency to blame someone else, even God.

After the man and woman disobeyed God's command in the garden of Eden, a conversation followed their transgression in which we glimpse the roots of today's proverb. As God approached the fearful couple, "they hid from the Lord God among the trees of the garden" (Genesis 3:8 NIV). When God asked Adam pointedly about the forbidden tree, "the man said, 'The woman whom You gave to be with me, she gave me some of the fruit of the tree, and I ate'" (Genesis 3:12 NASB). Adam's first instinct was to shift the blame for his folly to both God and his wife!

After wandering in the desert for forty years, Moses reminded the Israelites, "You rebelled against the command of the Lord your God and refused to go in. You complained in your tents and said, 'The Lord must hate us'" (Deuteronomy 1:26–27 NLT). The generation that died in the desert tried to find fault with God for their own rebellion.

In Christ, we have mercy and do not always face the full consequences of our actions. But He isn't to blame if we "ruin" our lives by foolish choices. Paul warned believers that "whoever sows to please their flesh, from the flesh will reap destruction" (Galatians 6:8 NIV). God isn't to blame if our own folly comes back upon us.

PRAY

Lord, rebuke me if I ever accuse You when I am the one who's to blame!

SELF-CONTROL

Read Proverbs 25:25–28

KEY VERSE

A man without self-control is like a city broken into and left without walls.
Proverbs 25:28 ESV

UNDERSTAND

- *What was the purpose of the city wall in ancient times?*
- *What would happen if those walls were breached or lay in ruin?*

APPLY

In ancient times, important cities were encircled by high walls for protection. Attacking armies would have to batter down the gates or breach the walls to gain access to the interior.

The most famous walled city in the Bible was Jericho. By God's divine judgment, the Israelites marched, trumpeted, and shouted "and the wall fell down flat, so that the [Israelites] went up into the city, every man straight before him, and they captured the city" (Joshua 6:20 ESV). While that situation was of God, the illustration works vividly as a metaphor for today's reading—the enemy of our souls would pour "straight" into our lives if some kind of wall wasn't in place. If "your adversary, the devil, prowls around like a roaring lion, seeking someone to devour" (1 Peter 5:8 NASB), you're going to need protection!

Self-control provides protection from being taken captive by sin, but a man who lacks it is basically a sitting duck. Temptation will find easy access from all directions to his inner man since there's nothing to slow it down. Even if there's only one broken section of the wall, that spot will invite constant attack by the enemy.

These walls of self-control, however, cannot be built by human effort alone since biblical self-control is a "fruit of the Spirit" (Galatians 5:22–23 ESV). Alone, the enemy's attacks will eventually batter down the stoutest defenses. But believing and walking by God's Spirit will strengthen us against all outside forces, "for God gave us a spirit not of fear but of power and love and self-control" (2 Timothy 1:7 ESV).

PRAY

Heavenly Father, thank You for Your Spirit, who strengthens me to exercise self-control.

PRESENT OR FUTURE TENSE

Read Malachi 1:11–14

KEY VERSE

"But my name is honored by people of other nations from morning till night. All around the world they offer sweet incense and pure offerings in honor of my name. For my name is great among the nations," says the LORD of Heaven's Armies. MALACHI 1:11 NLT

UNDERSTAND

- *In a footnote for today's key verse, the NLT translators say they used present tense but the prophet's meaning may have been future tense.*
- *In a footnote for this same verse, the ESV translators say they used future tense but the prophet's meaning may have been present tense.*

APPLY

Present or future tense? "Is" or "will be"? In exploring this small but important question, it's helpful to consider the following historical events described in great detail in God's Word:

- *Sometime near 600 BC, Nebuchadnezzar issued a public statement of praise to the Most High, the King of heaven (Daniel 4:34–37). This statement was well-known in Babylonia, but it also reached many other cities throughout his empire.*
- *In 538 BC, King Cyrus of Persia issued a statement in praise of the Lord, the God of heaven, throughout his kingdom (2 Chronicles 36:22–23; Ezra 1:1–4).*
- *Sometime near 535 BC, Darius the Mede sent a statement of praise to the God of Daniel to the people of every race and nation and language throughout the known world, which comprised at least 120 provinces (Daniel 6:25–27).*

This makes at least two worldwide statements of praise to the Lord God within ninety years of the writing of the book of Malachi, which a number of scholars believe was written in (or close to) 445 BC. That same year, King Artaxerxes issued letters to the governors of the regions west of the Euphrates River in support of Nehemiah's mission to rebuild Jerusalem (Nehemiah 2:7–9).

In Malachi's day, therefore, it's likely that the Lord's name truly "is" great and feared among the nations!

PRAY

Yes, Lord, I want to say "Thank You!" that Your great name has been feared all throughout history. Thanks too that Your desire is that none perish but that all come to repentance (2 Peter 3:9). Amen!

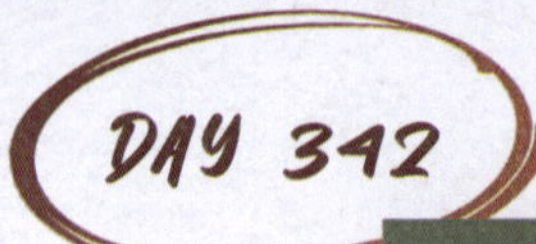

GOD'S DIRECTION MAKES COURAGEOUS DECISIONS POSSIBLE

Read Joshua 1:1–7

KEY VERSES

"Be strong and courageous, for you shall give this people possession of the land which I swore to their fathers to give them. Only be strong and very courageous; be careful to do according to all the Law which Moses My servant commanded you; do not turn from it to the right or to the left, so that you may achieve success wherever you go."

JOSHUA 1:6–7 NASB

UNDERSTAND

- *How does God's promise to Israel relate to the command to be strong and courageous?*
- *Why is obedience to the Law paired with the command to be courageous?*
- *How does God measure success in this exchange with Joshua? How does that compare to the ways that success is measured today?*

APPLY

In Exodus 33:11, we read that Joshua didn't depart from the tabernacle tent even after Moses retired for the evening. As Joshua was set to take charge of God's people, those quiet moments with the Lord started to pay off as he received His charge to "be strong and very courageous" during a time of uncertainty and conflict.

Taking quiet moments to be present with the Lord lays a foundation of attention to His voice and obedience to His commands that will be essential in your life today. The Lord's command to Joshua wasn't a general admonishment to be strong and courageous. He received a specific charge from God, and because he heard God's commands, he could confidently make the difficult and dangerous decisions ahead.

Your own challenge today is to discern what God is asking of you and to be receptive to the teachings of scripture. When you have confidence in God's calling and direction for you, it will be far easier to make the tough decisions that require courage and strength.

PRAY

Father, I ask that You would meet me in the private, quiet moments of my life and that I would hear Your voice calling me to pause and listen even during the storms of life. Help me to respond to today's challenges with faith and courage. Amen.

WISDOM HIMSELF

Read 1 Corinthians 1:26–31

KEY VERSE

God has united you with Christ Jesus. For our benefit God made him to be wisdom itself. Christ made us right with God; he made us pure and holy, and he freed us from sin.
1 Corinthians 1:30 NLT

UNDERSTAND

- *What does it mean to be "united" with Christ?*
- *Who is the very essence of wisdom?*
- *What does it mean to be made right with God?*

APPLY

To really apply the wisdom of God in our lives, we need to grasp the fact that Jesus Christ is wisdom embodied. He is its origin and its essence; He is its source and its goal. For us to understand any verse in the Bible about wisdom—from its role in the creation to Solomon's very specific instructions to Paul's discourse in 1 Corinthians on human philosophy—we must understand this most foundational truth.

Jesus made this dramatic claim about Himself: "I am the way, the truth, and the life. No one can come to the Father except through me" (John 14:6 NLT). He wasn't saying He could show us the way to the Father or that He knew the truth about God or was the path to new life, but that He was the living definition of those things. It's the same with wisdom. In other words, to speak of wisdom without Jesus Christ is to speak of something man-made, something limited and incomplete. Wisdom apart from Him is—at best—calling a shadow a real person.

Jesus is our wisdom, and nothing will make sense apart from Him.

PRAY

Father, You've united us with Your Son and have given us life! And in Him we find living wisdom! Thank You. Lead us to become more like Jesus, walking daily in His wisdom.

THE END AND THE MEANS

Read Genesis 3

KEY VERSE

The woman was convinced. She saw that the tree was beautiful and its fruit looked delicious, and she wanted the wisdom it would give her. So she took some of the fruit and ate it. Then she gave some to her husband, who was with her, and he ate it, too. Genesis 3:6 NLT

UNDERSTAND

- *Where was the man when the woman was having a conversation with the serpent?*
- *What about the fruit appealed to the woman?*

APPLY

In the garden of Eden everything was good. The woman was not wrong for desiring wisdom. But there were some serious problems with the way she pursued it. Before we lay all the blame on the woman, though, let's look at the whole story.

In Genesis 2:15–17, when God commanded the man not to eat of that *one* tree, he was alone; the command came prior to the woman's existence—so how did she know about it? From her husband. It was his responsibility to instruct her. When the serpent asked her, "Did God really say. . ." (Genesis 3:1 NIV), he was questioning her trust in her husband just as much as in God's command. And apparently the man added to God's prohibition, since the woman includes, "And you must not touch it" (Genesis 3:3 NIV) in her reply to the serpent's question. That may have been a wise addition, but nonetheless, in the critical moment, the man "who was with her" (verse 6) didn't step up. He sided with his wife's reasoning over God's command (Genesis 3:17).

They both missed something essential: True wisdom can't exist apart from simple obedience. No amount of rationalizing, even well-intentioned, can substitute for that. Whether we use our rational gifts to obey or justify our own path is the real test of wisdom.

PRAY

Lord God, protect me from my own imagination when it tries to compete with Your clear and loving commands!

SOLOMON'S PRAYER

Read 1 Kings 3:7–14

KEY VERSES

"Your servant is here among the people you have chosen, a great people, too numerous to count or number. So give your servant a discerning heart to govern your people and to distinguish between right and wrong. For who is able to govern this great people of yours?" The Lord was pleased that Solomon had asked for this. So God said to him, "Since you have asked for. . .discernment in administering justice, I will do what you have asked. I will give you a wise and discerning heart, so that there will never have been anyone like you, nor will there ever be." 1 Kings 3:8–12 NIV

UNDERSTAND

- *What was Solomon's attitude toward his new role as king?*
- *Why was God pleased with Solomon's request?*
- *What did God do in addition to granting Solomon's request?*

APPLY

Solomon had been king for a few years before God appeared to him in a vision—enough time to see how hard the job was! His father, David, had established the royal line after succeeding Saul, but Solomon still had significant challenges. For example, he faced opposition from his elder brother, Adonijah, and from hostile nations eager to test a young king.

But Solomon had been chosen by God to "build a house for my Name. He will be my son, and I will be his father. And I will establish the throne of his kingdom over Israel forever" (1 Chronicles 22:10 NIV). Solomon's request for wisdom was pleasing to God because it showed his dependence on God to do the job He had assigned. Likewise, we are chosen in Christ, and we embody that fact by calling on Him for wisdom and strength to fulfill our calling.

PRAY

Father, I want to please You by what I desire; ignore my pleas for worthless things!

GUARDING THE HEART

Read Proverbs 4:20–27

KEY VERSE

Guard your heart above all else, for it determines the course of your life.
PROVERBS 4:23 NLT

UNDERSTAND

- *What makes the heart so important for those who seek to please God?*
- *How does one guard the heart?*

APPLY

Knowing and doing don't always go hand in hand. A chain-smoker who tells his children not to smoke isn't wrong; he's just not taking his own advice. Likewise, Solomon had much to share about wisdom, though as we've seen, he fell short of living by his own advice.

The Hebrew word *lebab*, most often translated as "heart," is always used metaphorically, frequently overlapping with "mind," "soul," or "spirit." As in English, it refers to the deepest part of a man, combining his desires and choices. It can be hardened, stirred, discouraged; evil, noble, upright; tested, faint, thankful; it stores things up and brings things forth. The heart is about as "you" as you can get.

The man who honors God has no allies in this world or even his own flesh. But believers do have an "advocate to help you and be with you forever—the Spirit of truth. . . . You know him, for he lives with you and will be in you" (John 14:16–17 NIV). This is why Paul can advise believers, "Do not conform to the pattern of this world, but be transformed by the renewing of your mind. Then you will be able to test and approve what God's will is—his good, pleasing and perfect will" (Romans 12:2 NIV). To "be transformed" is a passive verb, meaning it happens to you as a result of something else—in this case, renewing the mind by the Spirit of truth. If we "keep in step with the Spirit" (Galatians 5:25 NIV), we never have to guard our hearts alone!

PRAY

Lord, You've given me a new heart in Christ. Teach me to guard that heart and to listen to Your Spirit.

LOVE IS REAL FREEDOM

Read Galatians 5:13–18

KEY VERSES

For you have been called to live in freedom, my brothers and sisters. But don't use your freedom to satisfy your sinful nature. Instead, use your freedom to serve one another in love. For the whole law can be summed up in this one command: "Love your neighbor as yourself." GALATIANS 5:13–14 NLT

UNDERSTAND

- *What does freedom mean to you right now? How does Paul want Christians to understand freedom and use it as a guide in their lives?*
- *Consider how you can depend on the Holy Spirit today to guide you through the competing desires to use your freedom either for your own indulgence or for loving service of others.*
- *How can a healthy love of yourself guide you today in making choices that benefit others?*

APPLY

Today, Paul is asking who guides your life and whether you are using your freedom and gifts for your own sake or for the sake of your neighbors. If you allow the Holy Spirit to guide you, there's a good chance you'll be able to make choices that benefit you and others and will lead you toward real freedom in Christ.

The problem is that "freedom" is often portrayed as doing what you want when you want regardless of how it impacts your neighbors. Even worse, this self-indulgence is a short-term path to peace and contentment, so self-centered freedom can become a trap that holds you back from God and others.

You have an open invitation today to ask God's Spirit to guide you, to entrust yourself to the safest, surest guide to freedom and joy. Today, you can discover that God's Spirit leads you to freedom you could have never found on your own.

PRAY

Holy Spirit, thank You for Your presence in my life and for Your compassion for me. Help me to see the ways I can remain aware of others and use my freedom to love and serve them. May I see the dead ends of personal indulgence today so that I can remain free in You. Amen.

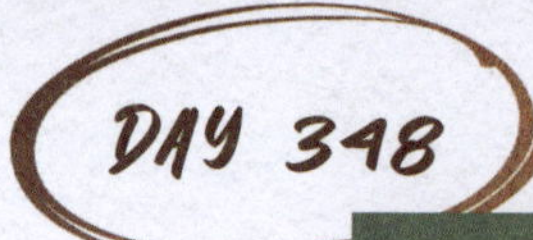

YOU ARE BLESSED TO BE A BLESSING

Read 2 Corinthians 9:6–15

KEY VERSE

You will be enriched in every way so that you can be generous on every occasion, and through us your generosity will result in thanksgiving to God. 2 CORINTHIANS 9:11 NIV

UNDERSTAND

- *Why does God bless you?*
- *When have you been the recipient of someone's generosity? What did it mean to you?*
- *What needs can you meet today?*

APPLY

We ask for and eagerly welcome God's blessings into our lives—food, shelter, clothing, money, to name a few—but why does God provide us with these things? One reason is that He enjoys giving good gifts to His children (see Matthew 7:11 and James 1:17), but another reason, explained in 2 Corinthians 9, is that God blesses us so we can be a blessing to others.

Think of it! God gives us the opportunity to pay forward the good gifts He gives to us. He invites us to follow His example and give generously, which not only blesses the receiver but enriches our lives and results in praise and thanks to God!

Be on the lookout for ways to be generous with your time, talent, and money. And in the meantime, prepare to be generous. Make time to do it. Save money to do it. God is blessing you—to be a blessing!

PRAY

Lord God, You are so good to me! Today I am not taking for granted everything You give to me. I am so blessed! Show me where You want me to be generous today. Keep my motives pure and my eyes open to Your will. My desire is for Your blessings to not stop here but to flow through me. Amen.

BE YOURSELF

Read Matthew 6:5–13

KEY VERSES

"When you pray, don't be like the hypocrites who love to pray publicly on street corners and in the synagogues where everyone can see them. . . . But when you pray, go away by yourself, shut the door behind you, and pray to your Father in private. Then your Father, who sees everything, will reward you. MATTHEW 6:5–6 NLT

UNDERSTAND

- *Why might someone be tempted to try to sound more spiritual than they really are?*
- *Do you use different words when you pray in public than when you pray silently? Why or why not?*

APPLY

God doesn't require eloquent speech, complete sentences, or even coherent thoughts in prayer. He wants to hear from your authentic self, speaking intimately and from your heart.

If you get the opportunity to pray aloud in public, be sure that your prayer motives are pure. God doesn't want a show, and He doesn't want you to pretend to be someone you aren't. In these instances, others—especially children—may look to you as an example of how to pray, and the best example you can set is one of a pure heart with a singular desire to connect with your heavenly Father.

Practice being authentic in prayer behind closed doors, and that authenticity will flow into other areas. Be yourself—perfectly loved and forgiven by God.

PRAY

Father, I come before You with no motive other than to be in Your presence. I am not pretending to be better than I am. I admit that I have no answers. I realize that I can't do life today without You. I need You, God. Please be near, and never leave me. Amen.

YOU ARE PART OF CHRIST'S BODY

Read 1 Corinthians 12:12–26

KEY VERSES

So God has put the body together such that extra honor and care are given to those parts that have less dignity. This makes for harmony among the members, so that all the members care for each other. If one part suffers, all the parts suffer with it, and if one part is honored, all the parts are glad. 1 CORINTHIANS 12:24–26 NLT

UNDERSTAND

- *How can you tell when your church is a healthy body of Christ?*
- *When have you experienced harmony among the members of the body of Christ?*
- *How have you been cared for by your church family?*

APPLY

Life for the Christian isn't meant to be an individual or private faith. Yes, we are made to be in a relationship with our Father God, but we live in this world together with other believers. Before Jesus returned to heaven, He established His church—what Paul describes in 1 Corinthians 12 as the body of Christ.

You are a unique part of your church, made with talents and passions and gifts, and you are cast in a role that only you can play. Body parts must work together and compensate when one part struggles, as well as celebrate and reap the benefits when one part is successful.

How's the health of your church as a whole? Are you doing life together, unified in faith? What practical steps can you take today to get involved in the lives of others?

PRAY

Jesus, I am thankful for my church. We are Your body, made up of flawed individuals, but You bind us together in unity, and we are better for it. Forgive me when I wrongly believe I am better on my own. Amen.

GOD KNOWS YOUR NEEDS BEFORE YOU PRAY

Read Matthew 6:1–8

KEY VERSES

"But when you pray, go into your room, close the door and pray to your Father, who is unseen. Then your Father, who sees what is done in secret, will reward you. And when you pray, do not keep on babbling like pagans, for they think they will be heard because of their many words." MATTHEW 6:6–7 NIV

UNDERSTAND

- *What do you long to receive as a result of your prayers and your Christian practices? How can you guard against craving accolades from others and instead trust God to be present and concerned about you when you pray?*
- *Why do you think it's so important to Jesus that you pray and practice your good deeds in secret?*
- *What are your expectations when you begin to pray? How could starting out with confidence that God knows exactly what you need change the way you pray?*

APPLY

How often do you see results right away when you pray? Prayer isn't a practice that usually brings immediate rewards or benefits. Instead, it's a long-term investment in a relationship with God. Oftentimes, a prayer may be answered in an unexpected way or on a timeline that is quite different from your own. It's tempting to see prayer and other spiritual practices as signs of your own holiness and goodness before others.

Today, Jesus asks you to take a big leap of faith, to trust that God not only hears your prayers and sees your good deeds but also knows exactly what you need before you even ask. When you do that, God will reward you for what you do in private, seen by Him alone. That calls for a lot of waiting and a lot of trust.

Even though God knows what you need, Jesus wants you to release your concerns and requests to Him. When you pray, you cultivate a relationship with God, one that benefits you as you share your hopes, fears, and concerns with Him. Not only that, you make yourself available to God in the secret, quiet place. The benefits of doing these things are beyond what you can imagine.

PRAY

Father, I trust that You know what I need before I ask and that You will reward me for what I do for You and for others in secret. May I turn my gaze away from what I can gain from others right now and instead entrust myself to Your kindness and generosity as I pray. Amen.

NO COMPLAINTS

Read Philippians 2:12–18

KEY VERSES

Do all things without grumbling or disputing, that you may be blameless and innocent, children of God without blemish in the midst of a crooked and twisted generation, among whom you shine as lights in the world. PHILIPPIANS 2:14–15 ESV

UNDERSTAND

- *How would your life be different if you did all things without grumbling?*
- *What is one thing you find yourself complaining about?*
- *Instead of complaining, how could you take your dissatisfaction and turn it into something positive?*

APPLY

Do you know anyone who has the gift of complaining? Instigators, party poopers, wet blankets, and Debbie Downers alike, these individuals bring down the mood with one well-placed criticism or grumble. Unfortunately, it's easier for a complainer to pull others down into their own mire than it is for others to raise them up to a more optimistic outlook.

As followers of Jesus, we are called to be better rather than bitter. And when we adopt the attitude of Christ and choose to neither complain nor argue, others will see something special and attractive in us. We'll shine brightly the love of God in a world dimmed by dissatisfaction, petty grumbling, and strife. When people ask what makes us different, we can point them straight to the love of Jesus.

Choose today to do *everything* without complaining and see how your outlook changes!

PRAY

God, I'm guilty of whining when I should be praising You for Your endless goodness to me. Forgive me. Take away any discontentment and bitterness in my heart and replace it with Your joy. Amen.

YOU ARE NEVER ALONE

Read John 14:15–26

KEY VERSES

"And I will ask the Father, and he will give you another Helper, to be with you forever, even the Spirit of truth, whom the world cannot receive, because it neither sees him nor knows him. You know him, for he dwells with you and will be in you." JOHN 14:16–17 ESV

UNDERSTAND

- *What does the Holy Spirit mean to you?*
- *Does the Spirit ever seem dormant inside you? Why do you think that is?*
- *What is one practical way you can engage with the Holy Spirit today?*

APPLY

Jesus' disciples must've felt panicked. Their beloved Rabbi had said repeatedly He would soon leave them. And if He was sincere in His promise, what would they do without Him, the Son of God who guided them on the path of truth, answered their questions, challenged them, and comforted them?

They couldn't understand it then, but the Helper that Jesus promised His Father would send would be so much more. Jesus came to earth to be God with us. The Spirit arrived to be God *in* us. Think of it! The same almighty, powerful God who spoke the world into existence has taken a home in your heart. . .forever!

You are not alone. You cannot be separated from God's love any more than you can be separated from His Spirit. Don't let this magnificent helper go unnoticed today! Breathe in the Spirit and ask for help to live out God's plan today.

PRAY

Spirit of God, sometimes You are a mystery to me. But I long to know You better. Come alive in my heart today and make Your presence known. Jesus said You are my helper. So I am asking for Your help. Help me even when I act like I don't need it. Amen.

BY GOD'S SIDE

Read Psalm 73

KEY VERSE

But as for me, it is good to be near God. I have made the Sovereign Lord *my refuge; I will tell of all your deeds.* Psalm 73:28 NIV

UNDERSTAND

- *When is it most difficult for you to feel near to God?*
- *When is it easiest for you to feel near to God?*
- *What is God doing in your life now? Who can you tell about it?*

APPLY

The writer of Psalm 73 is going through a hard time. All around him, he sees evil people prospering. While he struggles and wrestles with his faith and daily life, he sees wicked people living a carefree existence. And he's angry about it. Why would God make the lives of bad people *easy* while His chosen people work endlessly to keep a pure heart, doing the Lord's work?

Maybe you've felt this way. *What's all this work for*, you wonder, *when other people are living it up and having a much better life than I am?*

Don't give up. God is here, and just like the psalm writer, realize that His nearness is a blessed refuge to the challenges of life. Give Him your frustrations—He can take it. Lean into Him in quiet time, Bible study, and prayer. Remember His faithfulness in the past. Celebrate His devotion to you today. Look forward to His (and your) victory tomorrow and forever.

PRAY

God, I am here with You, and You are here with me. Make Your presence so real that I cannot deny that I am by Your side. Please give me a glimpse into Your plan, especially when I see situations that I simply do not understand. I long to understand what You are doing behind the scenes. I trust You, Father. Amen.

ARM YOURSELF FOR TODAY'S BATTLES

Read Ephesians 6:10–20

KEY VERSE

Therefore put on the full armor of God, so that when the day of evil comes, you may be able to stand your ground, and after you have done everything, to stand. Ephesians 6:13 NIV

UNDERSTAND

- *How have you seen the armor of God be helpful to you both spiritually and in practical, everyday life?*
- *Which piece of the armor of God is the easiest for you to take up? Which is the most challenging? Why?*

APPLY

You are powerful. Why? Because the Spirit of God lives inside you. And God has given us tools to meet life's challenges head-on with the armor of God.

So what are you facing today? When Satan whispers his lies that you aren't good enough, tighten the belt of God's truth around your waist and know that you are cherished and loved. Guard your heart with the breastplate of righteousness and stand firm in the peace of the gospel that Jesus came to earth to make a way for us to live with Him forever. Hold high that shield of faith that gives you hope even in hard times. Secure your helmet of salvation, and rest in the knowledge that you cannot lose God's saving grace. Grip tightly the hilt of the sword of the Spirit—your counterattack when Satan does his worst. And when you've done all you can today, stand, knowing that God wins every battle.

PRAY

Almighty God, I am not a fierce warrior, but Your Spirit makes me strong. When Satan charges at me, give me Your fearless bravery and the security to know that the power of Your Holy Spirit inside me has already prevailed over every kind of evil. I trust You, Father. Amen.

HOPE IN GOD BRINGS GLADNESS

Read Psalm 33:13–22

KEY VERSES

Our soul waits for the Lord; *he is our help and shield. Our heart is glad in him, because we trust in his holy name. Let your steadfast love, O* Lord, *be upon us, even as we hope in you.* Psalm 33:20–22 NRSV

UNDERSTAND

- *How would you describe your heart or emotions right now? What would you like to ask God to change?*
- *In whom or what do you most often find yourself placing your trust? How can you increase your hope and trust in God?*
- *Consider whether you're aware of God's love for you today. How does today's passage encourage you to think of God's love for you?*

APPLY

Today's reading is about adversity and about whom you depend on in the midst of it. Consider how people—those in your immediate circles and those in the wider culture—handle adversity and challenges. Who or what are they relying on for their hope?

Rather than looking at the size of the challenges before you today, consider that God is looking down on you and on everyone else from heaven. God has fashioned the hearts of men and knows everyone's secret deeds. When you rely on God and fear Him, you can count on Him seeing and caring for you in the midst of your adversity.

What you focus on today will go a long way toward determining your relationship with God. Today's reading ends with an image of God's love resting on His people. That can be a source of comfort for you today as you face challenges and adversity. If you depend on God and look to Him as your source of hope, you will find security and peace in the most challenging of times.

PRAY

Father, You are greater than anyone or anything, and Your power is unmatched. May I find peace, hope, and gladness in Your presence and power today, waiting patiently for Your intervention in my life. May Your steadfast love rest on me and my loved ones. Amen.

STOP AND THINK

Read Ephesians 4:25–32

KEY VERSE

"Don't sin by letting anger control you." Don't let the sun go down while you are still angry.
Ephesians 4:26 NLT

UNDERSTAND

- *What people or situations automatically get your hackles up?*
- *Have you ever been so angry that you felt out of control of your words, actions, or thoughts? What was the outcome?*
- *What practical safeguards can you take to remain silent and think when you are getting angry?*

APPLY

When anger rises, you may not *literally* see red, but we all know that feeling. Maybe you're reacting to a careless word said by another or an injustice that must be righted. Or it could be good, old-fashioned road rage. The kids are fighting. . .again. The dog eviscerated a new pair of shoes. Your wife did the thing that irritates you more than you like to admit. And here comes that blood-rushing, pulse-pounding, face-flushing, frustration-spiking wave of emotion called anger.

When anger comes—and it *will* come—you have a choice: You can explode in an emotion-fueled reaction or simply stop and think.

Simple? Yes. Easy? Not at all. But the Creator of our complex emotions understands anger, and He also knows such a strong emotion can lead us to sinful actions, words, and thoughts. So train your mind, heart, and tongue to stop, give control to the Holy Spirit, and then, at His prompting, react in love.

PRAY

Jesus, sometimes giving in to anger in the moment just feels good. But I also know that the destruction in the wake of an angry outburst is hard to clean up. I've hurt people I love in the past, and that's the last thing I want to do in the future. Give me wisdom to stop and think before reacting in anger today. Amen.

GUARD YOUR TONGUE

Read James 3:1–12

KEY VERSE

For if we could control our tongues, we would be perfect and could also control ourselves in every other way. James 3:2 NLT

UNDERSTAND

- *In what situations are you most likely to lose control of your tongue?*
- *James likens the tongue to a flame of fire (James 3:6). When have you seen words create devastation like an out-of-control fire?*
- *When have you held your tongue despite wanting to say something? How did it make you feel?*

APPLY

If you're doing this study early in the morning, maybe you haven't had a chance to open mouth, insert foot yet—the day is still young. James 3:7–8 tells us that unlike all kinds of animals, birds, reptiles, and fish that can be trained and tamed, no one can tame the tongue.

So if we can't tame it, we must keep it under lock and key.

Proverbs 21:23 (ESV) tells us, "Whoever keeps his mouth and his tongue keeps himself out of trouble." Psalm 34:13 (NLT) says to "keep your tongue from speaking evil and your lips from telling lies!" God has given us speech for a reason, and from our words can come encouraging, life-giving hope. But we must learn to listen first, consider second, and answer (when necessary) third. Ask God for the words He would have you say (or not say), and He will help you use your words wisely.

PRAY

Father, only You can help me get a handle on this powerful muscle in my mouth. My tongue gets me into trouble too often, but I also admit that I too often react with my tongue. Give me the wisdom to know when and what to speak and when to remain silent. Amen.

CHOOSE LOVE ABOVE ALL

Read 1 John 3:11–20

KEY VERSES

Dear children, let's not merely say that we love each other; let us show the truth by our actions. Our actions will show that we belong to the truth, so we will be confident when we stand before God. 1 John 3:18–19 NLT

UNDERSTAND

- *What action, when performed by another, makes you feel most loved?*
- *In what ways (actions) do you show others you love them?*
- *How do you best give love? How do you best receive love?*

APPLY

Our Father God shows us He loves us in so many ways. His Word tells us of His love and devotion for us. He listens to our prayers. He provides for our needs. And Jesus Christ became the very definition of love by laying down His life to make a way for each of us to be with Him for eternity.

So when John encourages us to go beyond just saying that we love each other, he tells us to display the truth of our words by putting love into action. Love displayed in multiple, tangible ways empowers relationships and makes us stronger together.

Who do you need to show some love to today? Don't let opportunities slip by for showing love in action. Love, in the name of God, is life-giving truth that can sustain us in the hardest times.

PRAY

Jesus, when I feel self-conscious and ill-equipped to show love in action, remind me of Your astounding act of humility on the cross. You showed me how to love perfectly, and I want to follow Your example. Put opportunities to love in my path today, Lord. My heart is open, and my hands are ready to do Your will. Amen.

SEE OTHERS AS JESUS SEES THEM

Read 1 Samuel 16:1–13

KEY VERSE

"The Lord doesn't see things the way you see them. People judge by outward appearance, but the Lord looks at the heart." 1 Samuel 16:7 NLT

UNDERSTAND

- *How does it feel to be judged by what you look like?*
- *Recall a time when you judged someone else's appearance and were surprised to find out your initial assessment was wrong. What did you learn from that experience?*
- *Why is the heart more important than physical appearance to God?*

APPLY

For those of us blessed with all five senses, sight, sound, smell, taste, and touch help us make sense of our environment. But while these senses can help us understand, experience, and appreciate the temporary, physical world, they don't help us understand the things that are important to God.

The prophet Samuel, sent by God to anoint the next king of Israel, put too much importance on his sense of sight. Surely the tallest, most attractive son of Jesse would be the next king, he thought. God assured Samuel that His interest was not in appearance but in the heart of the individual. And Jesse's youngest, smallest son, David, was the boy for the job.

Today is a day to resist snap judgments based on appearance alone. Do you owe someone a second chance to get to know them? Ask God to show you others through His eyes—straight to the heart.

PRAY

God, I admit that I judge others unfairly. But I also know the unfairness of being judged by my appearance. Give me a beautiful heart overflowing with love, joy, peace, patience, kindness, goodness, faithfulness, and self-control. And if others see any beauty in me, let it be because of You. Amen.

PRAY FOR THOSE WHO ARE SUFFERING

Read Nehemiah 1

KEY VERSES

"Remember, please, the word which You commanded Your servant Moses, saying, 'If you are unfaithful, I will scatter you among the peoples; but if you return to Me and keep My commandments and do them, though those of you who have been scattered were in the most remote part of the heavens, I will gather them from there and bring them to the place where I have chosen to have My name dwell.'" NEHEMIAH 1:8–9 NASB

UNDERSTAND

- *What can you learn about the people of Israel in this passage? How did Nehemiah act toward them in response to their situation?*
- *What does this passage teach about obedience vs. disobedience and the consequences God's people faced for their actions?*
- *It appeared that the worst had happened to the people of Israel. How did Nehemiah go about making things right with God?*

APPLY

Consider those who are suffering or struggling today. They may be facing the consequences of their actions, or they may be swept up into circumstances beyond their control. Suffering and loss happen for a variety of reasons. Regardless, Nehemiah saw that the people of Israel were suffering because of their unfaithfulness, but he still interceded in prayer for them.

Nehemiah was the cupbearer to King Artaxerxes of Persia, and he had every reason to focus on the seemingly more important issues of the palace. Although he lived in a foreign land, he had comfort and influence. Yet he took time to learn about the remnant living in Israel, and he prayed with compassion for them when he learned of their suffering. His example is a reminder to show concern for those suffering regardless of their circumstances, especially if you are living in comfort and plenty.

Nehemiah's intercession for his people is also worthy of notice because he modeled an awareness of God's commands, a humility in acknowledging the sin of Israel, and a plea for mercy based on God's character. As you intercede for yourself and for others, Nehemiah's prayer is a good example of repentance and of full trust in God.

PRAY

Father, You will not abandon Your people to their sins and failures if they repent and pray. I ask for Your mercy for my faults. May I show awareness and compassion toward others who are suffering shame and deprivation today. Amen.

GOD KNOWS YOUR FUTURE

Read Jeremiah 29:1–23

KEY VERSE

"For I know the plans I have for you," says the Lord. "They are plans for good and not for disaster, to give you a future and a hope." JEREMIAH 29:11 NLT

UNDERSTAND

- *When in the past did God work in a way that you did not expect?*
- *What do you fear about the future? Are your fears rational or irrational, and do you have any control over the outcome you fear?*

APPLY

Whether we admit it or not, we all like to be in control. From deciding whether or not to buy a house to determining at what temperature to set the thermostat, there's nothing too big or too small that wouldn't like to have our say in.

What does the future hold? We may have plans and hopes and dreams, but the truth is we have little control over what happens today, tomorrow, or a decade from now. Left unchecked, our desire for control can cause sleepless nights or even strife in our relationships, and worry may spiral into despair.

But God, in His infinite wisdom and knowledge of all that has been and all that will be, cares about your future. Even when you are struggling with stress and uncertainty, God is working out your today for a hope-filled tomorrow. Live in His goodness, in His grace, and in His love.

PRAY

God, I give my future to You. Forgive me for acting as if I am in control, because I'm not. You're much better at it. I believe You have good plans for my today and my tomorrows. Align my desires with Your will so that I am living today and every day in You. Please be the Lord of my life, Father. Amen.

WHERE WILL YOU BE AT THE END OF TODAY?

Read Philippians 3:7–21

KEY VERSES

I focus on this one thing: Forgetting the past and looking forward to what lies ahead, I press on to reach the end of the race and receive the heavenly prize for which God, through Christ Jesus, is calling us. PHILIPPIANS 3:13–14 NLT

UNDERSTAND

- *What can you realistically accomplish today?*
- *What goals are worth pursuing today? Are there others that aren't worth the time?*
- *What do you need to forget to allow you to move forward to the future?*

APPLY

What's the state of your to-do list? Whether it's a mile long or blessedly under control, life is busy. Stay up late or get up early, we each have only twenty-four hours a day to get everything done.

There are tasks and responsibilities we must attend to, but the apostle Paul writing to the Philippian church challenges us to focus on the bigger picture—to make it our priority to know Jesus and experience the mighty power that raised Him from the dead.

How can you come closer to that goal today? You're starting out the day right by spending time in His Word and in prayer. Lean on Him throughout the day and ask Him to guide your steps, your thoughts, your words, and your actions. Commit to seeking Him every morning, taking a step (or a leap) closer to the glory of your brother, Jesus.

PRAY

Jesus, I'm forgetting about my past when I struggled to know my true goals from day to day. Now I'm running toward You. Give me the wisdom to continue in that race while I pursue daily responsibilities. I know that when I am doing both, my life can and will glorify You! Amen.

CHOOSE TO BE A SERVANT

Read Galatians 5:1–15

KEY VERSE

For you have been called to live in freedom, my brothers and sisters. But don't use your freedom to satisfy your sinful nature. Instead, use your freedom to serve one another in love.
GALATIANS 5:13 NLT

UNDERSTAND

- *What does freedom mean to you?*
- *Servants/slaves, by definition, don't have complete freedom, yet Paul reminds the Galatians that they are free in Christ, and in the very next sentence tells them to use that freedom to serve one another. What does this mean to you?*

APPLY

The world sees our faith as a list of rules to be followed—ancient stone tablets filled with "thou shalts" and—even worse in the world's eyes—the unending "thou shalt nots" sure to rain on every parade.

While God's Word does provide guidance in many areas of life along with guardrails to keep us on His perfect path for us, the truth is that the freedom we have because of Jesus' sacrifice gives us unparalleled joy to experience life to the fullest.

One way we can experience that full life is to pour our lives into serving others. Even better, we can follow the example of Jesus by loving our neighbors through our actions. You are free to serve today. Serve your family. Serve your friends. Serve your enemies. It seems counterintuitive, but when we willingly become servants of others, we will experience the true freedom of Christ Jesus.

PRAY

Jesus, today I choose to live in Your freedom. Forgive me for living too often with the shackles of sin around my wrists and ankles by satisfying my own desires. Show me ways to serve and love others today. I am Your willing servant, Lord, who will be Your hands and feet. Amen.

DAY 365

USE YOUR WORDS AS BUILDING BLOCKS

Read 1 Thessalonians 5:1–11

KEY VERSE

So encourage each other and build each other up, just as you are already doing.
1 THESSALONIANS 5:11 NLT

UNDERSTAND

- *Who encourages you with their words?*
- *When have you been encouraged at just the right time? What did it mean to you?*
- *How can you best encourage others with words?*

APPLY

Small children know the time it takes to build a tower of blocks and the single moment it takes for a bully to come and knock it down. In a similar way, research shows that for every negative message we hear about ourselves, it takes many more positive messages to rebuild confidence. That's just one of the reasons why encouragement is so important.

Your words have power. The words you use to talk, text, and write to others can energize and empower them. The words you use to talk to yourself are just as mighty. Well-used words are building blocks that can construct a fortress of confidence and hope able to withstand the inevitable destruction of criticism and negativity that Satan spews our way.

Today, use encouraging words to build up the people around you. Have a conversation. Send a thoughtful text. Mail a note telling the recipient what they mean to you. Don't wait for signs that someone is struggling and in need of a pick-me-up. The truth is we all need encouragement, and we need it all the time.

PRAY

Father God, thank You for Your Word. The Bible as a whole and individual scriptures are such an encouragement to me. Today I am asking You to inhabit my words as I seek to encourage others the way You encourage me. Give me eyes to see those around me as You see them. Amen.

CONTRIBUTORS

Ed Cyzewski is the author of *Reconnect: Spiritual Restoration from Digital Distraction* and *Flee, Be Silent, Pray: Ancient Prayers for Anxious Christians* and is the coauthor of *Unfollowers: Unlikely Lessons on Faith from Those Who Doubted Jesus*. He writes about prayer and imperfectly following Jesus at www.edcyzewski.com.

Quentin Guy writes from the high desert of New Mexico to encourage and equip people to know and serve God. He currently works in publishing for Calvary Church and has cowritten such books as *Weird and Gross Bible Stuff* and *The 2:52 Boys Bible*, both of which are stuck in future classic status. A former middle school teacher, he serves with his wife as marriage prep mentors and trusts God that his children will survive their teenage years.

Jess MacCallum is president of Professional Printers, Inc., in Columbia, South Carolina. He has authored three books—two on marriage and one on raising daughters—and has twice been featured on "Family Life Today" with Dr. Dennis Rainey. He also works with two leadership organizations as an executive coach and is a regular contributor to HealthyLeaders.com. Jess has been married for more than thirty years and has three grown children.

David Sanford served on the leadership team at Corban University, which is consistently ranked by *U.S. News Best Colleges* as one of the top ten colleges in the West. Among his many credits, David served as executive editor of *Holy Bible: Mosaic*, general editor of the popular *Handbook on Thriving as an Adoptive Family*, coauthor of the bestselling *God Is Relevant*, and author of *If God Disappears*.

SCRIPTURE INDEX

THE OLD TESTAMENT

THE NEW TESTAMENT

John

Acts

Romans

1 Corinthians

2 Corinthians

Galatians